mate
nus

Takako Shigematsu

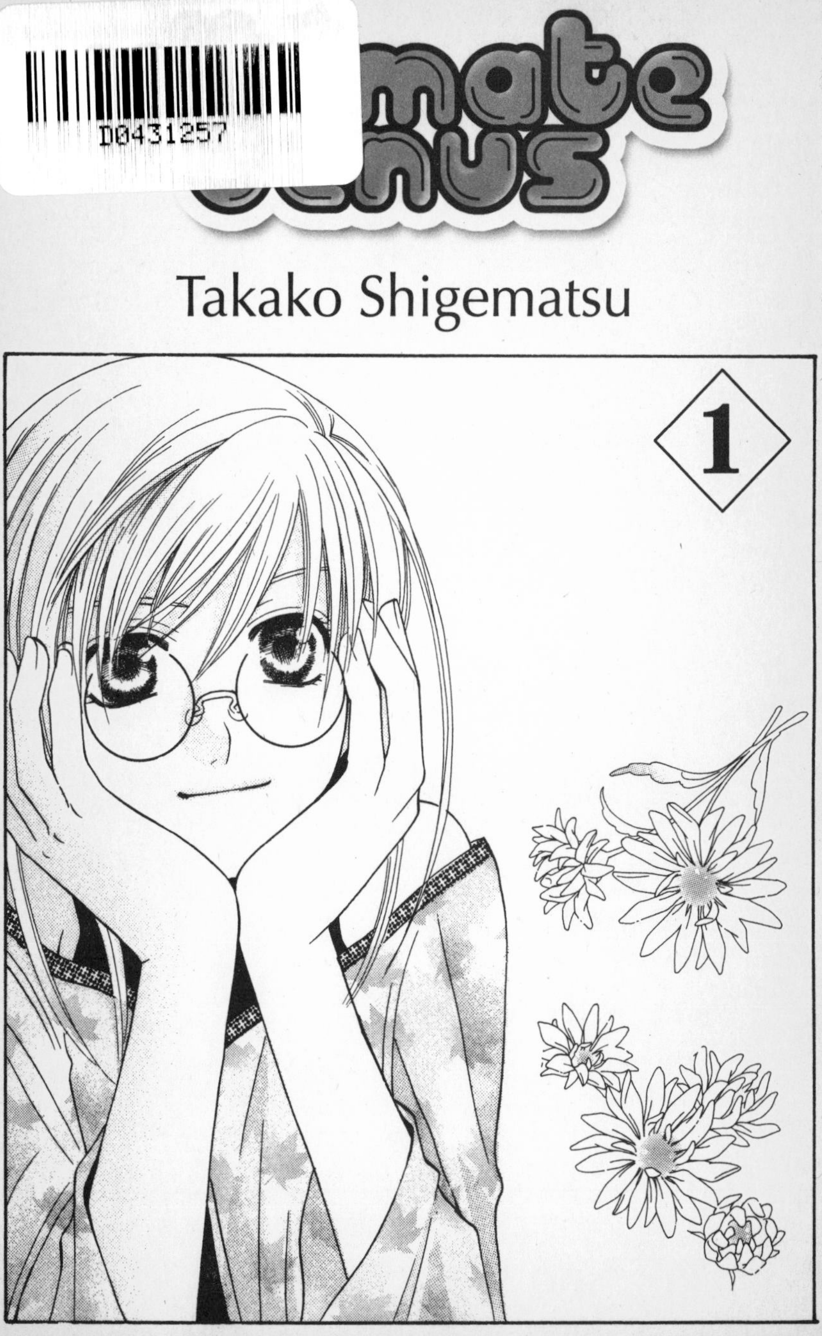
1

Translation –Christine Schilling
Adaptation – Brynne Chandler
Editorial Assistant – Mallory Reaves
Lettering & Retouch – Erika T.
Production Manager – James Dashiell
Production Assistant – Suzy Wells
Editor – Brynne Chandler

A Go! Comi manga

Published by Go! Media Entertainment, LLC

Kyukyoku Venus Volume 1
© TAKAKO SHIGEMATSU 2007
Originally published in Japan in 2007 by Akita Publishing Co., Ltd., Tokyo.
English translation rights arranged with Akita Publishing Co., Ltd.
through TOHAN CORPORATION, Tokyo.

Visit us online at www.gocomi.com
e-mail: info@gocomi.com

ISBN 978-1-933617-88-6

First printed in June 2008

1 2 3 4 5 6 7 8 9

Manufactured in the United States of America

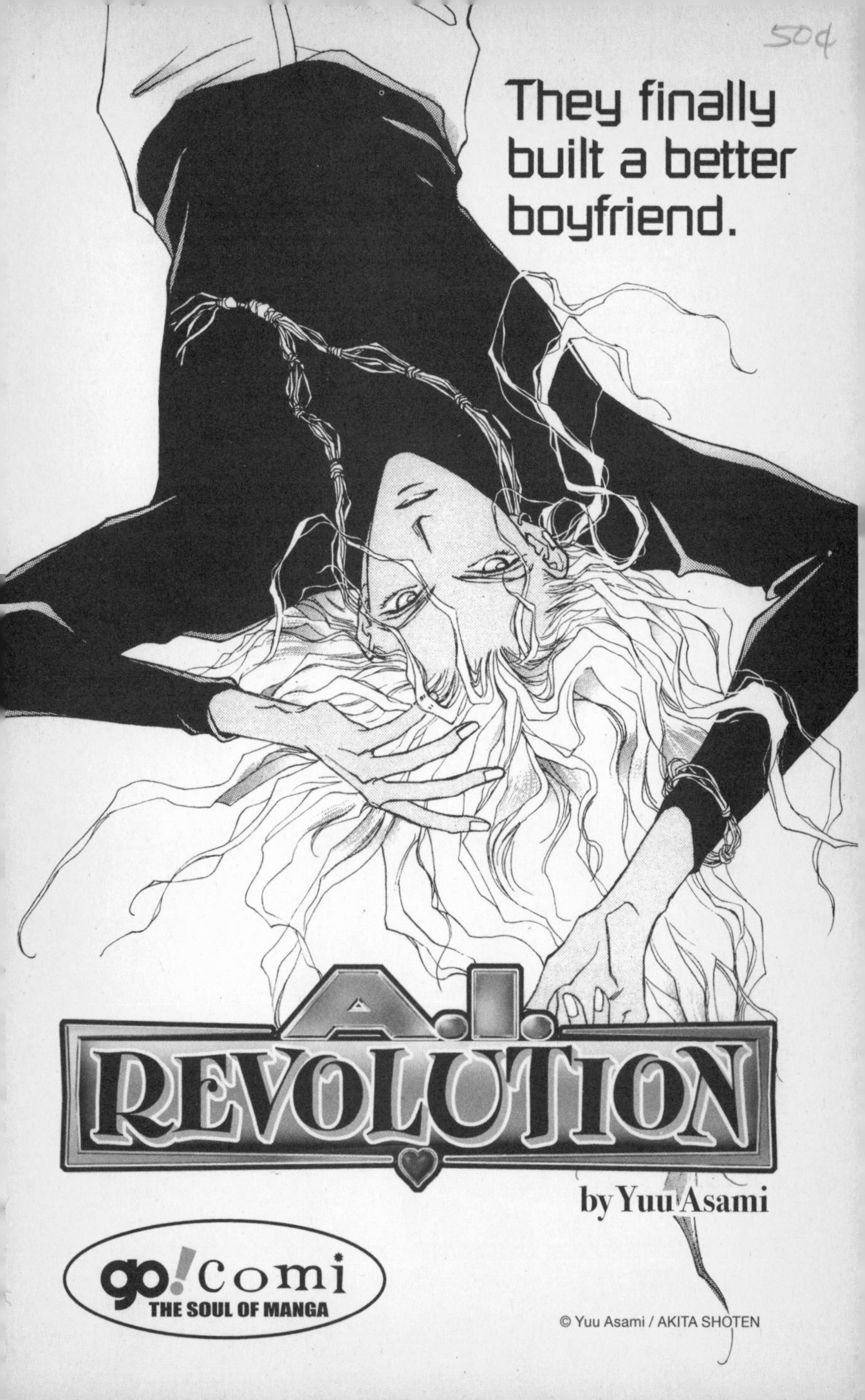
They finally built a better boyfriend.
A.I. REVOLUTION
by Yuu Asami
go!comi
THE SOUL OF MANGA
© Yuu Asami / AKITA SHOTEN

AFTER SCHOOL NIGHTMARE
This dream draws blood.
"Enthralling!" – Library Journal
"An absolute must-buy! I haven't been this blown away by a first volume of a series in a long time."
– Anime on DVD
go!comi
THE SOUL OF MANGA
© 2005 Setona Mizushiro/AKITASHOTEN

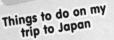

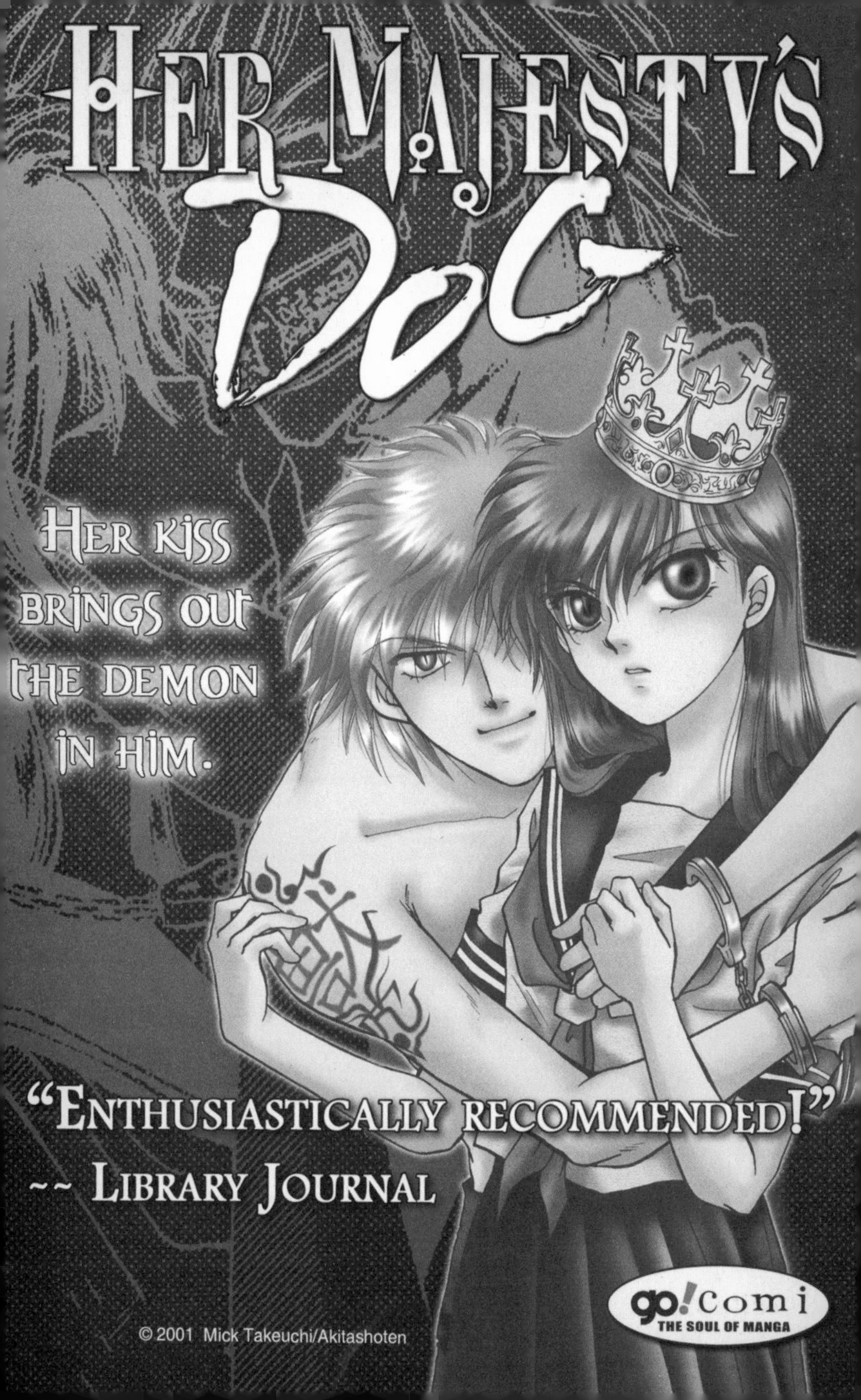
HER MAJESTY'S DOG
HER KISS BRINGS OUT THE DEMON IN HIM.
"ENTHUSIASTICALLY RECOMMENDED!"
~~ LIBRARY JOURNAL
go!comi THE SOUL OF MANGA
© 2001 Mick Takeuchi/Akitashoten

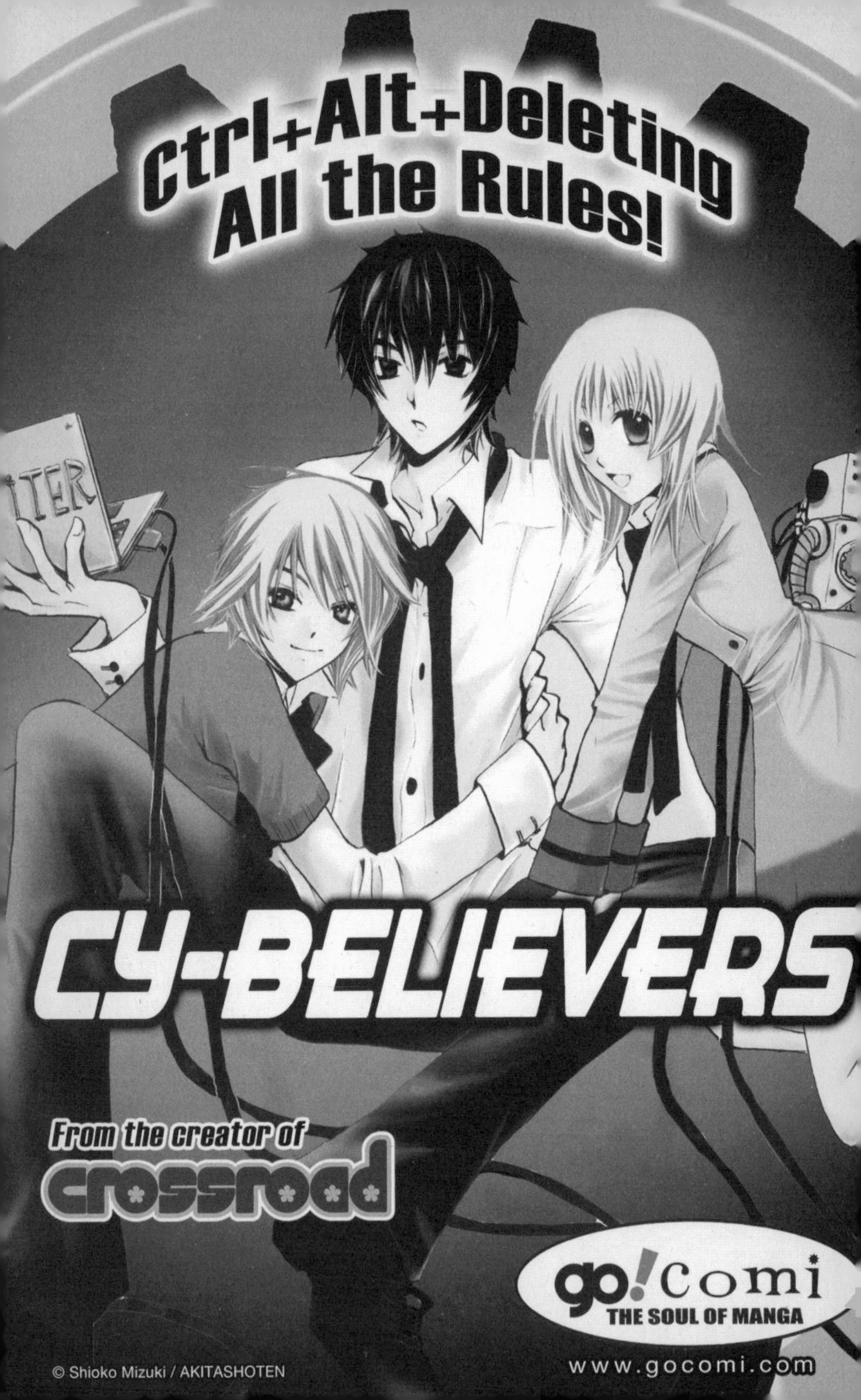

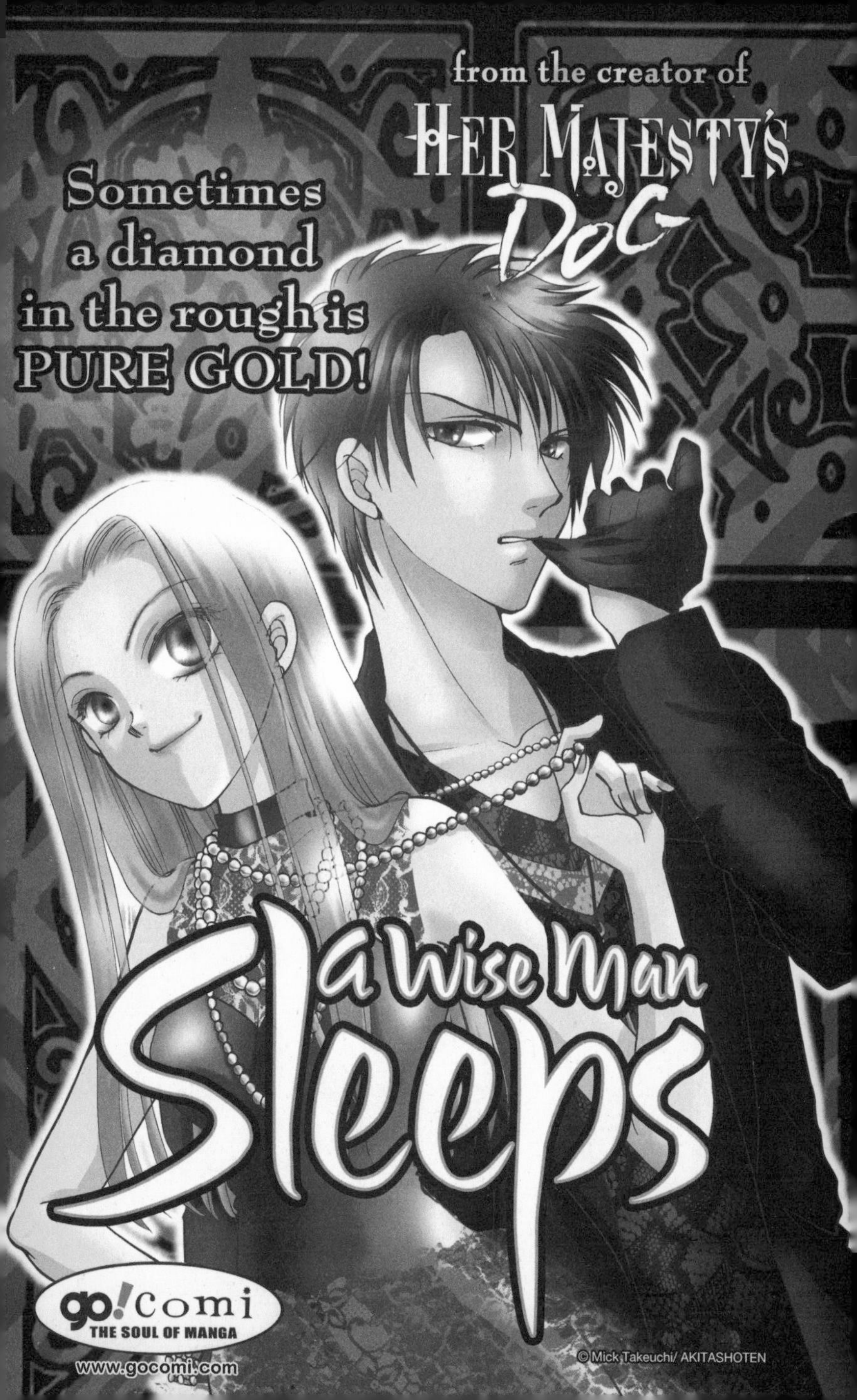
from the creator of
HER MAJESTY'S DOG
Sometimes a diamond in the rough is PURE GOLD!
A Wise Man Sleeps
go!comi
THE SOUL OF MANGA
www.gocomi.com
© Mick Takeuchi/ AKITASHOTEN

Reading. 'Riting. 'Rithmetic.

Romance.

LOVE MASTER

by Kyoko Hashimoto

A

by
Takako Shigematsu

Volume 1

go!comi

ultimate venus

VOLUME:1

CONTENTS

YAAWN

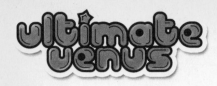

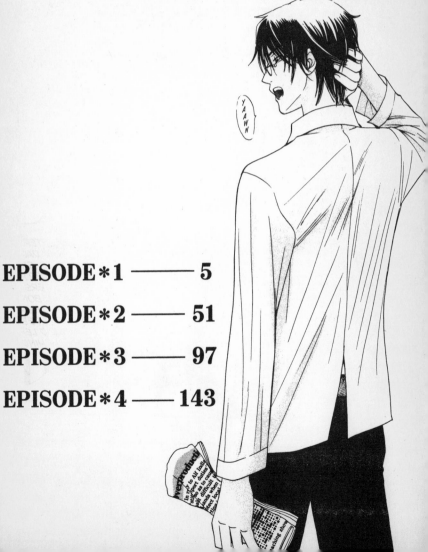

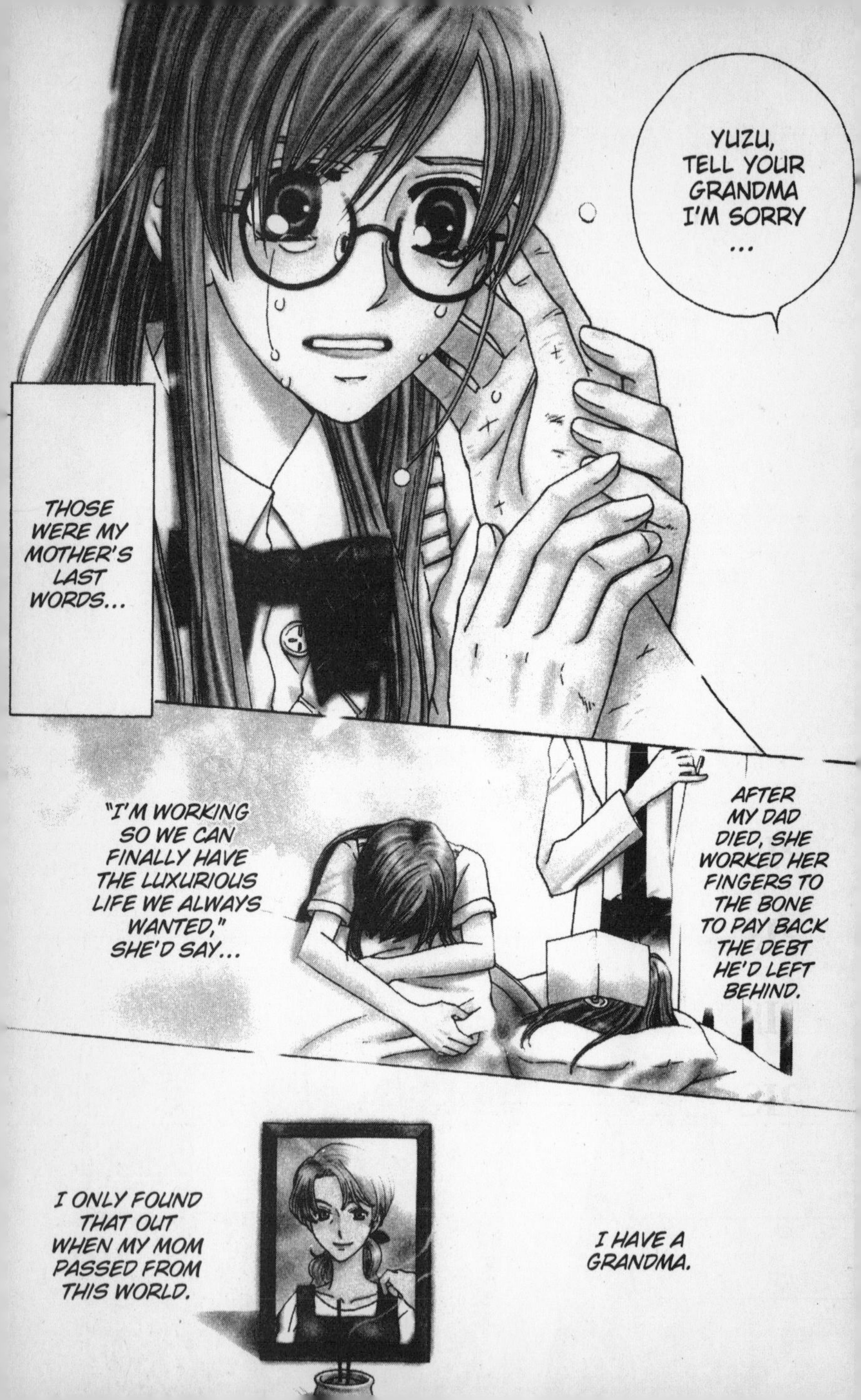
YUZU, TELL YOUR GRANDMA I'M SORRY ...
THOSE WERE MY MOTHER'S LAST WORDS...
AFTER MY DAD DIED, SHE WORKED HER FINGERS TO THE BONE TO PAY BACK THE DEBT HE'D LEFT BEHIND.
"I'M WORKING SO WE CAN FINALLY HAVE THE LUXURIOUS LIFE WE ALWAYS WANTED," SHE'D SAY...
I HAVE A GRANDMA.
I ONLY FOUND THAT OUT WHEN MY MOM PASSED FROM THIS WORLD.

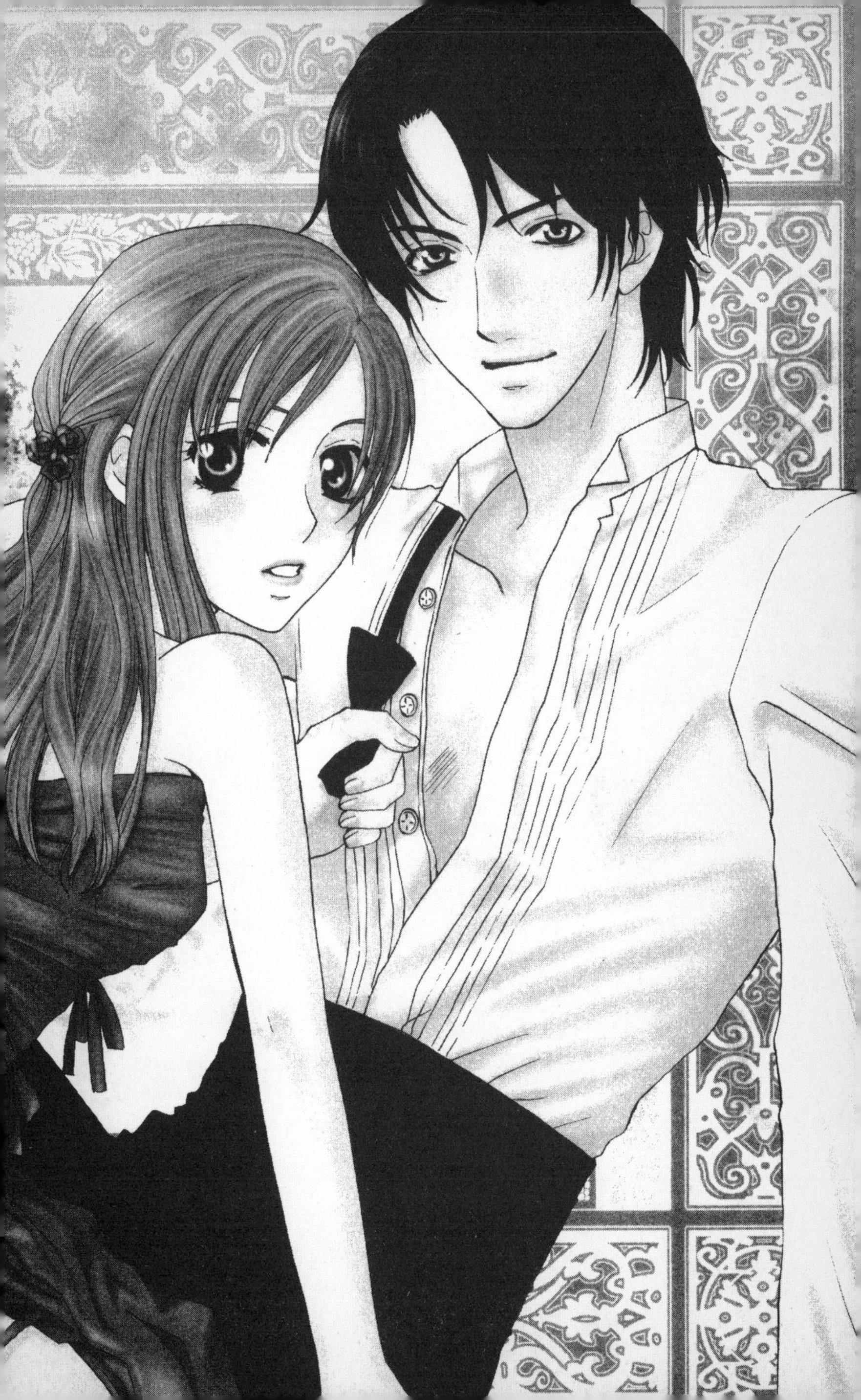

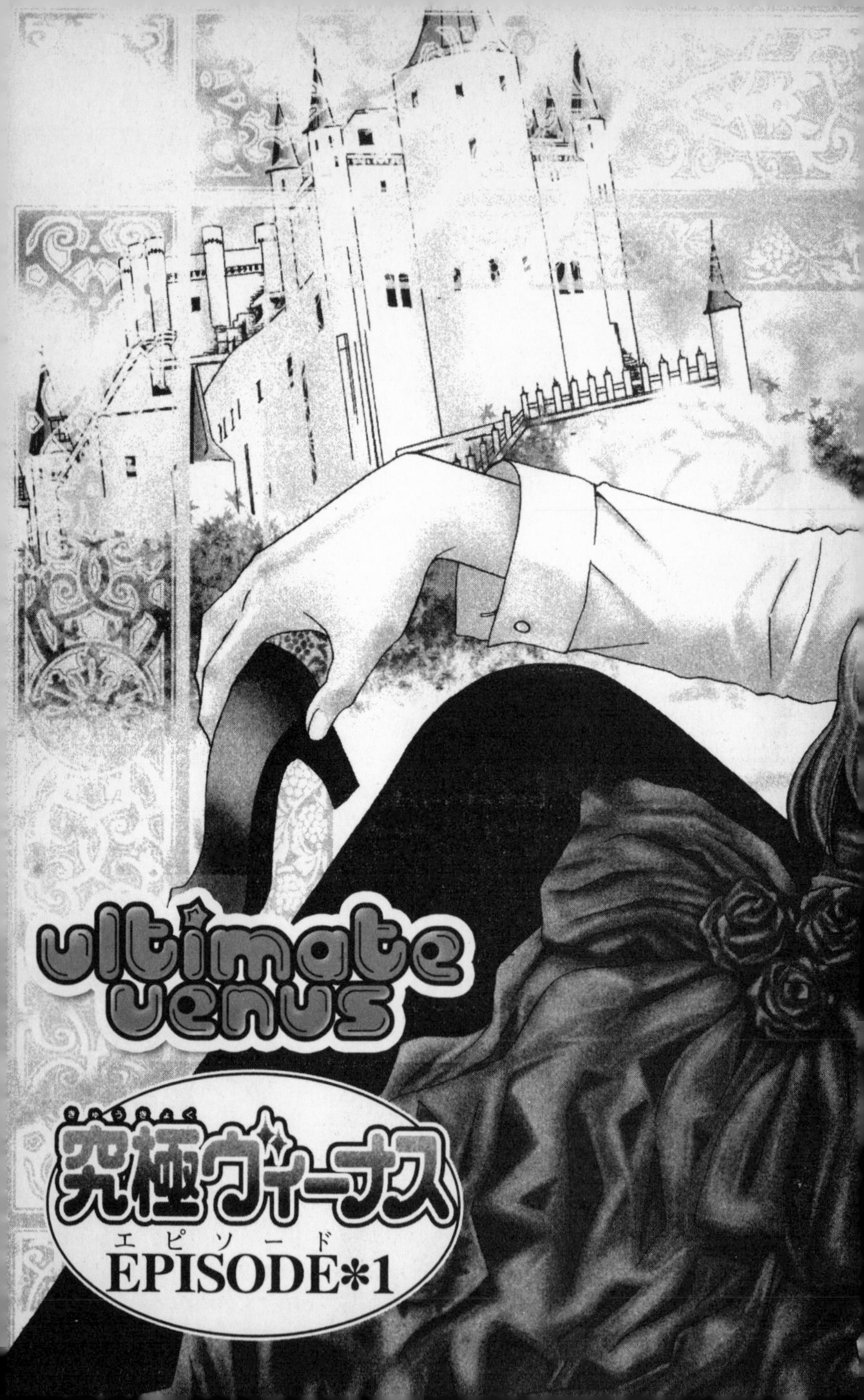
ultimate venus
究極ヴィーナス
EPISODE*1

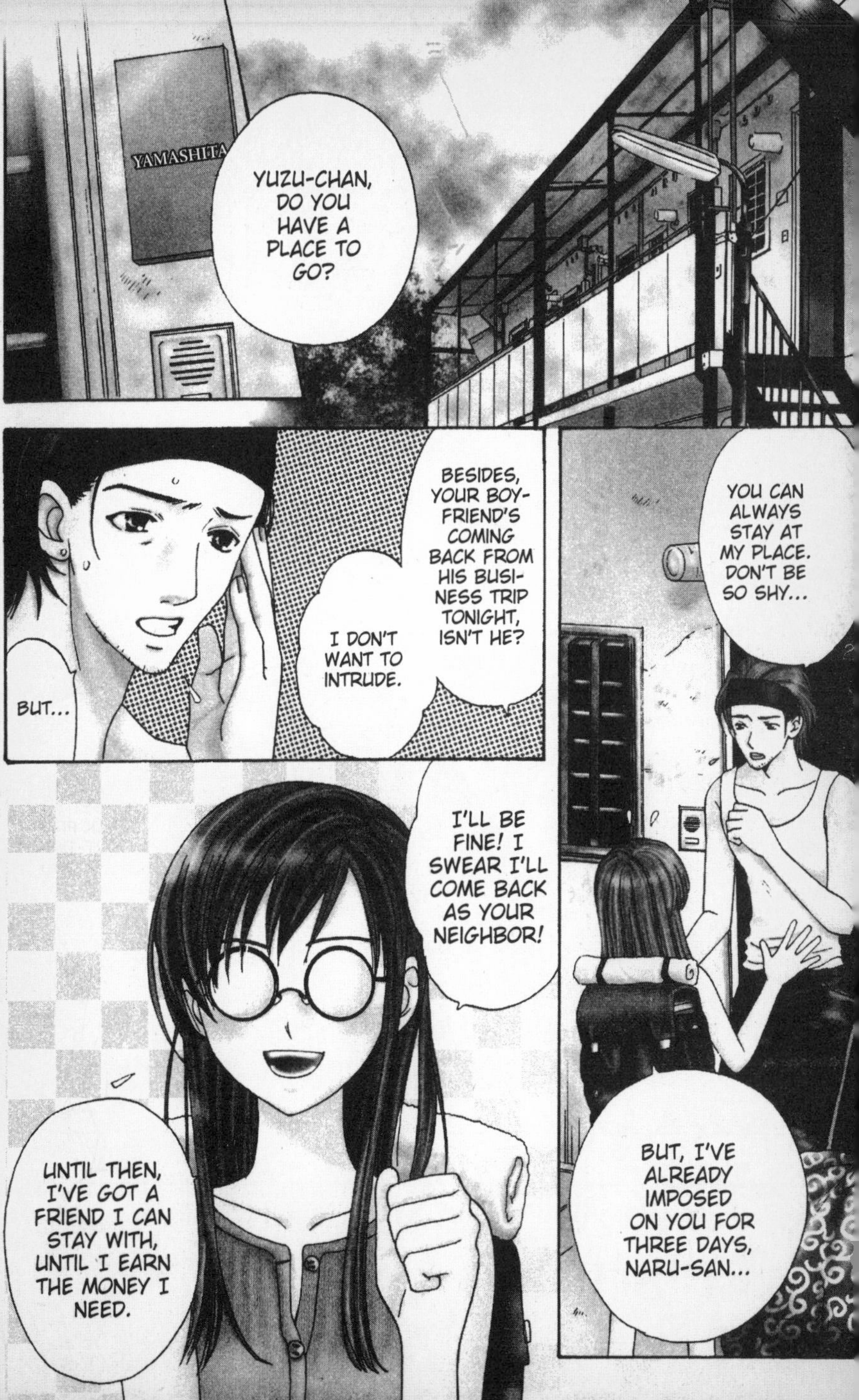
YAMASHITA
YUZU-CHAN, DO YOU HAVE A PLACE TO GO?
YOU CAN ALWAYS STAY AT MY PLACE. DON'T BE SO SHY...
BUT, I'VE ALREADY IMPOSED ON YOU FOR THREE DAYS, NARU-SAN...
BESIDES, YOUR BOY-FRIEND'S COMING BACK FROM HIS BUSI-NESS TRIP TONIGHT, ISN'T HE?
I DON'T WANT TO INTRUDE.
BUT...
I'LL BE FINE! I SWEAR I'LL COME BACK AS YOUR NEIGHBOR!
UNTIL THEN, I'VE GOT A FRIEND I CAN STAY WITH, UNTIL I EARN THE MONEY I NEED.

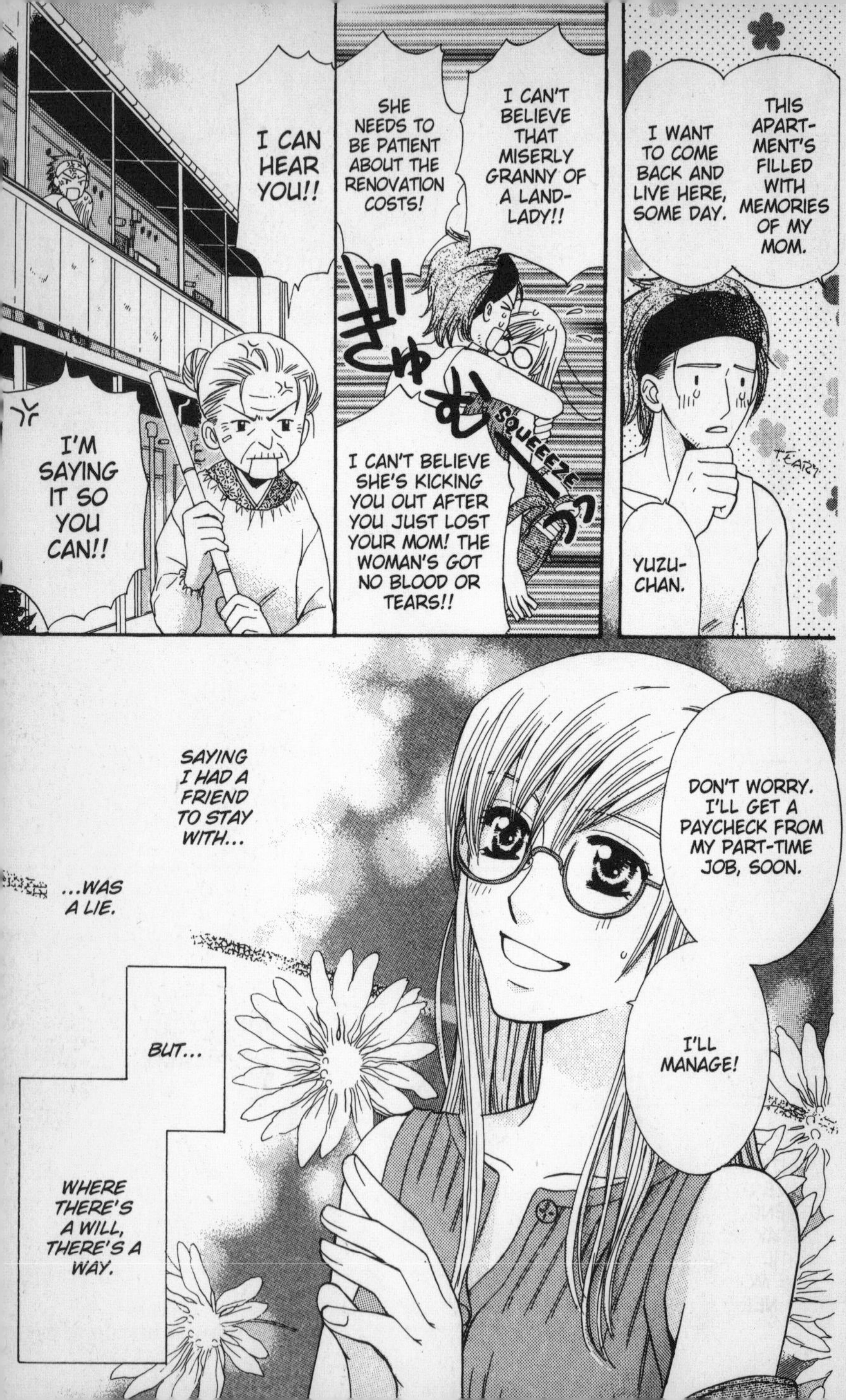
THIS APART-MENT'S FILLED WITH MEMORIES OF MY MOM.
I WANT TO COME BACK AND LIVE HERE, SOME DAY.
TEARY
YUZU-CHAN.
I CAN'T BELIEVE THAT MISERLY GRANNY OF A LAND-LADY!!
SHE NEEDS TO BE PATIENT ABOUT THE RENOVATION COSTS!
SQUEEEZE
I CAN'T BELIEVE SHE'S KICKING YOU OUT AFTER YOU JUST LOST YOUR MOM! THE WOMAN'S GOT NO BLOOD OR TEARS!!
I CAN HEAR YOU!!
I'M SAYING IT SO YOU CAN!!
DON'T WORRY. I'LL GET A PAYCHECK FROM MY PART-TIME JOB, SOON.
I'LL MANAGE!
SAYING I HAD A FRIEND TO STAY WITH...
...WAS A LIE.
BUT...
WHERE THERE'S A WILL, THERE'S A WAY.

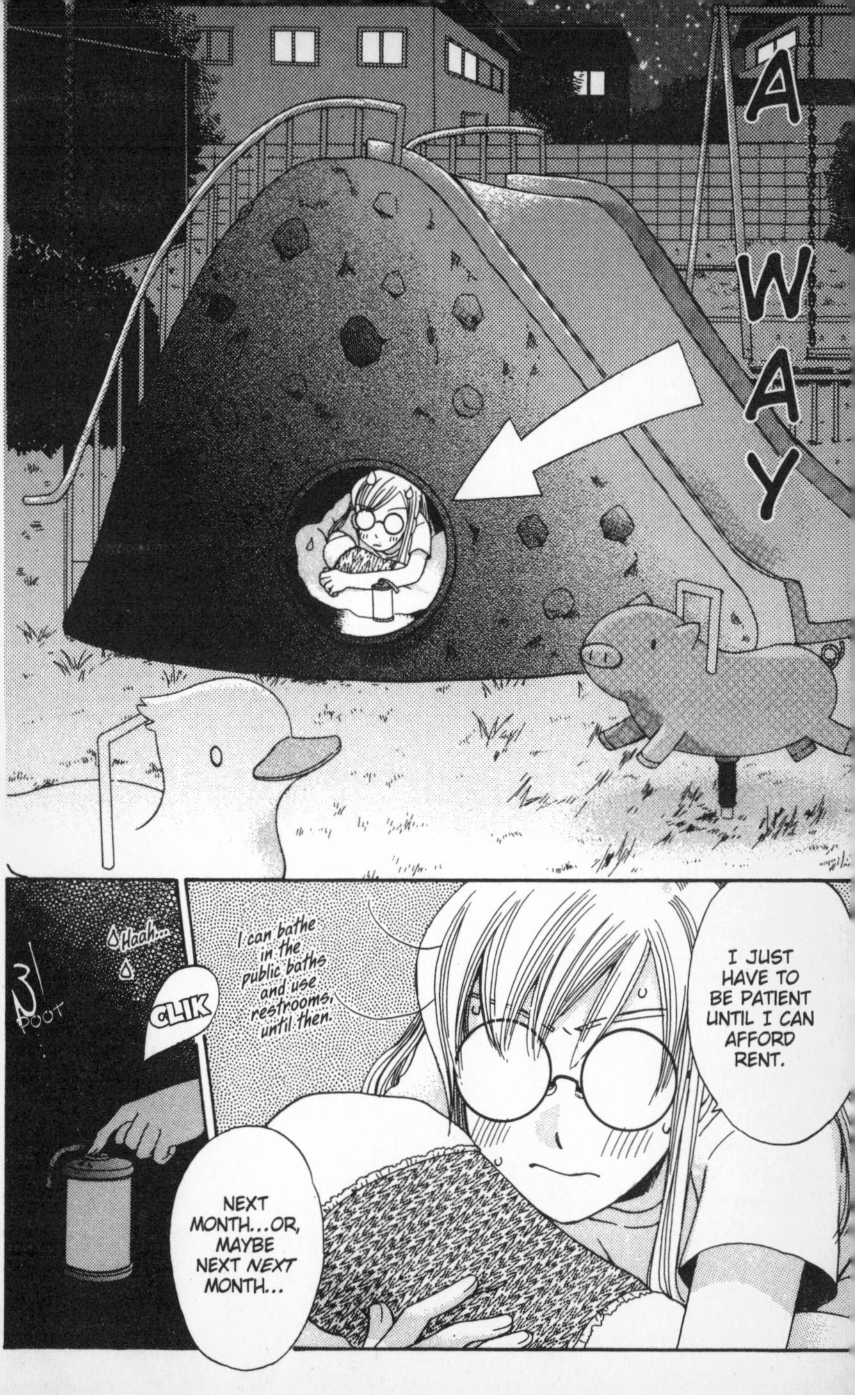
AWAY
I JUST HAVE TO BE PATIENT UNTIL I CAN AFFORD RENT.
I can bathe in the public baths and use restrooms, until then.
NEXT MONTH...OR, MAYBE NEXT *NEXT* MONTH...
CLIK
Haah...
POOT

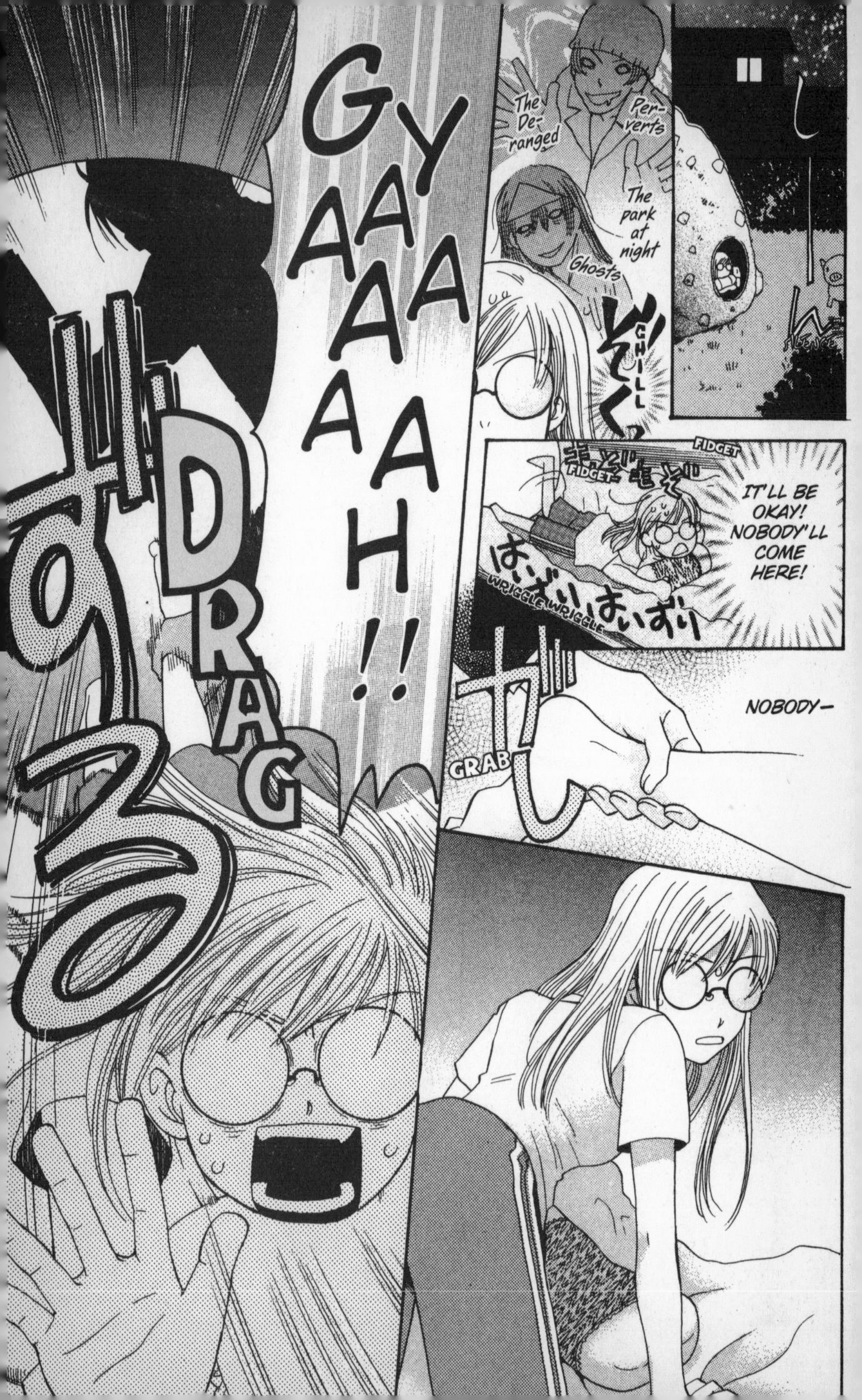
SILENCE
Per-verts
The De-ranged
The park at night
Ghosts
CHILL
FIDGET
FIDGET
IT'LL BE OKAY! NOBODY'LL COME HERE!
WRIGGLE WRIGGLE
NOBODY—
GRAB
GYAAAAAAH!!
DRAG

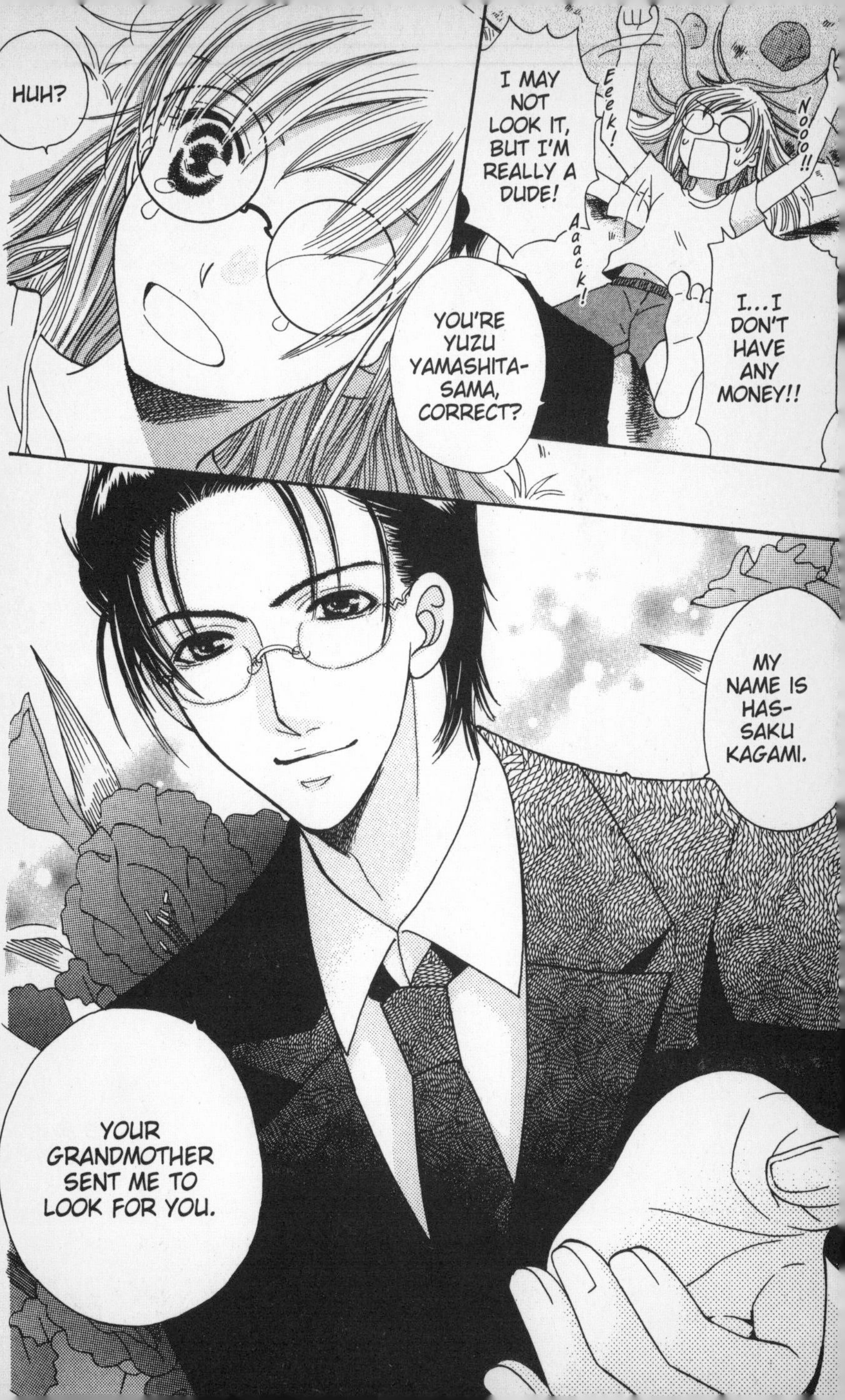
Noooo!!
Eeeek!
I MAY NOT LOOK IT, BUT I'M REALLY A DUDE!
Aaack!
I...I DON'T HAVE ANY MONEY!!
YOU'RE YUZU YAMASHITA-SAMA, CORRECT?
HUH?
MY NAME IS HAS-SAKU KAGAMI.
YOUR GRANDMOTHER SENT ME TO LOOK FOR YOU.

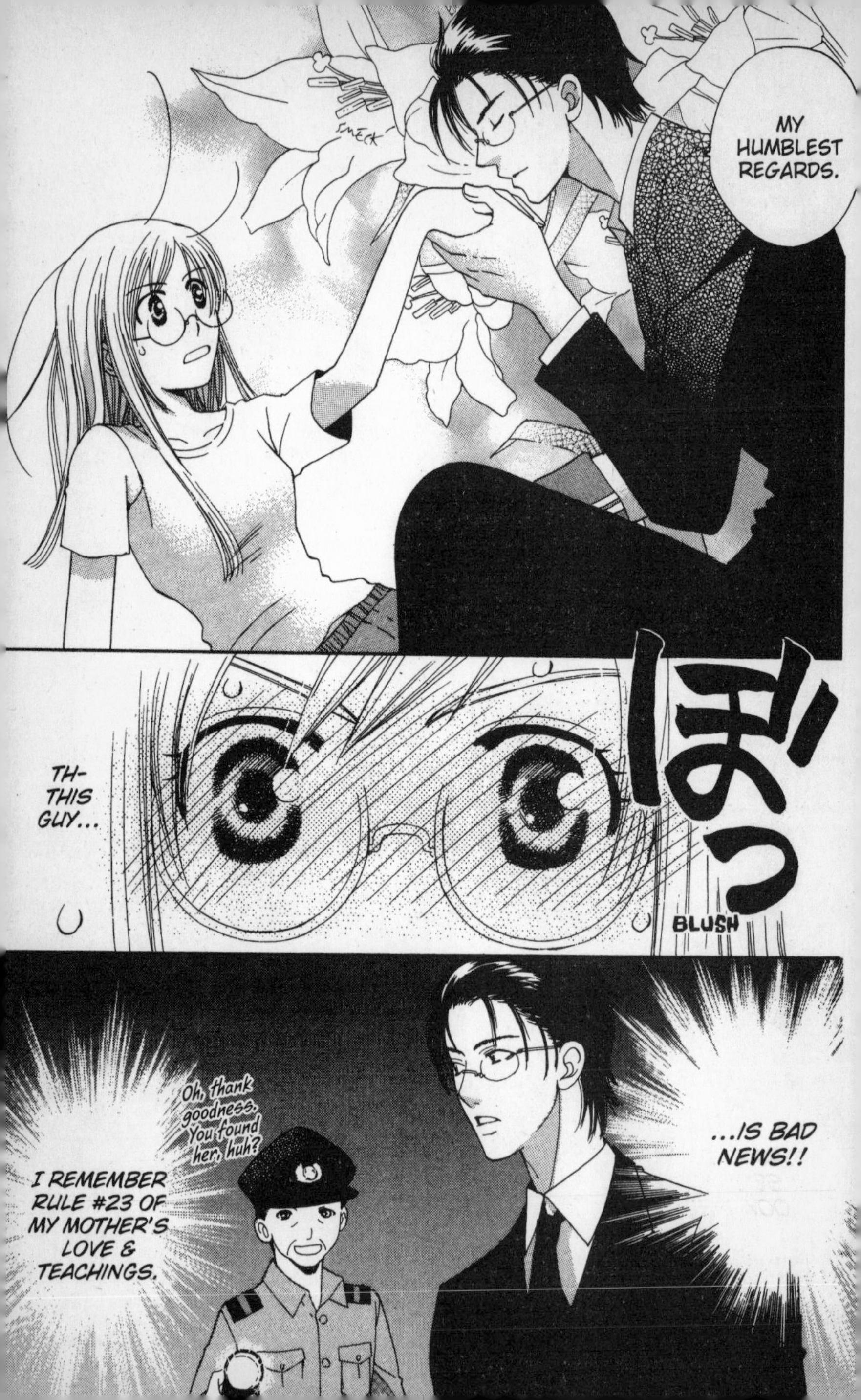
MY HUMBLEST REGARDS.
SMECK
ぼっ
BLUSH
TH- THIS GUY...
...IS BAD NEWS!!
Oh, thank goodness. You found her, huh?
I REMEMBER RULE #23 OF MY MOTHER'S LOVE & TEACHINGS.

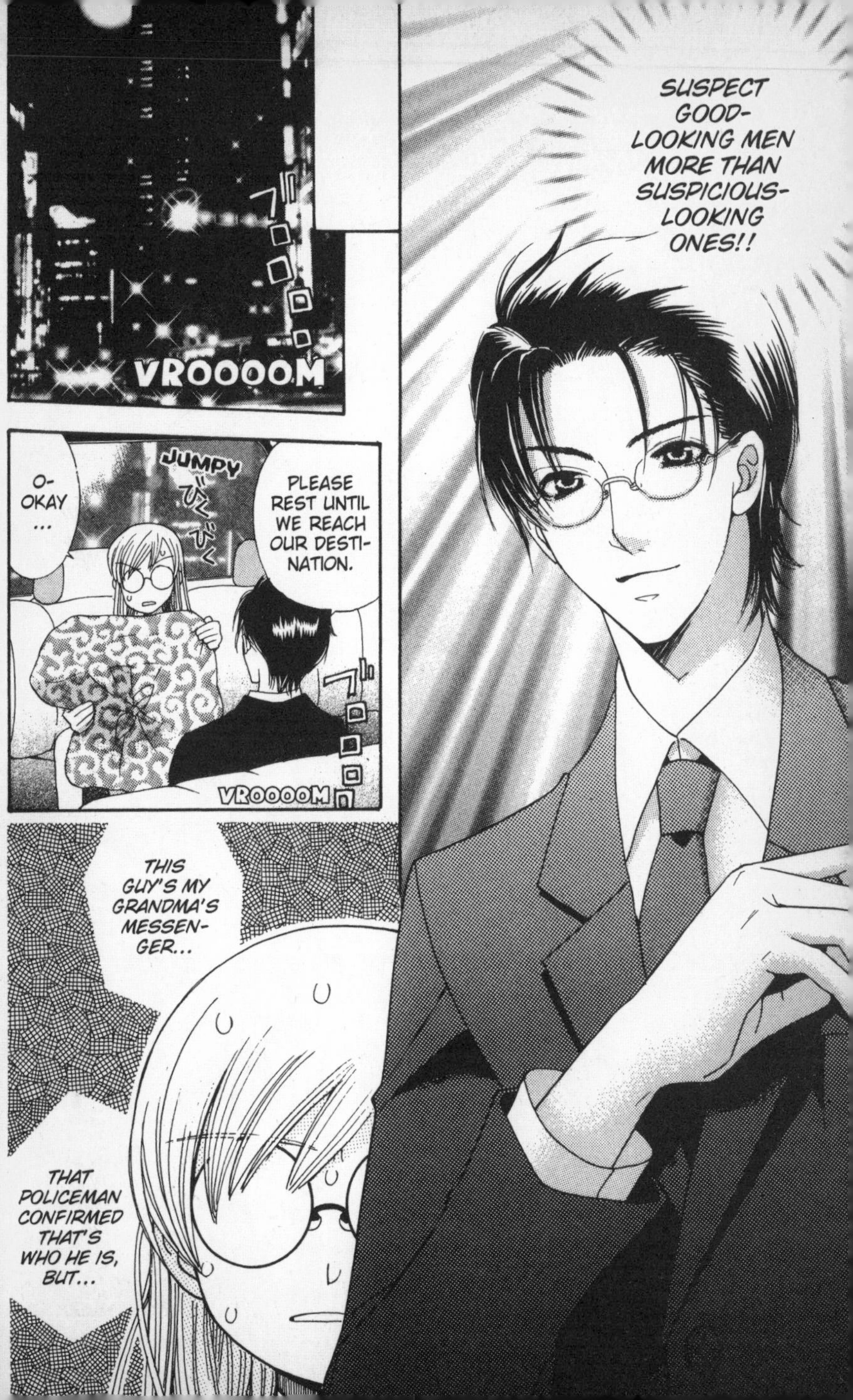
SUSPECT GOOD-LOOKING MEN MORE THAN SUSPICIOUS-LOOKING ONES!!
VROOOOM
PLEASE REST UNTIL WE REACH OUR DESTINATION.
JUMPY
O-OKAY ...
VROOOOM
THIS GUY'S MY GRANDMA'S MESSENGER...
THAT POLICEMAN CONFIRMED THAT'S WHO HE IS, BUT...

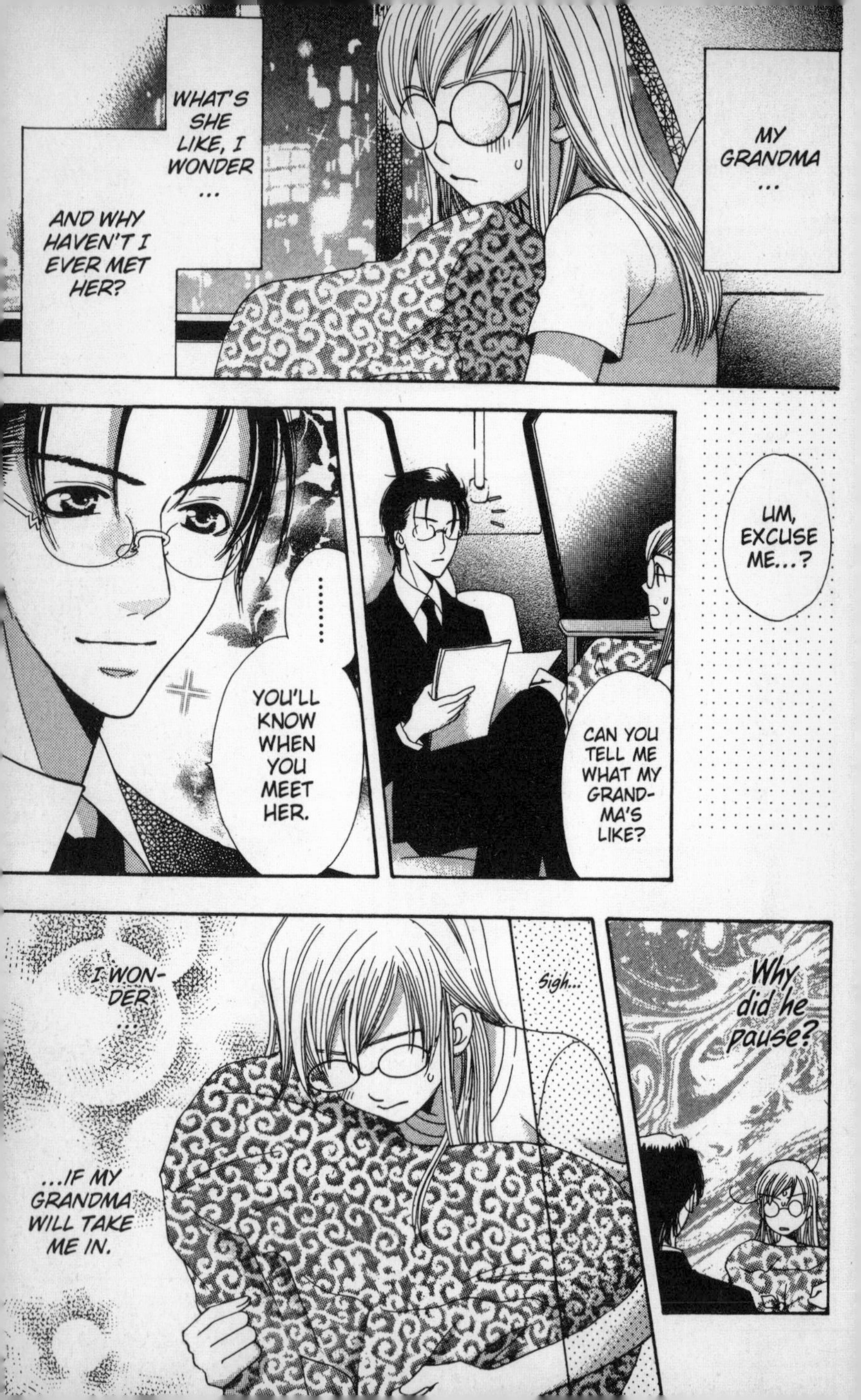
MY GRANDMA ...
WHAT'S SHE LIKE, I WONDER ...
AND WHY HAVEN'T I EVER MET HER?
UM, EXCUSE ME...?
CAN YOU TELL ME WHAT MY GRAND-MA'S LIKE?
......
YOU'LL KNOW WHEN YOU MEET HER.
Why did he pause?
Sigh...
I WON-DER ...
...IF MY GRANDMA WILL TAKE ME IN.

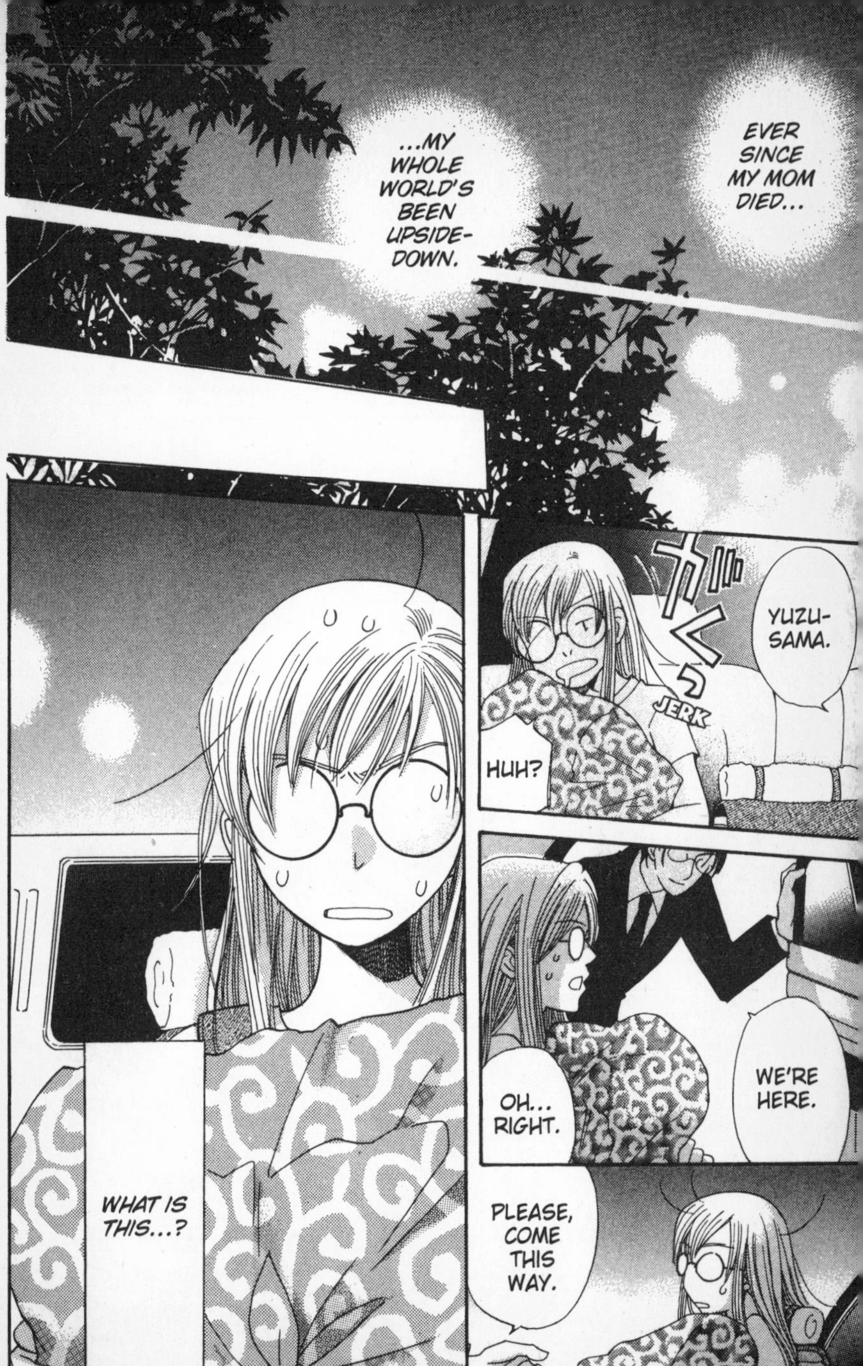
EVER SINCE MY MOM DIED...
...MY WHOLE WORLD'S BEEN UPSIDE-DOWN.
YUZU-SAMA.
JERK
HUH?
WE'RE HERE.
OH... RIGHT.
PLEASE, COME THIS WAY.
WHAT IS THIS...?

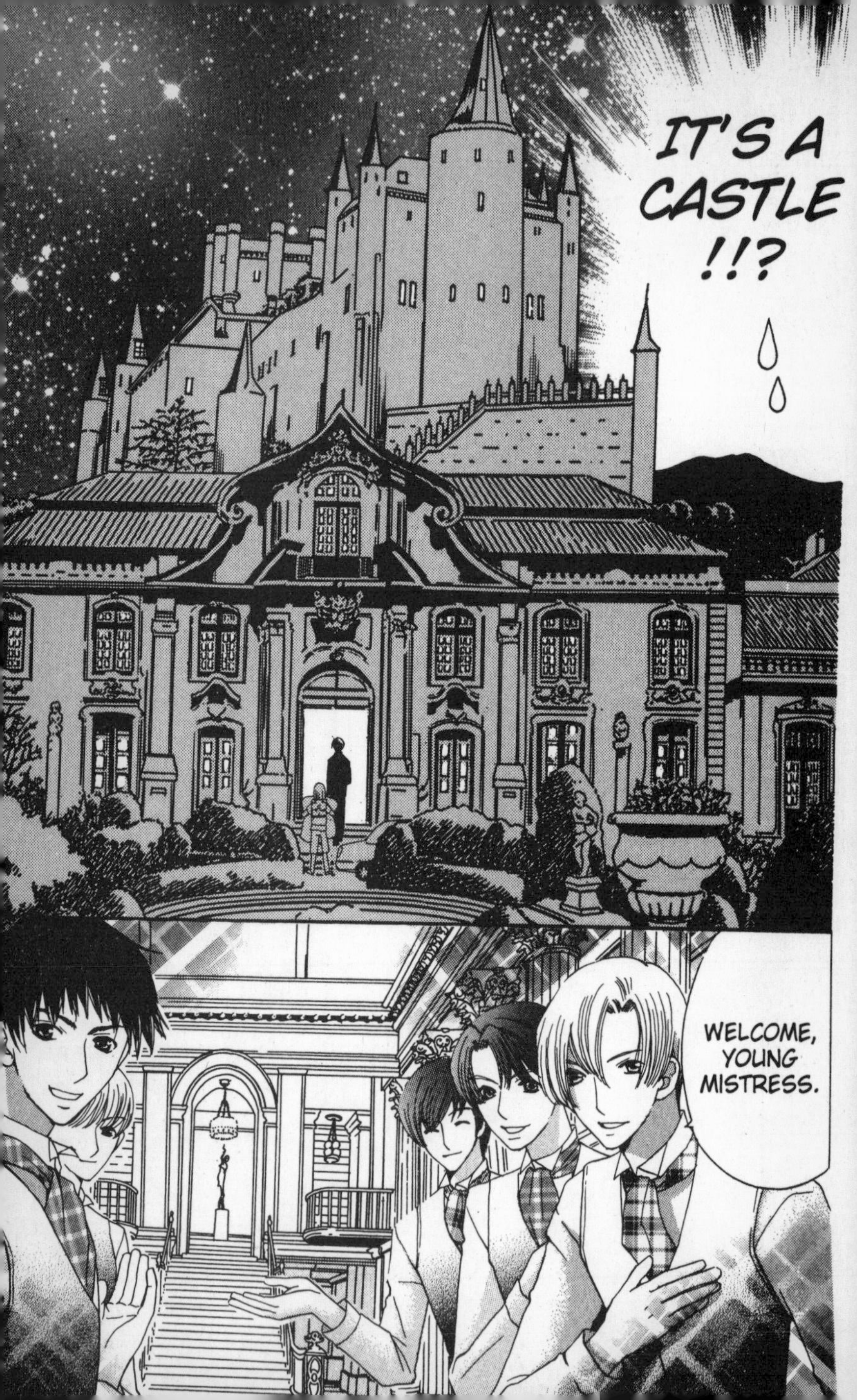
IT'S A CASTLE !!?
WELCOME, YOUNG MISTRESS.

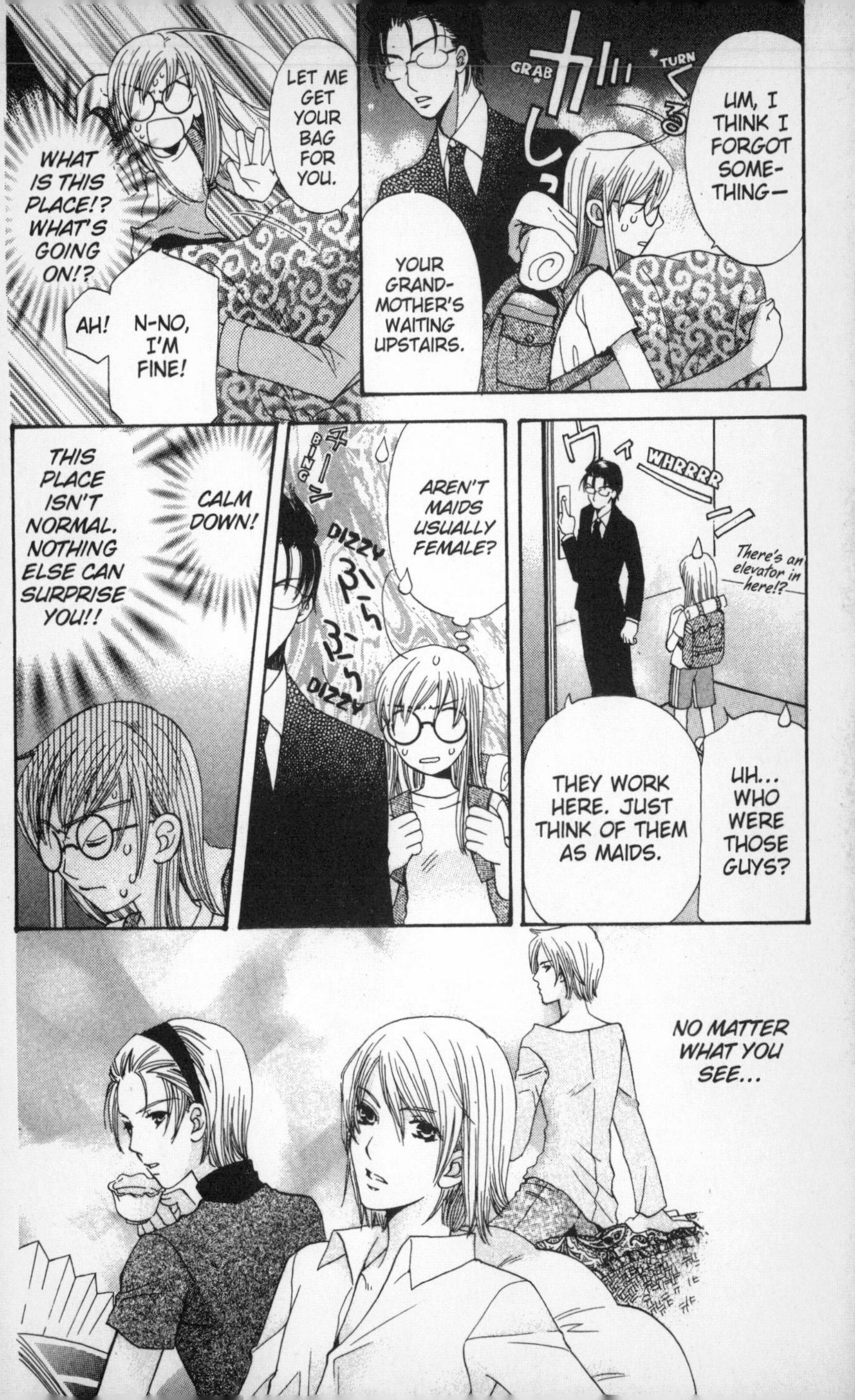
GRAB
TURN
UM, I THINK I FORGOT SOME-THING—
YOUR GRAND-MOTHER'S WAITING UPSTAIRS.
LET ME GET YOUR BAG FOR YOU.
WHAT IS THIS PLACE!? WHAT'S GOING ON!?
AH!
N-NO, I'M FINE!
WHRRRR
There's an elevator in here!?
UH... WHO WERE THOSE GUYS?
THEY WORK HERE. JUST THINK OF THEM AS MAIDS.
BING
AREN'T MAIDS USUALLY FEMALE?
DIZZY
DIZZY
CALM DOWN!
THIS PLACE ISN'T NORMAL. NOTHING ELSE CAN SURPRISE YOU!!
NO MATTER WHAT YOU SEE...

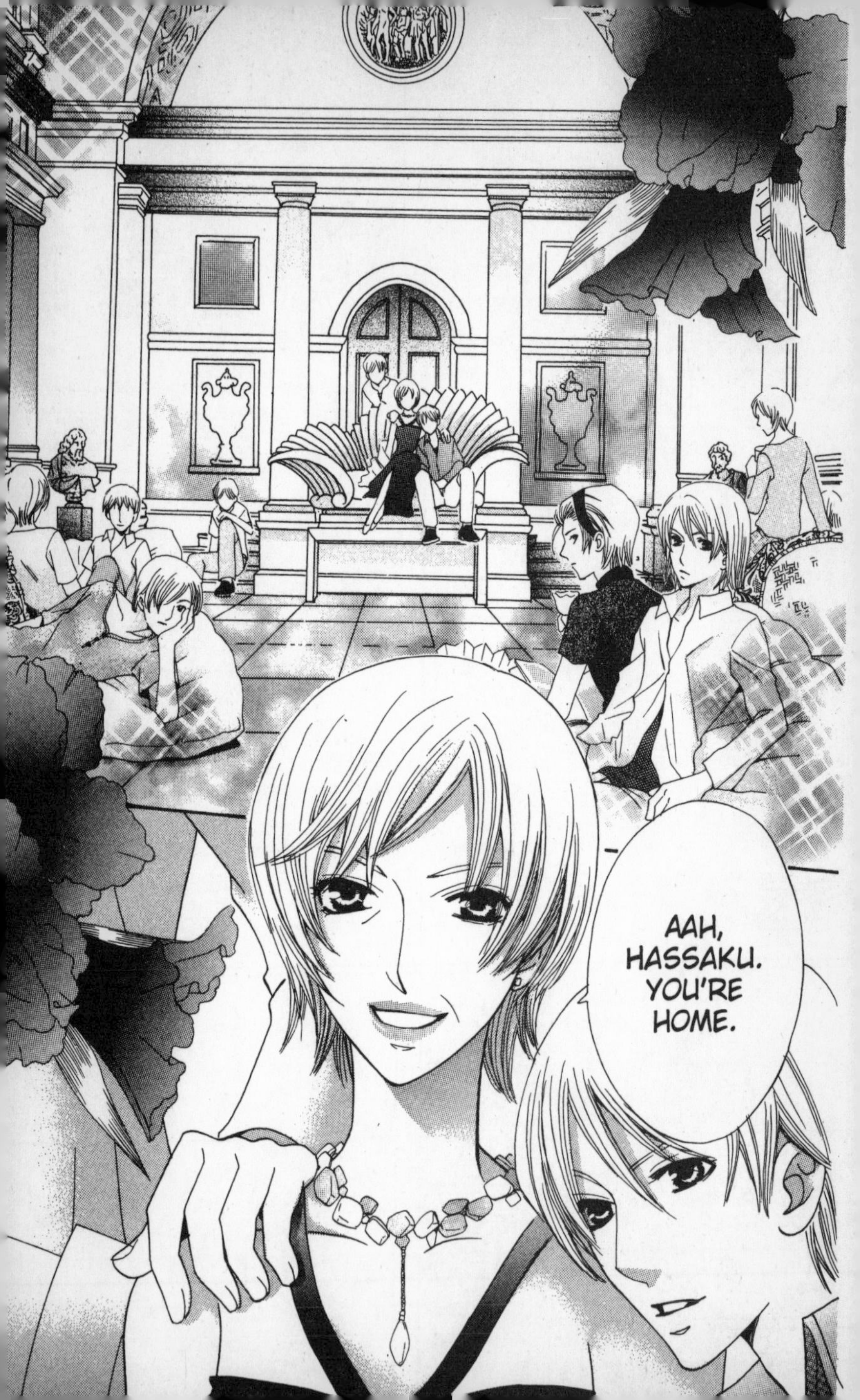
AAH, HASSAKU. YOU'RE HOME.

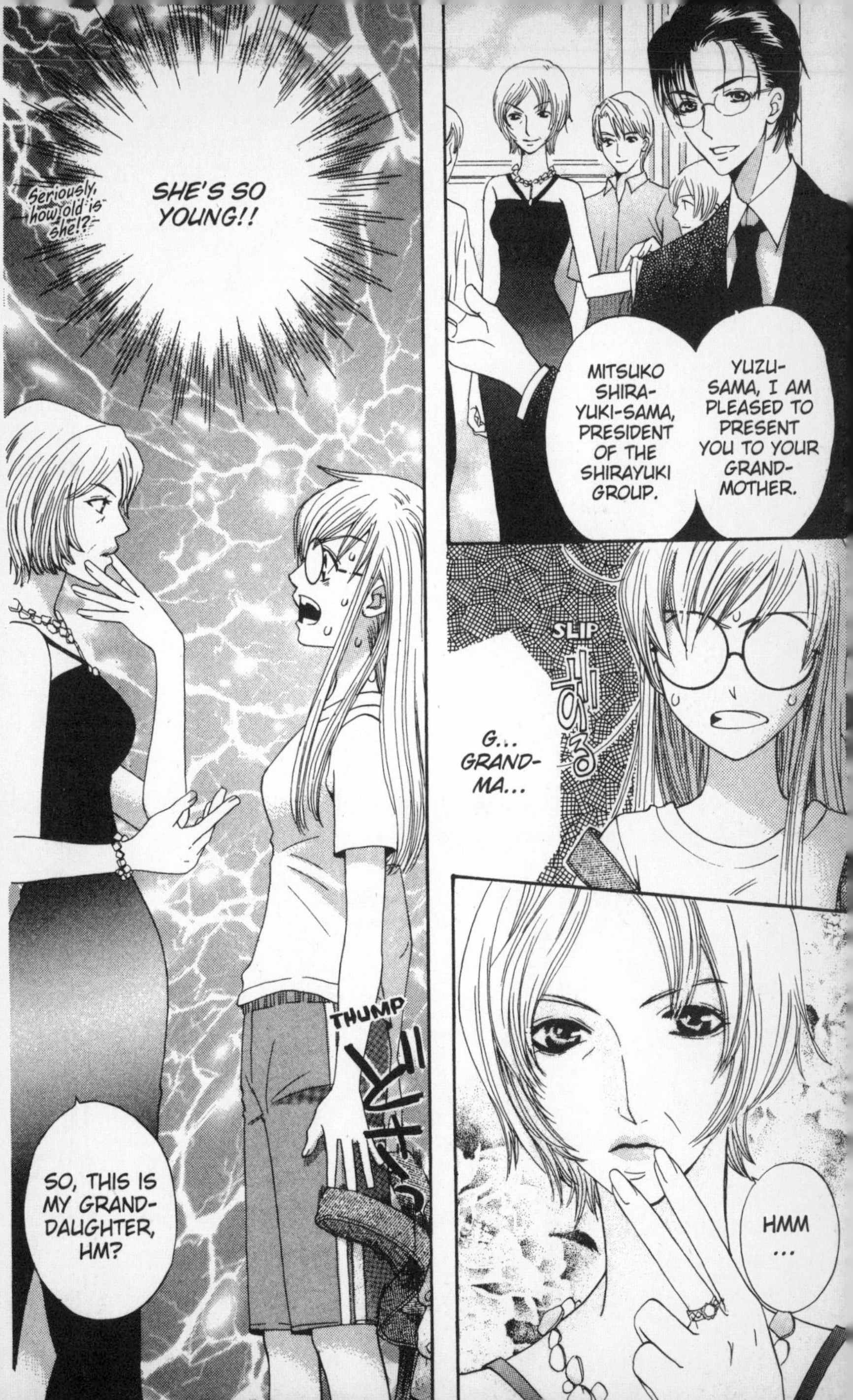
YUZU-SAMA, I AM PLEASED TO PRESENT YOU TO YOUR GRAND-MOTHER.
MITSUKO SHIRA-YUKI-SAMA, PRESIDENT OF THE SHIRAYUKI GROUP.
SLIP
G... GRAND-MA...
HMM ...
SHE'S SO YOUNG!!
Seriously, how old is she!?
THUMP
SO, THIS IS MY GRAND-DAUGHTER, HM?

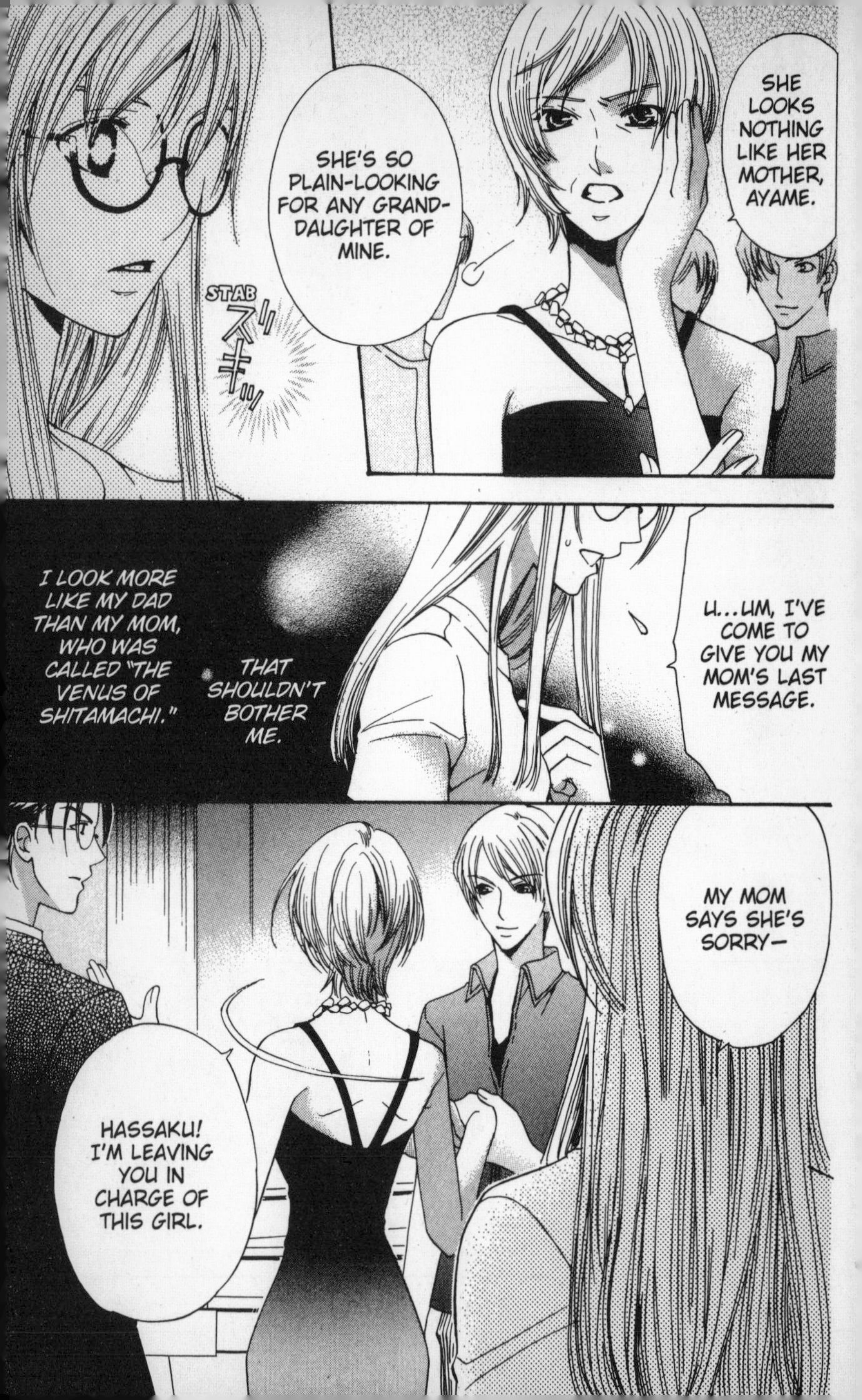
SHE LOOKS NOTHING LIKE HER MOTHER, AYAME.
SHE'S SO PLAIN-LOOKING FOR ANY GRAND-DAUGHTER OF MINE.
STAB
U...UM, I'VE COME TO GIVE YOU MY MOM'S LAST MESSAGE.
I LOOK MORE LIKE MY DAD THAN MY MOM, WHO WAS CALLED "THE VENUS OF SHITAMACHI."
THAT SHOULDN'T BOTHER ME.
MY MOM SAYS SHE'S SORRY—
HASSAKU! I'M LEAVING YOU IN CHARGE OF THIS GIRL.

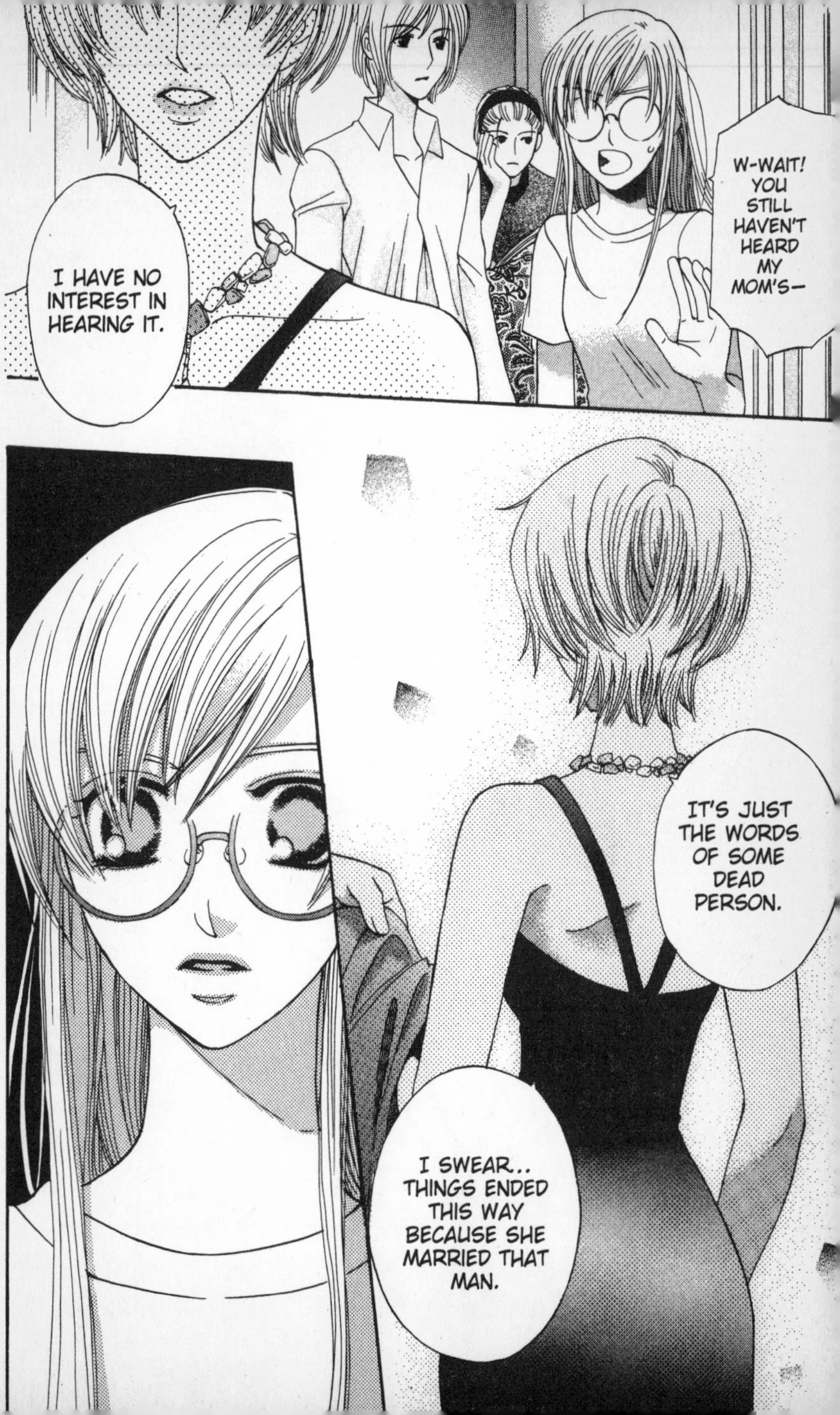
W-WAIT! YOU STILL HAVEN'T HEARD MY MOM'S—
I HAVE NO INTEREST IN HEARING IT.
IT'S JUST THE WORDS OF SOME DEAD PERSON.
I SWEAR... THINGS ENDED THIS WAY BECAUSE SHE MARRIED THAT MAN.

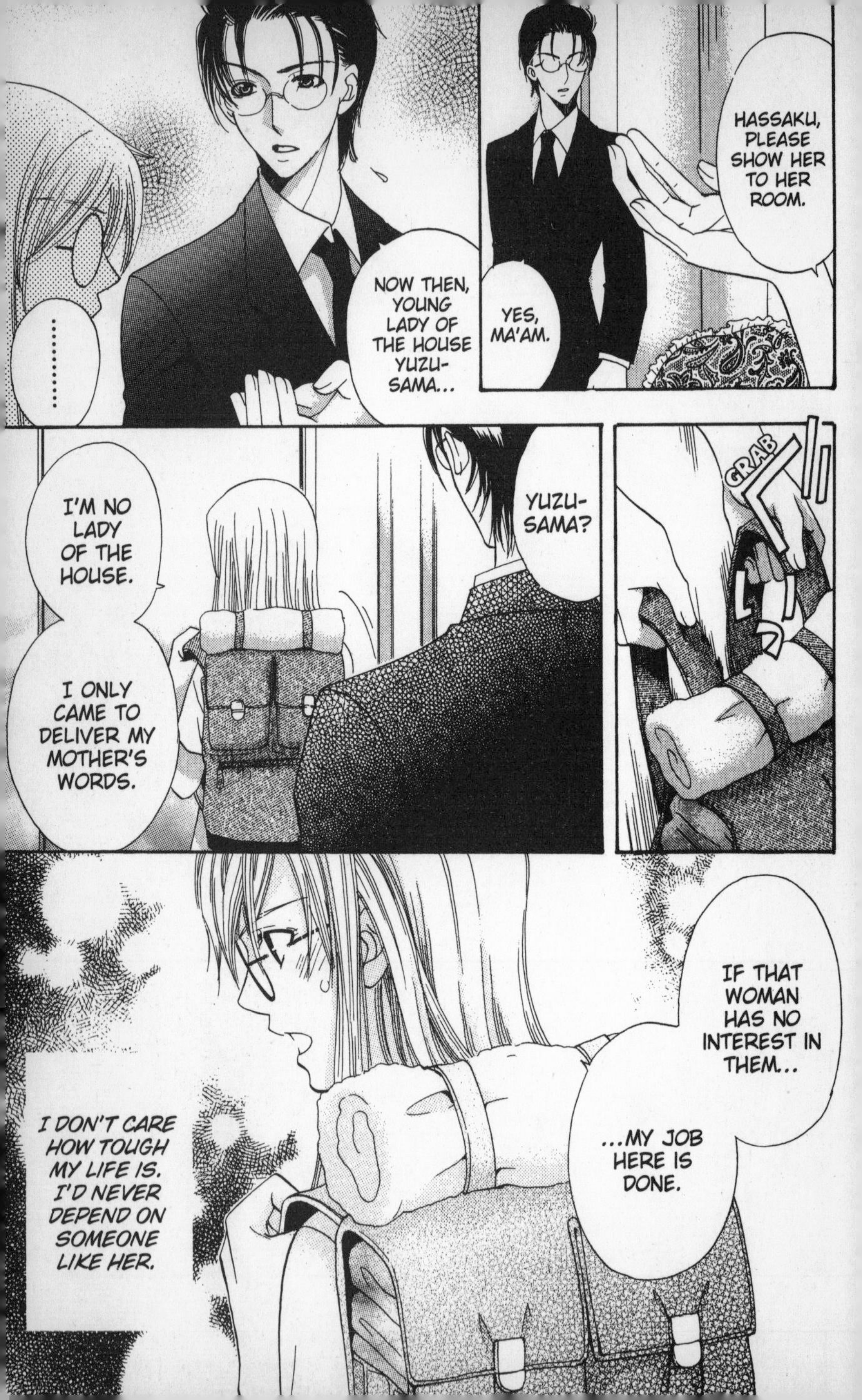
HASSAKU, PLEASE SHOW HER TO HER ROOM.
YES, MA'AM.
NOW THEN, YOUNG LADY OF THE HOUSE YUZU-SAMA...
......
GRAB
YUZU-SAMA?
I'M NO LADY OF THE HOUSE.
I ONLY CAME TO DELIVER MY MOTHER'S WORDS.
IF THAT WOMAN HAS NO INTEREST IN THEM...
...MY JOB HERE IS DONE.
I DON'T CARE HOW TOUGH MY LIFE IS. I'D NEVER DEPEND ON SOMEONE LIKE HER.

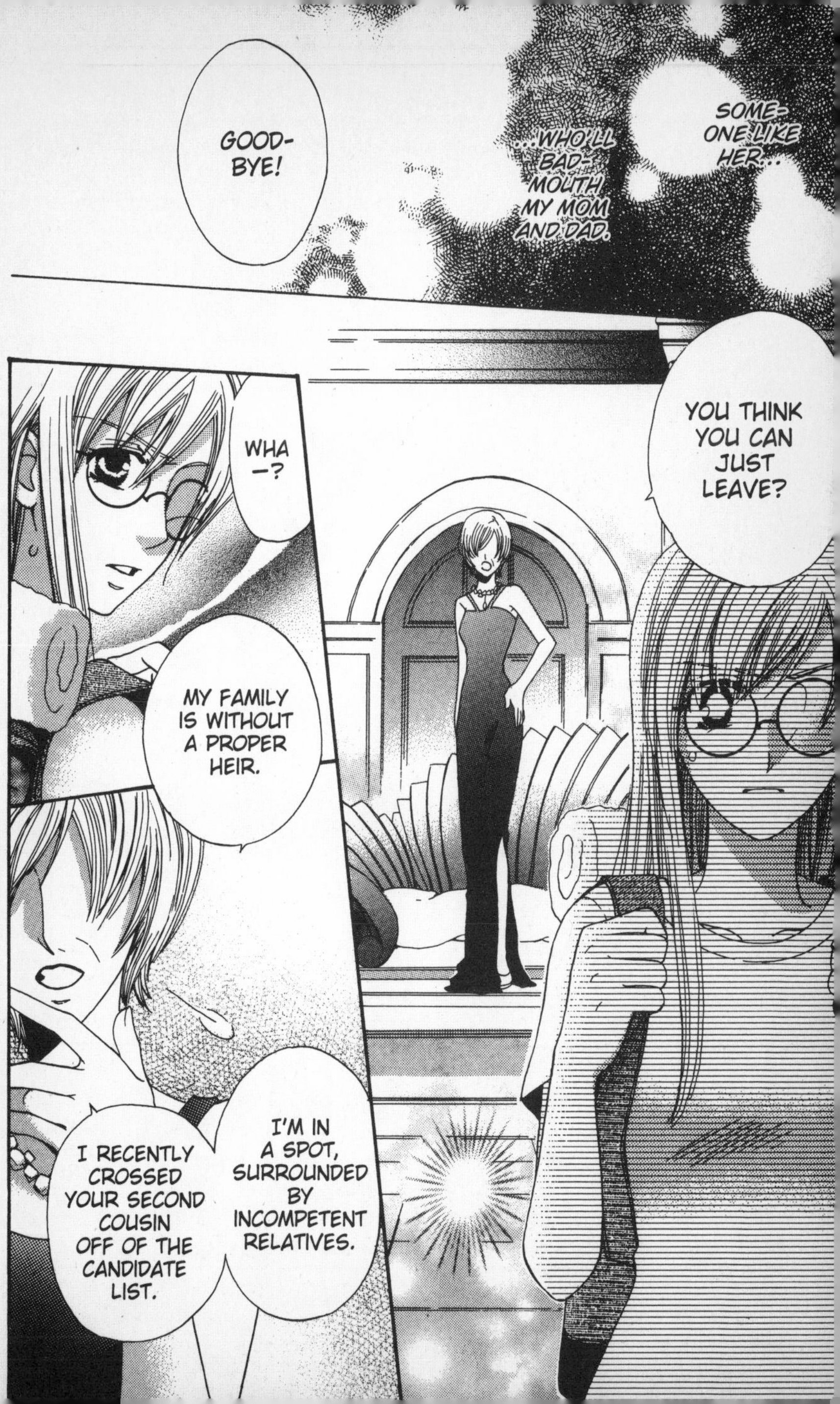
SOME-ONE LIKE HER...
...WHO'LL BAD-MOUTH MY MOM AND DAD.
GOOD-BYE!
YOU THINK YOU CAN JUST LEAVE?
WHA—?
MY FAMILY IS WITHOUT A PROPER HEIR.
I'M IN A SPOT, SURROUNDED BY INCOMPETENT RELATIVES.
I RECENTLY CROSSED YOUR SECOND COUSIN OFF OF THE CANDIDATE LIST.

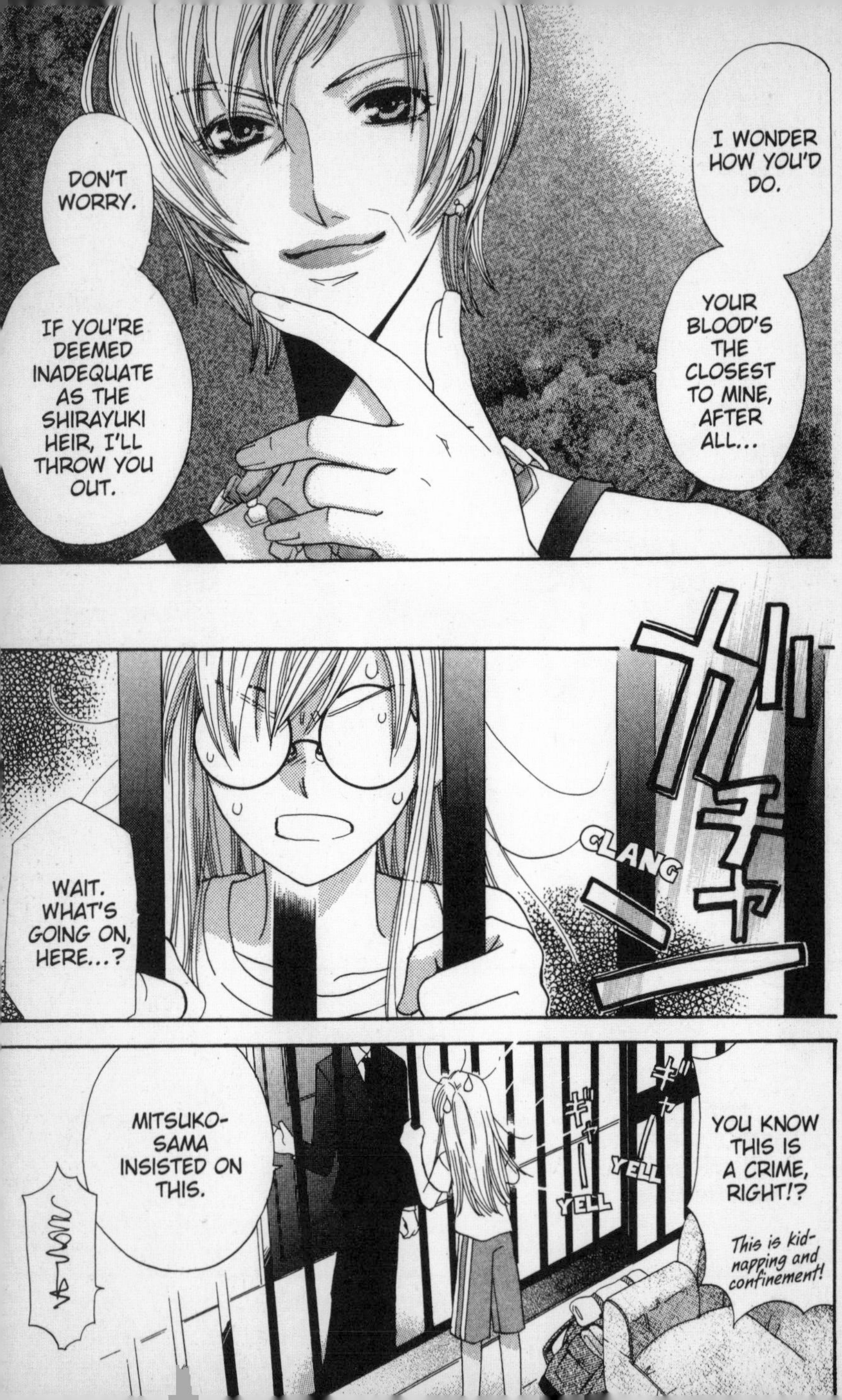
I WONDER HOW YOU'D DO.
YOUR BLOOD'S THE CLOSEST TO MINE, AFTER ALL...
DON'T WORRY.
IF YOU'RE DEEMED INADEQUATE AS THE SHIRAYUKI HEIR, I'LL THROW YOU OUT.
CLANG
WAIT. WHAT'S GOING ON, HERE...?
YOU KNOW THIS IS A CRIME, RIGHT!?
This is kid-napping and confinement!
YELL
YELL
MITSUKO-SAMA INSISTED ON THIS.

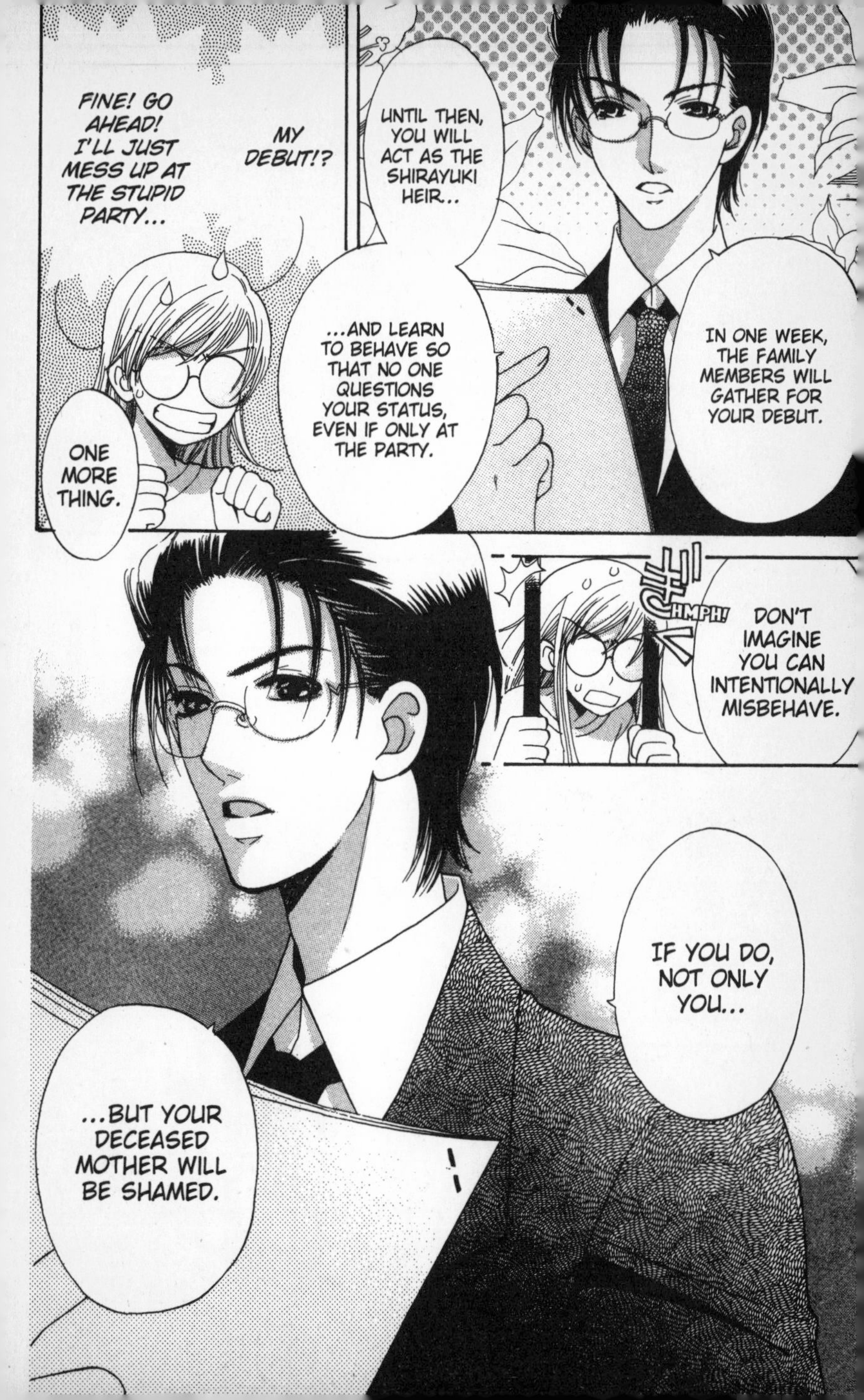
IN ONE WEEK, THE FAMILY MEMBERS WILL GATHER FOR YOUR DEBUT.
UNTIL THEN, YOU WILL ACT AS THE SHIRAYUKI HEIR...
...AND LEARN TO BEHAVE SO THAT NO ONE QUESTIONS YOUR STATUS, EVEN IF ONLY AT THE PARTY.
MY DEBUT!?
FINE! GO AHEAD! I'LL JUST MESS UP AT THE STUPID PARTY...
ONE MORE THING.
DON'T IMAGINE YOU CAN INTENTIONALLY MISBEHAVE.
HMPH!
IF YOU DO, NOT ONLY YOU...
...BUT YOUR DECEASED MOTHER WILL BE SHAMED.

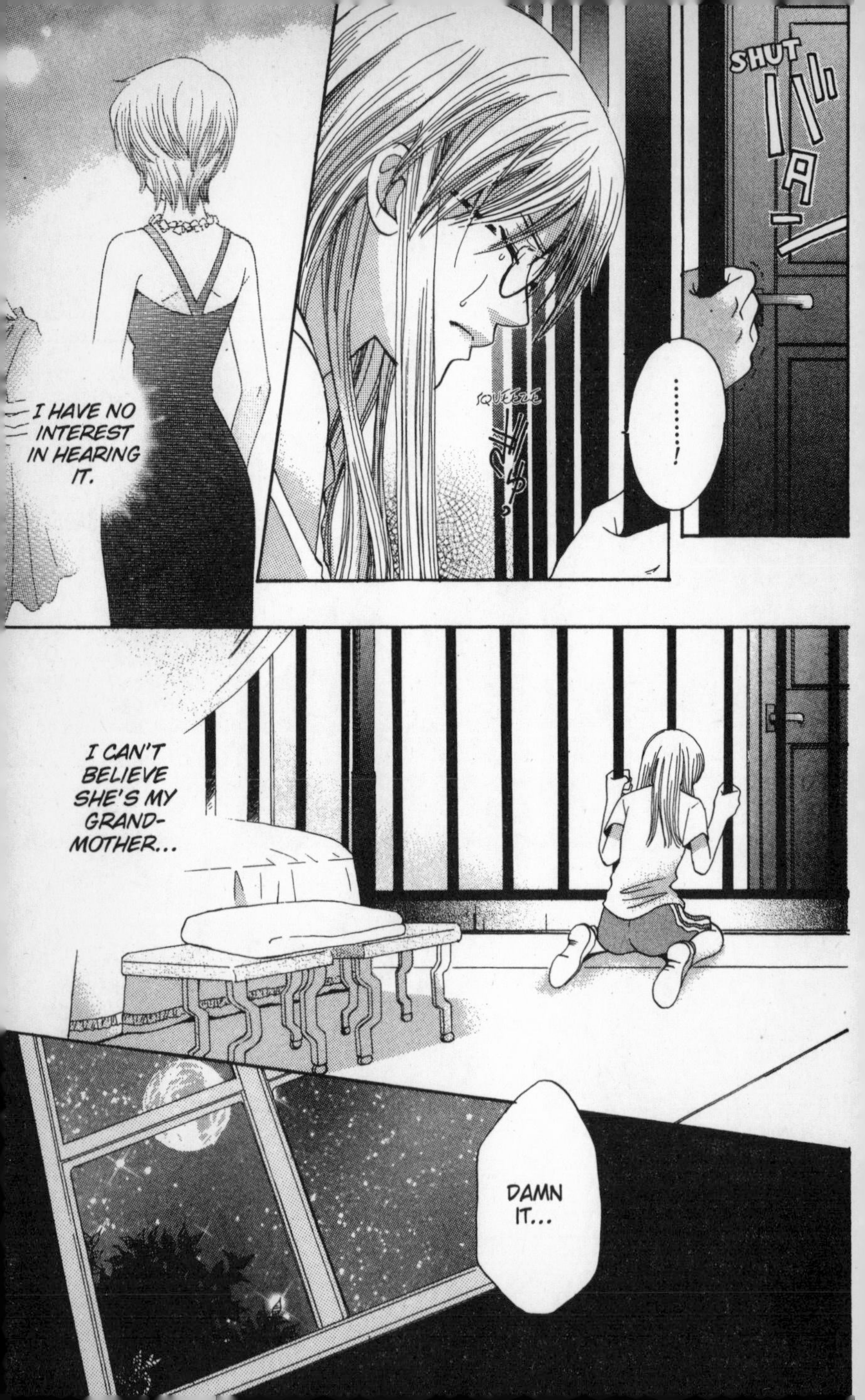
SHUT
SQUEEZE
......!
I HAVE NO INTEREST IN HEARING IT.
I CAN'T BELIEVE SHE'S MY GRANDMOTHER...
DAMN IT...

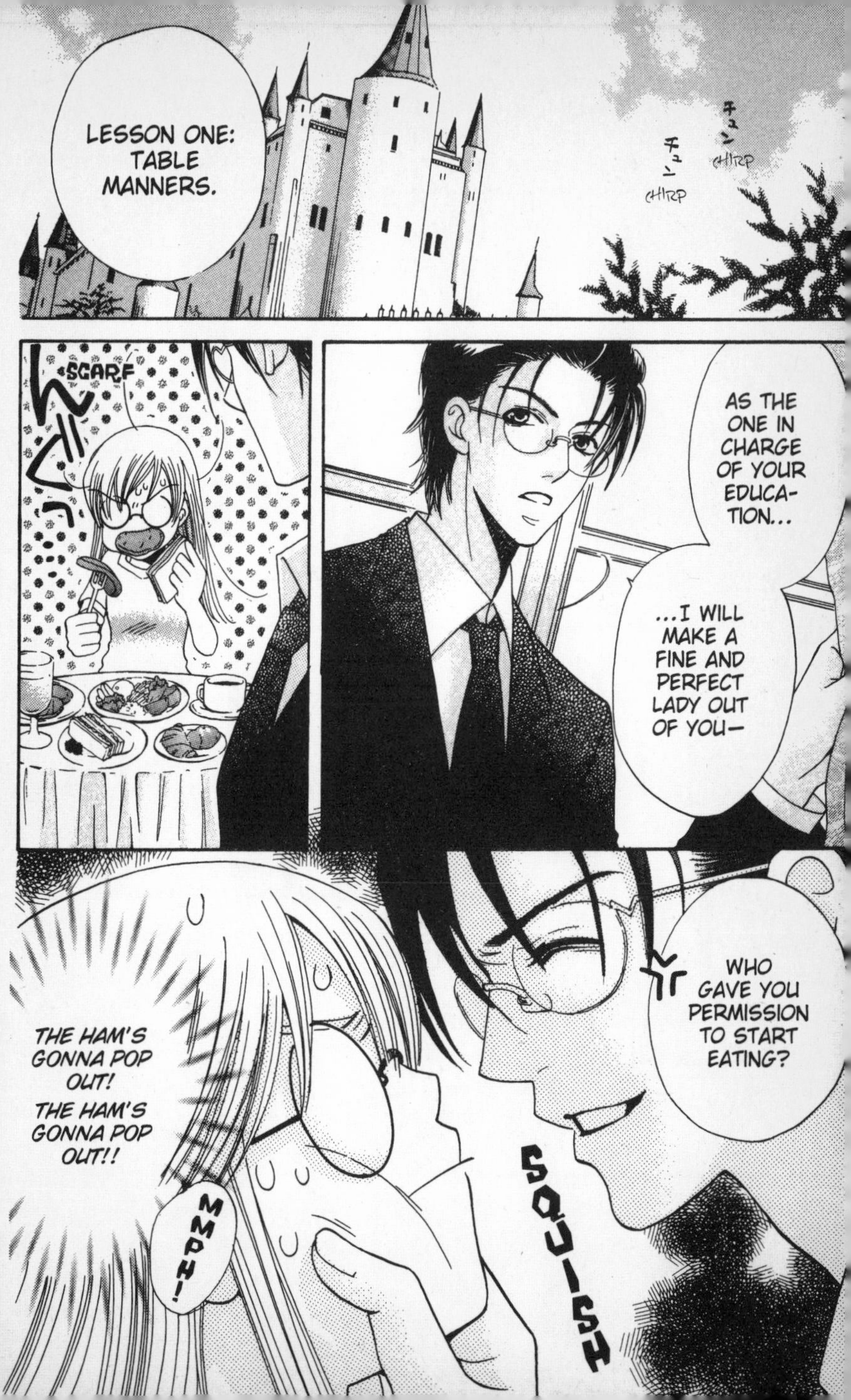
LESSON ONE: TABLE MANNERS.
チュン CHIRP
チュン CHIRP
AS THE ONE IN CHARGE OF YOUR EDUCATION...
...I WILL MAKE A FINE AND PERFECT LADY OUT OF YOU—
SCARF
WHO GAVE YOU PERMISSION TO START EATING?
SQUISH
THE HAM'S GONNA POP OUT!
THE HAM'S GONNA POP OUT!!
MMPH!

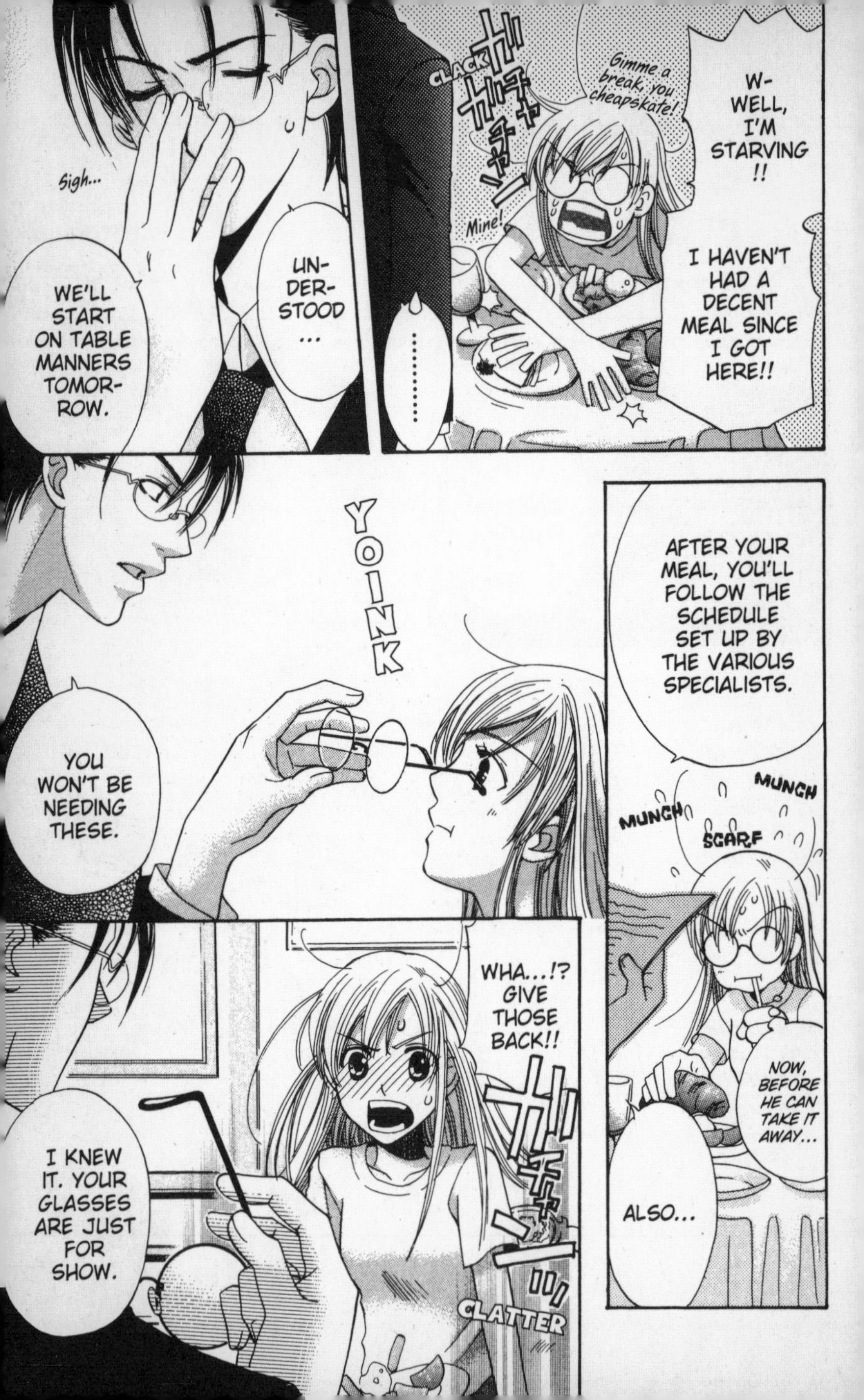
W-WELL, I'M STARVING!!
Gimme a break, you cheapskate!
CLACK
Mine!
I HAVEN'T HAD A DECENT MEAL SINCE I GOT HERE!!
UN-DER-STOOD...
......
Sigh...
WE'LL START ON TABLE MANNERS TOMORROW.
AFTER YOUR MEAL, YOU'LL FOLLOW THE SCHEDULE SET UP BY THE VARIOUS SPECIALISTS.
MUNCH
MUNCH
SCARF
NOW, BEFORE HE CAN TAKE IT AWAY...
ALSO...
YOINK
YOU WON'T BE NEEDING THESE.
WHA...!? GIVE THOSE BACK!!
CLATTER
I KNEW IT. YOUR GLASSES ARE JUST FOR SHOW.

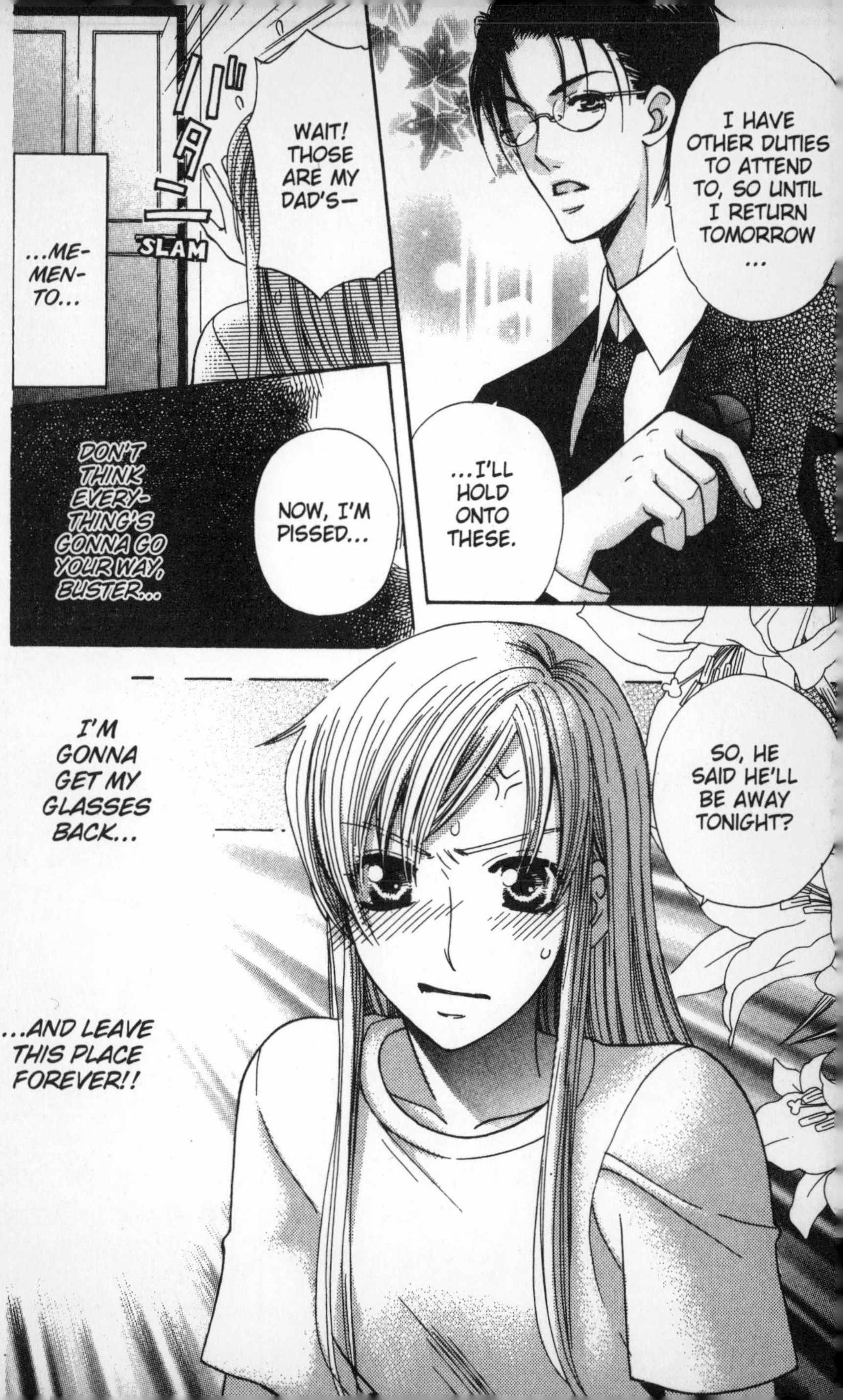

I HAVE OTHER DUTIES TO ATTEND TO, SO UNTIL I RETURN TOMORROW ...
...I'LL HOLD ONTO THESE.
WAIT! THOSE ARE MY DAD'S—
SLAM
...ME-MEN-TO...
NOW, I'M PISSED...
DON'T THINK EVERY-THING'S GONNA GO YOUR WAY, BUSTER...
SO, HE SAID HE'LL BE AWAY TONIGHT?
I'M GONNA GET MY GLASSES BACK...
...AND LEAVE THIS PLACE FOREVER!!

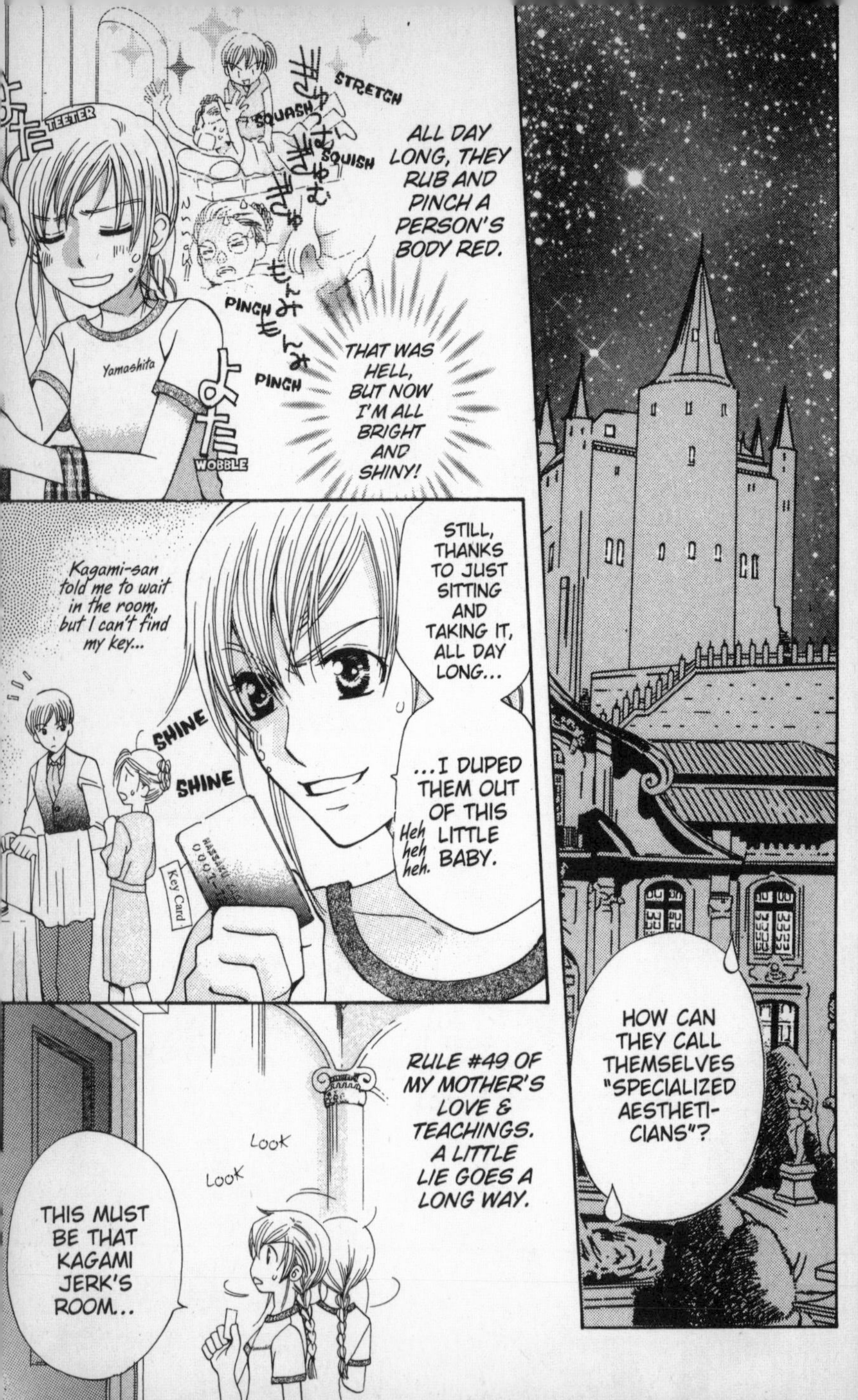
HOW CAN THEY CALL THEMSELVES "SPECIALIZED AESTHETICIANS"?
STRETCH
SQUASH
SQUISH
TEETER
ALL DAY LONG, THEY RUB AND PINCH A PERSON'S BODY RED.
PINCH
PINCH
Yamashita
WOBBLE
THAT WAS HELL, BUT NOW I'M ALL BRIGHT AND SHINY!
STILL, THANKS TO JUST SITTING AND TAKING IT, ALL DAY LONG...
...I DUPED THEM OUT OF THIS LITTLE BABY.
Heh heh heh.
Kagami-san told me to wait in the room, but I can't find my key...
SHINE
SHINE
Key Card
RULE #49 OF MY MOTHER'S LOVE & TEACHINGS. A LITTLE LIE GOES A LONG WAY.
Look
Look
THIS MUST BE THAT KAGAMI JERK'S ROOM...

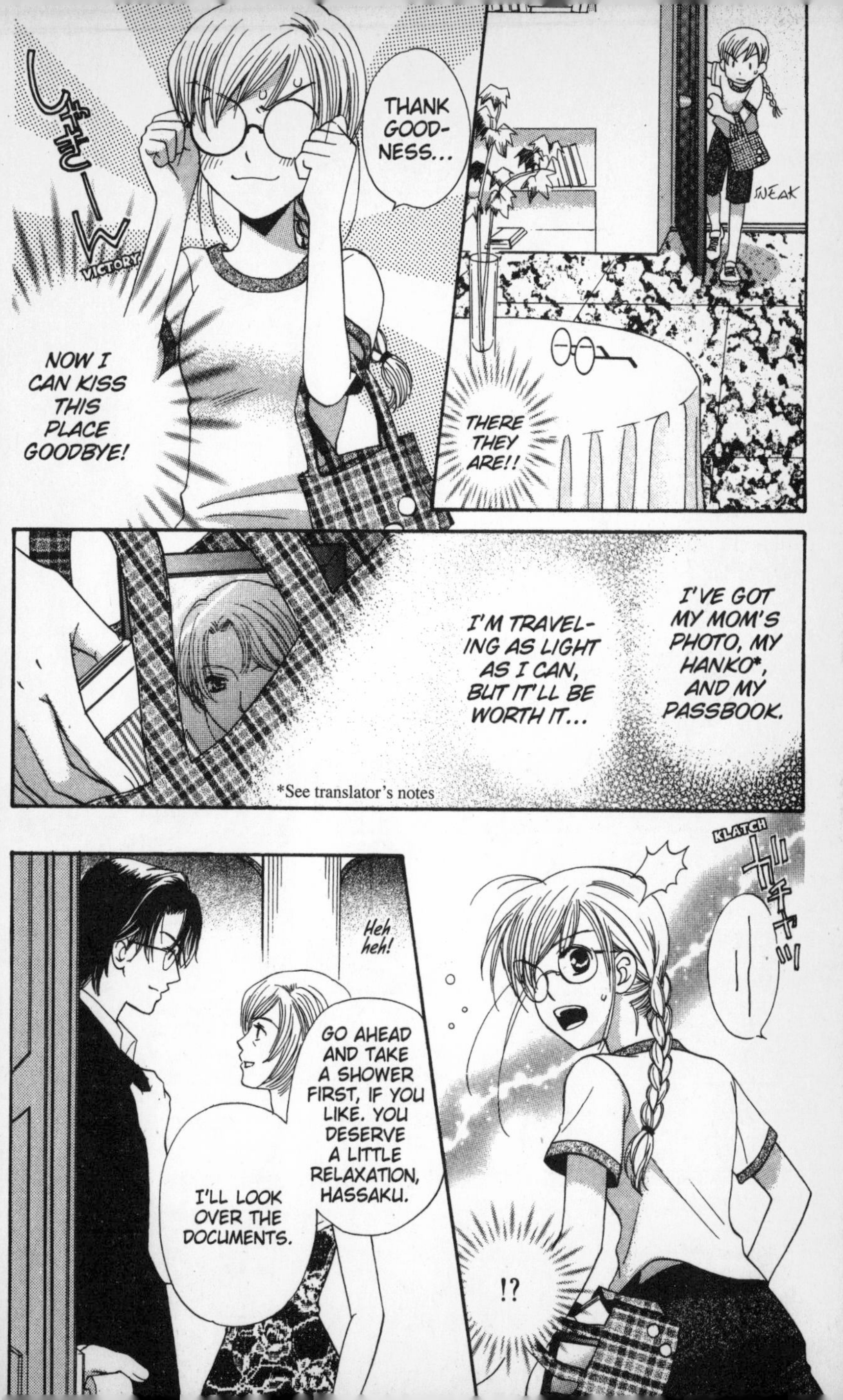
SNEAK
THERE THEY ARE!!
THANK GOOD-NESS...
しゃきーん
VICTORY
NOW I CAN KISS THIS PLACE GOODBYE!
I'VE GOT MY MOM'S PHOTO, MY HANKO*, AND MY PASSBOOK.
I'M TRAVEL-ING AS LIGHT AS I CAN, BUT IT'LL BE WORTH IT...
*See translator's notes
KLATCH
ガチャ
!?
Heh heh!
GO AHEAD AND TAKE A SHOWER FIRST, IF YOU LIKE. YOU DESERVE A LITTLE RELAXATION, HASSAKU.
I'LL LOOK OVER THE DOCUMENTS.

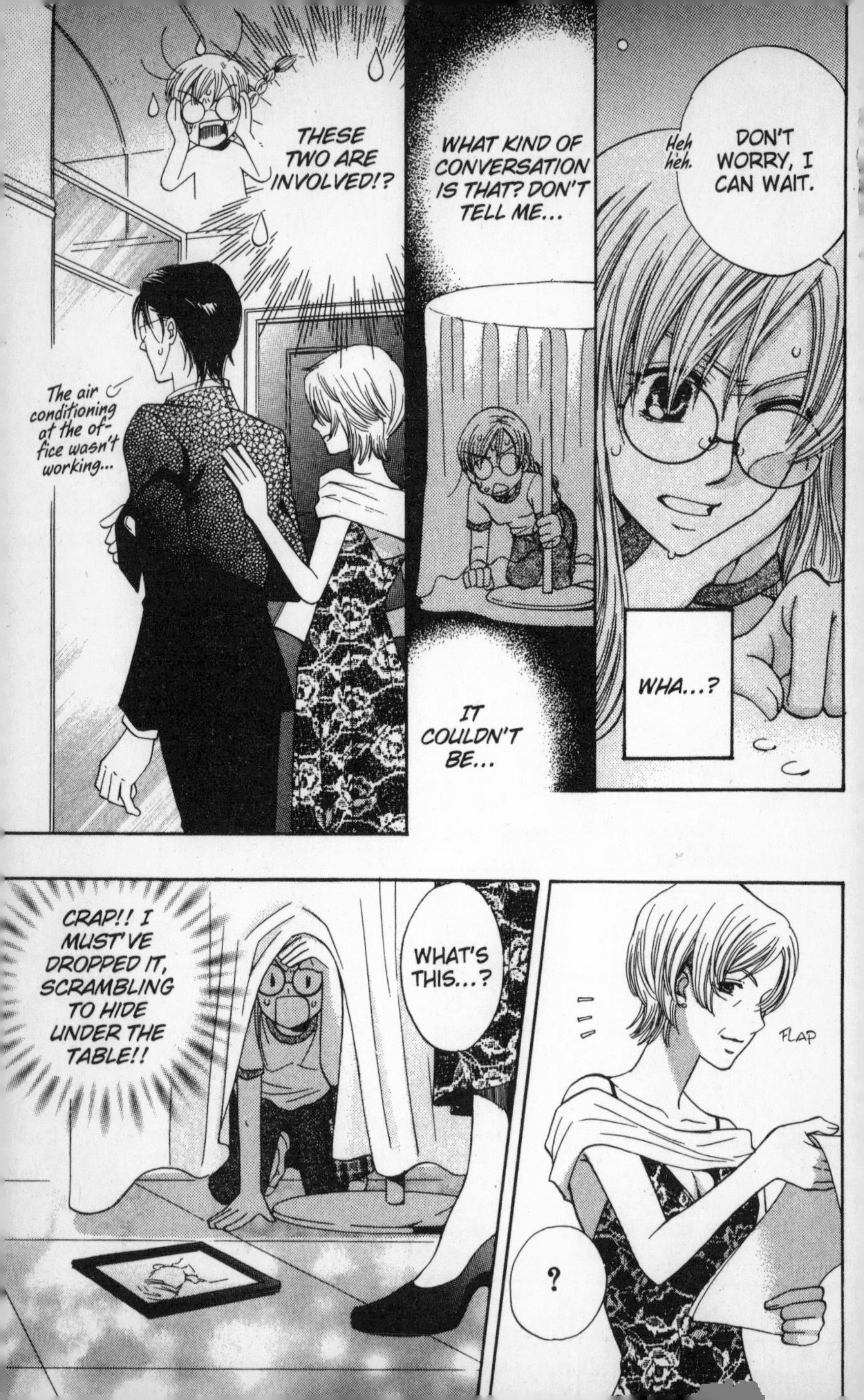
Heh heh.
DON'T WORRY, I CAN WAIT.
WHA...?
WHAT KIND OF CONVERSATION IS THAT? DON'T TELL ME...
IT COULDN'T BE...
THESE TWO ARE INVOLVED!?
The air conditioning at the office wasn't working...
FLAP
?
WHAT'S THIS...?
CRAP!! I MUST'VE DROPPED IT, SCRAMBLING TO HIDE UNDER THE TABLE!!

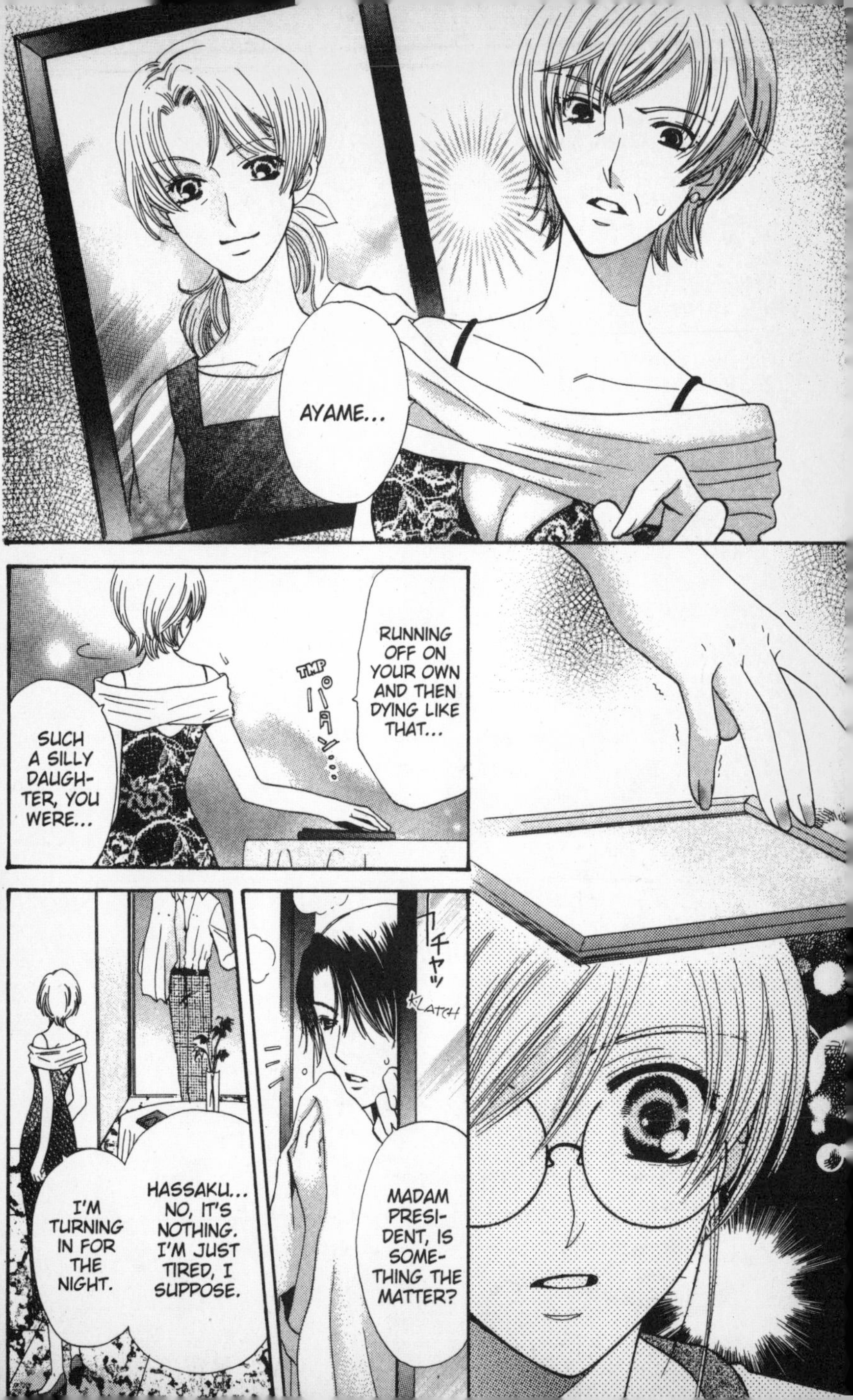
AYAME...
RUNNING OFF ON YOUR OWN AND THEN DYING LIKE THAT...
TMP
パタン...
SUCH A SILLY DAUGHTER, YOU WERE...
MADAM PRESIDENT, IS SOMETHING THE MATTER?
カチャッ
KLATCH
HASSAKU... NO, IT'S NOTHING. I'M JUST TIRED, I SUPPOSE.
I'M TURNING IN FOR THE NIGHT.

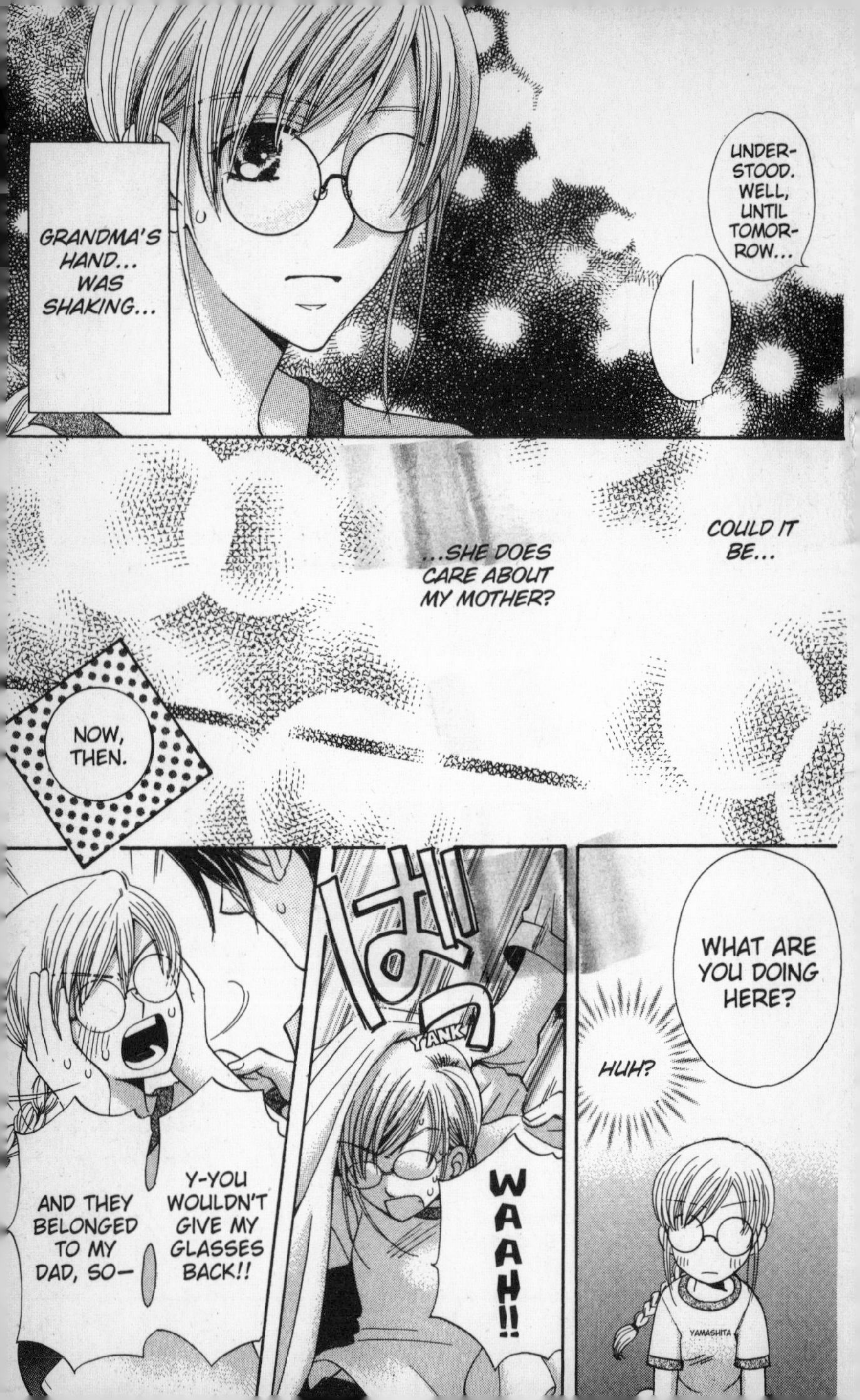
UNDER-STOOD. WELL, UNTIL TOMOR-ROW...
GRANDMA'S HAND... WAS SHAKING...
COULD IT BE...
...SHE DOES CARE ABOUT MY MOTHER?
NOW, THEN.
WHAT ARE YOU DOING HERE?
HUH?
YAMASHITA
YANK
WAAAH!!
Y-YOU WOULDN'T GIVE MY GLASSES BACK!!
AND THEY BELONGED TO MY DAD, SO—

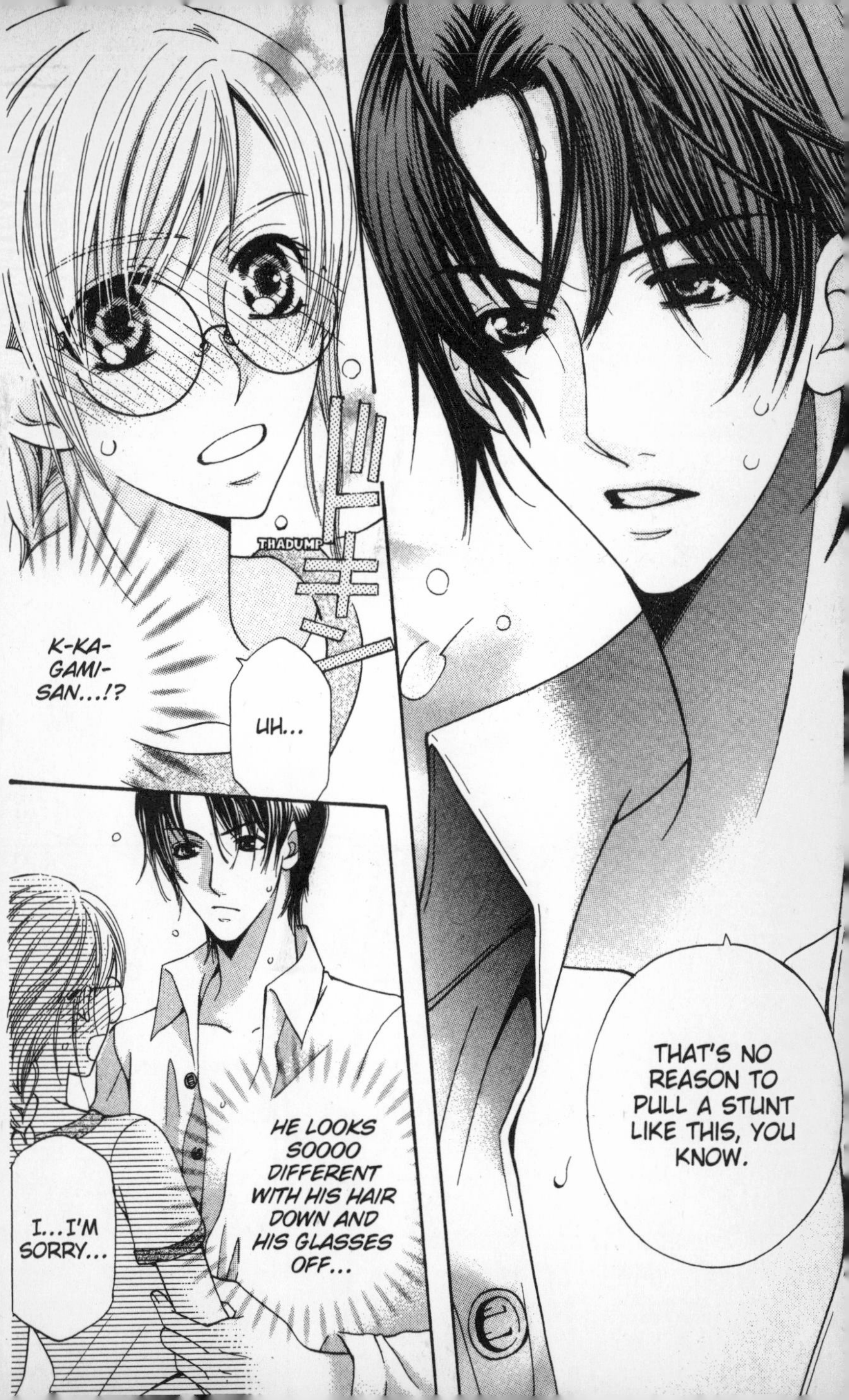
THAT'S NO REASON TO PULL A STUNT LIKE THIS, YOU KNOW.
THADUMP
UH...
K-KA-GAMI-SAN...!?
HE LOOKS SOOOO DIFFERENT WITH HIS HAIR DOWN AND HIS GLASSES OFF...
I...I'M SORRY...

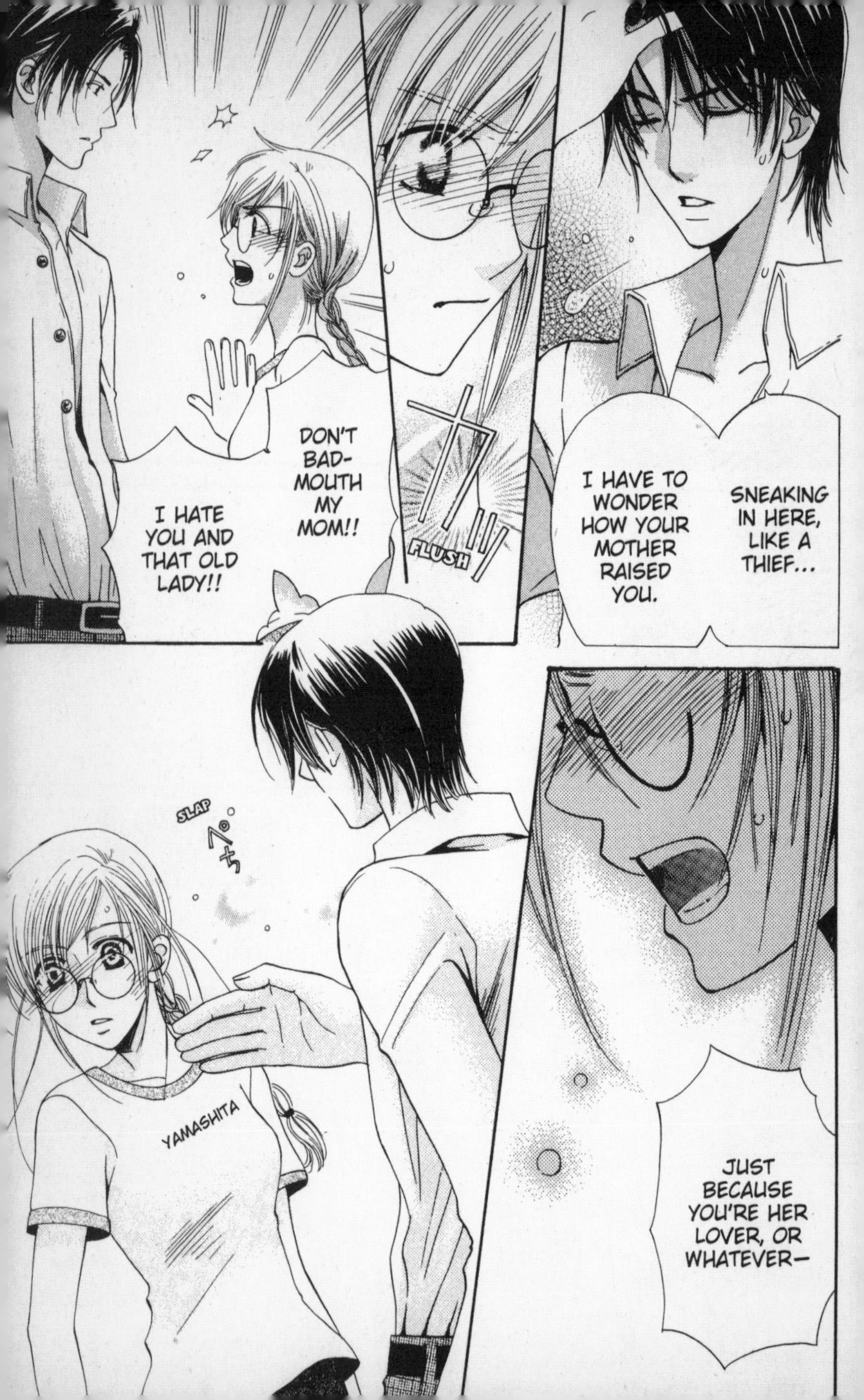
SNEAKING IN HERE, LIKE A THIEF...
I HAVE TO WONDER HOW YOUR MOTHER RAISED YOU.
FLUSH
DON'T BAD-MOUTH MY MOM!!
I HATE YOU AND THAT OLD LADY!!
JUST BECAUSE YOU'RE HER LOVER, OR WHATEVER—
SLAP
YAMASHITA

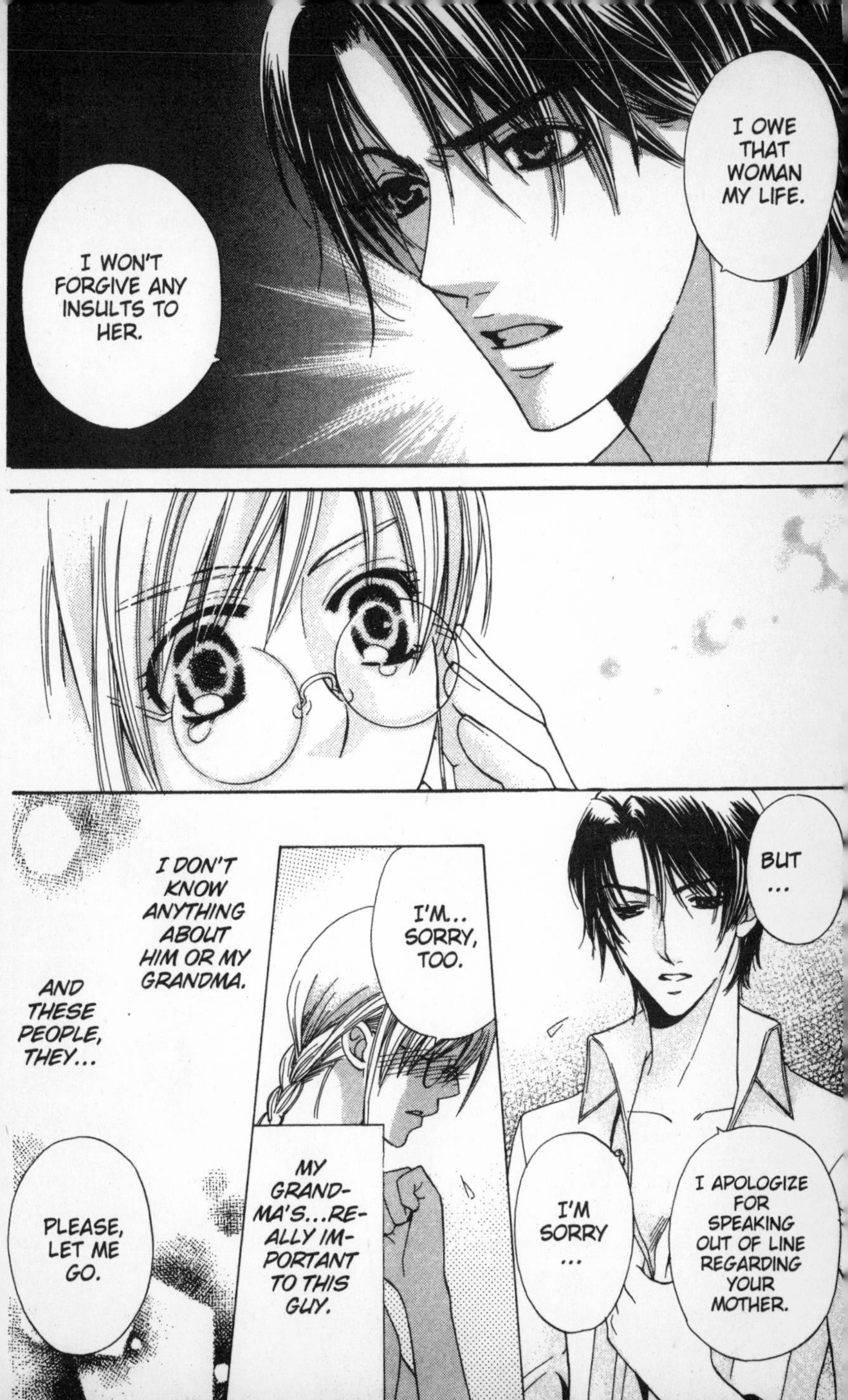
I OWE THAT WOMAN MY LIFE.
I WON'T FORGIVE ANY INSULTS TO HER.
BUT ...
I APOLOGIZE FOR SPEAKING OUT OF LINE REGARDING YOUR MOTHER.
I'M SORRY ...
I'M... SORRY, TOO.
MY GRAND-MA'S...RE-ALLY IM-PORTANT TO THIS GUY.
I DON'T KNOW ANYTHING ABOUT HIM OR MY GRANDMA.
AND THESE PEOPLE, THEY...
PLEASE, LET ME GO.

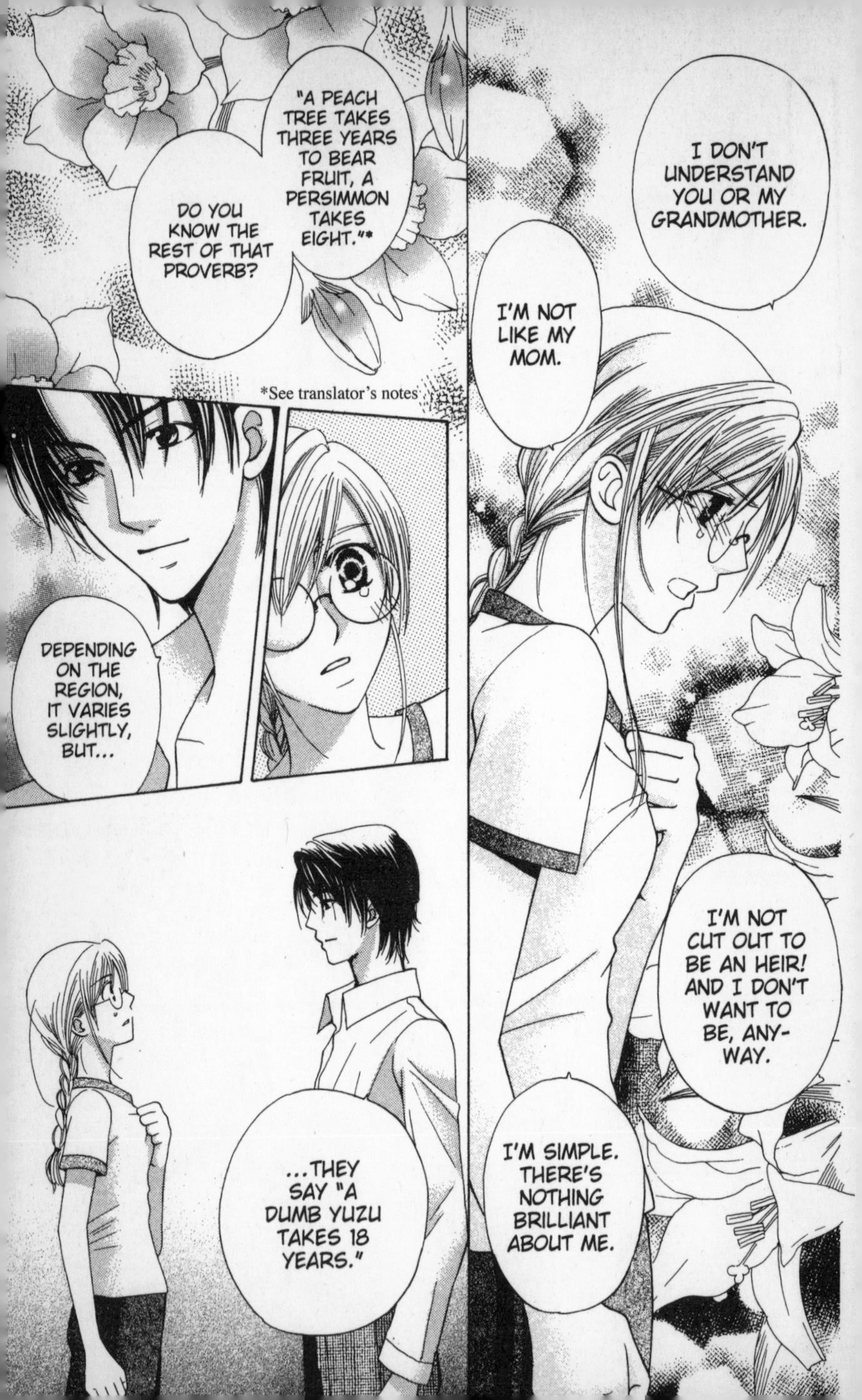
I DON'T UNDERSTAND YOU OR MY GRANDMOTHER.
I'M NOT LIKE MY MOM.
I'M NOT CUT OUT TO BE AN HEIR! AND I DON'T WANT TO BE, ANY-WAY.
I'M SIMPLE. THERE'S NOTHING BRILLIANT ABOUT ME.
"A PEACH TREE TAKES THREE YEARS TO BEAR FRUIT, A PERSIMMON TAKES EIGHT."*
DO YOU KNOW THE REST OF THAT PROVERB?
*See translator's notes
DEPENDING ON THE REGION, IT VARIES SLIGHTLY, BUT...
...THEY SAY "A DUMB YUZU TAKES 18 YEARS."

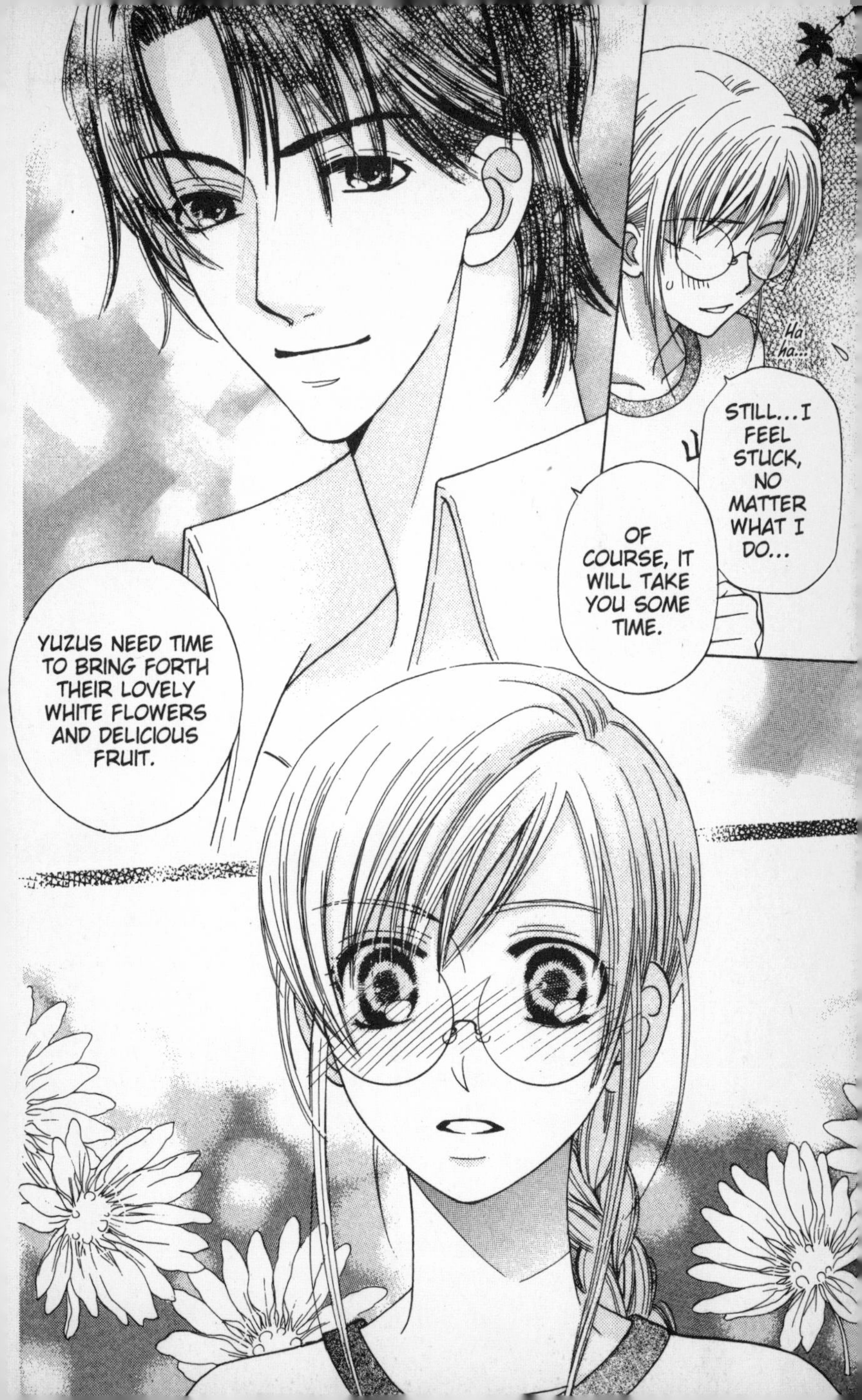
Ha ha...
STILL...I FEEL STUCK, NO MATTER WHAT I DO...
OF COURSE, IT WILL TAKE YOU SOME TIME.
YUZUS NEED TIME TO BRING FORTH THEIR LOVELY WHITE FLOWERS AND DELICIOUS FRUIT.

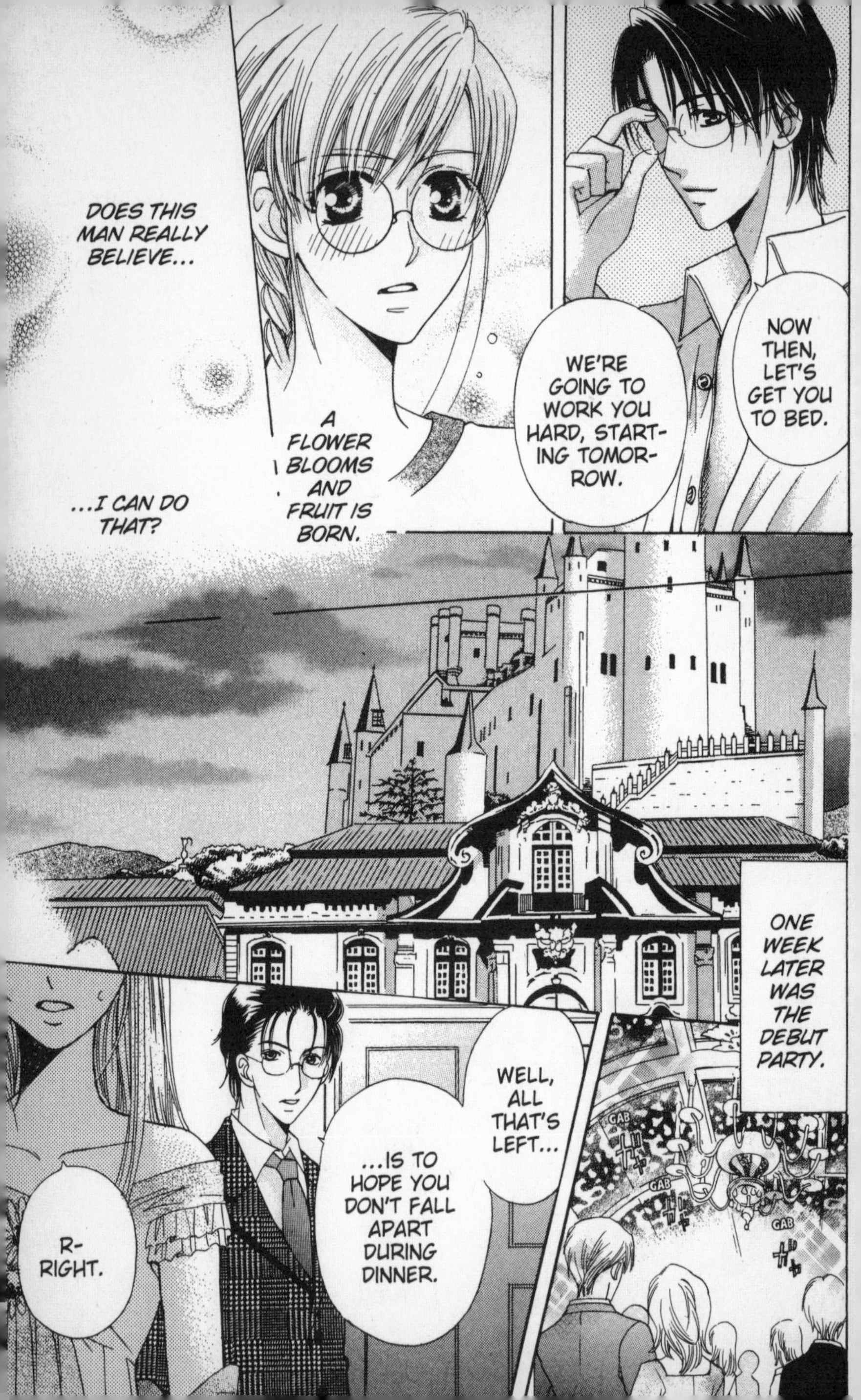
NOW THEN, LET'S GET YOU TO BED.
WE'RE GOING TO WORK YOU HARD, START-ING TOMOR-ROW.
DOES THIS MAN REALLY BELIEVE...
A FLOWER BLOOMS AND FRUIT IS BORN.
...I CAN DO THAT?
ONE WEEK LATER WAS THE DEBUT PARTY.
GAB
GAB
GAB
WELL, ALL THAT'S LEFT...
...IS TO HOPE YOU DON'T FALL APART DURING DINNER.
R-RIGHT.

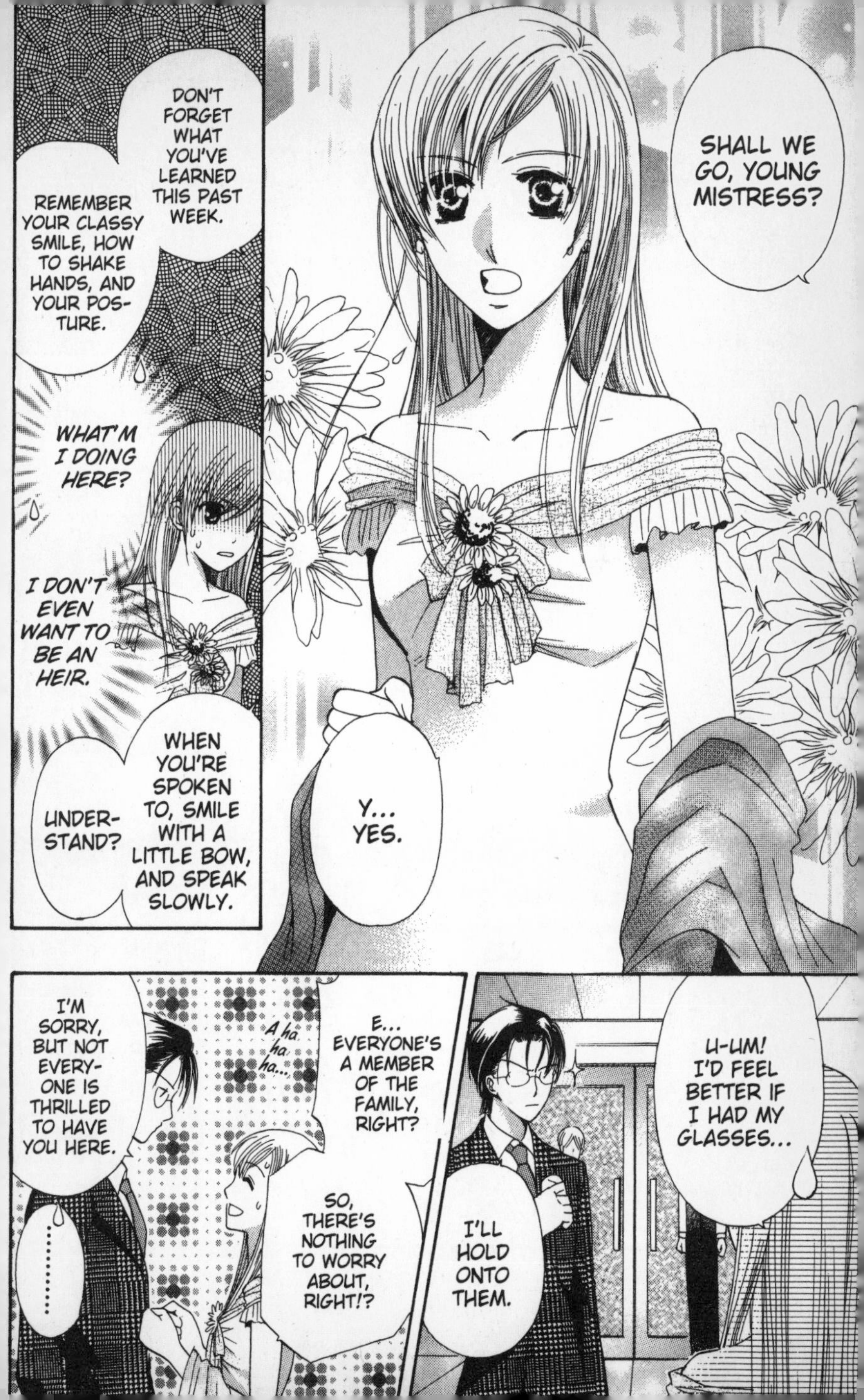
SHALL WE GO, YOUNG MISTRESS?
Y... YES.
DON'T FORGET WHAT YOU'VE LEARNED THIS PAST WEEK.
REMEMBER YOUR CLASSY SMILE, HOW TO SHAKE HANDS, AND YOUR POS-TURE.
WHAT'M I DOING HERE?
I DON'T EVEN WANT TO BE AN HEIR.
WHEN YOU'RE SPOKEN TO, SMILE WITH A LITTLE BOW, AND SPEAK SLOWLY.
UNDER-STAND?
U-UM! I'D FEEL BETTER IF I HAD MY GLASSES...
I'LL HOLD ONTO THEM.
E... EVERYONE'S A MEMBER OF THE FAMILY, RIGHT?
A ha ha ha...
I'M SORRY, BUT NOT EVERY-ONE IS THRILLED TO HAVE YOU HERE.
SO, THERE'S NOTHING TO WORRY ABOUT, RIGHT!?
......

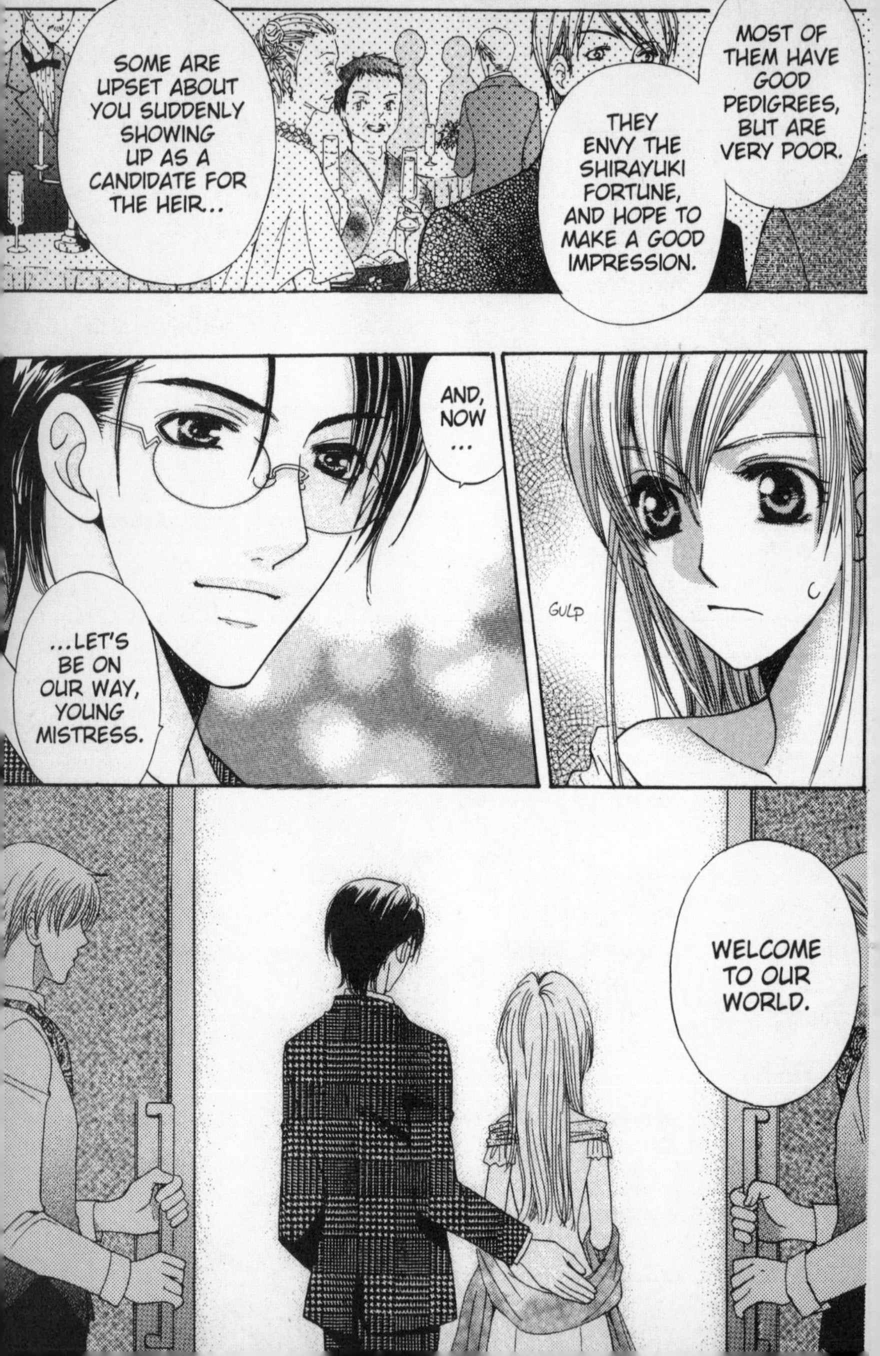
MOST OF THEM HAVE GOOD PEDIGREES, BUT ARE VERY POOR.
THEY ENVY THE SHIRAYUKI FORTUNE, AND HOPE TO MAKE A GOOD IMPRESSION.
SOME ARE UPSET ABOUT YOU SUDDENLY SHOWING UP AS A CANDIDATE FOR THE HEIR...
GULP
AND, NOW...
...LET'S BE ON OUR WAY, YOUNG MISTRESS.
WELCOME TO OUR WORLD.

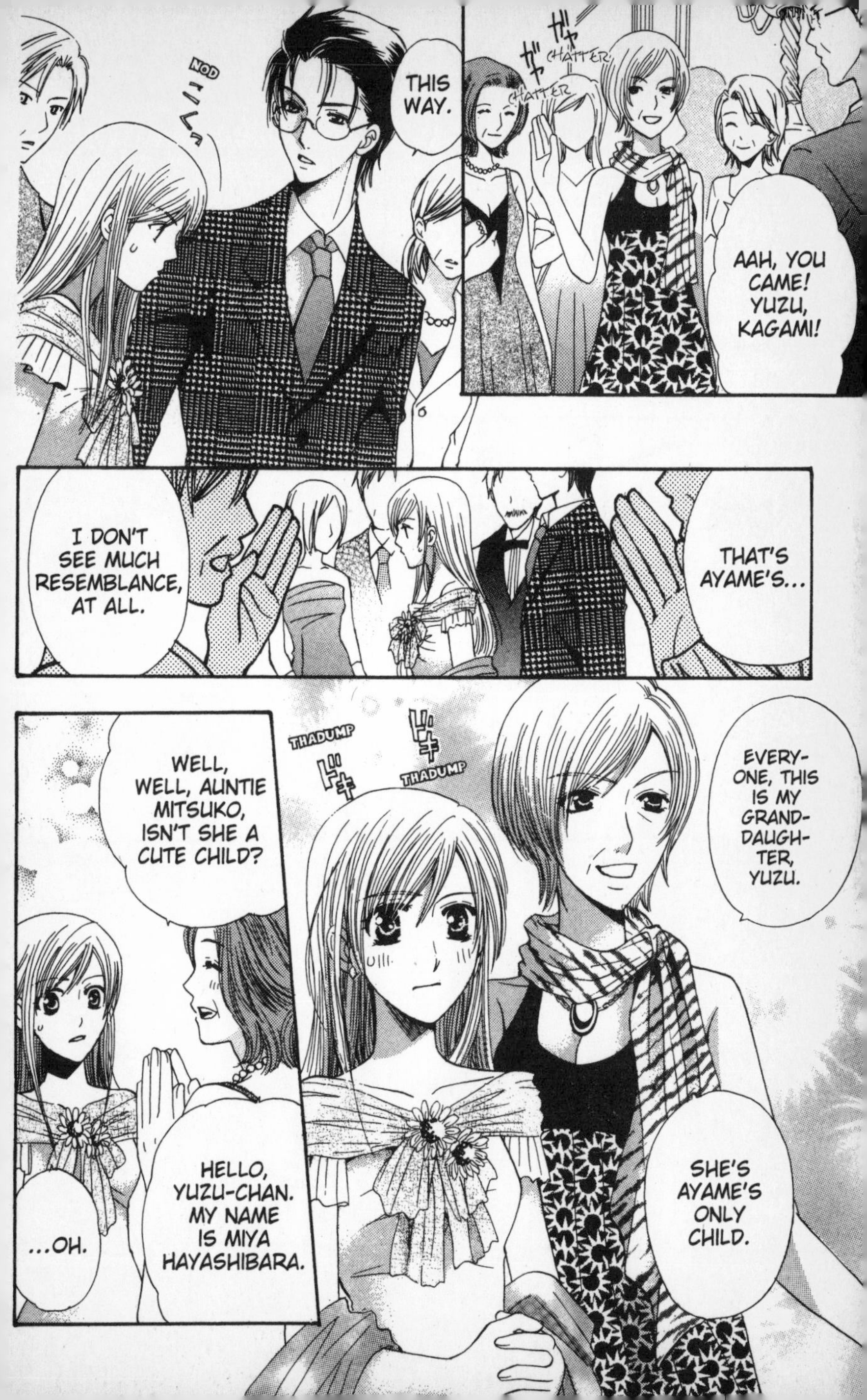
CHATTER
CHATTER
AAH, YOU CAME! YUZU, KAGAMI!
THIS WAY.
NOD
THAT'S AYAME'S...
I DON'T SEE MUCH RESEMBLANCE, AT ALL.
EVERY-ONE, THIS IS MY GRAND-DAUGH-TER, YUZU.
THADUMP
THADUMP
SHE'S AYAME'S ONLY CHILD.
WELL, WELL, AUNTIE MITSUKO, ISN'T SHE A CUTE CHILD?
HELLO, YUZU-CHAN. MY NAME IS MIYA HAYASHIBARA.
...OH.

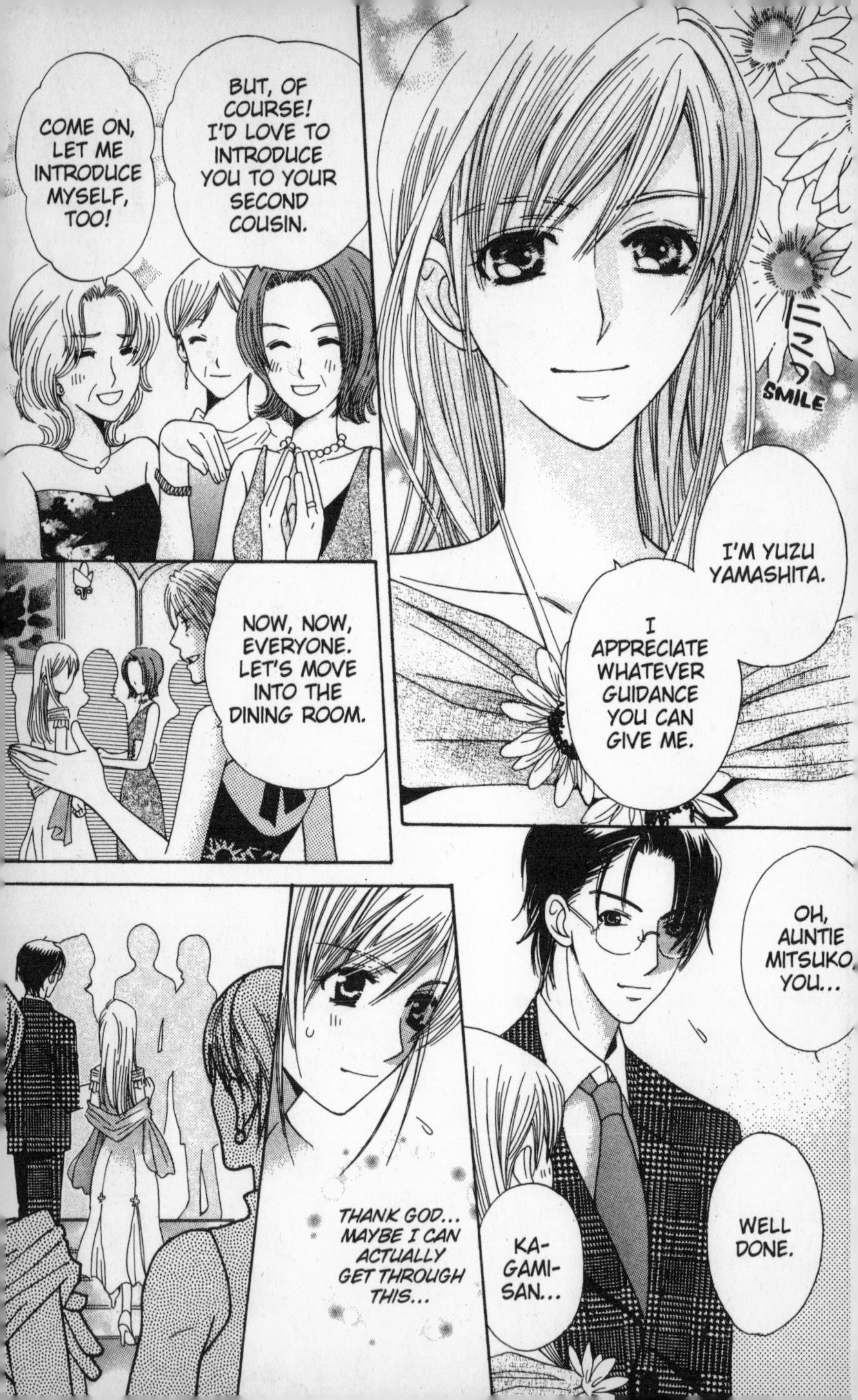
SMILE
I'M YUZU YAMASHITA.
I APPRECIATE WHATEVER GUIDANCE YOU CAN GIVE ME.
BUT, OF COURSE! I'D LOVE TO INTRODUCE YOU TO YOUR SECOND COUSIN.
COME ON, LET ME INTRODUCE MYSELF, TOO!
NOW, NOW, EVERYONE. LET'S MOVE INTO THE DINING ROOM.
OH, AUNTIE MITSUKO, YOU...
WELL DONE.
KA-GAMI-SAN...
THANK GOD... MAYBE I CAN ACTUALLY GET THROUGH THIS...

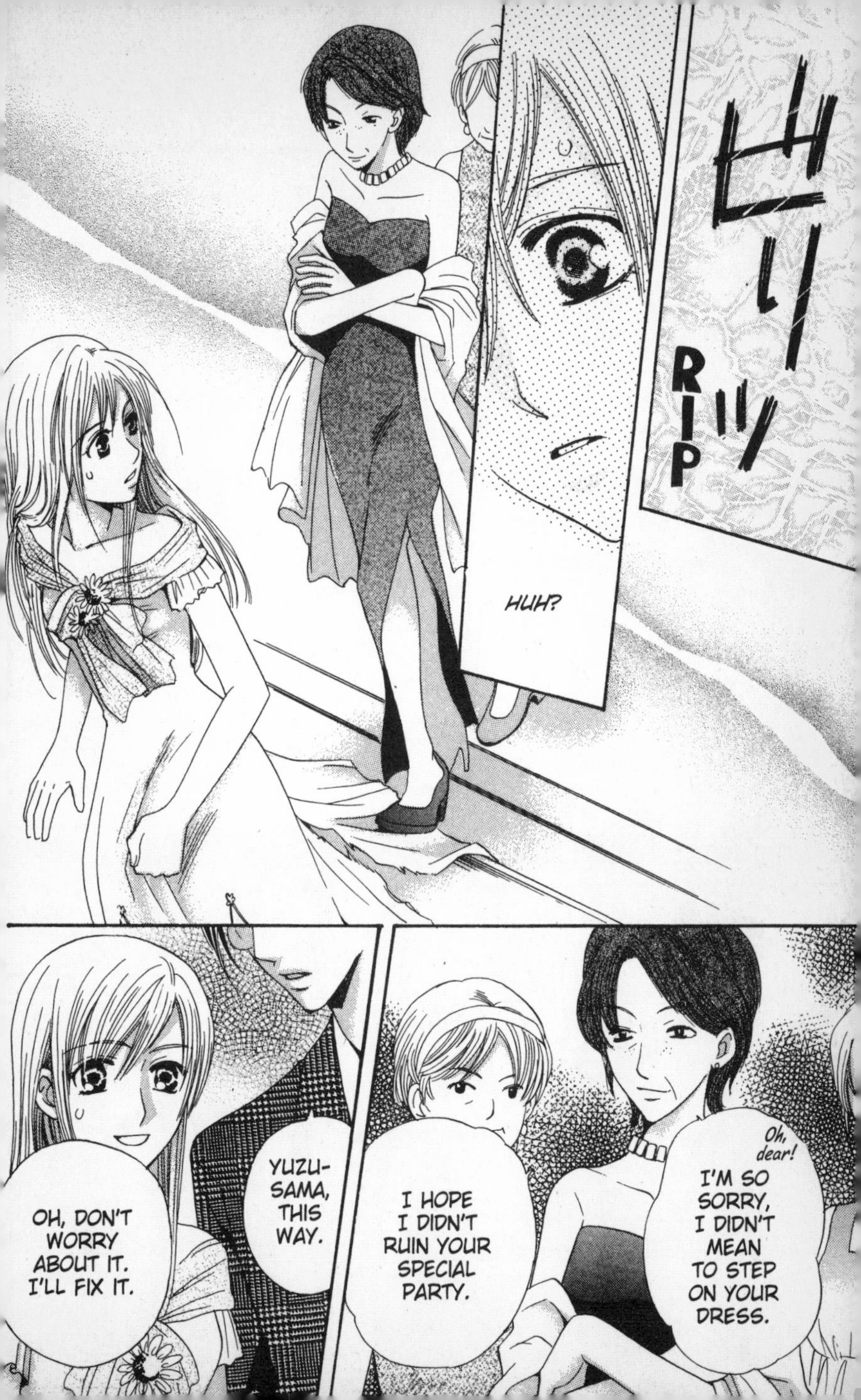
ビリッ
RIP
HUH?
Oh, dear!
I'M SO SORRY, I DIDN'T MEAN TO STEP ON YOUR DRESS.
I HOPE I DIDN'T RUIN YOUR SPECIAL PARTY.
YUZU-SAMA, THIS WAY.
OH, DON'T WORRY ABOUT IT. I'LL FIX IT.

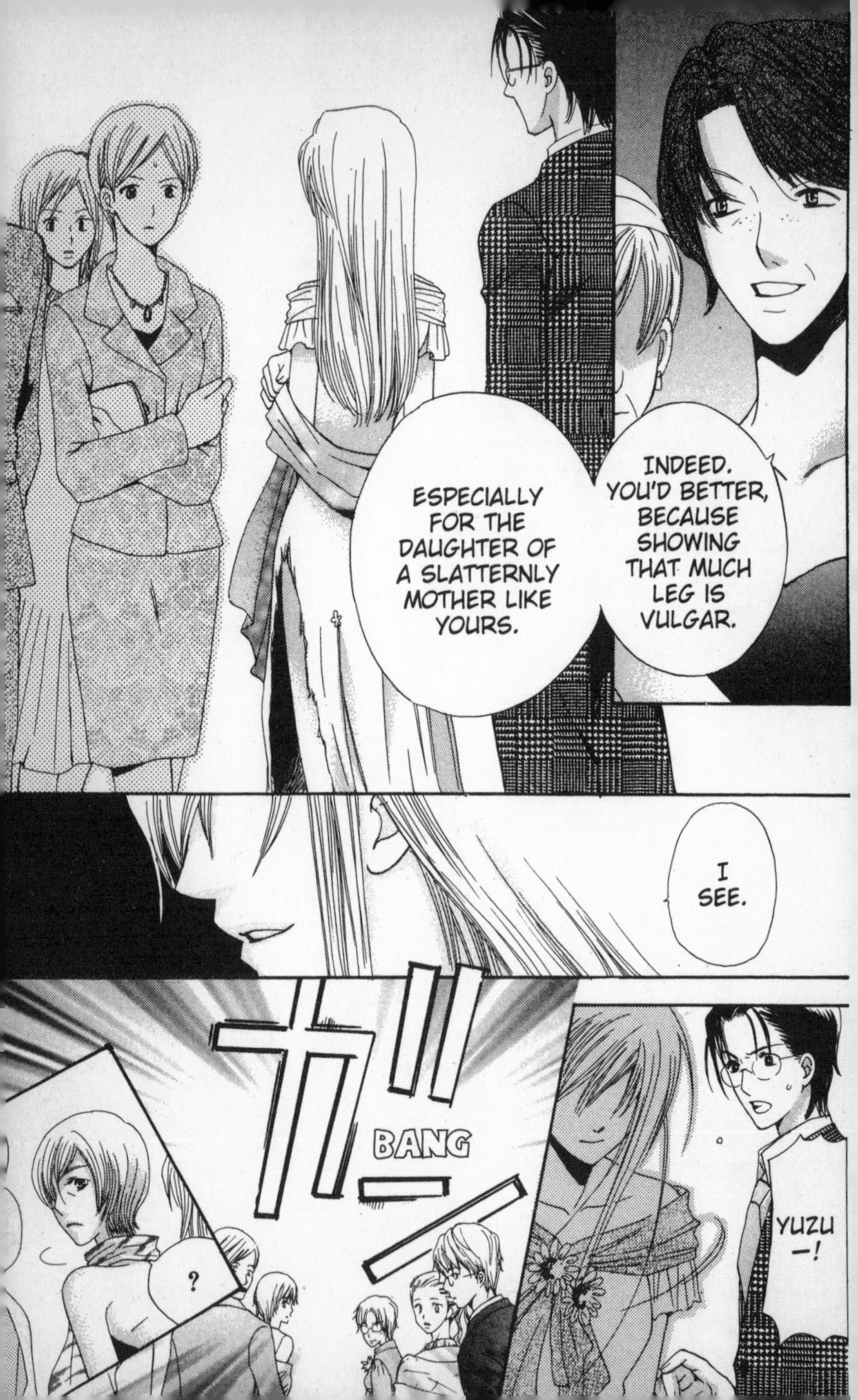
INDEED. YOU'D BETTER, BECAUSE SHOWING THAT MUCH LEG IS VULGAR.
ESPECIALLY FOR THE DAUGHTER OF A SLATTERNLY MOTHER LIKE YOURS.
I SEE.
YUZU—!
BANG
?

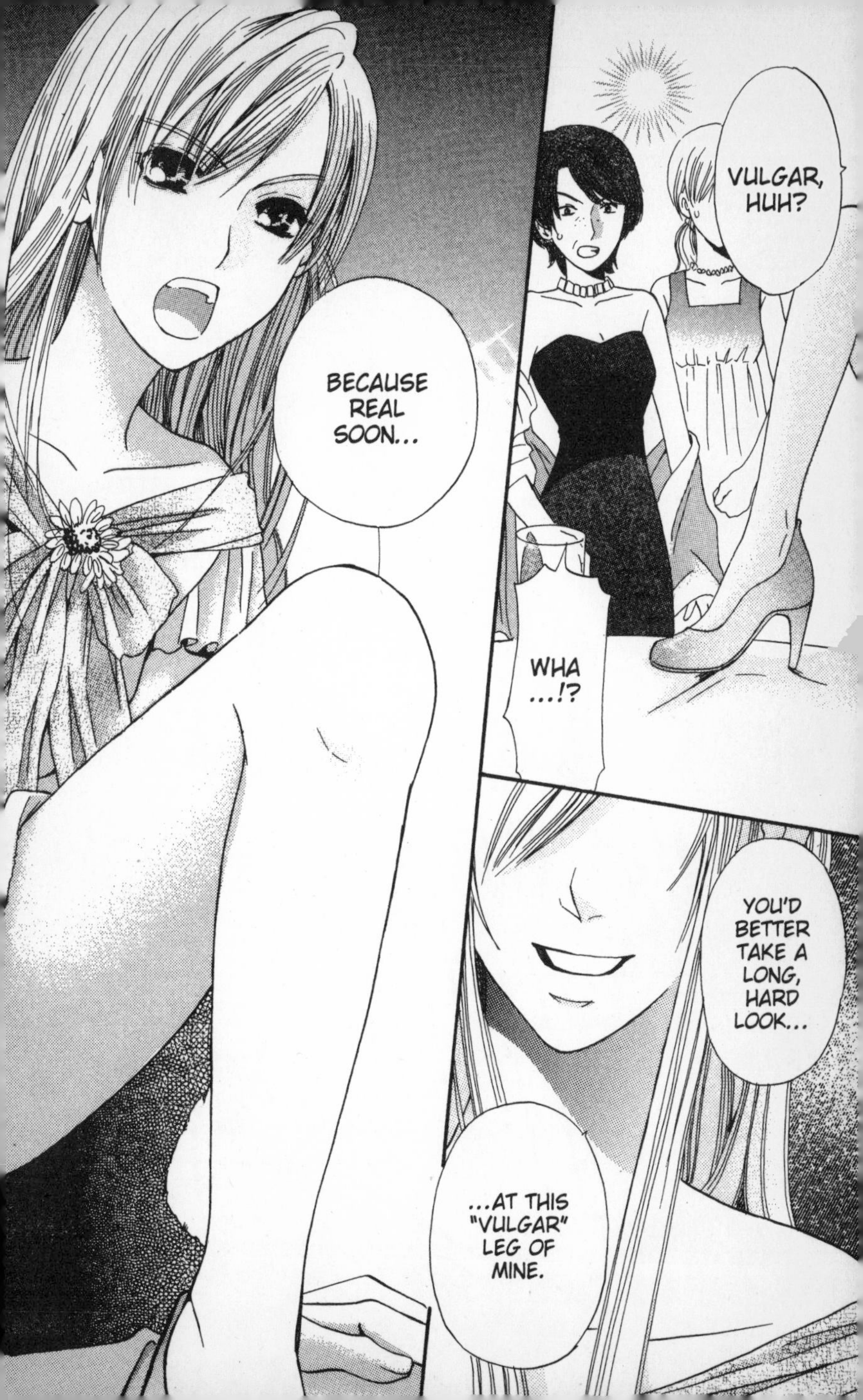
VULGAR, HUH?
WHA...!?
YOU'D BETTER TAKE A LONG, HARD LOOK...
...AT THIS "VULGAR" LEG OF MINE.
BECAUSE REAL SOON...

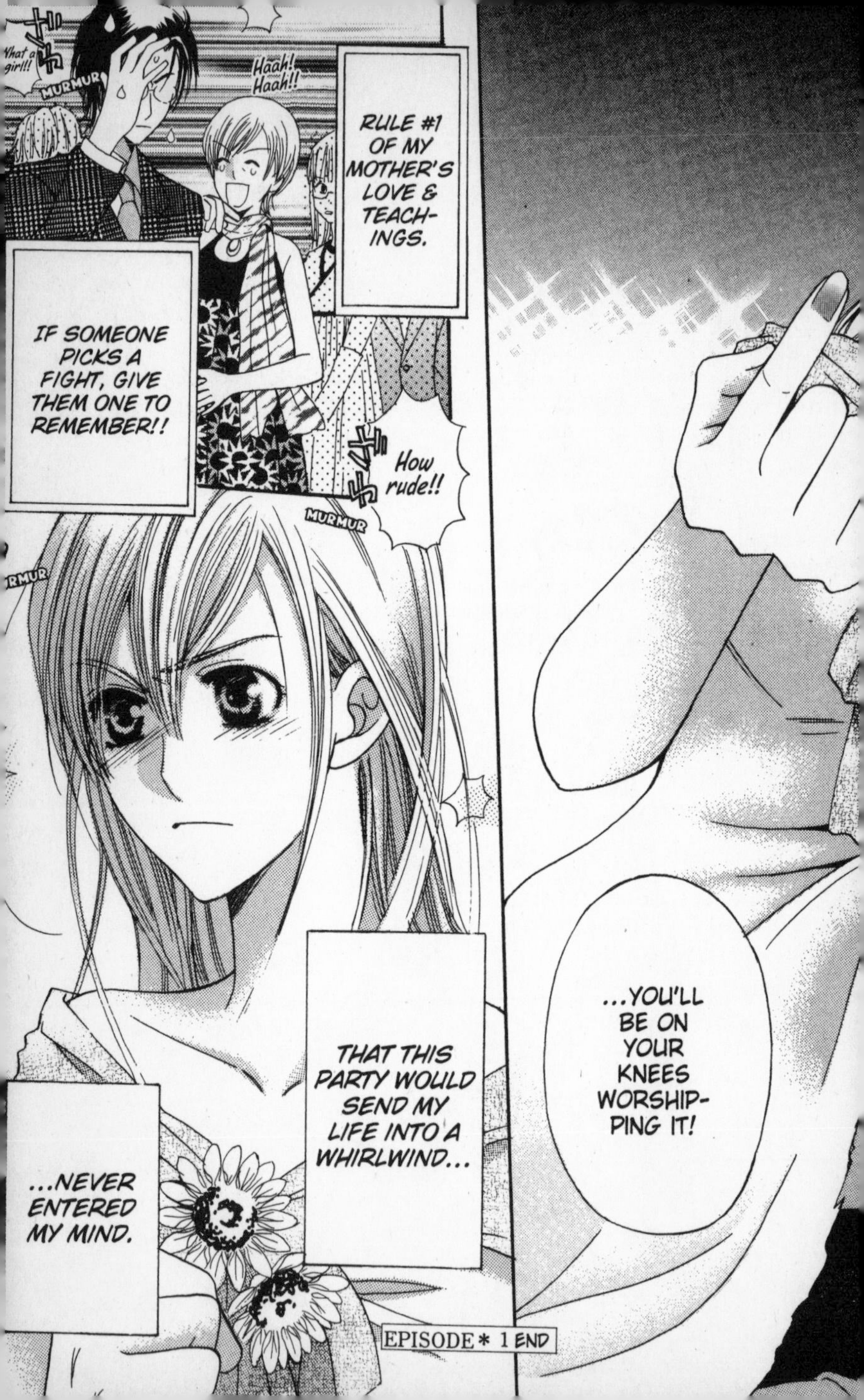
...YOU'LL BE ON YOUR KNEES WORSHIP-PING IT!
RULE #1 OF MY MOTHER'S LOVE & TEACH-INGS.
Haah! Haah!!
What a girl!!
MURMUR
IF SOMEONE PICKS A FIGHT, GIVE THEM ONE TO REMEMBER!!
How rude!!
MURMUR
MURMUR
THAT THIS PARTY WOULD SEND MY LIFE INTO A WHIRLWIND...
...NEVER ENTERED MY MIND.
EPISODE * 1 END

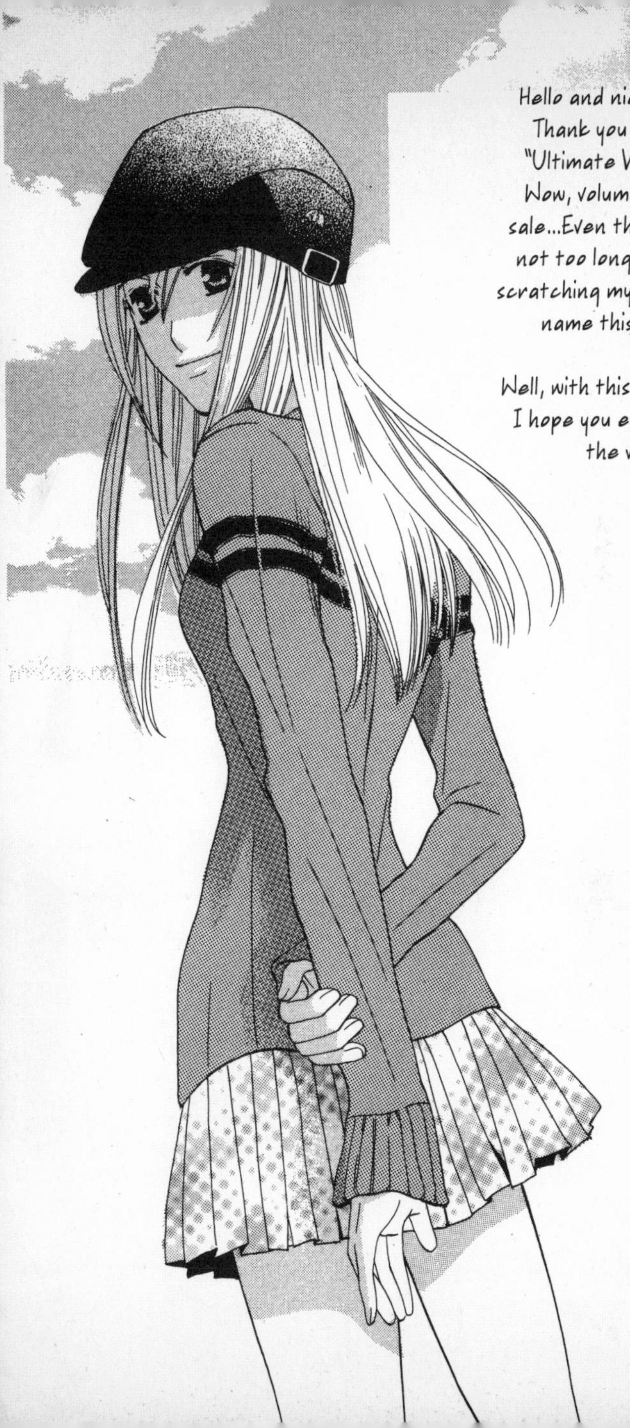

Hello and nice to meet you.
Thank you for picking up
"Ultimate Venus" volume 1!
Wow, volume 1's already on
sale...Even though it feels like
not too long ago when I was
scratching my head over how to
name this new series...

Well, with this feeling and that,
I hope you enjoy this work to
the very end.

November 16,
2006

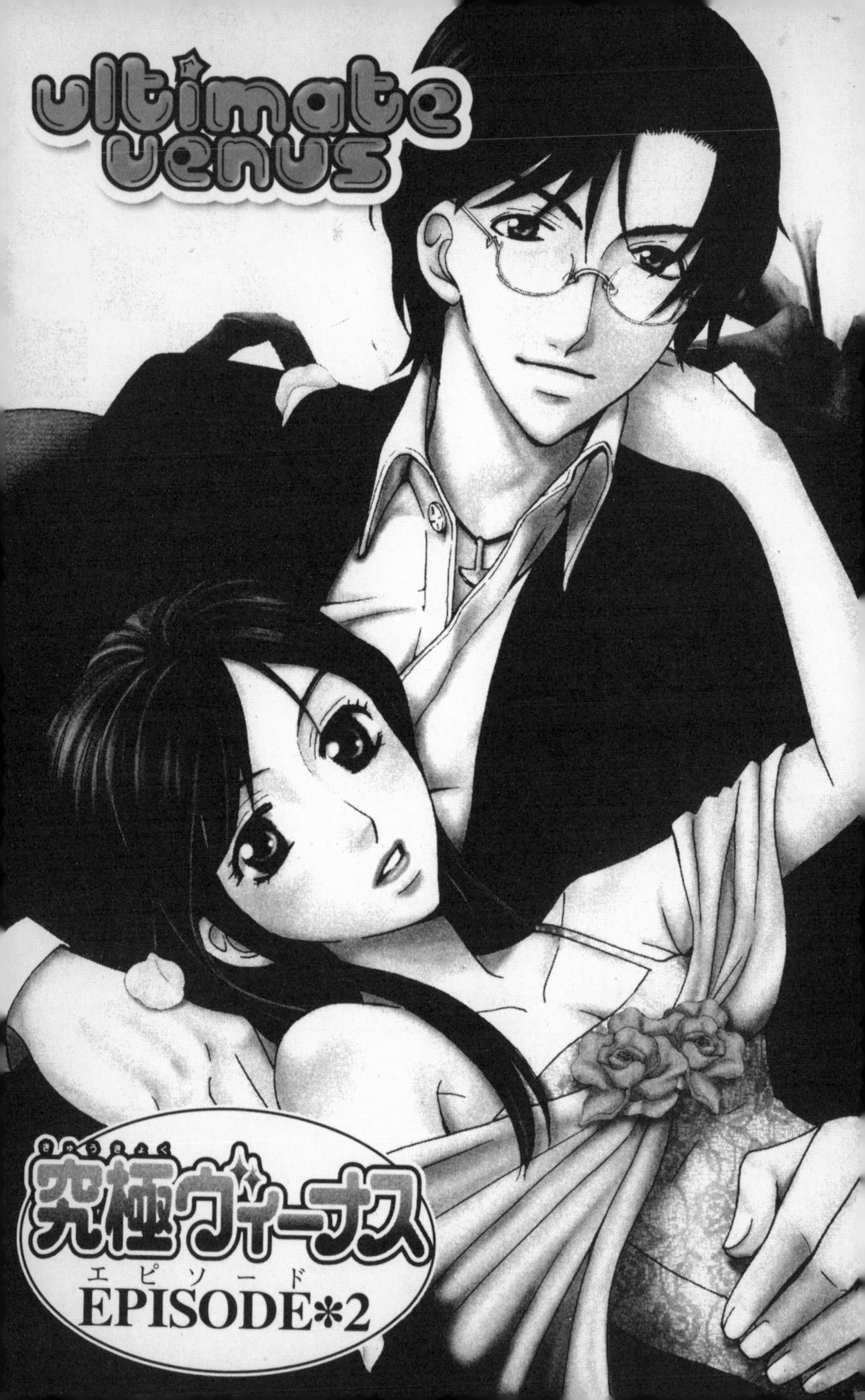
ultimate venus
究極ウィーナス
EPISODE*2

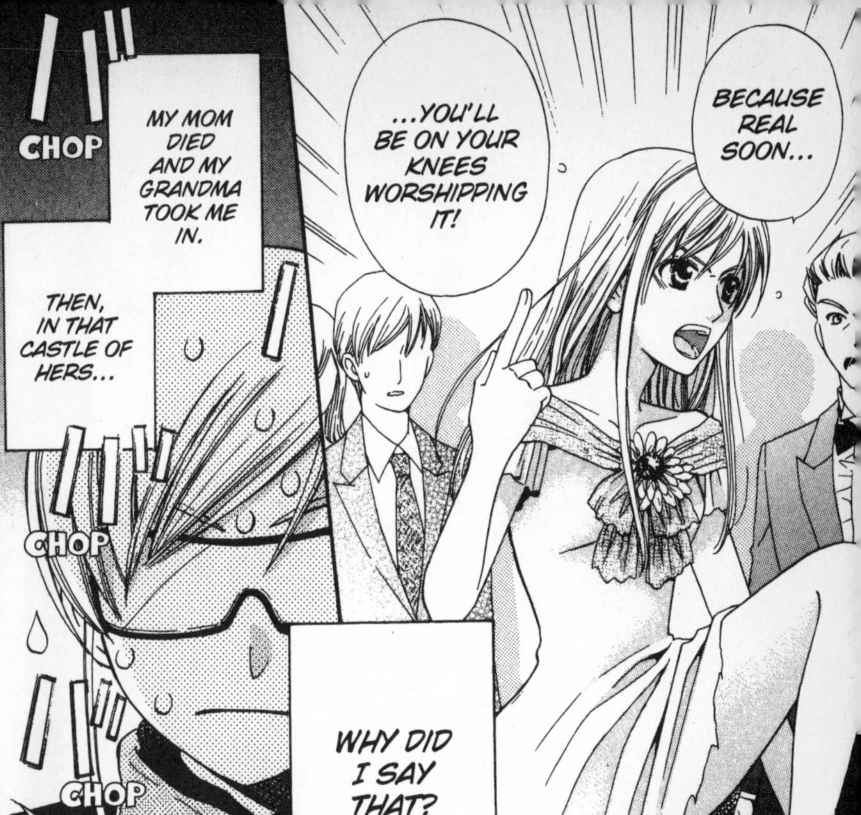
BECAUSE REAL SOON...
...YOU'LL BE ON YOUR KNEES WORSHIPPING IT!
WHY DID I SAY THAT?
MY MOM DIED AND MY GRANDMA TOOK ME IN.
THEN, IN THAT CASTLE OF HERS...
CHOP
CHOP
CHOP
YUZU, YOU READY?
CHOP

Yuzu Yamashita (age 15)

Birthday: December 24th

Blood Type: A

Hobby: Horticulture
(well, the family vegetable garden)

Favorites: Natto, piggy banks with coins in them. The woman she looks up to is her mom. She's got a mother-complex and a father-complex.

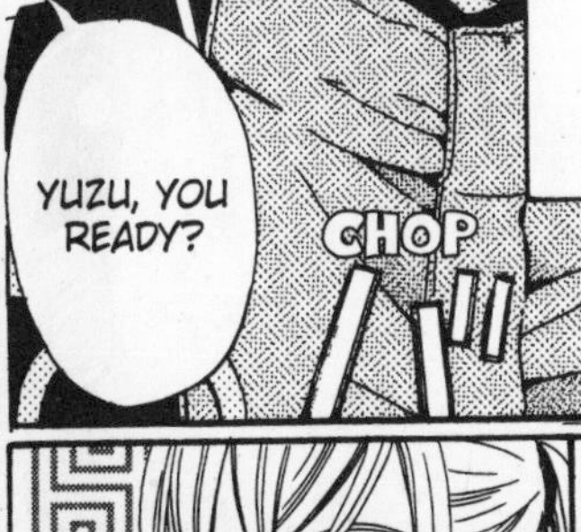

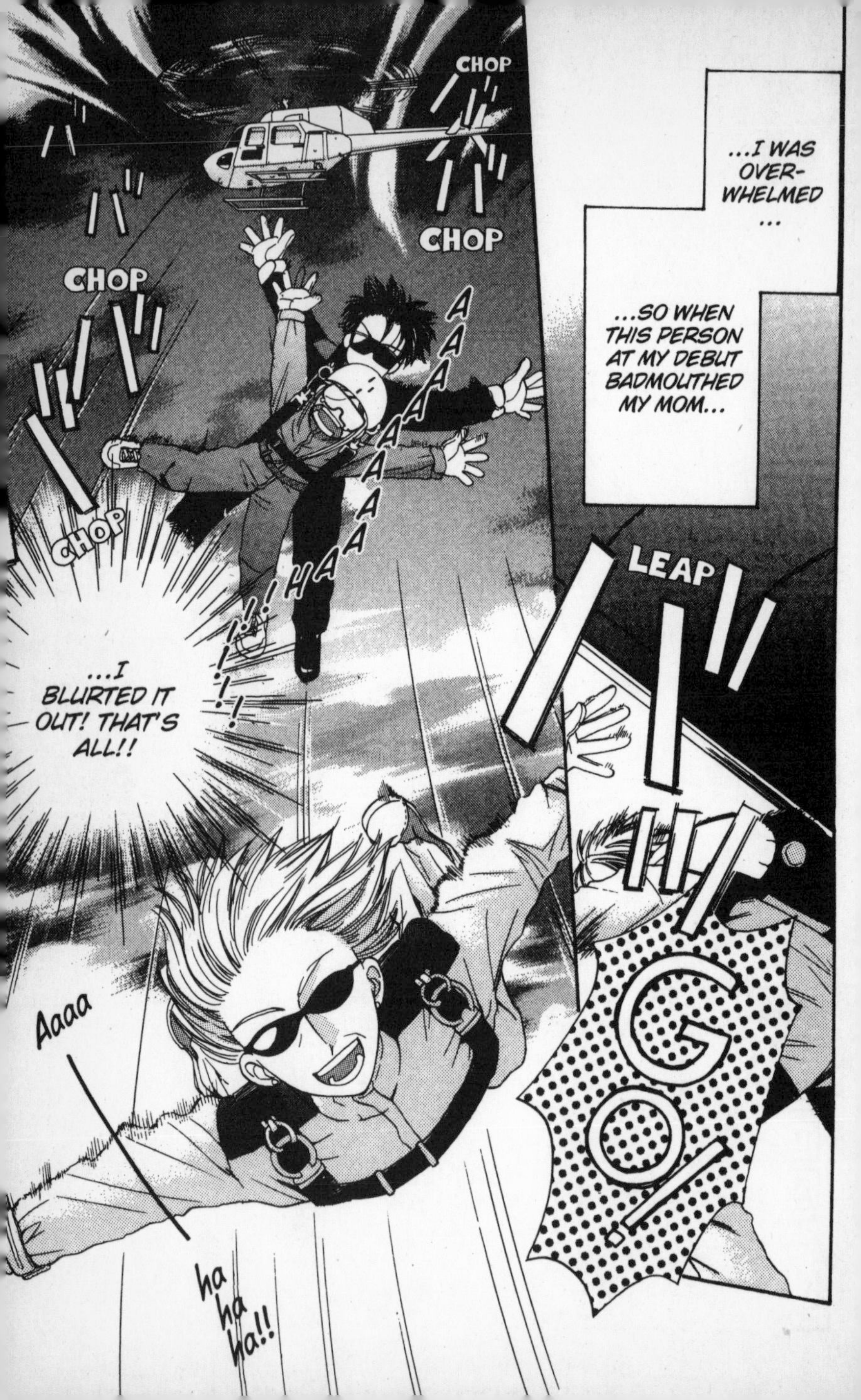
...I WAS OVER-WHELMED ...
...SO WHEN THIS PERSON AT MY DEBUT BADMOUTHED MY MOM...
CHOP
CHOP
CHOP
CHOP
AAAAAAAAAAAHA!!!!!
...I BLURTED IT OUT! THAT'S ALL!!
LEAP
GO!
Aaaa
ha ha ha!!

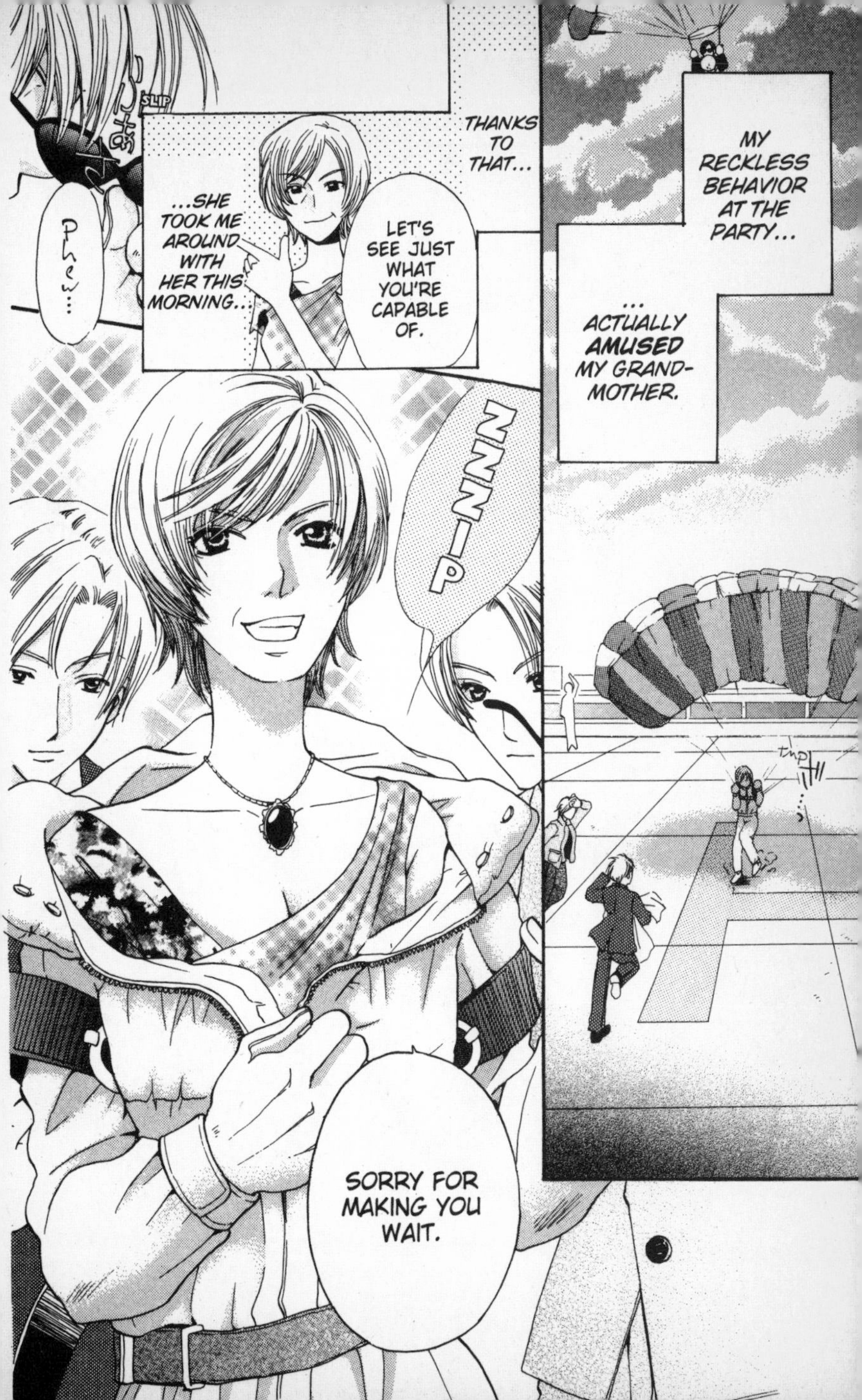
MY RECKLESS BEHAVIOR AT THE PARTY...
...ACTUALLY **AMUSED** MY GRANDMOTHER.
tmp
SLIP
Phew...
THANKS TO THAT...
...SHE TOOK ME AROUND WITH HER THIS MORNING...
LET'S SEE JUST WHAT YOU'RE CAPABLE OF.
ZZZIP
SORRY FOR MAKING YOU WAIT.

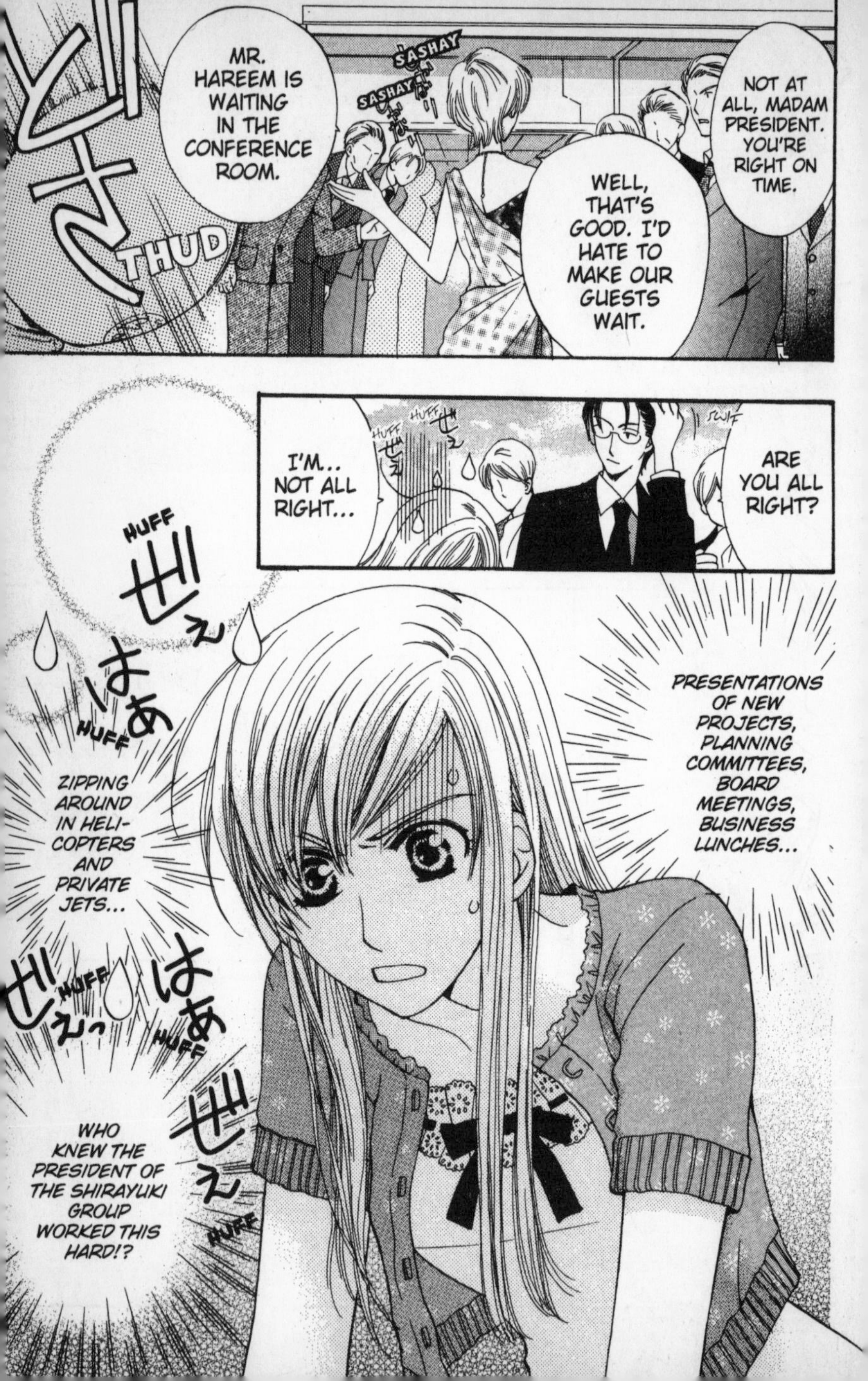
NOT AT ALL, MADAM PRESIDENT. YOU'RE RIGHT ON TIME.
WELL, THAT'S GOOD. I'D HATE TO MAKE OUR GUESTS WAIT.
SASHAY
SASHAY
MR. HAREEM IS WAITING IN THE CONFERENCE ROOM.
THUD
ARE YOU ALL RIGHT?
SWIF
HUFF
HUFF
I'M... NOT ALL RIGHT...
PRESENTATIONS OF NEW PROJECTS, PLANNING COMMITTEES, BOARD MEETINGS, BUSINESS LUNCHES...
HUFF
HUFF
ZIPPING AROUND IN HELI-COPTERS AND PRIVATE JETS...
HUFF
HUFF
HUFF
WHO KNEW THE PRESIDENT OF THE SHIRAYUKI GROUP WORKED THIS HARD!?

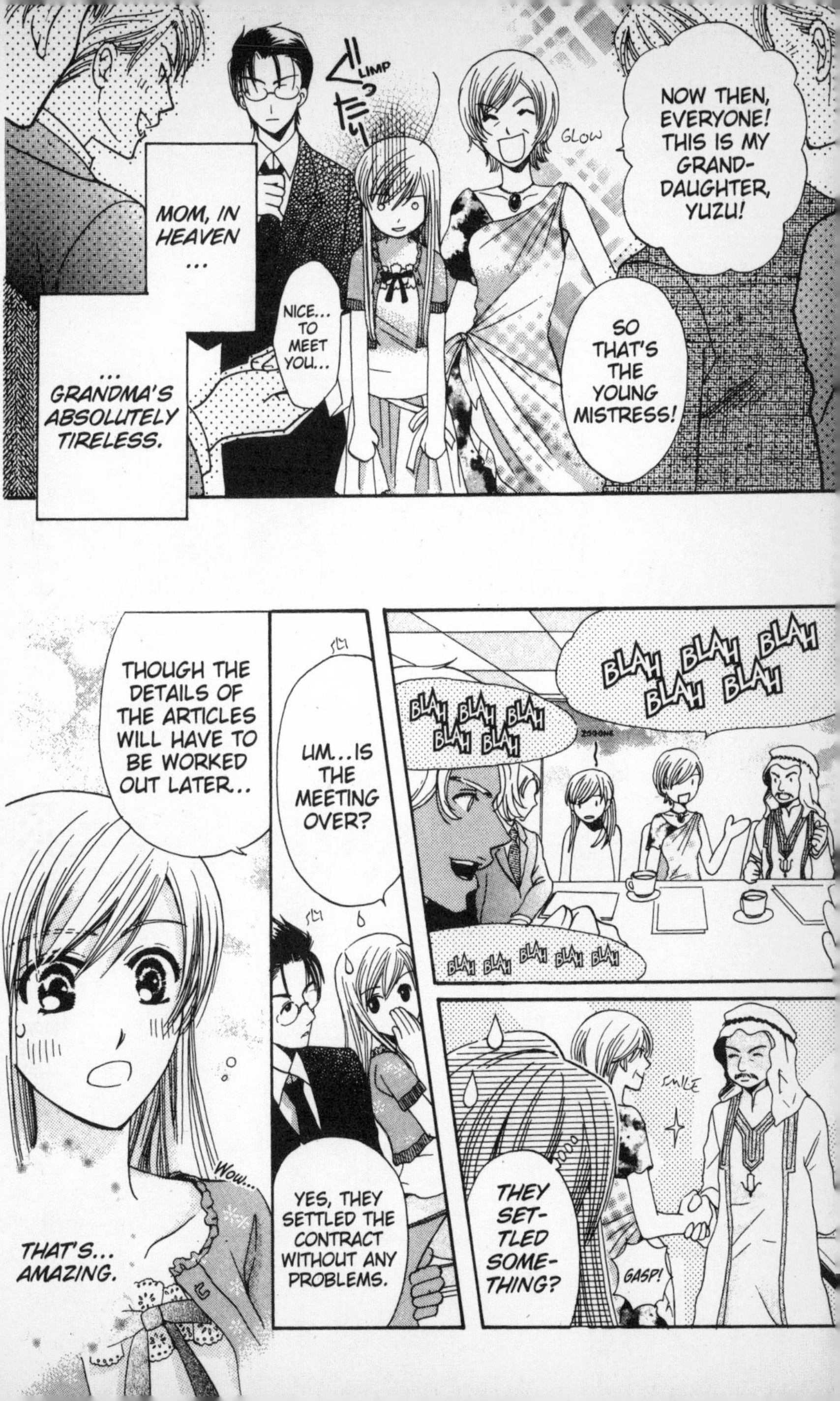
NOW THEN, EVERYONE! THIS IS MY GRAND-DAUGHTER, YUZU!
GLOW
SO THAT'S THE YOUNG MISTRESS!
LIMP
NICE... TO MEET YOU...
MOM, IN HEAVEN ...
... GRANDMA'S ABSOLUTELY TIRELESS.
BLAH BLAH BLAH BLAH BLAH
BLAH BLAH BLAH BLAH BLAH
BLAH BLAH BLAH BLAH BLAH
THEY SET-TLED SOME-THING?
SMILE
GASP!
UM...IS THE MEETING OVER?
YES, THEY SETTLED THE CONTRACT WITHOUT ANY PROBLEMS.
THOUGH THE DETAILS OF THE ARTICLES WILL HAVE TO BE WORKED OUT LATER...
WOW...
THAT'S... AMAZING.

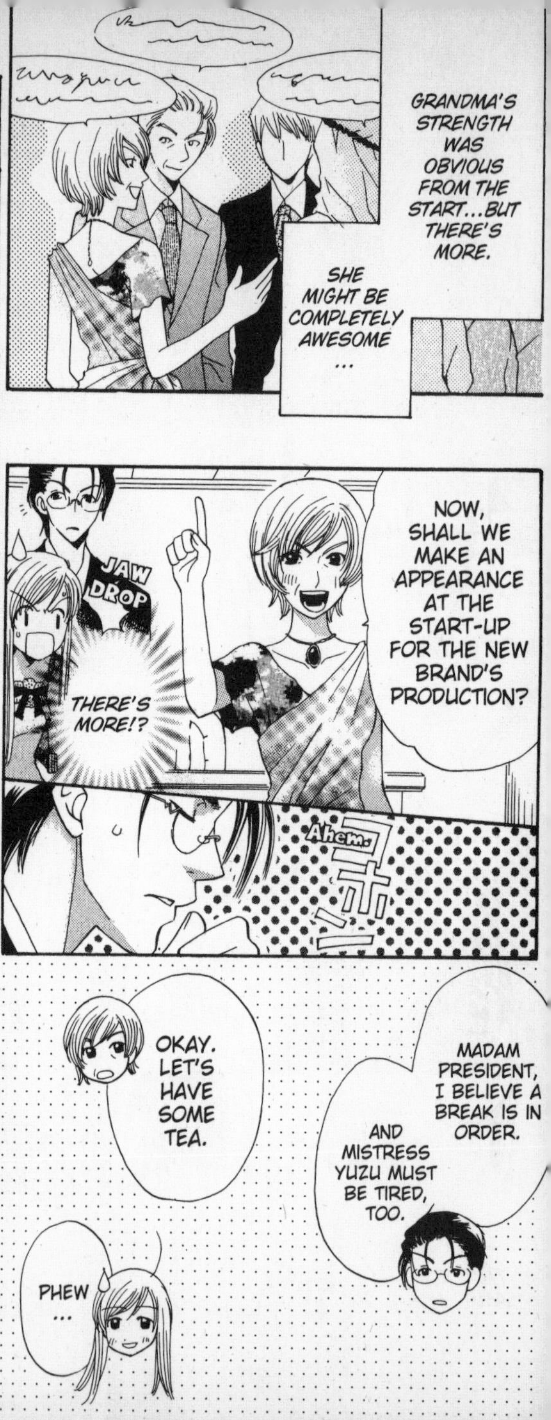
GRANDMA'S STRENGTH WAS OBVIOUS FROM THE START...BUT THERE'S MORE.
SHE MIGHT BE COMPLETELY AWESOME ...
NOW, SHALL WE MAKE AN APPEARANCE AT THE START-UP FOR THE NEW BRAND'S PRODUCTION?
JAW DROP
THERE'S MORE!?
Ahem.
MADAM PRESIDENT, I BELIEVE A BREAK IS IN ORDER.
AND MISTRESS YUZU MUST BE TIRED, TOO.
OKAY. LET'S HAVE SOME TEA.
PHEW ...

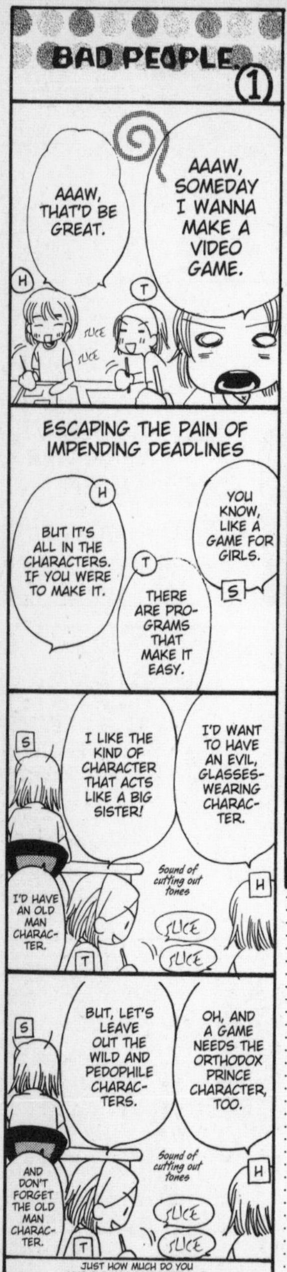
BAD PEOPLE 1
AAAW, SOMEDAY I WANNA MAKE A VIDEO GAME.
AAAW, THAT'D BE GREAT.
SLICE
SLICE
ESCAPING THE PAIN OF IMPENDING DEADLINES
YOU KNOW, LIKE A GAME FOR GIRLS.
BUT IT'S ALL IN THE CHARACTERS. IF YOU WERE TO MAKE IT.
THERE ARE PROGRAMS THAT MAKE IT EASY.
I'D WANT TO HAVE AN EVIL, GLASSES-WEARING CHARACTER.
I LIKE THE KIND OF CHARACTER THAT ACTS LIKE A BIG SISTER!
Sound of cutting out tones
I'D HAVE AN OLD MAN CHARACTER.
SLICE
SLICE
OH, AND A GAME NEEDS THE ORTHODOX PRINCE CHARACTER, TOO.
BUT, LET'S LEAVE OUT THE WILD AND PEDOPHILE CHARACTERS.
Sound of cutting out tones
AND DON'T FORGET THE OLD MAN CHARACTER.
SLICE
SLICE
JUST HOW MUCH DO YOU LIKE OLD MAN CHARACTERS...?

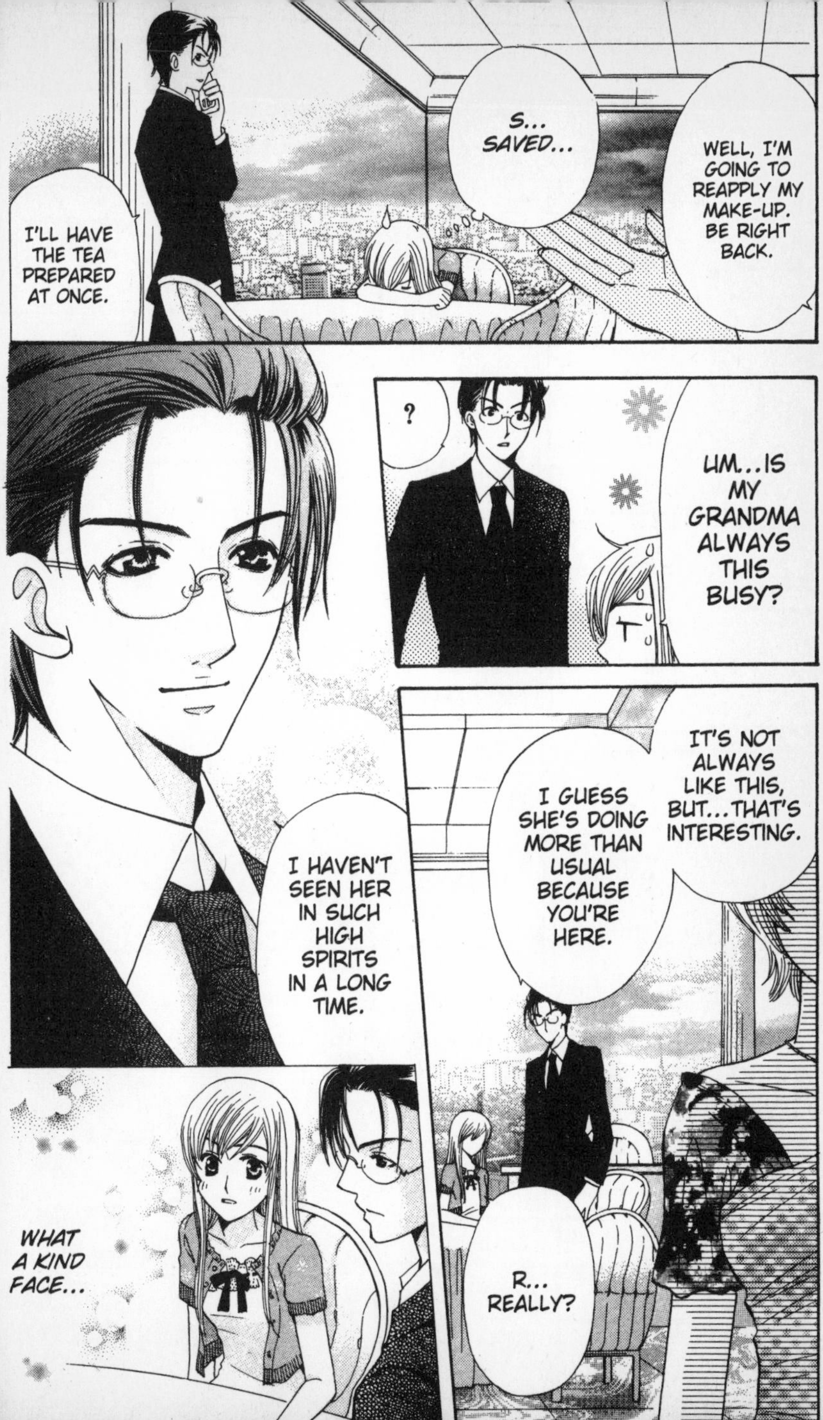
WELL, I'M GOING TO REAPPLY MY MAKE-UP. BE RIGHT BACK.
S... SAVED...
I'LL HAVE THE TEA PREPARED AT ONCE.
UM...IS MY GRANDMA ALWAYS THIS BUSY?
?
IT'S NOT ALWAYS LIKE THIS, BUT...THAT'S INTERESTING.
I GUESS SHE'S DOING MORE THAN USUAL BECAUSE YOU'RE HERE.
R... REALLY?
I HAVEN'T SEEN HER IN SUCH HIGH SPIRITS IN A LONG TIME.
WHAT A KIND FACE...

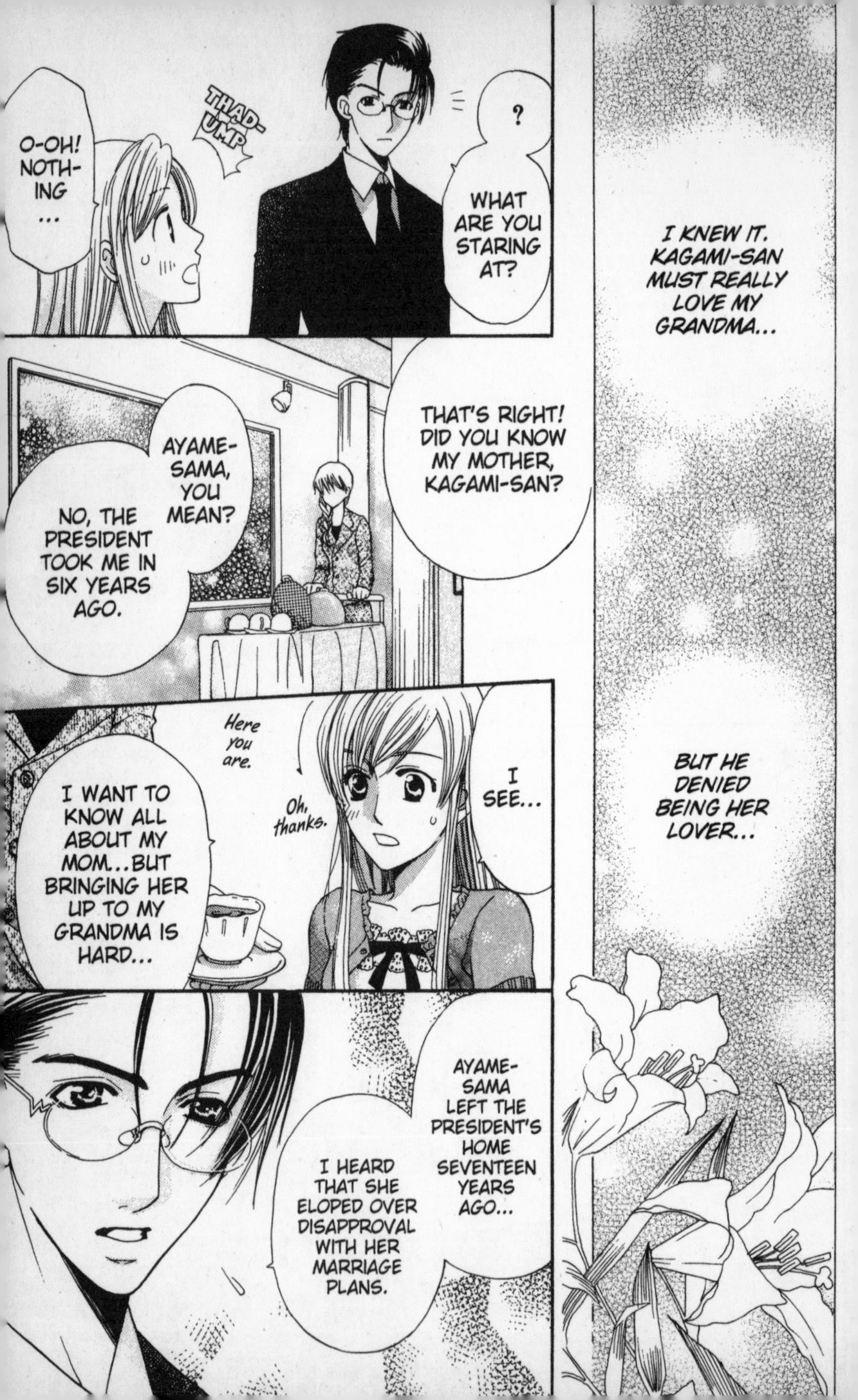
I KNEW IT. KAGAMI-SAN MUST REALLY LOVE MY GRANDMA...
BUT HE DENIED BEING HER LOVER...
?
WHAT ARE YOU STARING AT?
THAD-UMP
O-OH! NOTHING-ING...
THAT'S RIGHT! DID YOU KNOW MY MOTHER, KAGAMI-SAN?
AYAME-SAMA, YOU MEAN?
NO, THE PRESIDENT TOOK ME IN SIX YEARS AGO.
I SEE...
Here you are.
Oh, thanks.
I WANT TO KNOW ALL ABOUT MY MOM...BUT BRINGING HER UP TO MY GRANDMA IS HARD...
AYAME-SAMA LEFT THE PRESIDENT'S HOME SEVENTEEN YEARS AGO...
I HEARD THAT SHE ELOPED OVER DISAPPROVAL WITH HER MARRIAGE PLANS.

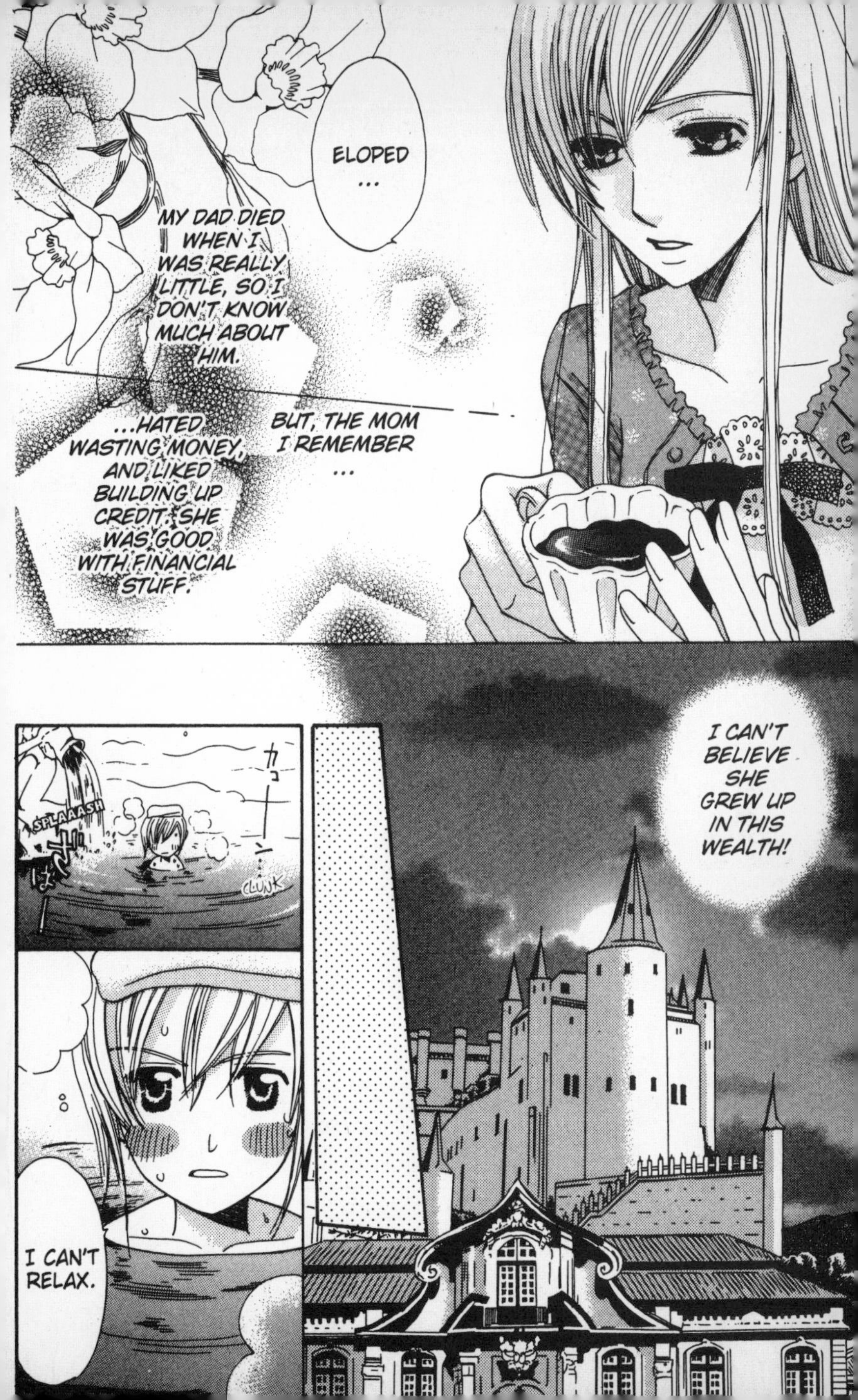
ELOPED ...
MY DAD DIED WHEN I WAS REALLY LITTLE, SO I DON'T KNOW MUCH ABOUT HIM.
BUT, THE MOM I REMEMBER ...
...HATED WASTING MONEY, AND LIKED BUILDING UP CREDIT. SHE WAS GOOD WITH FINANCIAL STUFF.
I CAN'T BELIEVE SHE GREW UP IN THIS WEALTH!
SPLAAASH
CLUNK
I CAN'T RELAX.

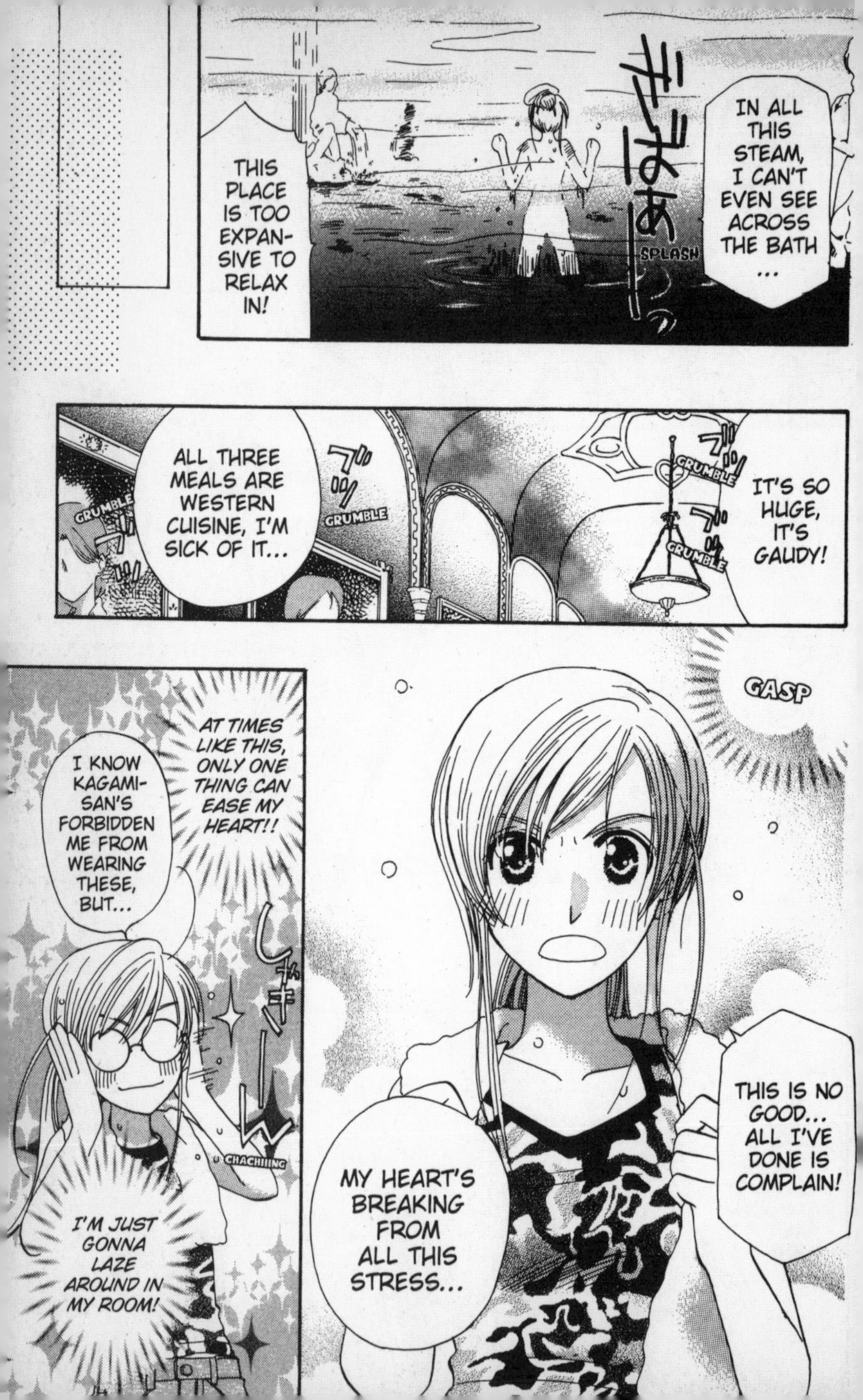
IN ALL THIS STEAM, I CAN'T EVEN SEE ACROSS THE BATH...
SPLASH
THIS PLACE IS TOO EXPANSIVE TO RELAX IN!
IT'S SO HUGE, IT'S GAUDY!
GRUMBLE
GRUMBLE
GRUMBLE
ALL THREE MEALS ARE WESTERN CUISINE, I'M SICK OF IT...
GRUMBLE
GASP
THIS IS NO GOOD... ALL I'VE DONE IS COMPLAIN!
MY HEART'S BREAKING FROM ALL THIS STRESS...
AT TIMES LIKE THIS, ONLY ONE THING CAN EASE MY HEART!!
I KNOW KAGAMI-SAN'S FORBIDDEN ME FROM WEARING THESE, BUT...
CHACHIIING
I'M JUST GONNA LAZE AROUND IN MY ROOM!

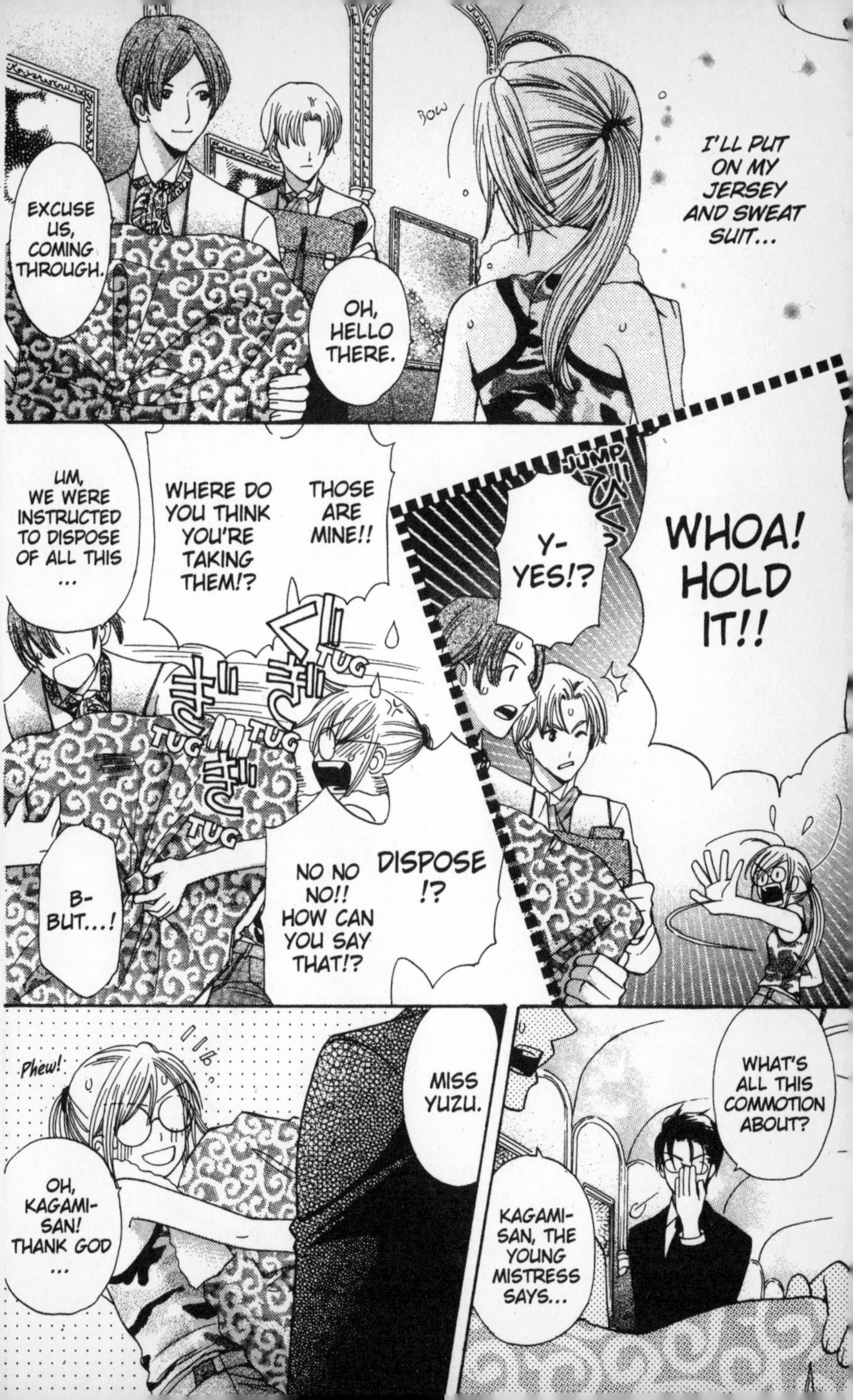
I'LL PUT ON MY JERSEY AND SWEAT SUIT...
BOW
OH, HELLO THERE.
EXCUSE US, COMING THROUGH.
WHOA! HOLD IT!!
JUMP
Y- YES!?
THOSE ARE MINE!!
WHERE DO YOU THINK YOU'RE TAKING THEM!?
UM, WE WERE INSTRUCTED TO DISPOSE OF ALL THIS ...
TUG
TUG
TUG
TUG
DISPOSE !?
NO NO NO!! HOW CAN YOU SAY THAT!?
B- BUT...!
WHAT'S ALL THIS COMMOTION ABOUT?
KAGAMI-SAN, THE YOUNG MISTRESS SAYS...
MISS YUZU.
Phew!
OH, KAGAMI-SAN! THANK GOD ...

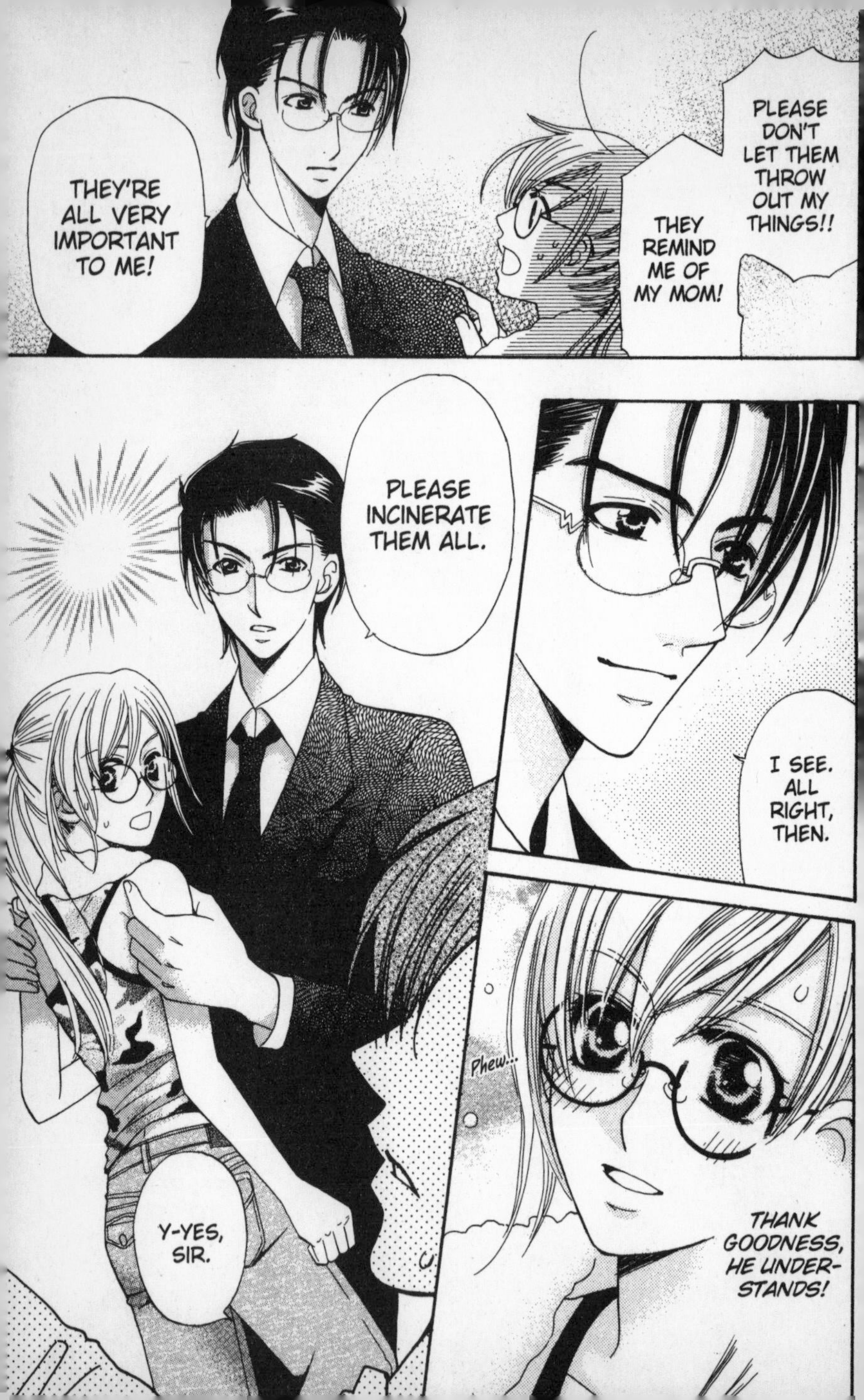
PLEASE DON'T LET THEM THROW OUT MY THINGS!!
THEY REMIND ME OF MY MOM!
THEY'RE ALL VERY IMPORTANT TO ME!
I SEE. ALL RIGHT, THEN.
Phew...
THANK GOODNESS, HE UNDER-STANDS!
PLEASE INCINERATE THEM ALL.
Y-YES, SIR.

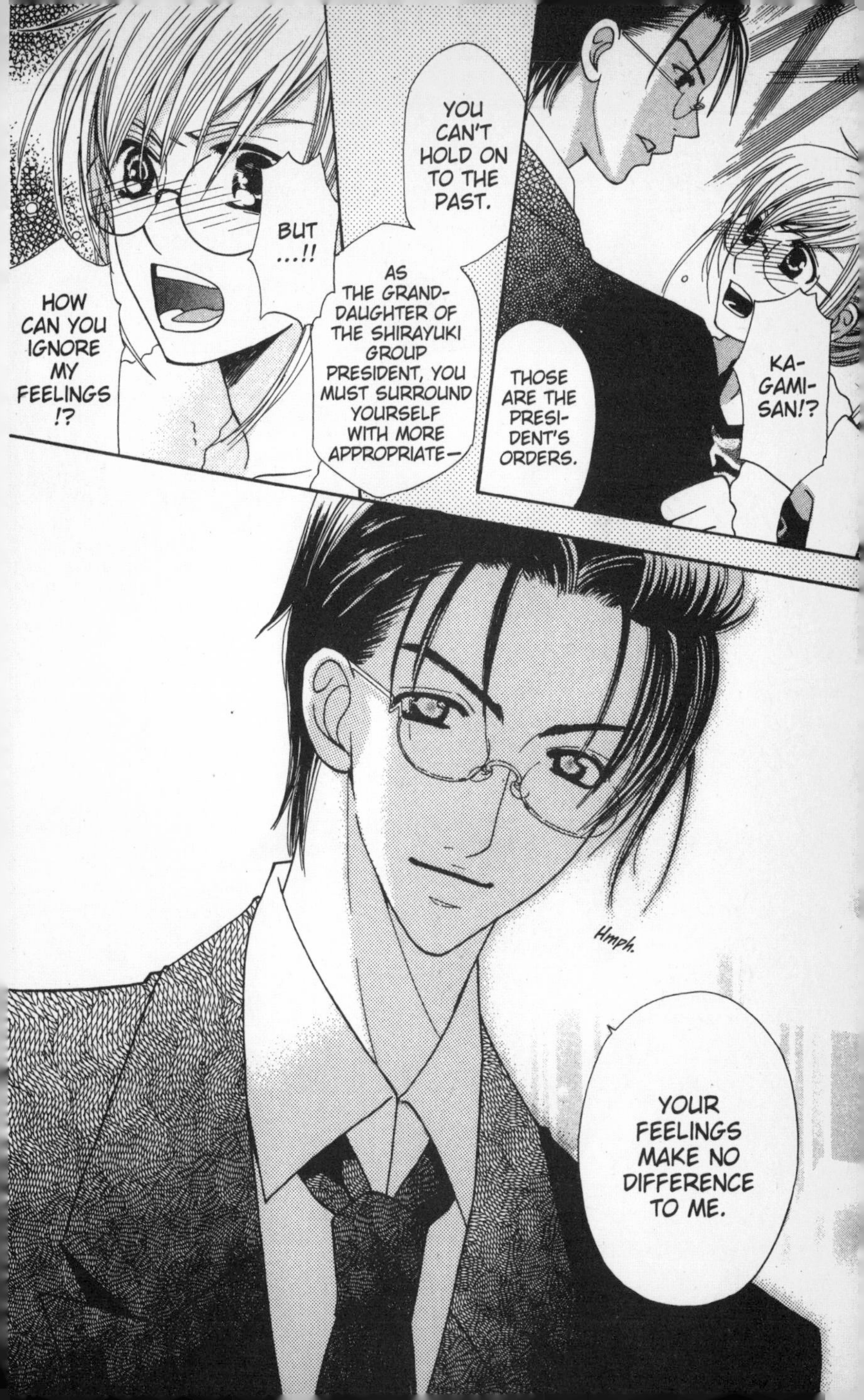
KA-GAMI-SAN!?
THOSE ARE THE PRESI-DENT'S ORDERS.
YOU CAN'T HOLD ON TO THE PAST.
AS THE GRAND-DAUGHTER OF THE SHIRAYUKI GROUP PRESIDENT, YOU MUST SURROUND YOURSELF WITH MORE APPROPRIATE—
BUT ...!!
HOW CAN YOU IGNORE MY FEELINGS !?
Hmph.
YOUR FEELINGS MAKE NO DIFFERENCE TO ME.

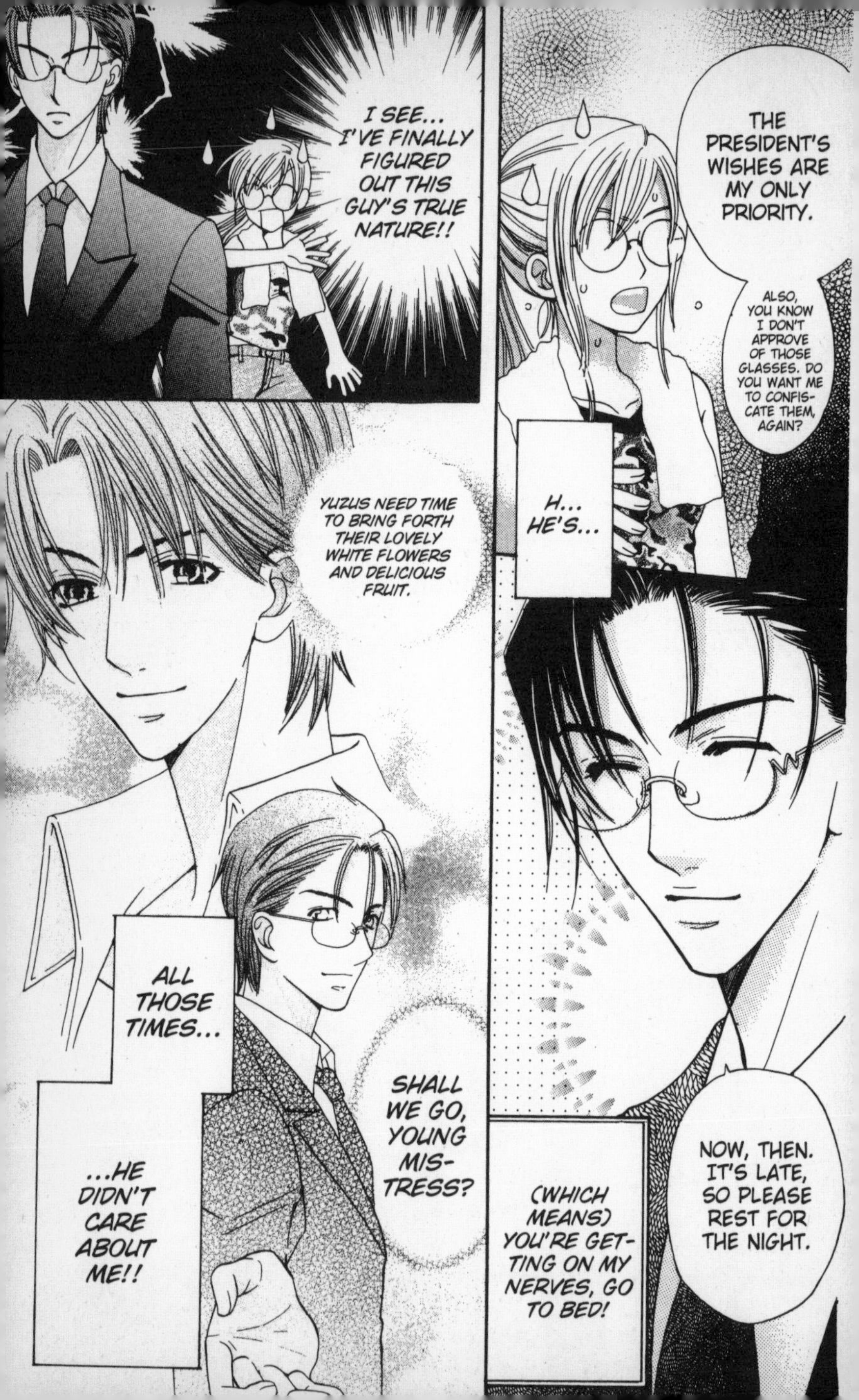
THE PRESIDENT'S WISHES ARE MY ONLY PRIORITY.
ALSO, YOU KNOW I DON'T APPROVE OF THOSE GLASSES. DO YOU WANT ME TO CONFISCATE THEM, AGAIN?
H... HE'S...
NOW, THEN. IT'S LATE, SO PLEASE REST FOR THE NIGHT.
(WHICH MEANS) YOU'RE GETTING ON MY NERVES, GO TO BED!
I SEE... I'VE FINALLY FIGURED OUT THIS GUY'S TRUE NATURE!!
YUZUS NEED TIME TO BRING FORTH THEIR LOVELY WHITE FLOWERS AND DELICIOUS FRUIT.
SHALL WE GO, YOUNG MISTRESS?
ALL THOSE TIMES...
...HE DIDN'T CARE ABOUT ME!!

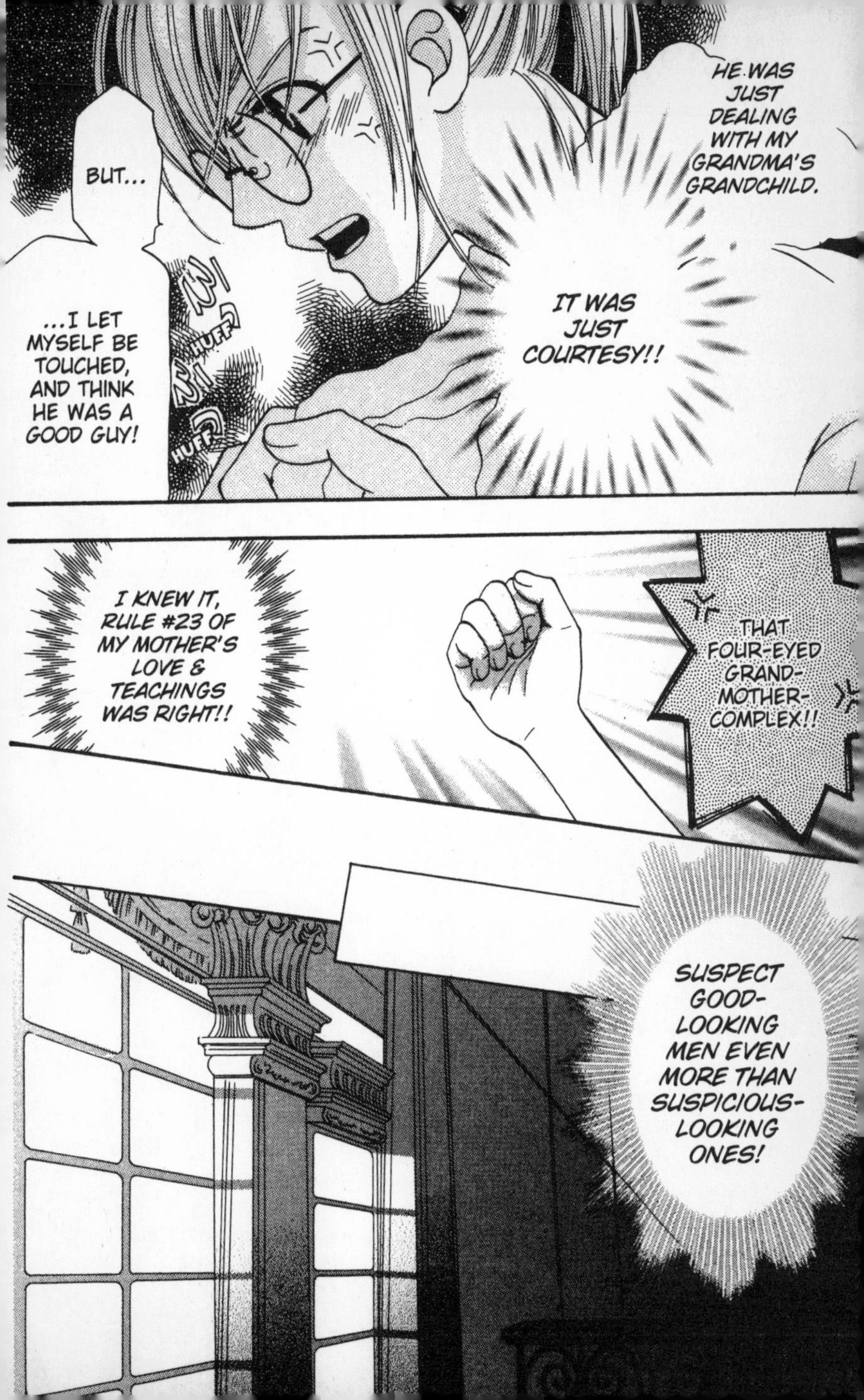
HE WAS JUST DEALING WITH MY GRANDMA'S GRANDCHILD.
IT WAS JUST COURTESY!!
BUT...
...I LET MYSELF BE TOUCHED, AND THINK HE WAS A GOOD GUY!
HUFF
HUFF
THAT FOUR-EYED GRAND-MOTHER-COMPLEX!!
I KNEW IT, RULE #23 OF MY MOTHER'S LOVE & TEACHINGS WAS RIGHT!!
SUSPECT GOOD-LOOKING MEN EVEN MORE THAN SUSPICIOUS-LOOKING ONES!

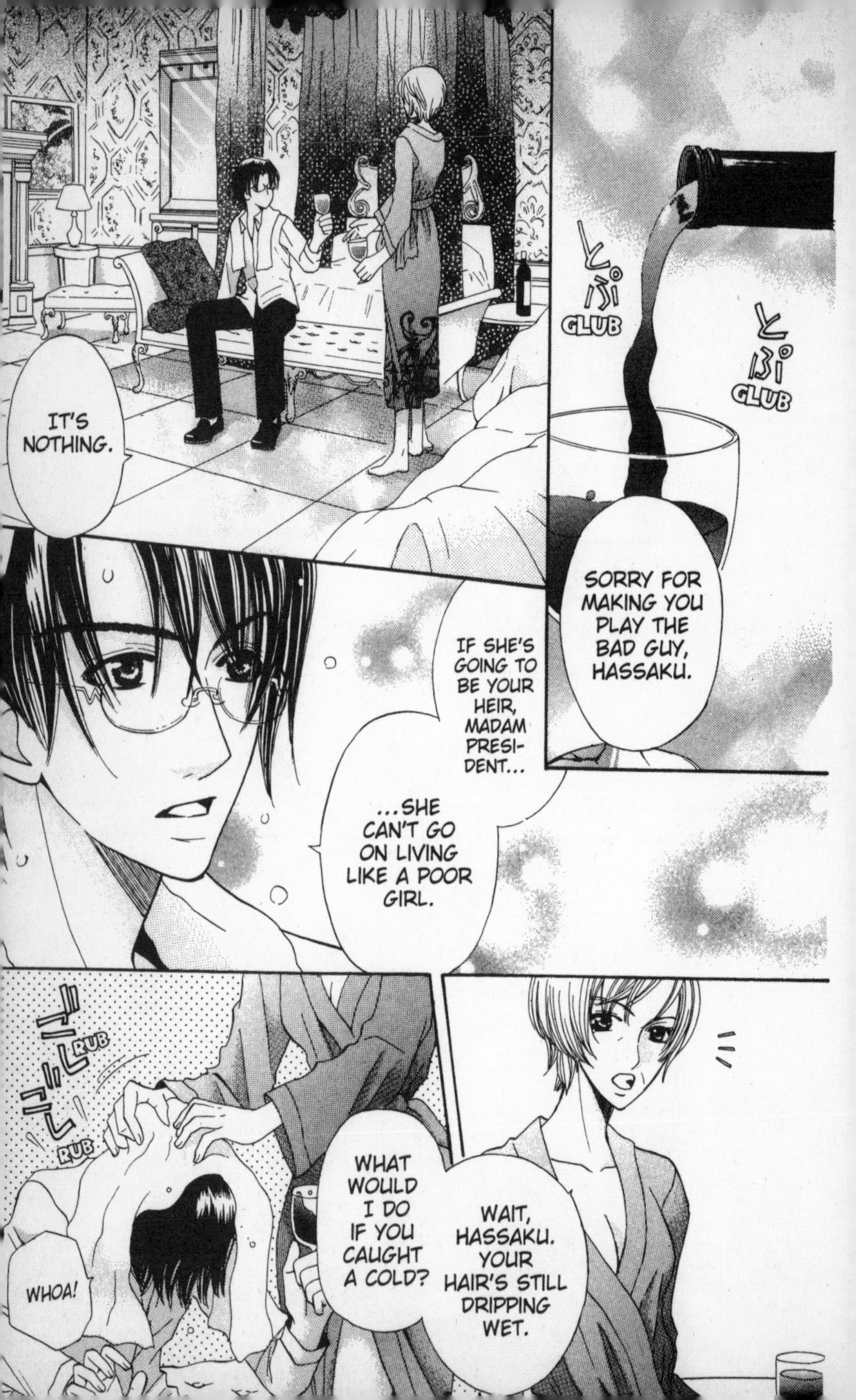
とぷ
GLUB
とぷ
GLUB
SORRY FOR MAKING YOU PLAY THE BAD GUY, HASSAKU.
IT'S NOTHING.
IF SHE'S GOING TO BE YOUR HEIR, MADAM PRESIDENT...
...SHE CAN'T GO ON LIVING LIKE A POOR GIRL.
WAIT, HASSAKU. YOUR HAIR'S STILL DRIPPING WET.
WHAT WOULD I DO IF YOU CAUGHT A COLD?
RUB
RUB
WHOA!

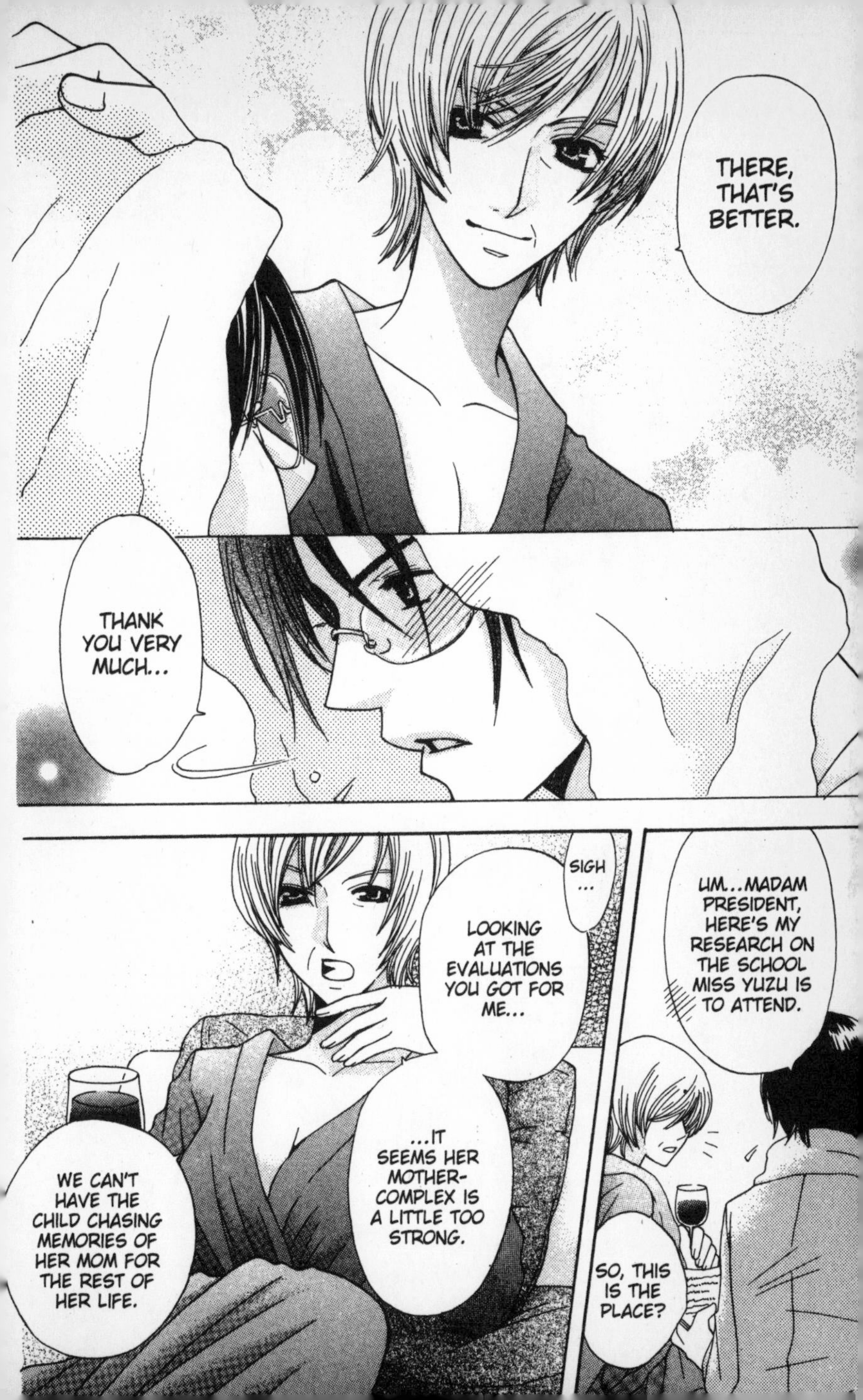

THERE, THAT'S BETTER.
THANK YOU VERY MUCH...
UM...MADAM PRESIDENT, HERE'S MY RESEARCH ON THE SCHOOL MISS YUZU IS TO ATTEND.
SO, THIS IS THE PLACE?
SIGH...
LOOKING AT THE EVALUATIONS YOU GOT FOR ME...
...IT SEEMS HER MOTHER-COMPLEX IS A LITTLE TOO STRONG.
WE CAN'T HAVE THE CHILD CHASING MEMORIES OF HER MOM FOR THE REST OF HER LIFE.

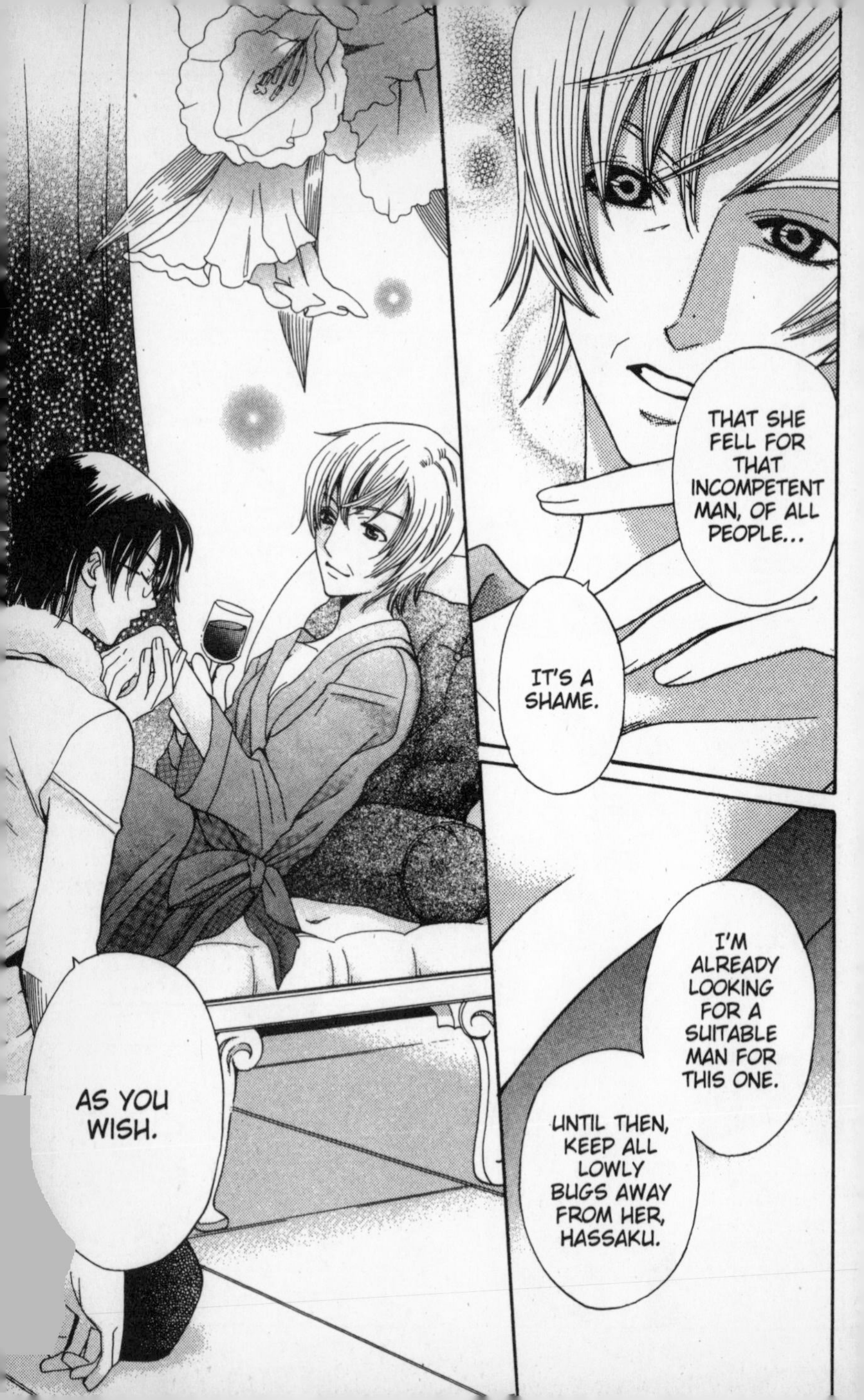
THAT SHE FELL FOR THAT INCOMPETENT MAN, OF ALL PEOPLE...
IT'S A SHAME.
I'M ALREADY LOOKING FOR A SUITABLE MAN FOR THIS ONE.
UNTIL THEN, KEEP ALL LOWLY BUGS AWAY FROM HER, HASSAKU.
AS YOU WISH.

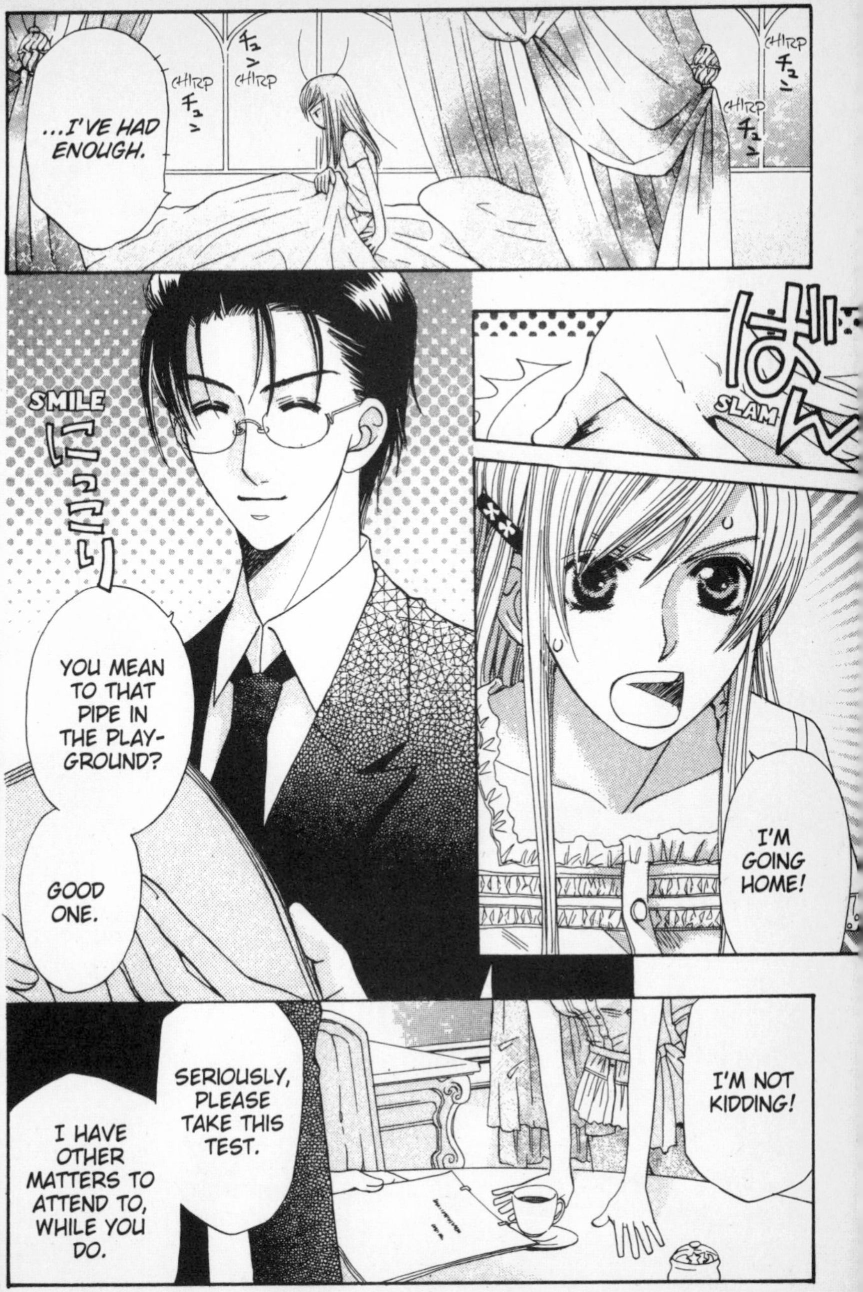
CHIRP
CHIRP
CHIRP
CHIRP
...I'VE HAD ENOUGH.
SLAM
I'M GOING HOME!
SMILE
YOU MEAN TO THAT PIPE IN THE PLAY-GROUND?
GOOD ONE.
I'M NOT KIDDING!
SERIOUSLY, PLEASE TAKE THIS TEST.
I HAVE OTHER MATTERS TO ATTEND TO, WHILE YOU DO.

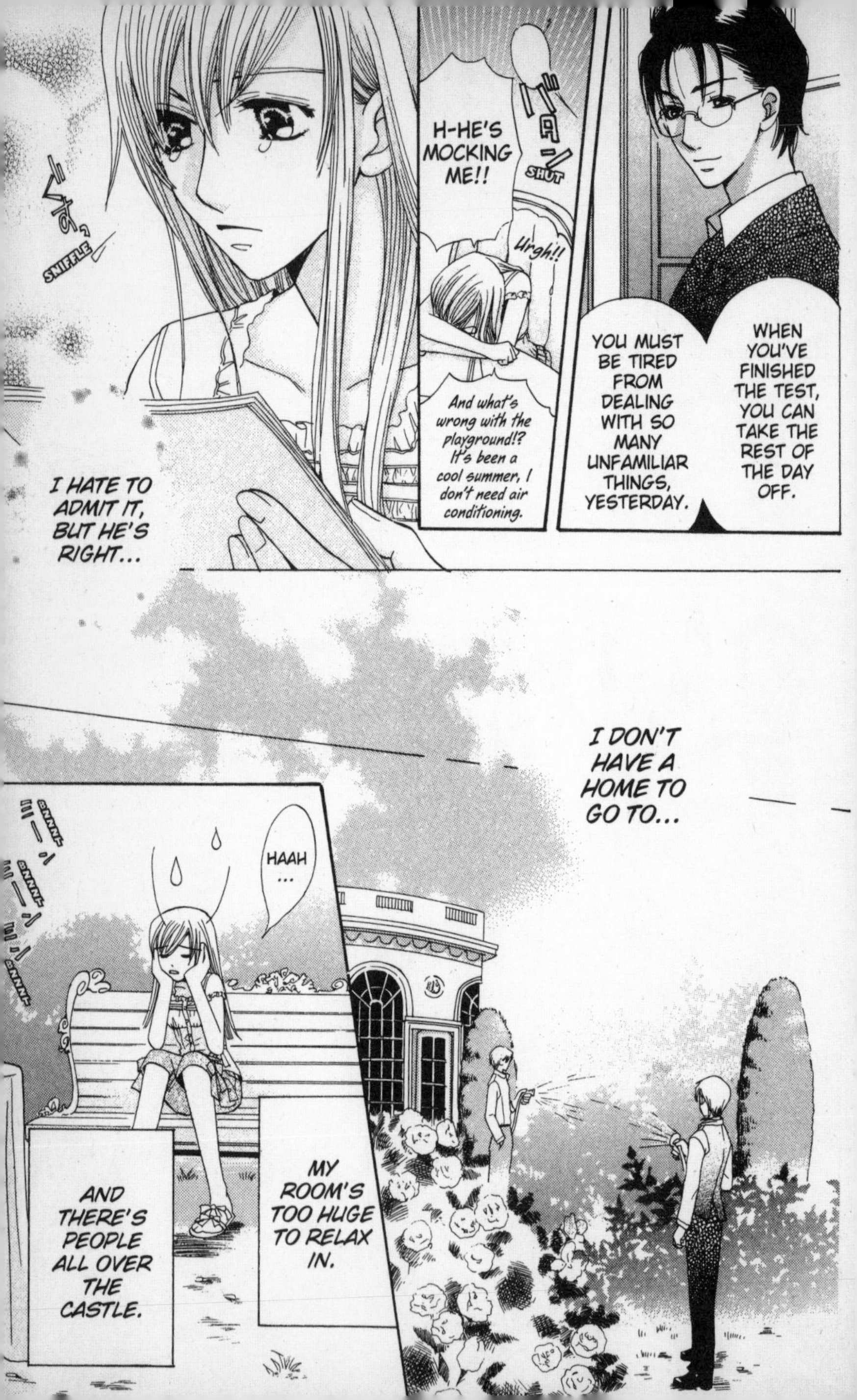
WHEN YOU'VE FINISHED THE TEST, YOU CAN TAKE THE REST OF THE DAY OFF.
YOU MUST BE TIRED FROM DEALING WITH SO MANY UNFAMILIAR THINGS, YESTERDAY.
SHUT
H-HE'S MOCKING ME!!
Urgh!!
And what's wrong with the playground!? It's been a cool summer, I don't need air conditioning.
SNIFFLE
I HATE TO ADMIT IT, BUT HE'S RIGHT...
I DON'T HAVE A HOME TO GO TO...
HAAH ...
GNNNT
GNNNT
GNNNT
MY ROOM'S TOO HUGE TO RELAX IN.
AND THERE'S PEOPLE ALL OVER THE CASTLE.

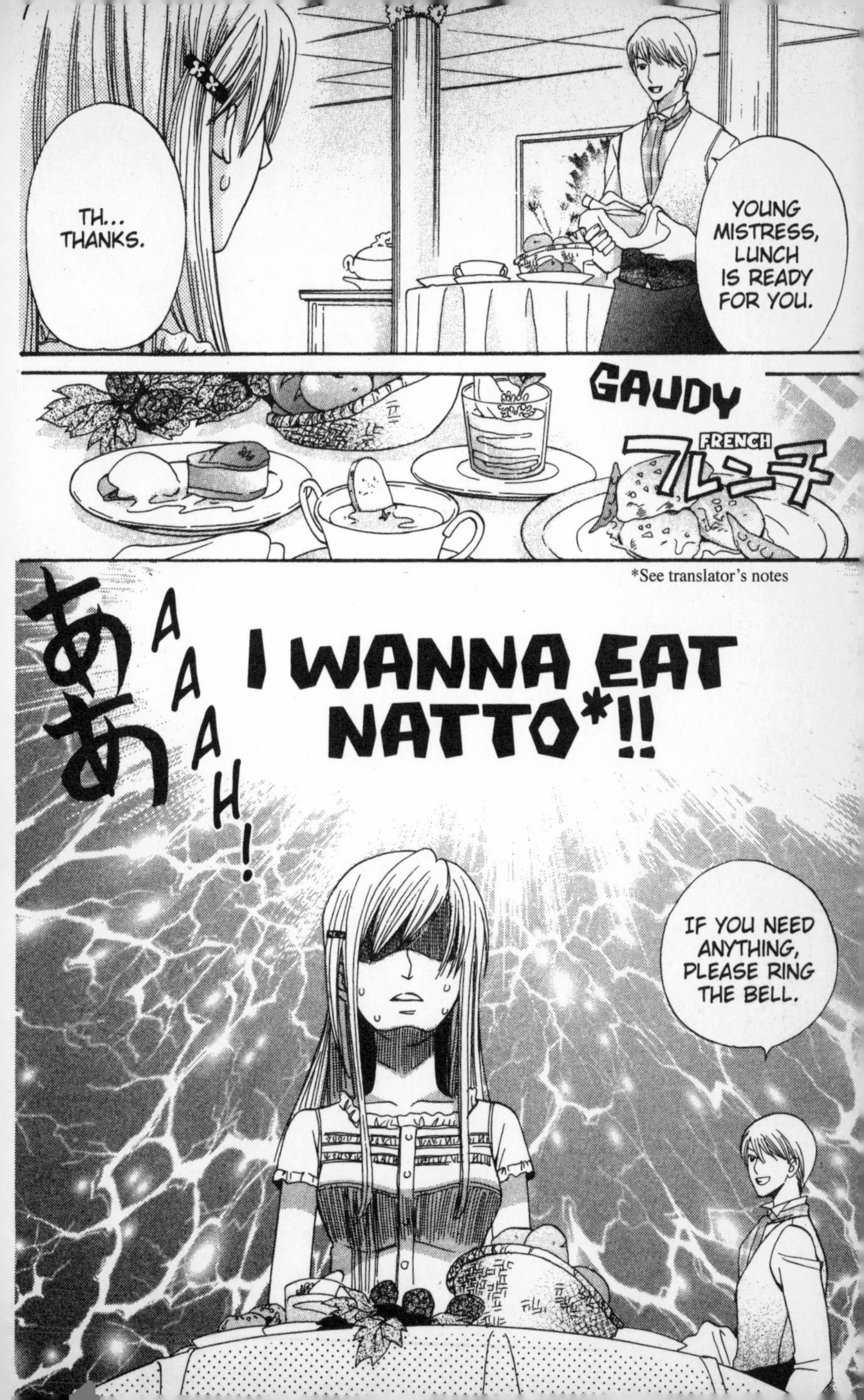
YOUNG MISTRESS, LUNCH IS READY FOR YOU.
TH... THANKS.
GAUDY
FRENCH
フレンチ
*See translator's notes
ああ
AAAH!
I WANNA EAT NATTO*!!
IF YOU NEED ANYTHING, PLEASE RING THE BELL.

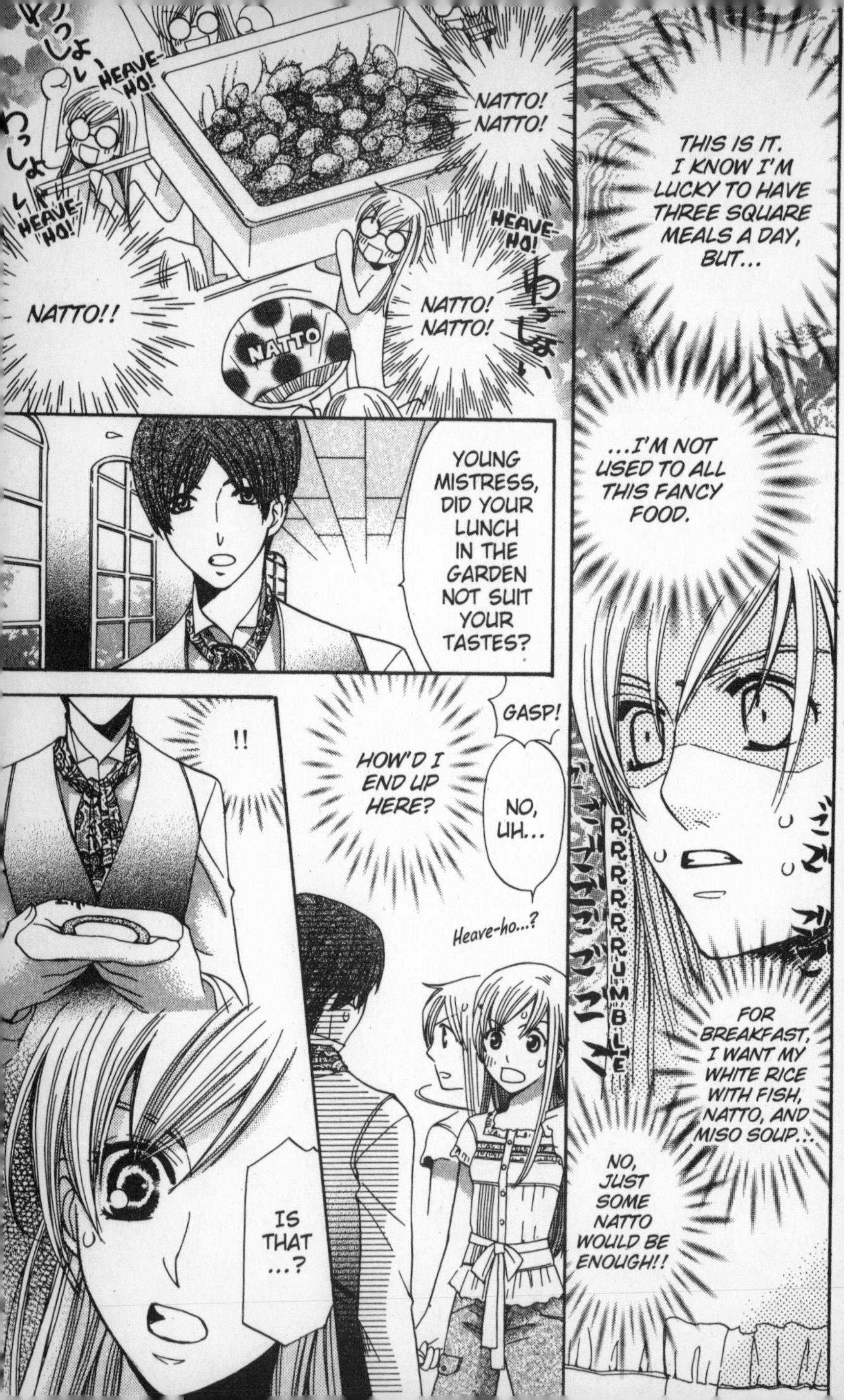
THIS IS IT. I KNOW I'M LUCKY TO HAVE THREE SQUARE MEALS A DAY, BUT...
...I'M NOT USED TO ALL THIS FANCY FOOD.
RRRRRUMBLE
FOR BREAKFAST, I WANT MY WHITE RICE WITH FISH, NATTO, AND MISO SOUP...
NO, JUST SOME NATTO WOULD BE ENOUGH!!
NATTO! NATTO!
HEAVE-HO!
わっしょい
HEAVE-HO!
わっしょい
HEAVE-HO!
わっしょい
NATTO! NATTO!
NATTO
NATTO!!
YOUNG MISTRESS, DID YOUR LUNCH IN THE GARDEN NOT SUIT YOUR TASTES?
GASP!
!!
HOW'D I END UP HERE?
NO, UH...
Heave-ho...?
IS THAT ...?

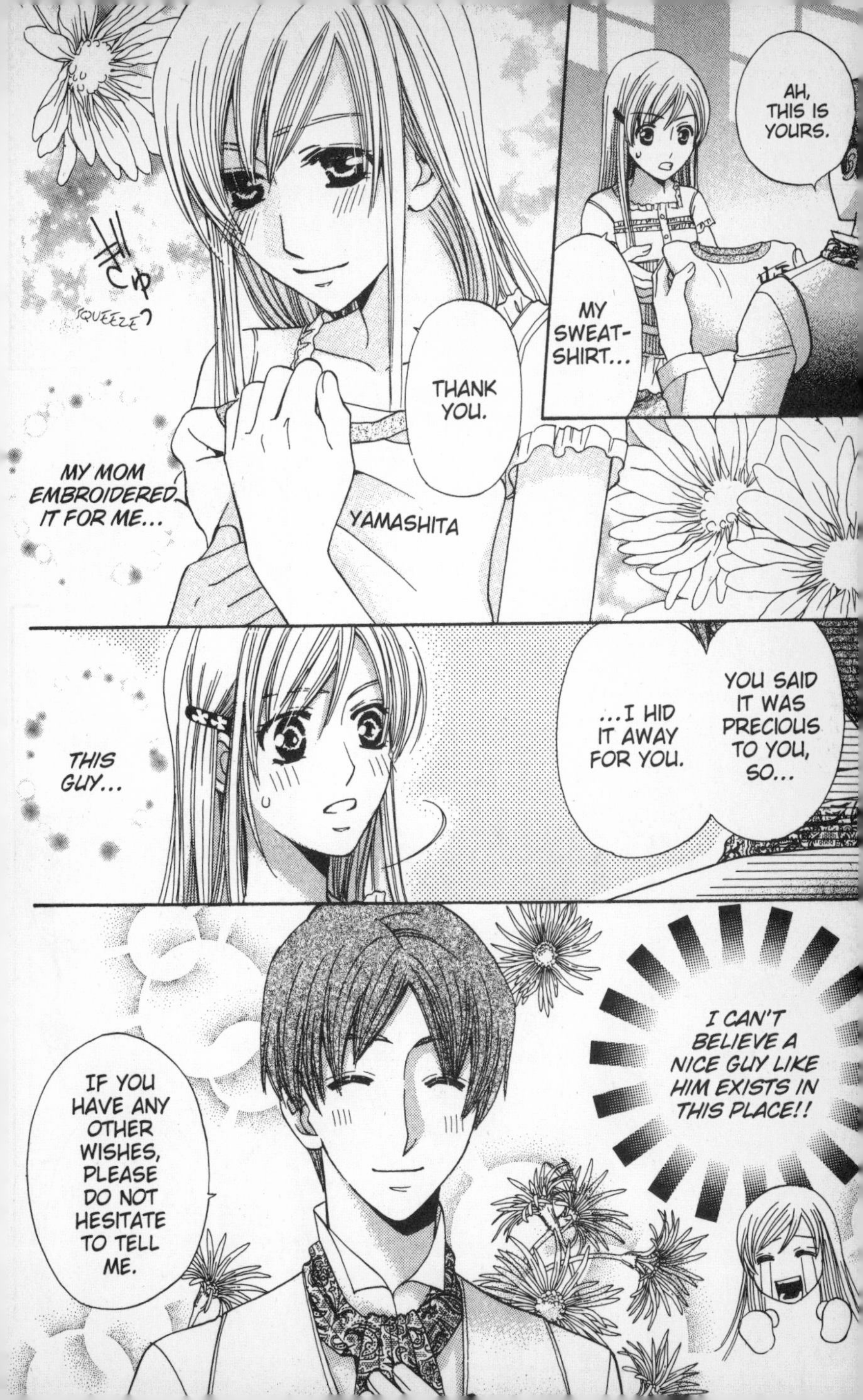
AH, THIS IS YOURS.
MY SWEAT-SHIRT...
SQUEEZE
THANK YOU.
YAMASHITA
MY MOM EMBROIDERED IT FOR ME...
YOU SAID IT WAS PRECIOUS TO YOU, SO...
...I HID IT AWAY FOR YOU.
THIS GUY...
I CAN'T BELIEVE A NICE GUY LIKE HIM EXISTS IN THIS PLACE!!
IF YOU HAVE ANY OTHER WISHES, PLEASE DO NOT HESITATE TO TELL ME.

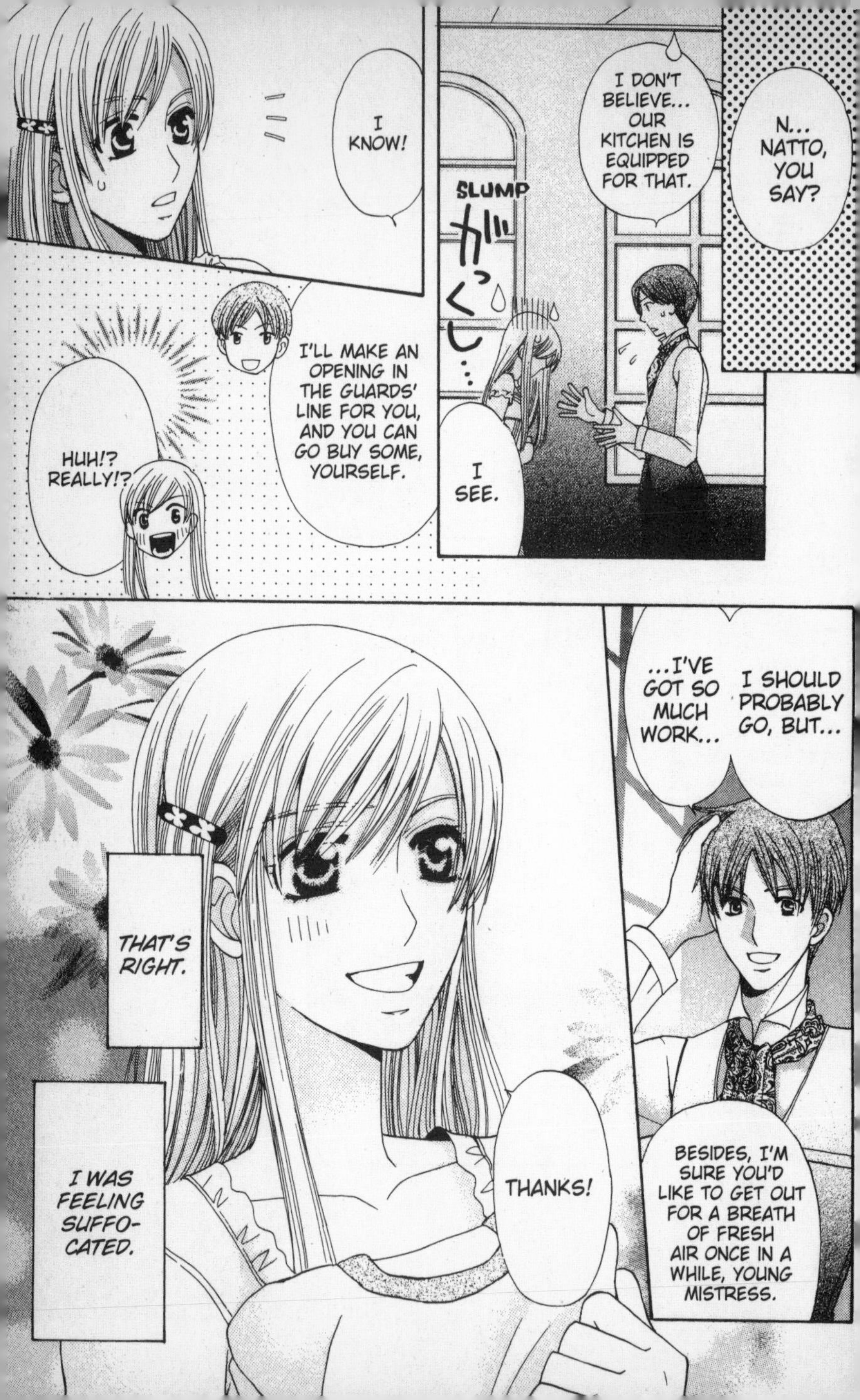
N... NATTO, YOU SAY?
I DON'T BELIEVE... OUR KITCHEN IS EQUIPPED FOR THAT.
SLUMP
がっくし...
I SEE.
I KNOW!
I'LL MAKE AN OPENING IN THE GUARDS' LINE FOR YOU, AND YOU CAN GO BUY SOME, YOURSELF.
HUH!? REALLY!?
I SHOULD PROBABLY GO, BUT...
...I'VE GOT SO MUCH WORK...
BESIDES, I'M SURE YOU'D LIKE TO GET OUT FOR A BREATH OF FRESH AIR ONCE IN A WHILE, YOUNG MISTRESS.
THANKS!
THAT'S RIGHT.
I WAS FEELING SUFFOCATED.

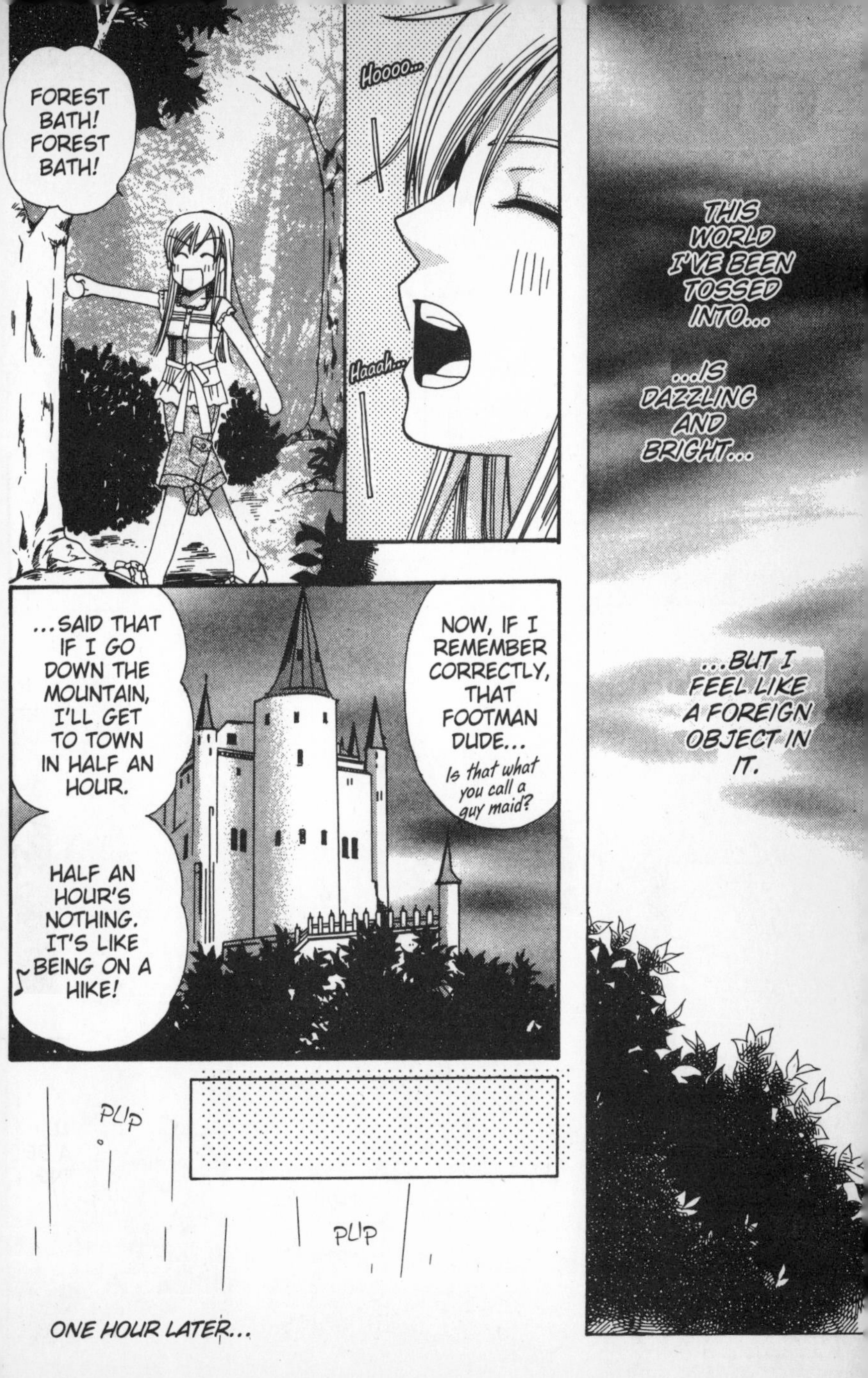
THIS WORLD I'VE BEEN TOSSED INTO...
...IS DAZZLING AND BRIGHT...
...BUT I FEEL LIKE A FOREIGN OBJECT IN IT.
Hoooo...
Haaah...
FOREST BATH! FOREST BATH!
NOW, IF I REMEMBER CORRECTLY, THAT FOOTMAN DUDE...
Is that what you call a guy maid?
...SAID THAT IF I GO DOWN THE MOUNTAIN, I'LL GET TO TOWN IN HALF AN HOUR.
HALF AN HOUR'S NOTHING. IT'S LIKE BEING ON A HIKE!
PLIP
PLIP
ONE HOUR LATER...

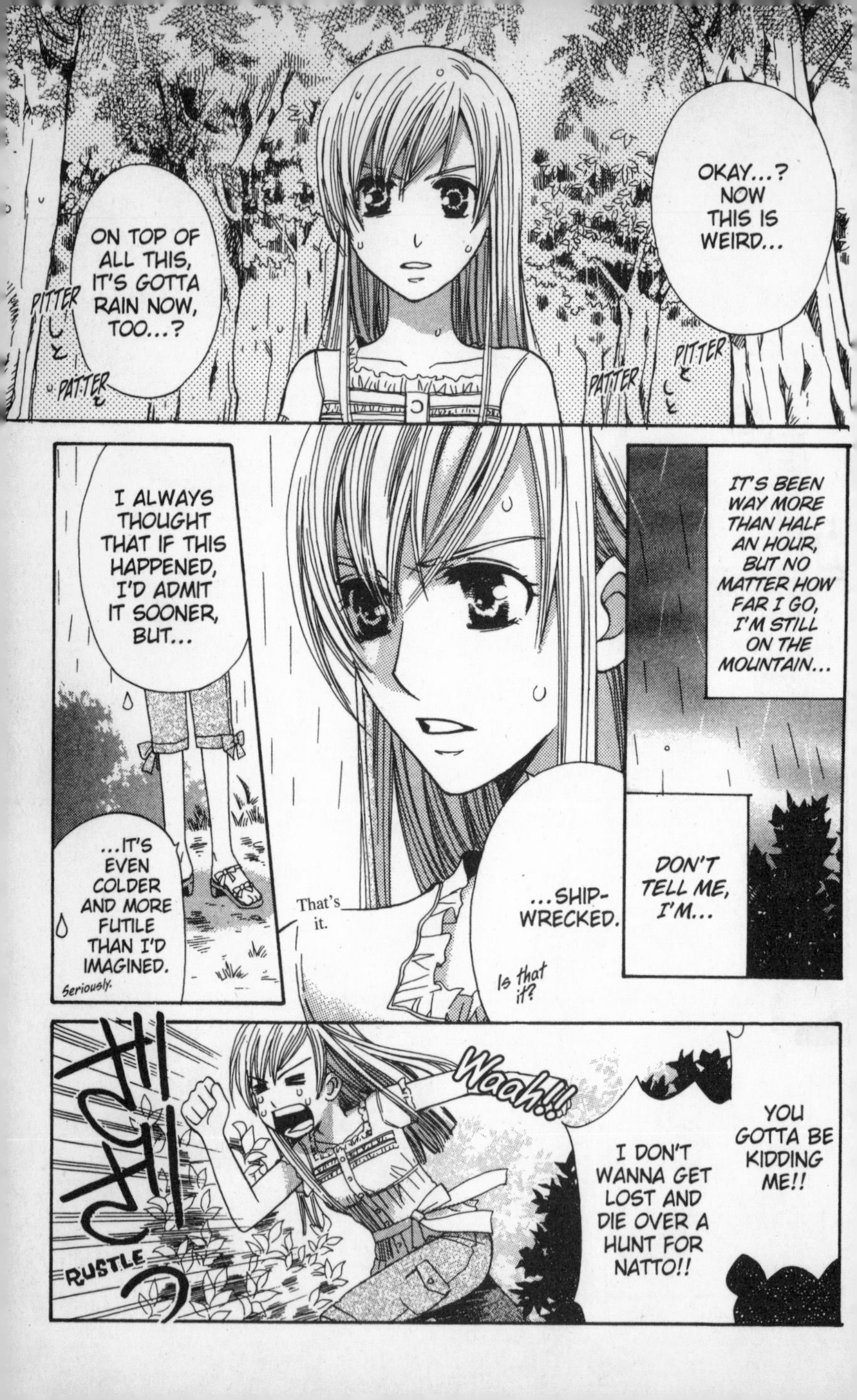
OKAY...? NOW THIS IS WEIRD...
ON TOP OF ALL THIS, IT'S GOTTA RAIN NOW, TOO...?
PITTER PATTER
PITTER PATTER
IT'S BEEN WAY MORE THAN HALF AN HOUR, BUT NO MATTER HOW FAR I GO, I'M STILL ON THE MOUNTAIN...
DON'T TELL ME, I'M...
...SHIP-WRECKED.
Is that it?
That's it.
I ALWAYS THOUGHT THAT IF THIS HAPPENED, I'D ADMIT IT SOONER, BUT...
...IT'S EVEN COLDER AND MORE FUTILE THAN I'D IMAGINED.
Seriously.
YOU GOTTA BE KIDDING ME!!
I DON'T WANNA GET LOST AND DIE OVER A HUNT FOR NATTO!!
Waah!!
RUSTLE

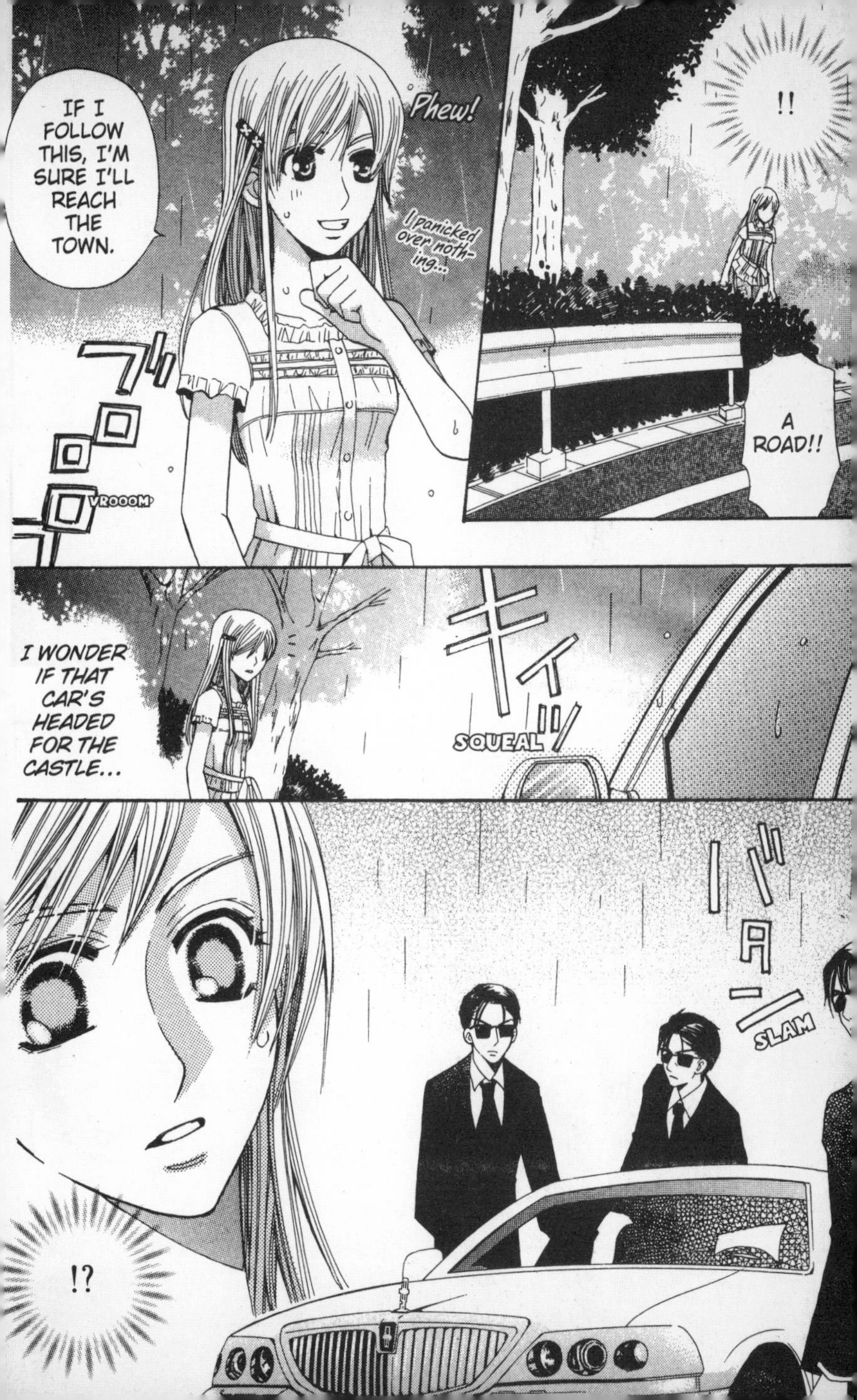
!!
A ROAD!!
IF I FOLLOW THIS, I'M SURE I'LL REACH THE TOWN.
Phew!
I panicked over nothing...
VROOOM
I WONDER IF THAT CAR'S HEADED FOR THE CASTLE...
SQUEAL
SLAM
!?

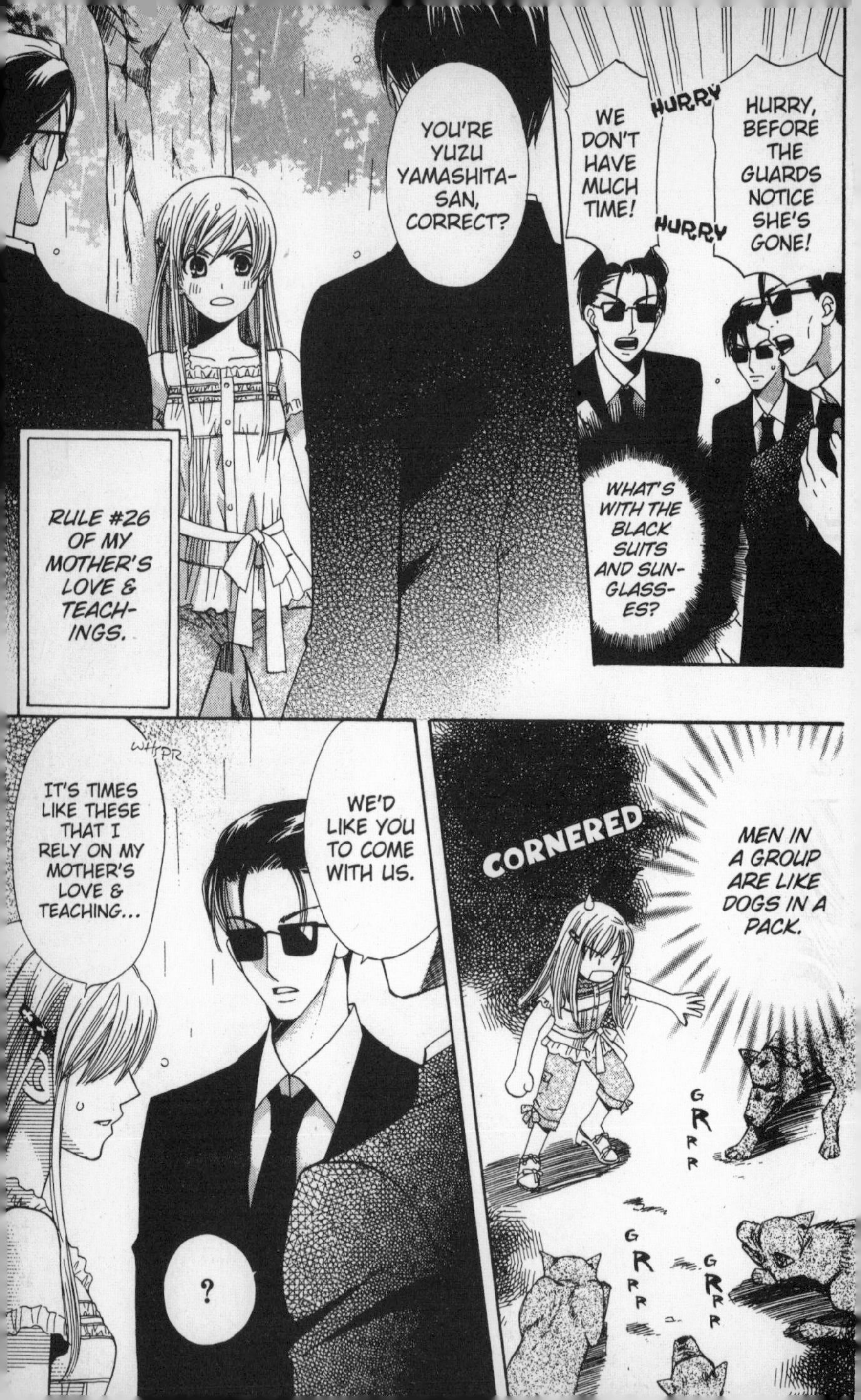
HURRY, BEFORE THE GUARDS NOTICE SHE'S GONE!
HURRY
WE DON'T HAVE MUCH TIME!
HURRY
WHAT'S WITH THE BLACK SUITS AND SUN-GLASS-ES?
YOU'RE YUZU YAMASHITA-SAN, CORRECT?
RULE #26 OF MY MOTHER'S LOVE & TEACH-INGS.
MEN IN A GROUP ARE LIKE DOGS IN A PACK.
CORNERED
GRRR
GRRR
GRRR
WE'D LIKE YOU TO COME WITH US.
WHSPR
IT'S TIMES LIKE THESE THAT I RELY ON MY MOTHER'S LOVE & TEACHING...
?

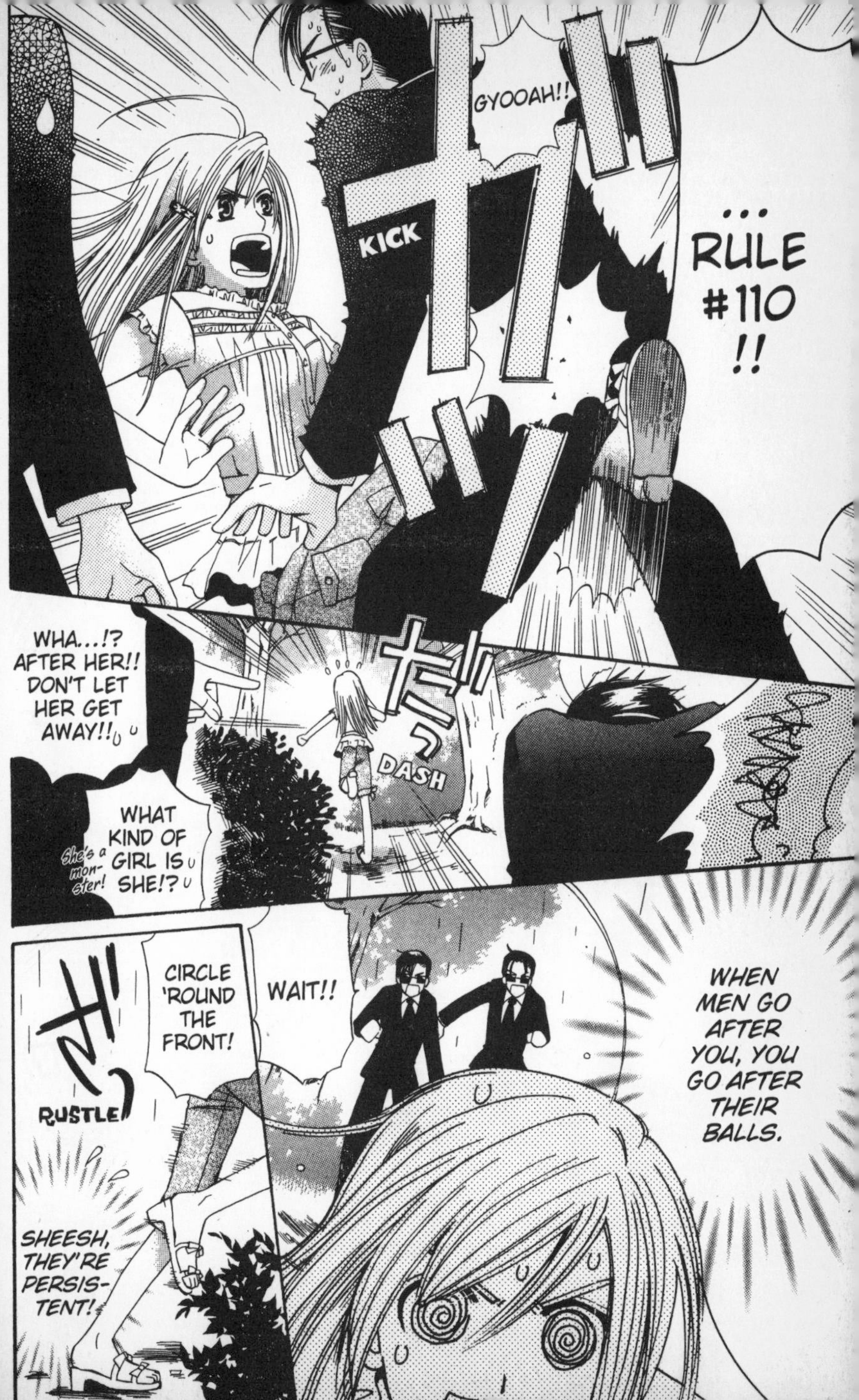
GYOOAH!!
... RULE #110 !!
KICK
DASH
WHA...!? AFTER HER!! DON'T LET HER GET AWAY!!
WHAT KIND OF GIRL IS SHE!?
She's a mon-ster!
WHEN MEN GO AFTER YOU, YOU GO AFTER THEIR BALLS.
WAIT!!
CIRCLE 'ROUND THE FRONT!
RUSTLE
SHEESH, THEY'RE PERSIS-TENT!

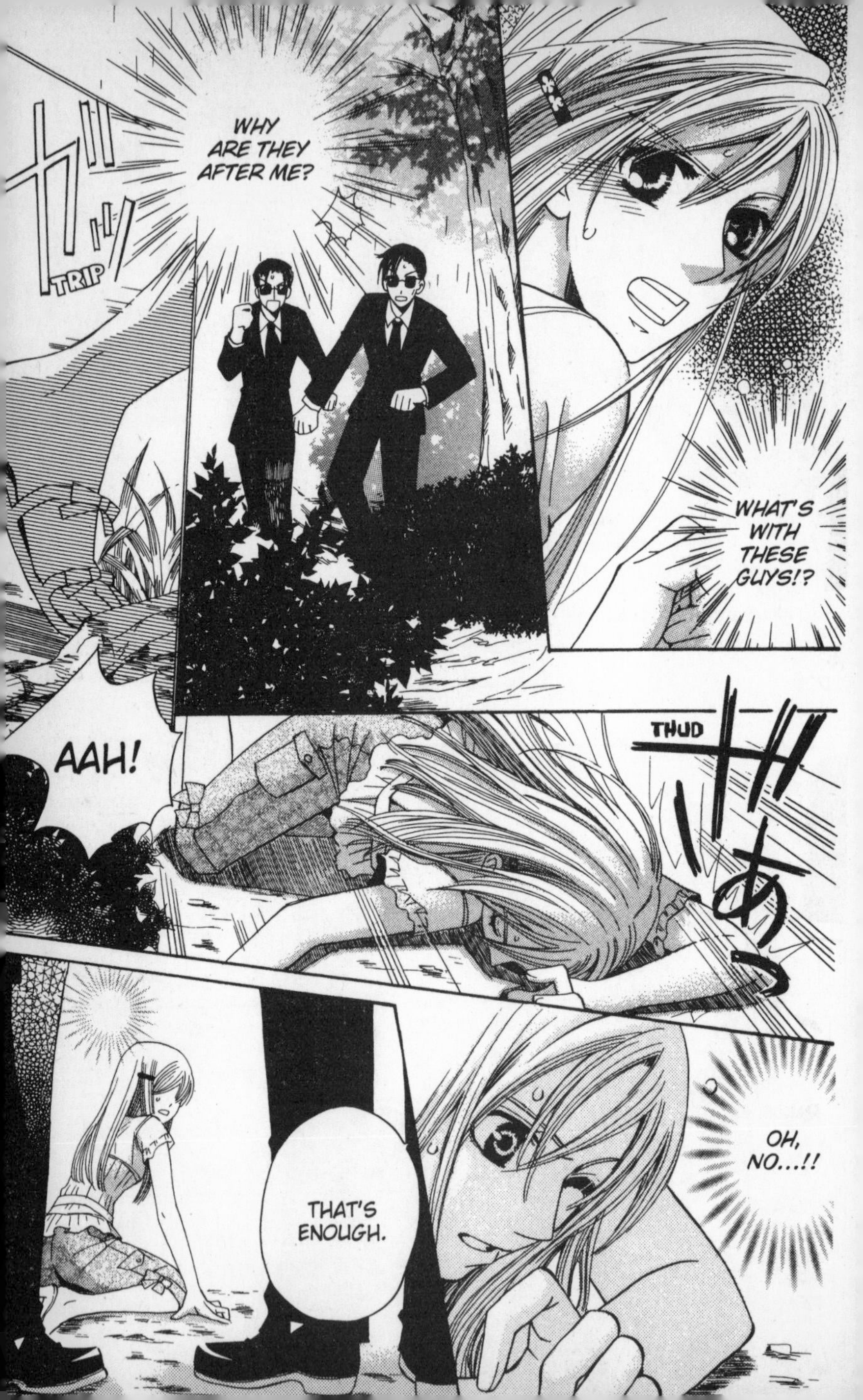

WHAT'S WITH THESE GUYS!?
WHY ARE THEY AFTER ME?
TRIP
AAH!
THUD
OH, NO...!!
THAT'S ENOUGH.

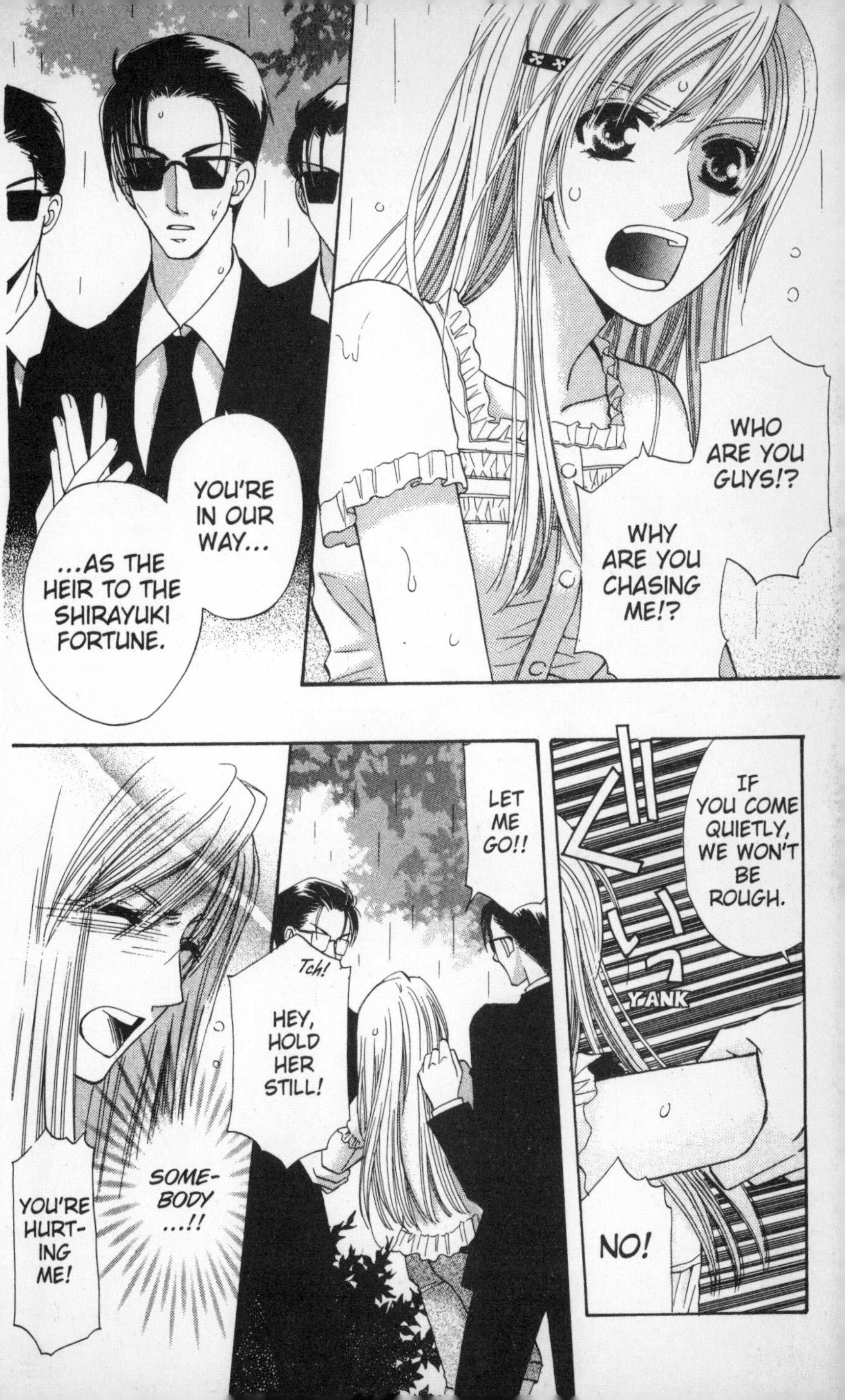
WHO ARE YOU GUYS!?
WHY ARE YOU CHASING ME!?
YOU'RE IN OUR WAY...
...AS THE HEIR TO THE SHIRAYUKI FORTUNE.
IF YOU COME QUIETLY, WE WON'T BE ROUGH.
YANK
NO!
LET ME GO!!
Tch!
HEY, HOLD HER STILL!
SOME-BODY ...!!
YOU'RE HURT-ING ME!

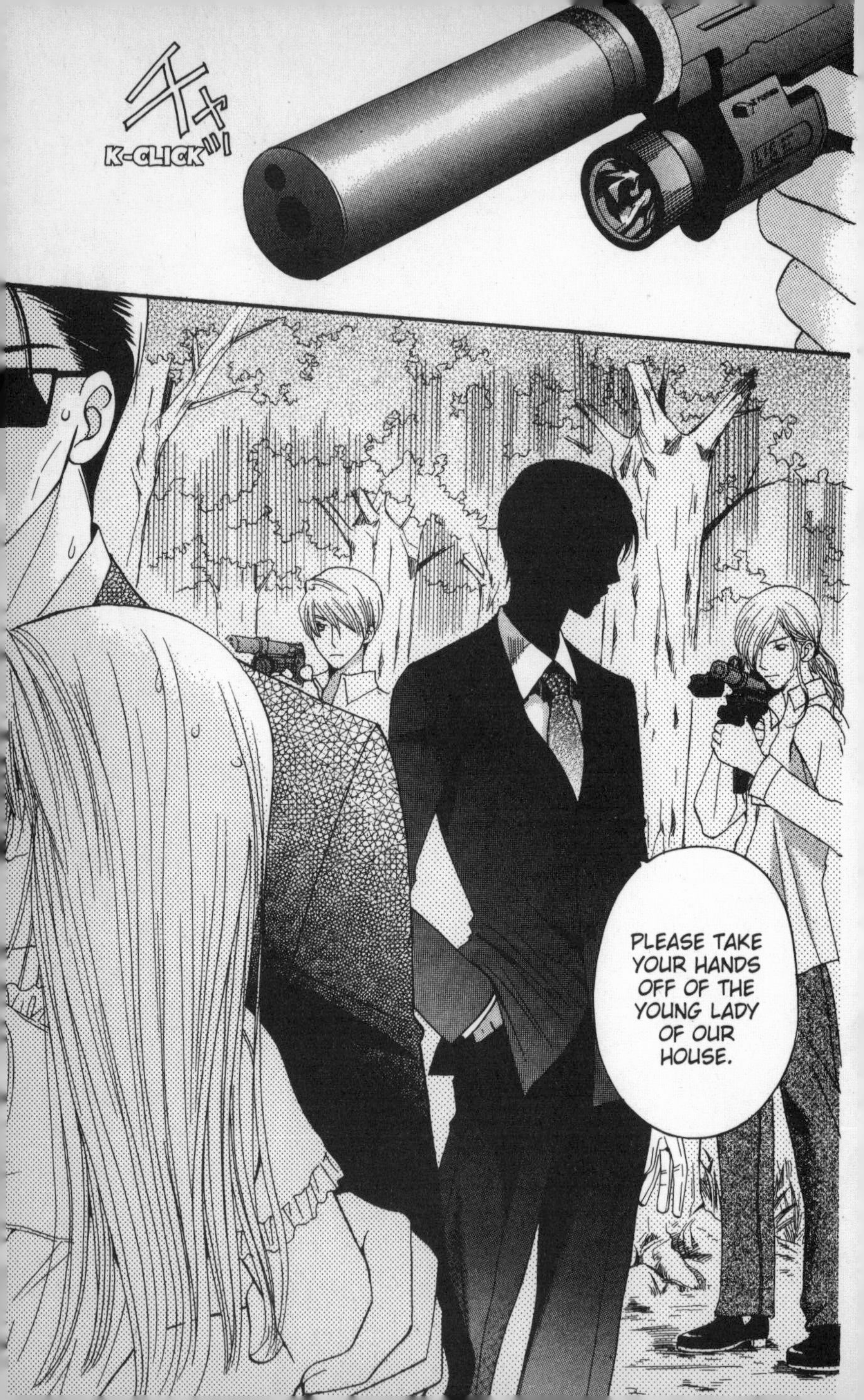
チャ
K-CLICK
PLEASE TAKE YOUR HANDS OFF OF THE YOUNG LADY OF OUR HOUSE.

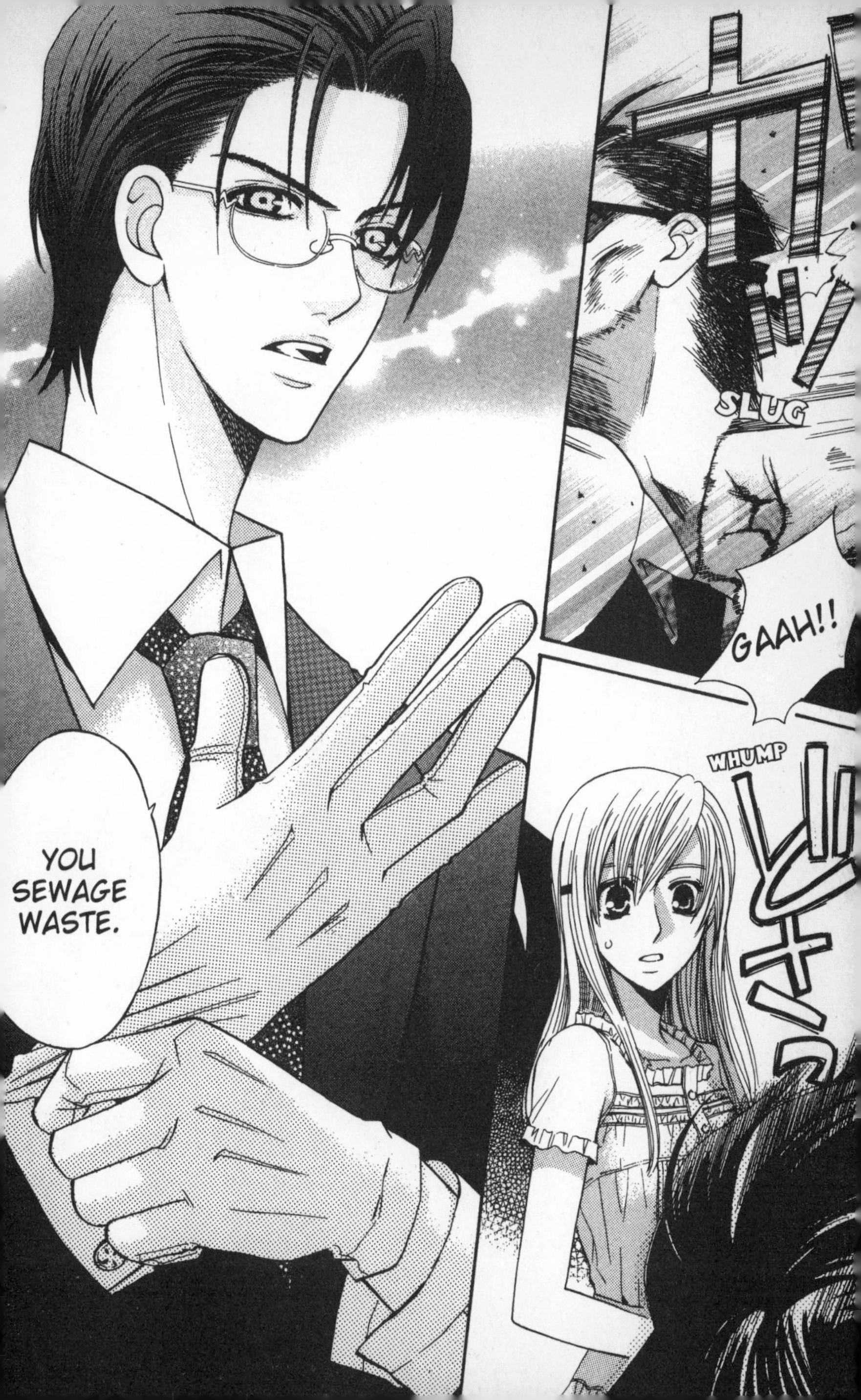
SLUG
GAAH!!
WHUMP
YOU SEWAGE WASTE.

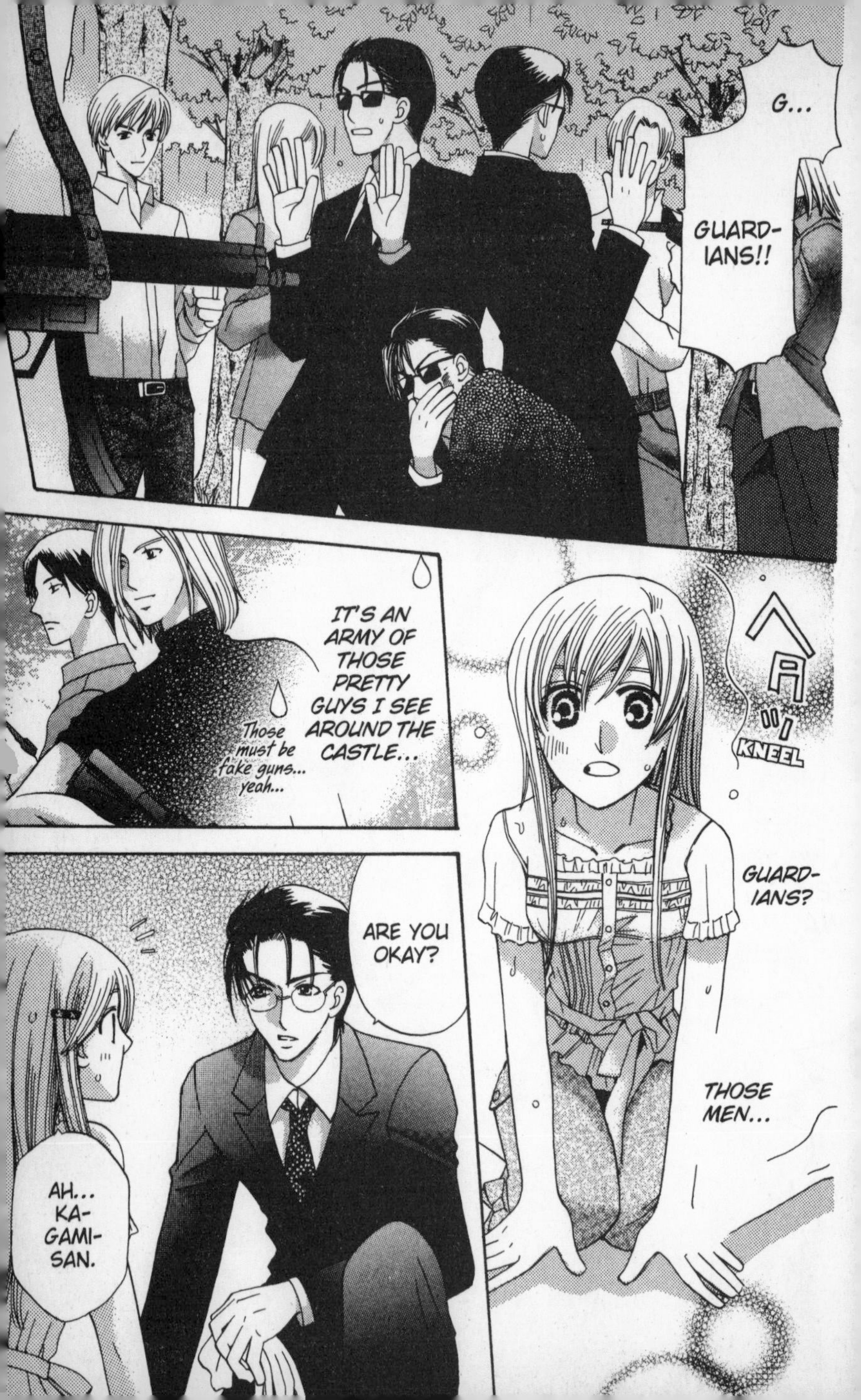
G...
GUARD-IANS!!
KNEEL
GUARD-IANS?
THOSE MEN...
IT'S AN ARMY OF THOSE PRETTY GUYS I SEE AROUND THE CASTLE...
Those must be fake guns... yeah...
ARE YOU OKAY?
AH... KA-GAMI-SAN.

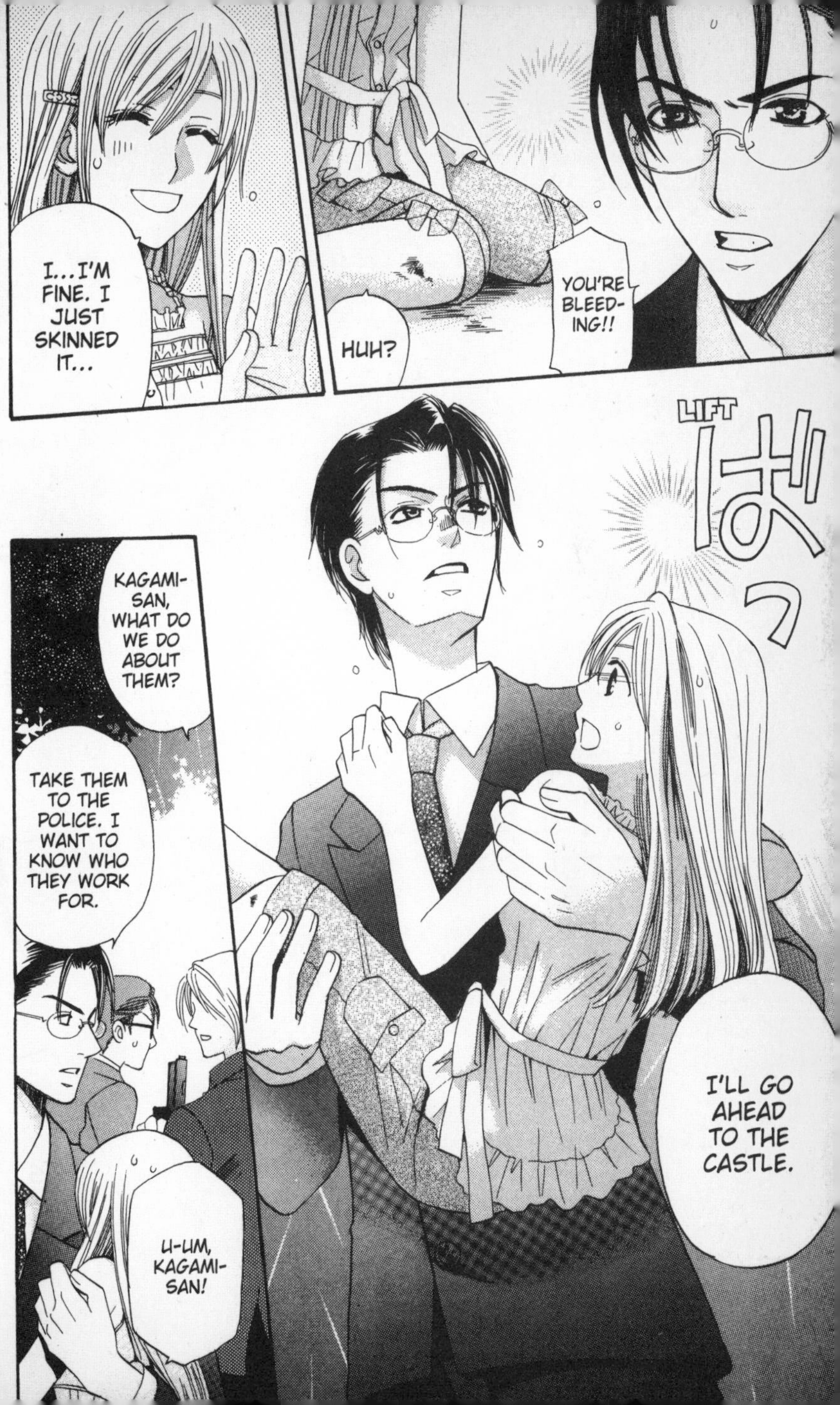
YOU'RE BLEEDING!!
HUH?
I...I'M FINE. I JUST SKINNED IT...
LIFT
ぱっ
I'LL GO AHEAD TO THE CASTLE.
KAGAMI-SAN, WHAT DO WE DO ABOUT THEM?
TAKE THEM TO THE POLICE. I WANT TO KNOW WHO THEY WORK FOR.
U-UM, KAGAMI-SAN!

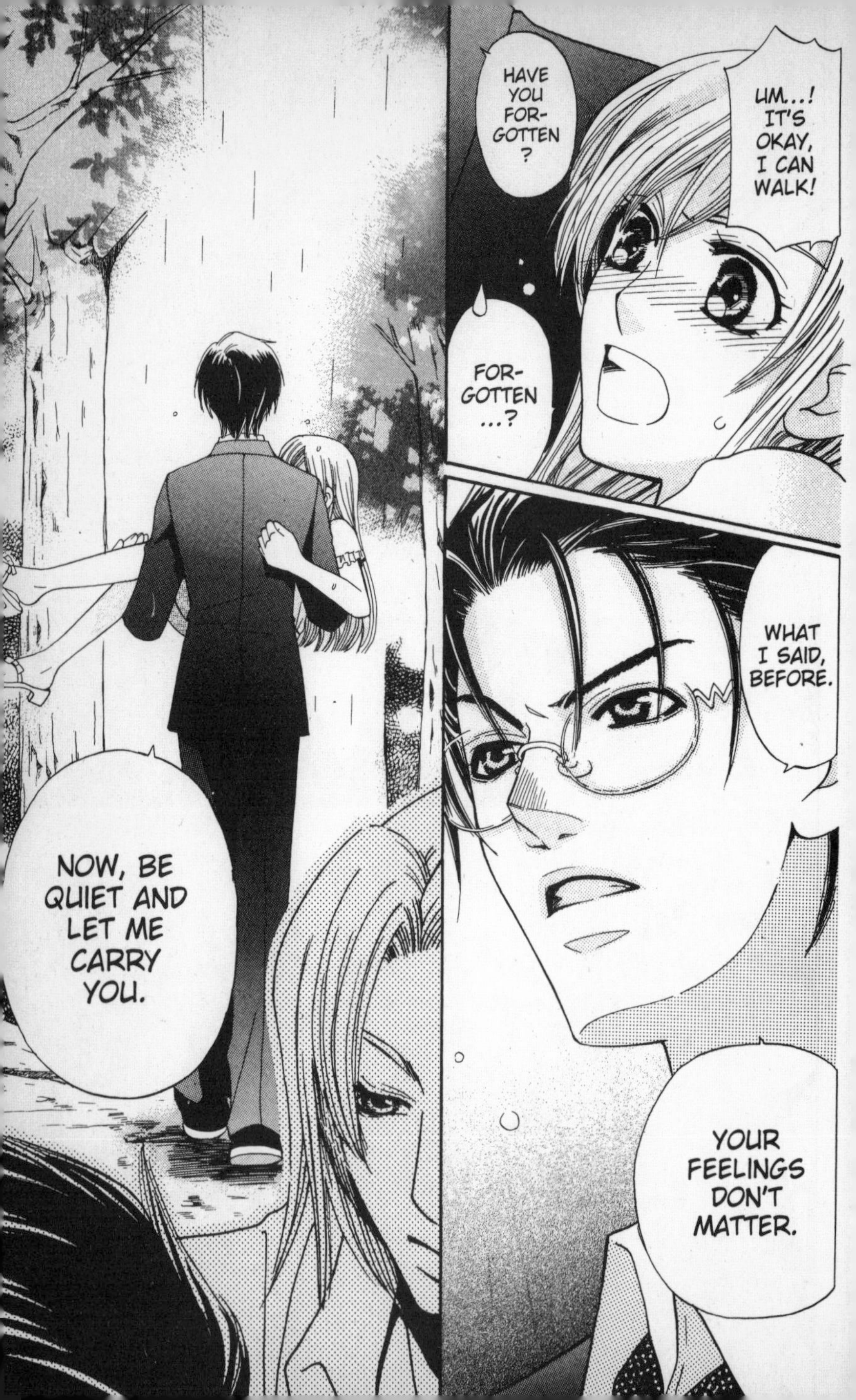
UM...! IT'S OKAY, I CAN WALK!
HAVE YOU FOR-GOTTEN?
FOR-GOTTEN...?
WHAT I SAID, BEFORE.
YOUR FEELINGS DON'T MATTER.
NOW, BE QUIET AND LET ME CARRY YOU.

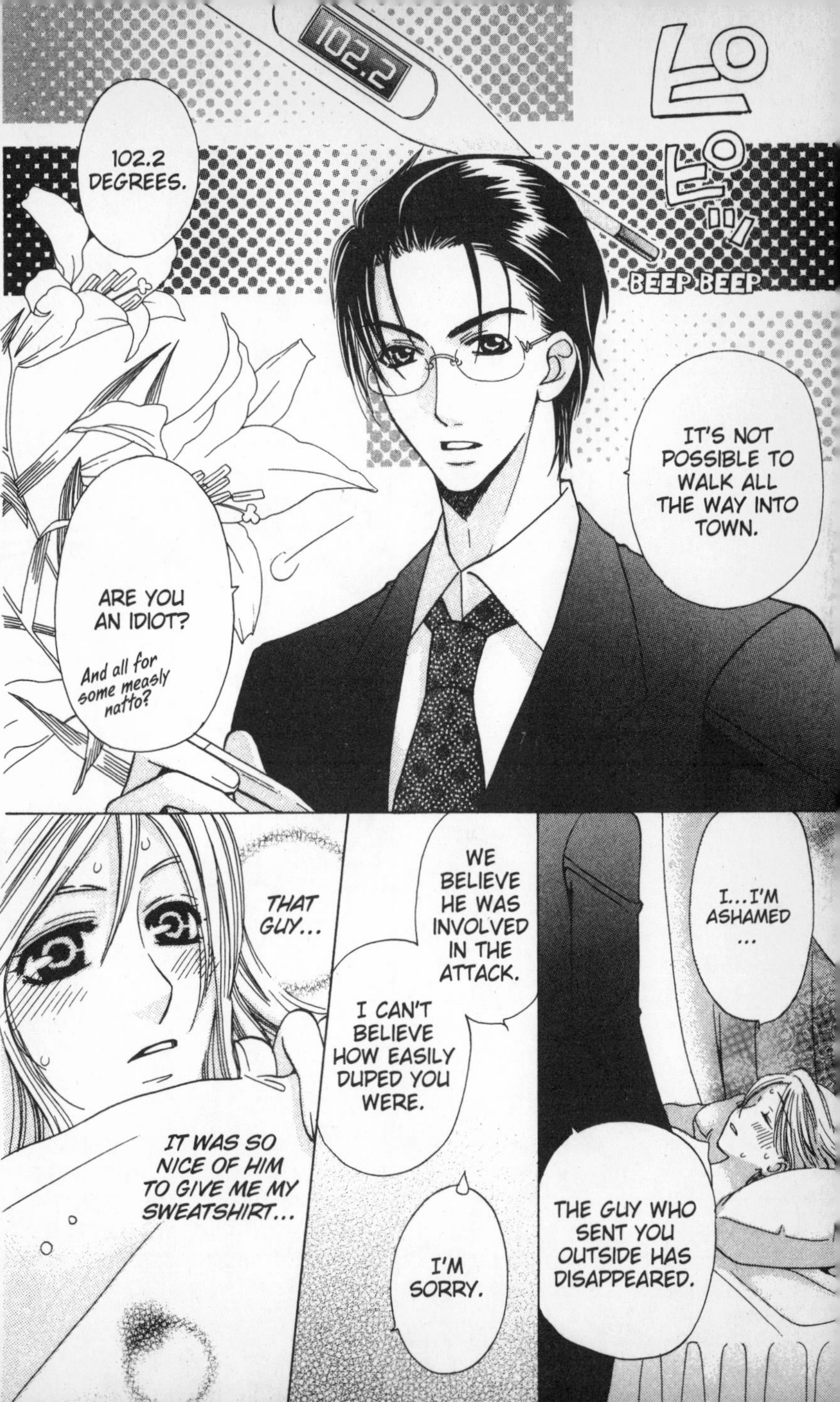
102.2
ピピッ
BEEP BEEP
102.2 DEGREES.
IT'S NOT POSSIBLE TO WALK ALL THE WAY INTO TOWN.
ARE YOU AN IDIOT?
And all for some measly natto?
I...I'M ASHAMED...
THE GUY WHO SENT YOU OUTSIDE HAS DISAPPEARED.
WE BELIEVE HE WAS INVOLVED IN THE ATTACK.
I CAN'T BELIEVE HOW EASILY DUPED YOU WERE.
I'M SORRY.
THAT GUY...
IT WAS SO NICE OF HIM TO GIVE ME MY SWEATSHIRT...

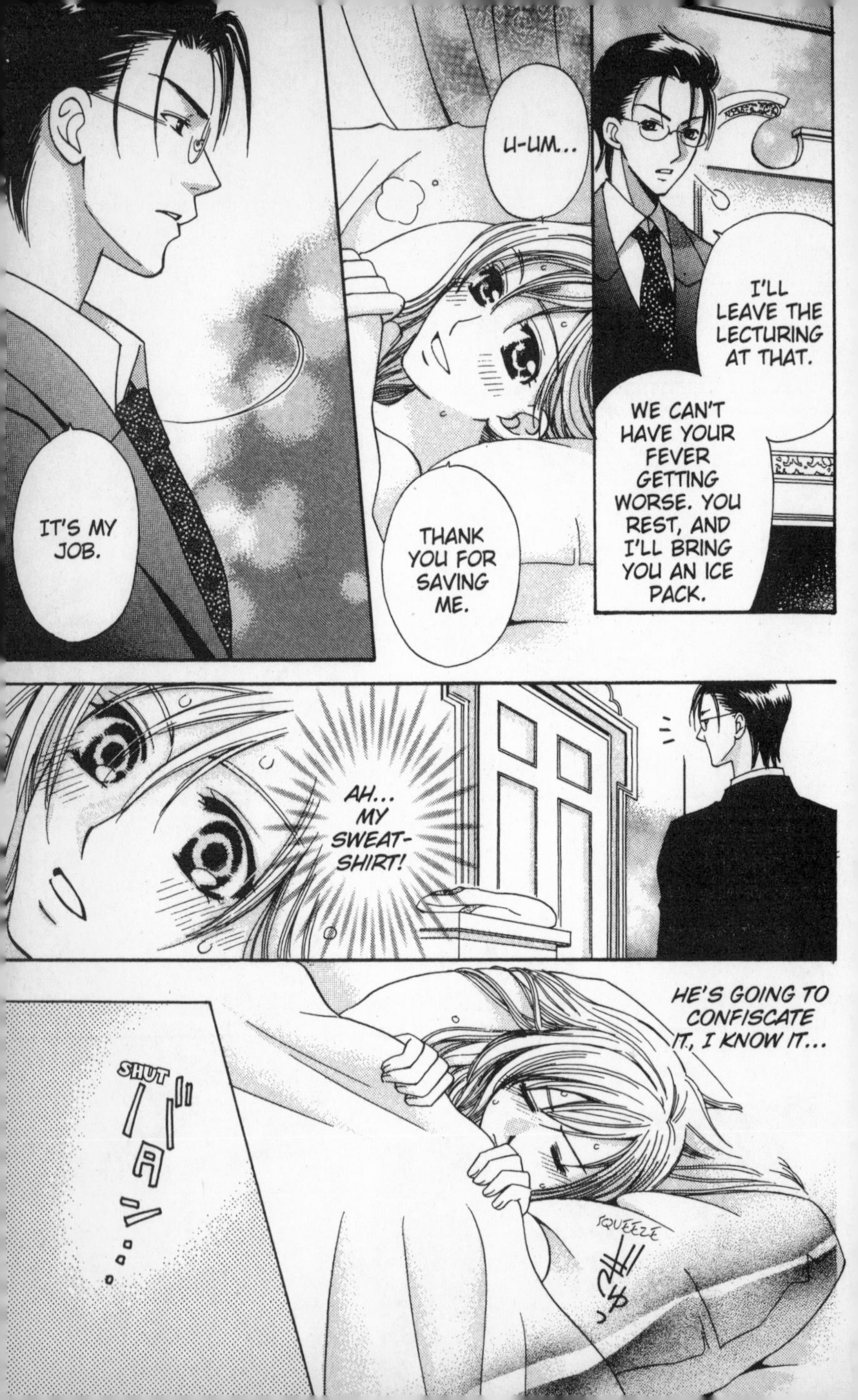
I'LL LEAVE THE LECTURING AT THAT.
WE CAN'T HAVE YOUR FEVER GETTING WORSE. YOU REST, AND I'LL BRING YOU AN ICE PACK.
U-UM...
THANK YOU FOR SAVING ME.
IT'S MY JOB.
AH... MY SWEAT-SHIRT!
HE'S GOING TO CONFISCATE IT, I KNOW IT...
SQUEEZE
SHUT

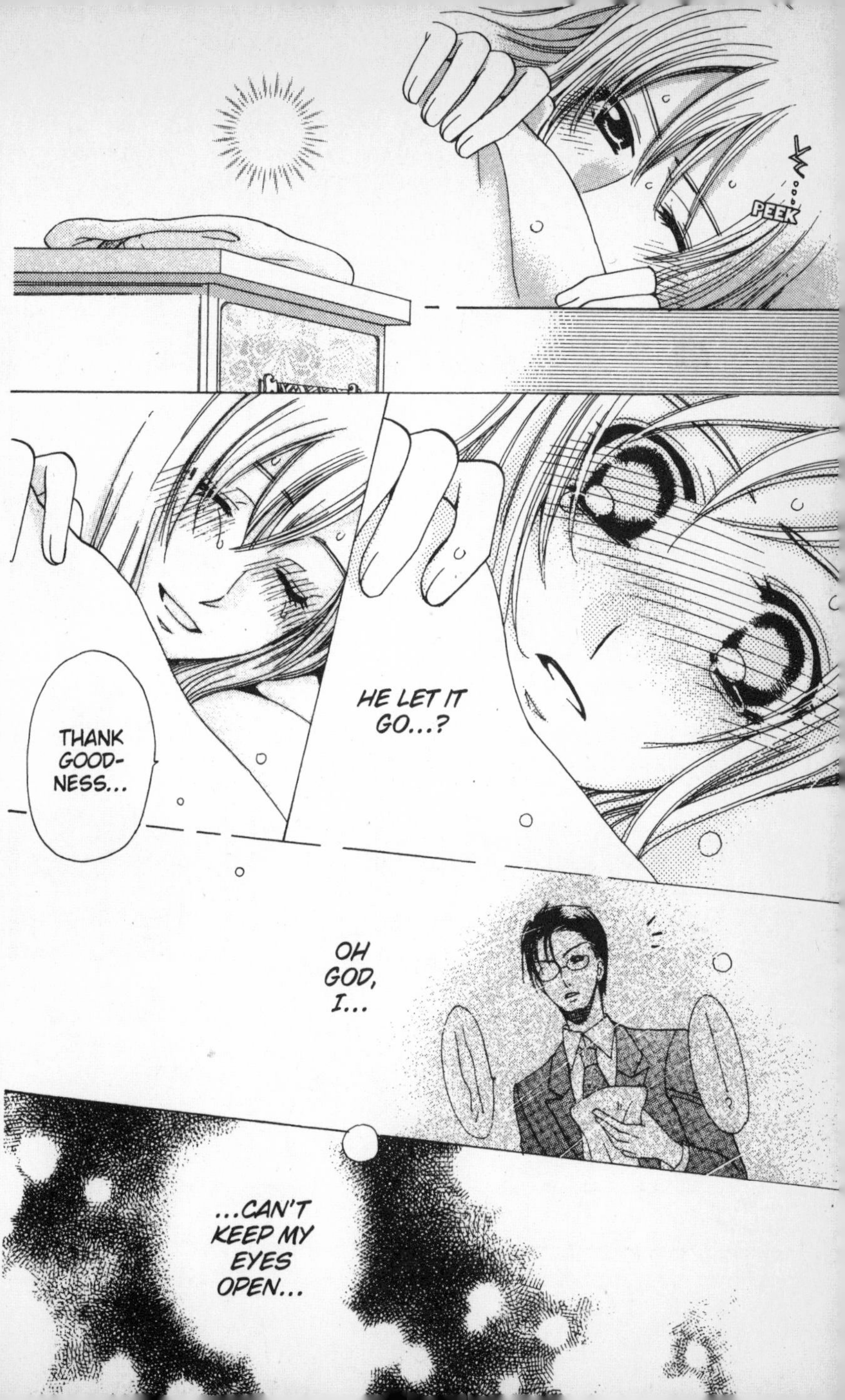
PEEK
HE LET IT GO...?
THANK GOOD-NESS...
OH GOD, I...
...CAN'T KEEP MY EYES OPEN...

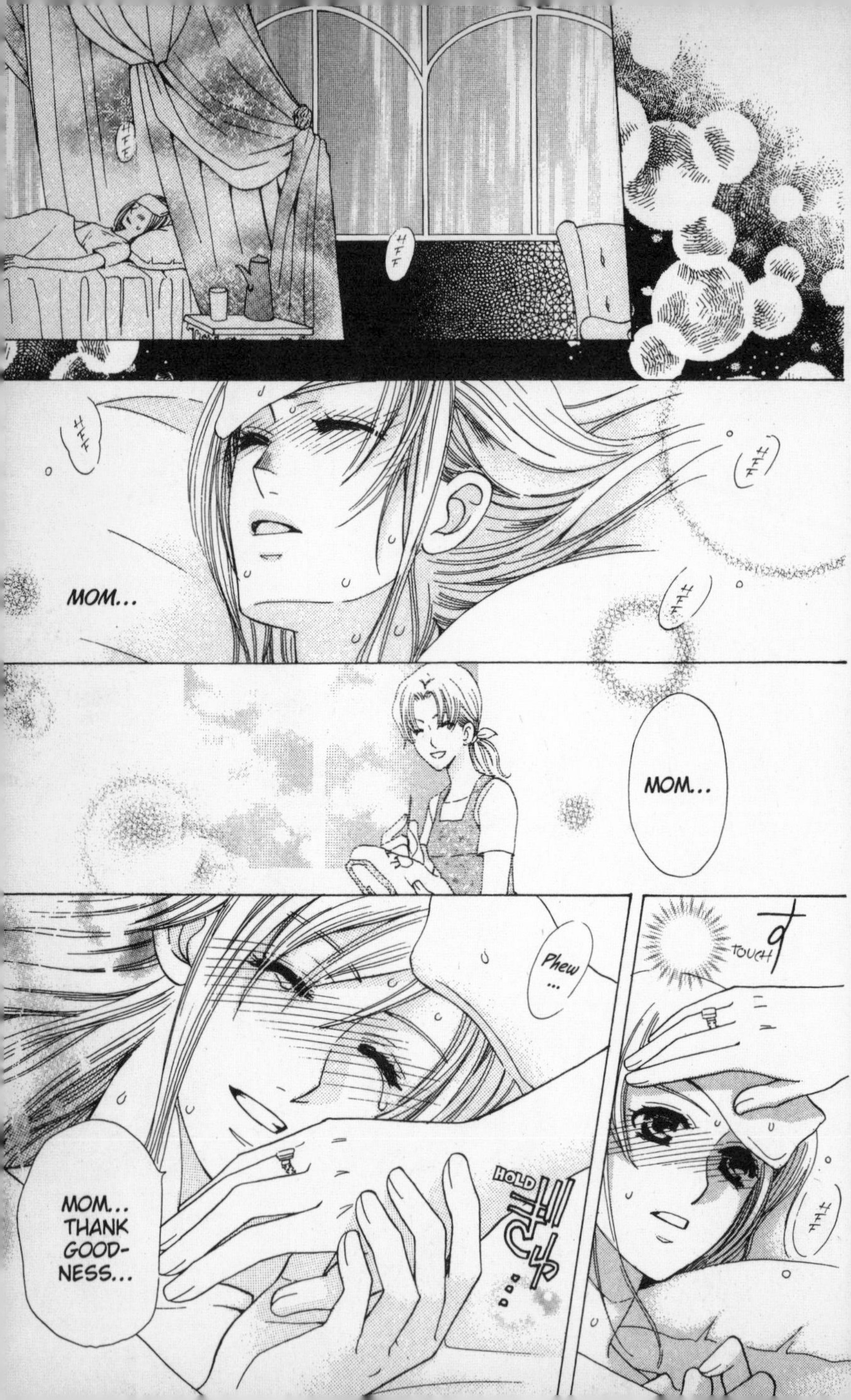
HFF
HFF
HFF
HFF
HFF
MOM...
MOM...
TOUCH
HFF
Phew...
HOLD
MOM... THANK GOODNESS...

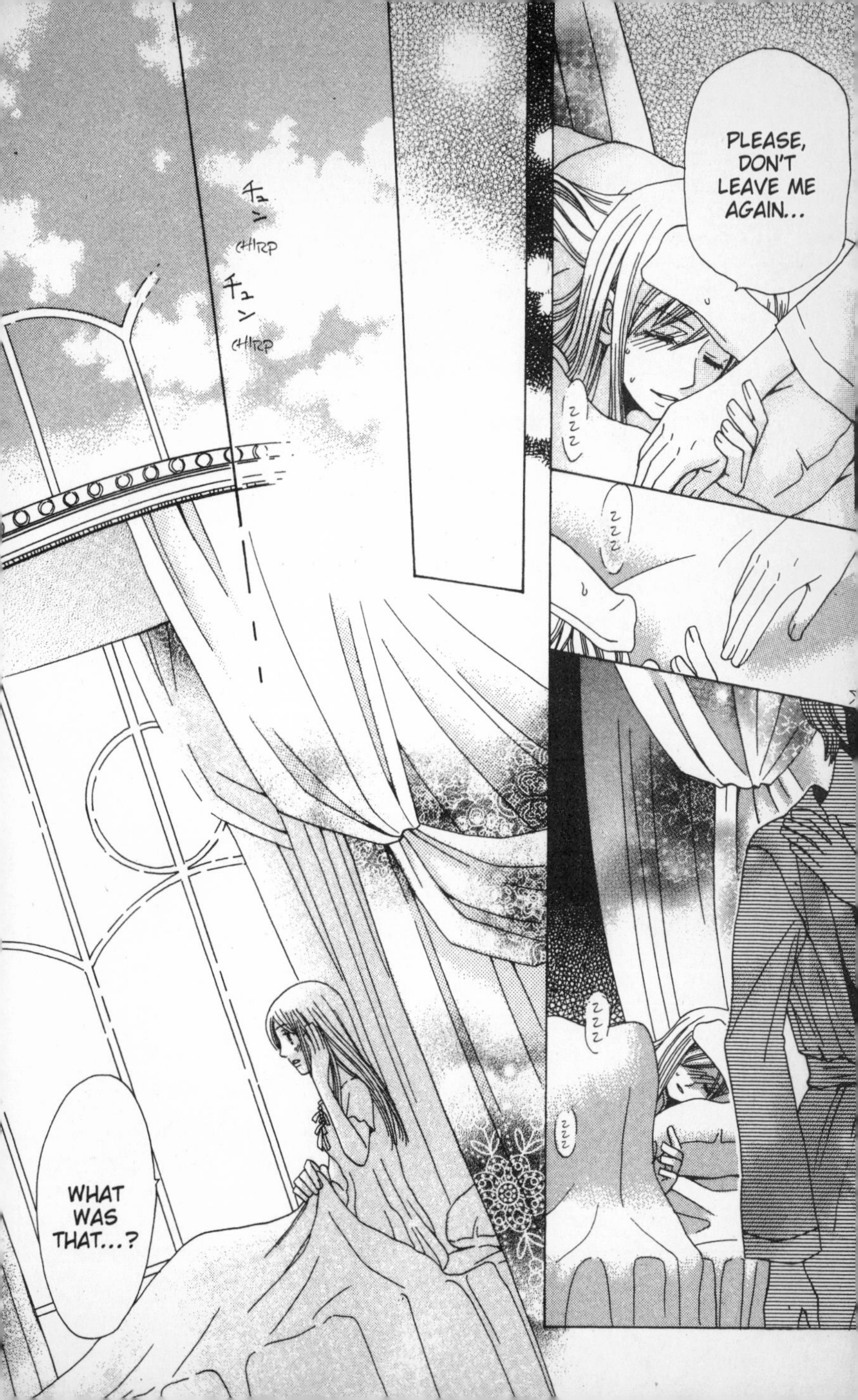
PLEASE, DON'T LEAVE ME AGAIN...
zzz
zzz
zzz
zzz
チュン
CHIRP
チュン
CHIRP
WHAT WAS THAT...?

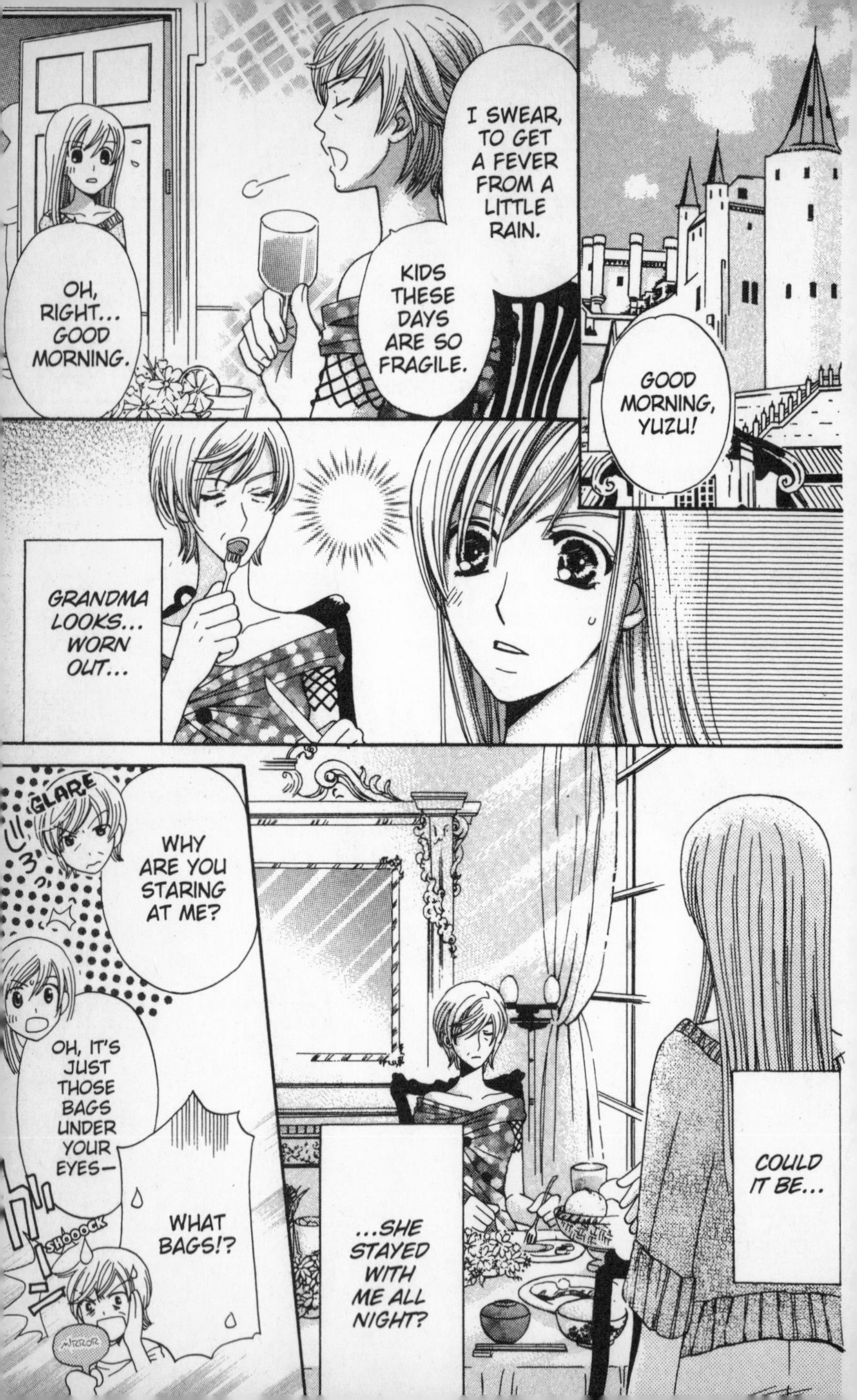
GOOD MORNING, YUZU!
I SWEAR, TO GET A FEVER FROM A LITTLE RAIN.
KIDS THESE DAYS ARE SO FRAGILE.
OH, RIGHT... GOOD MORNING.
GRANDMA LOOKS... WORN OUT...
COULD IT BE...
...SHE STAYED WITH ME ALL NIGHT?
GLARE
WHY ARE YOU STARING AT ME?
OH, IT'S JUST THOSE BAGS UNDER YOUR EYES—
WHAT BAGS!?
SHOOOCK
MIRROR

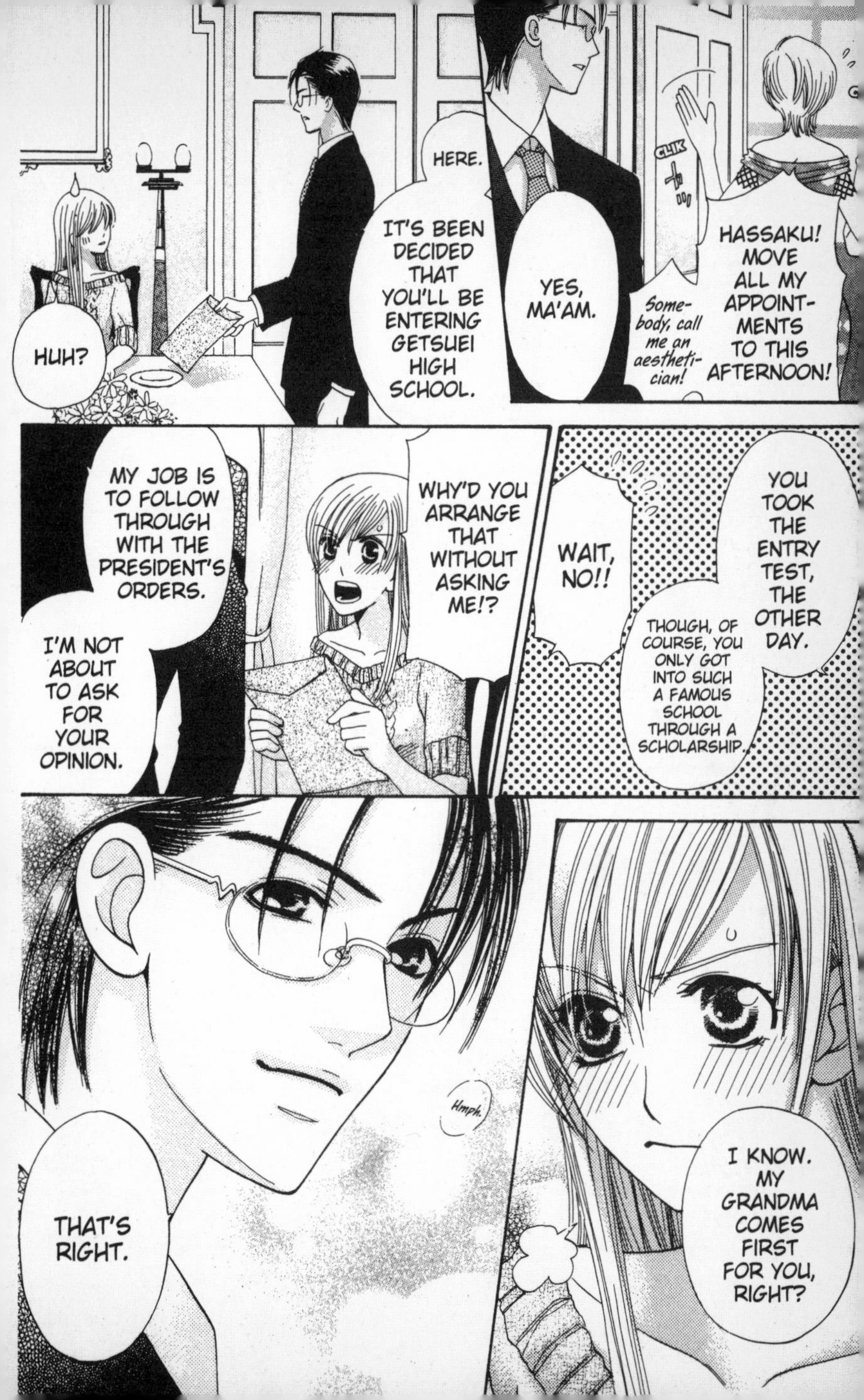
HASSAKU! MOVE ALL MY APPOINTMENTS TO THIS AFTERNOON!
Somebody, call me an aesthetician!
CLIK
YES, MA'AM.
HERE.
IT'S BEEN DECIDED THAT YOU'LL BE ENTERING GETSUEI HIGH SCHOOL.
HUH?
YOU TOOK THE ENTRY TEST, THE OTHER DAY.
THOUGH, OF COURSE, YOU ONLY GOT INTO SUCH A FAMOUS SCHOOL THROUGH A SCHOLARSHIP.
WAIT, NO!!
WHY'D YOU ARRANGE THAT WITHOUT ASKING ME!?
MY JOB IS TO FOLLOW THROUGH WITH THE PRESIDENT'S ORDERS.
I'M NOT ABOUT TO ASK FOR YOUR OPINION.
I KNOW. MY GRANDMA COMES FIRST FOR YOU, RIGHT?
Hmph.
THAT'S RIGHT.

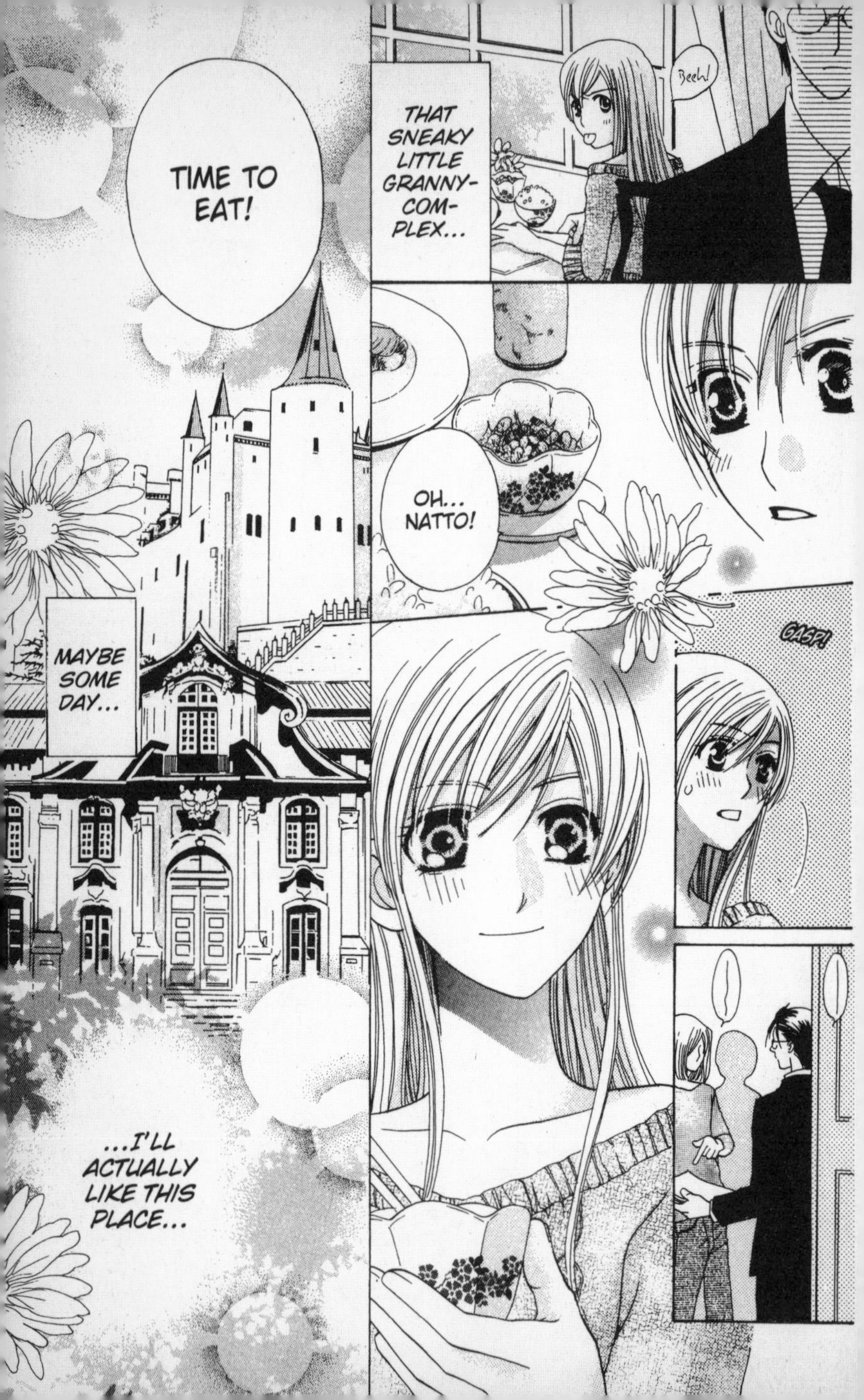
Beeh!
THAT SNEAKY LITTLE GRANNY-COMPLEX...
OH... NATTO!
GASP!
TIME TO EAT!
MAYBE SOME DAY...
...I'LL ACTUALLY LIKE THIS PLACE...

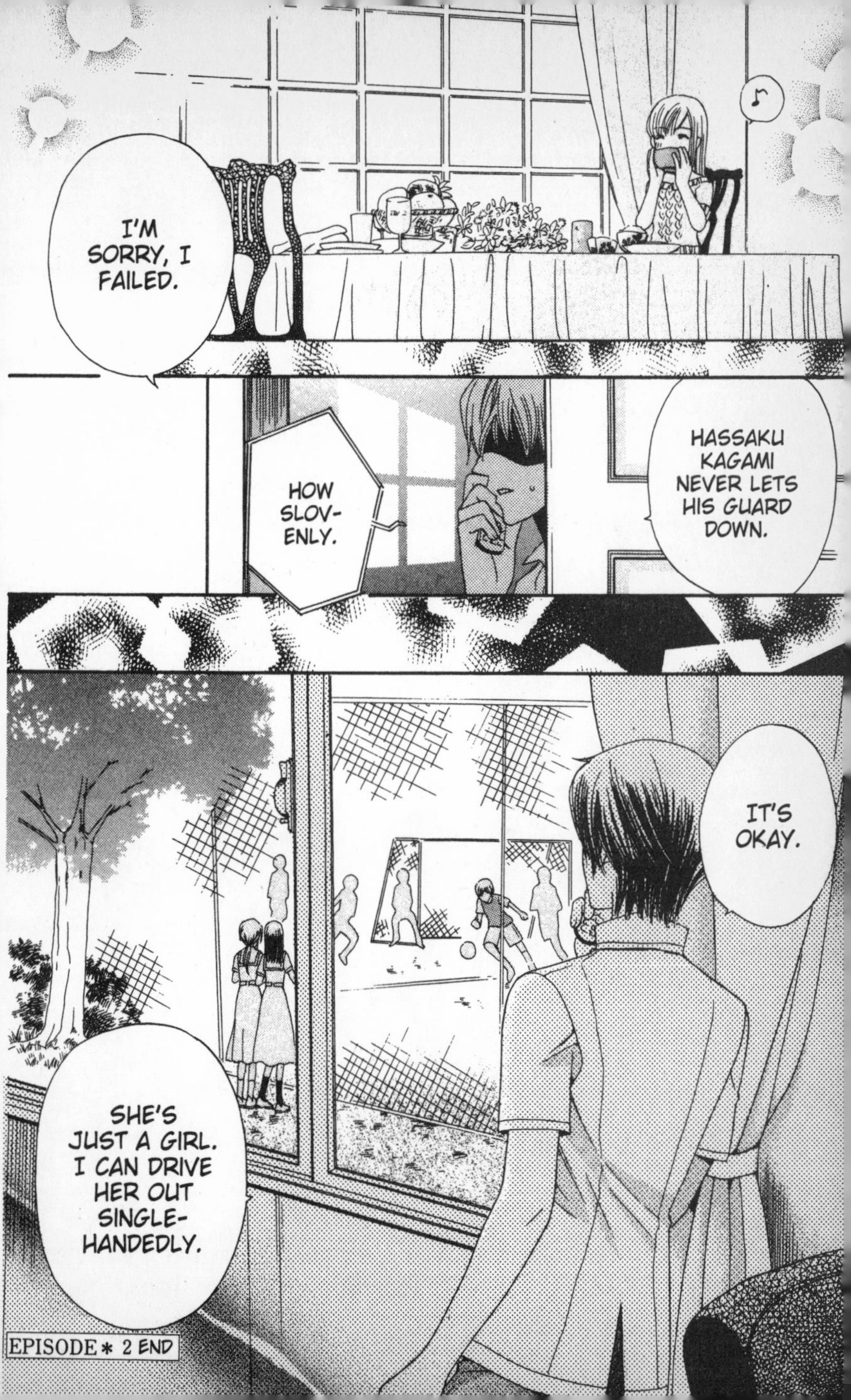
♪
I'M SORRY, I FAILED.
HASSAKU KAGAMI NEVER LETS HIS GUARD DOWN.
HOW SLOV-ENLY.
IT'S OKAY.
SHE'S JUST A GIRL. I CAN DRIVE HER OUT SINGLE-HANDEDLY.
EPISODE * 2 END

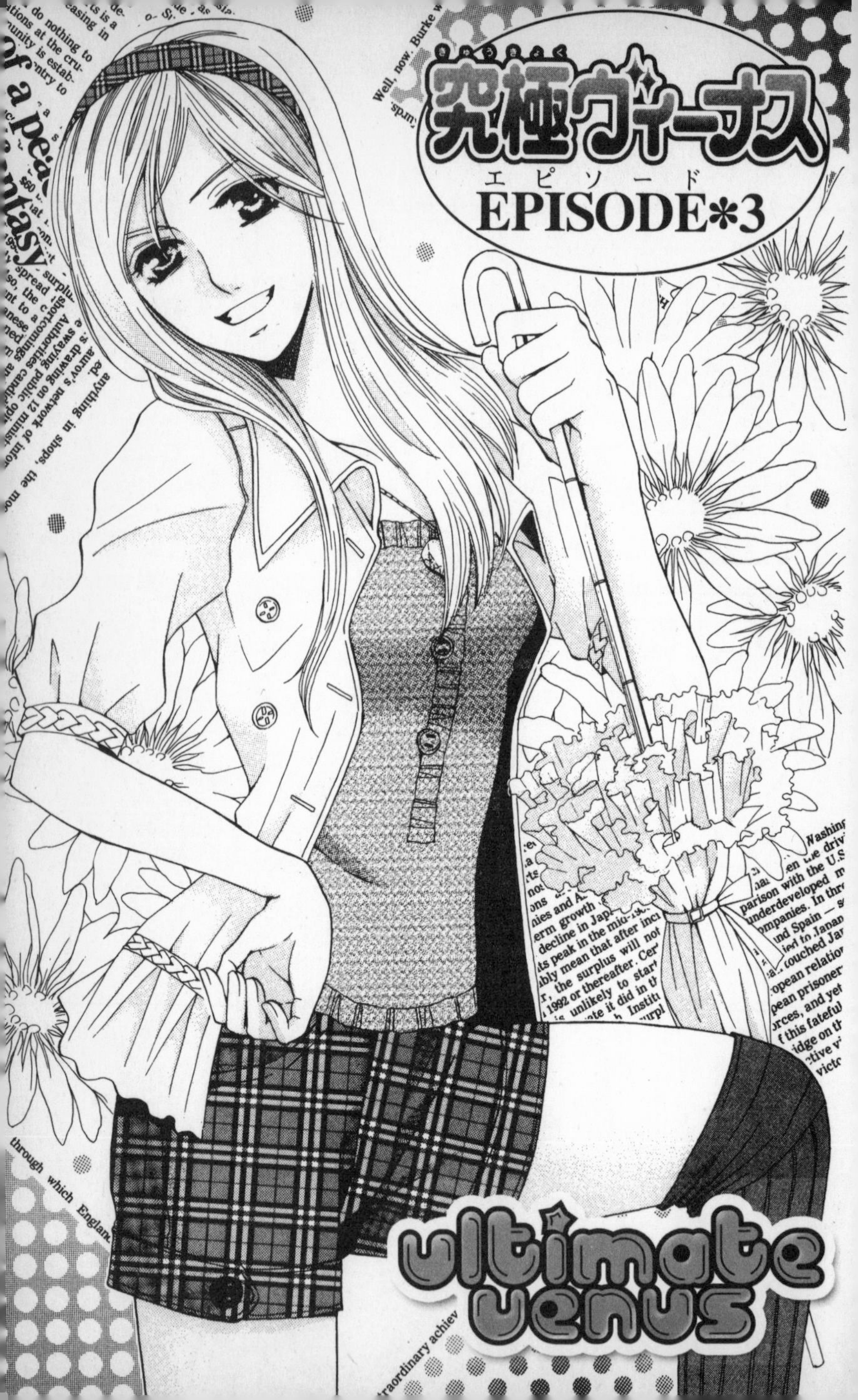
きゅうきょく
究極ヴィーナス
エピソード
EPISODE*3
ultimate venus

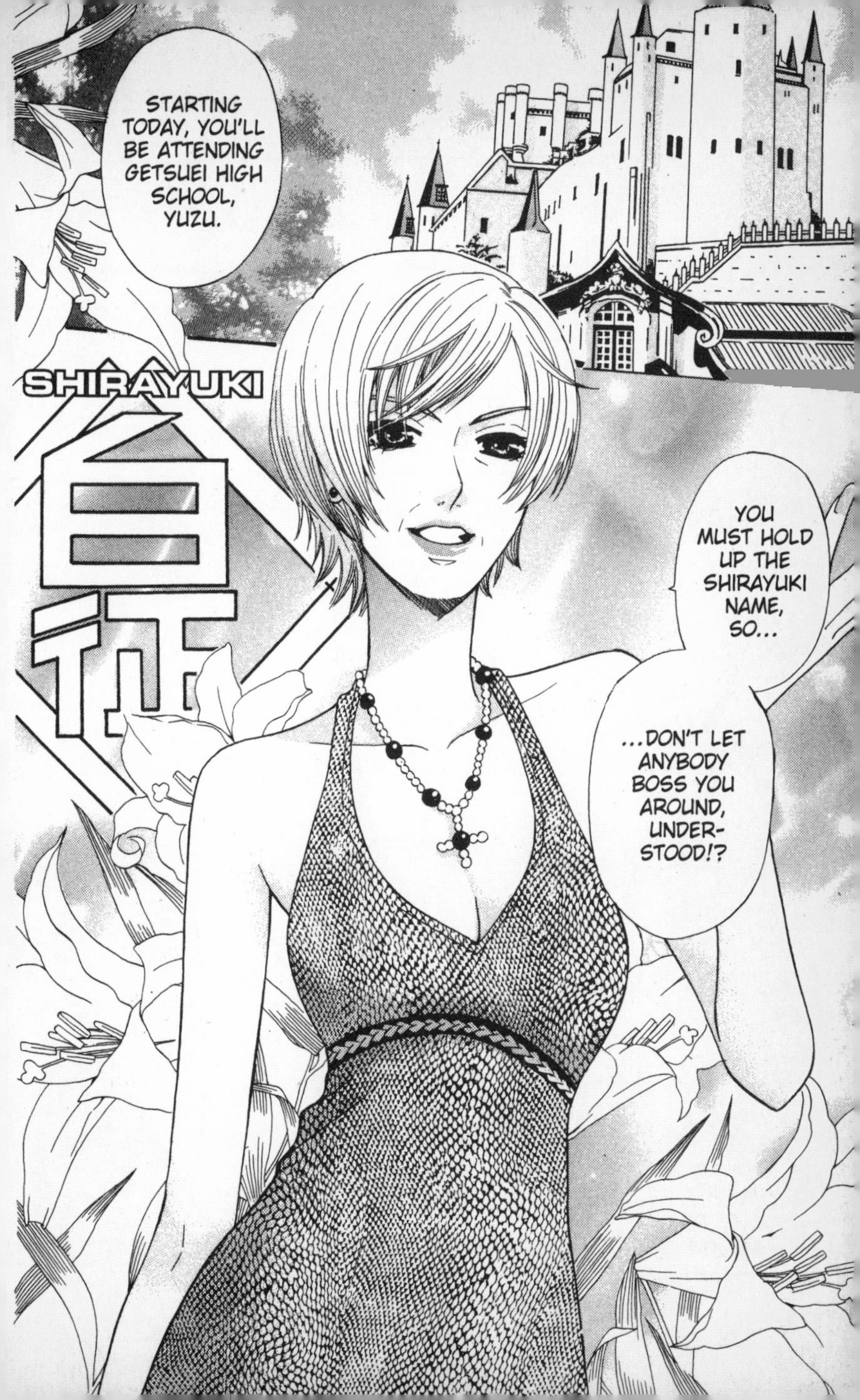
STARTING TODAY, YOU'LL BE ATTENDING GETSUEI HIGH SCHOOL, YUZU.
SHIRAYUKI
YOU MUST HOLD UP THE SHIRAYUKI NAME, SO...
...DON'T LET ANYBODY BOSS YOU AROUND, UNDER-STOOD!?

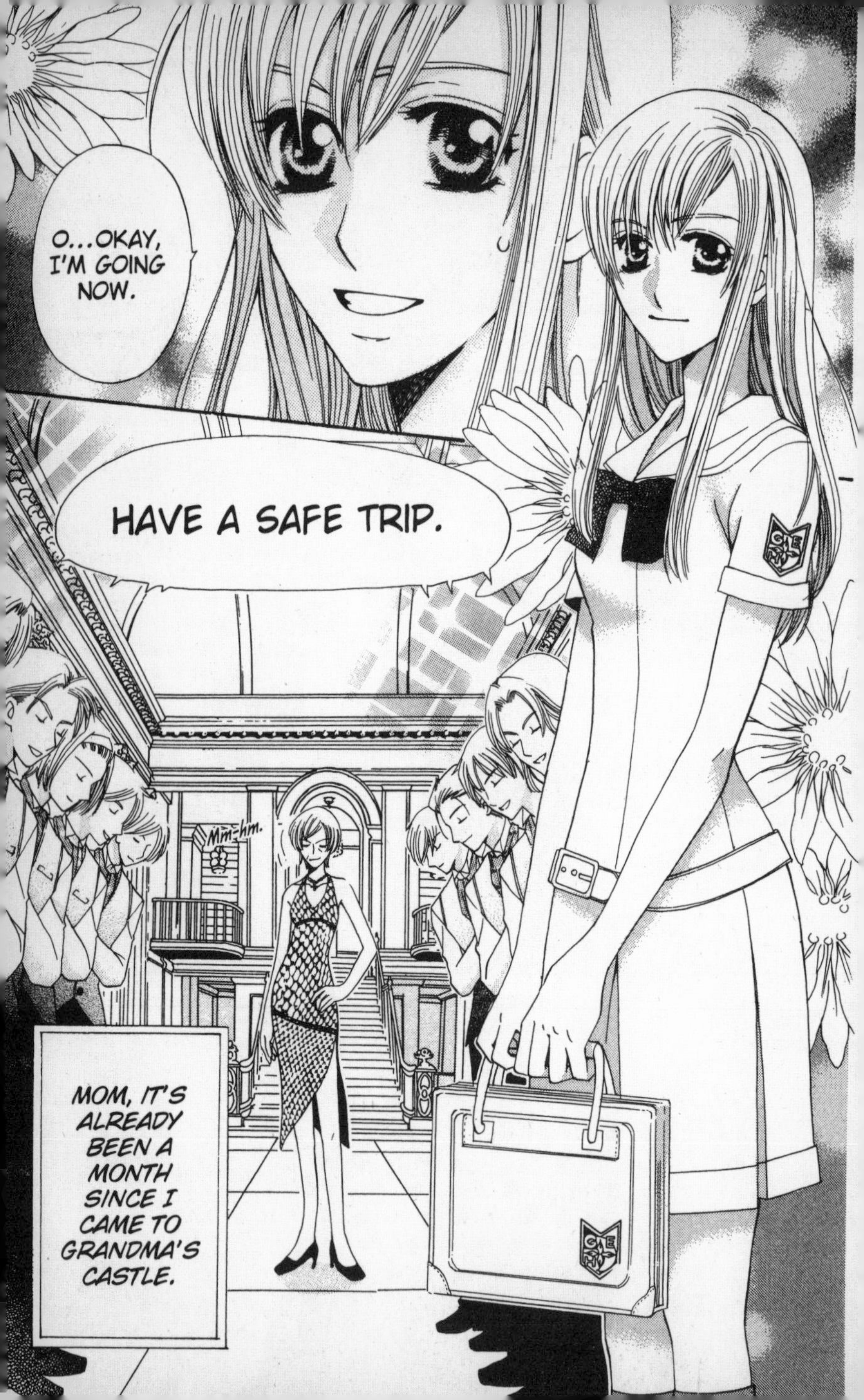
O...OKAY, I'M GOING NOW.
HAVE A SAFE TRIP.
Mm-hm.
MOM, IT'S ALREADY BEEN A MONTH SINCE I CAME TO GRANDMA'S CASTLE.

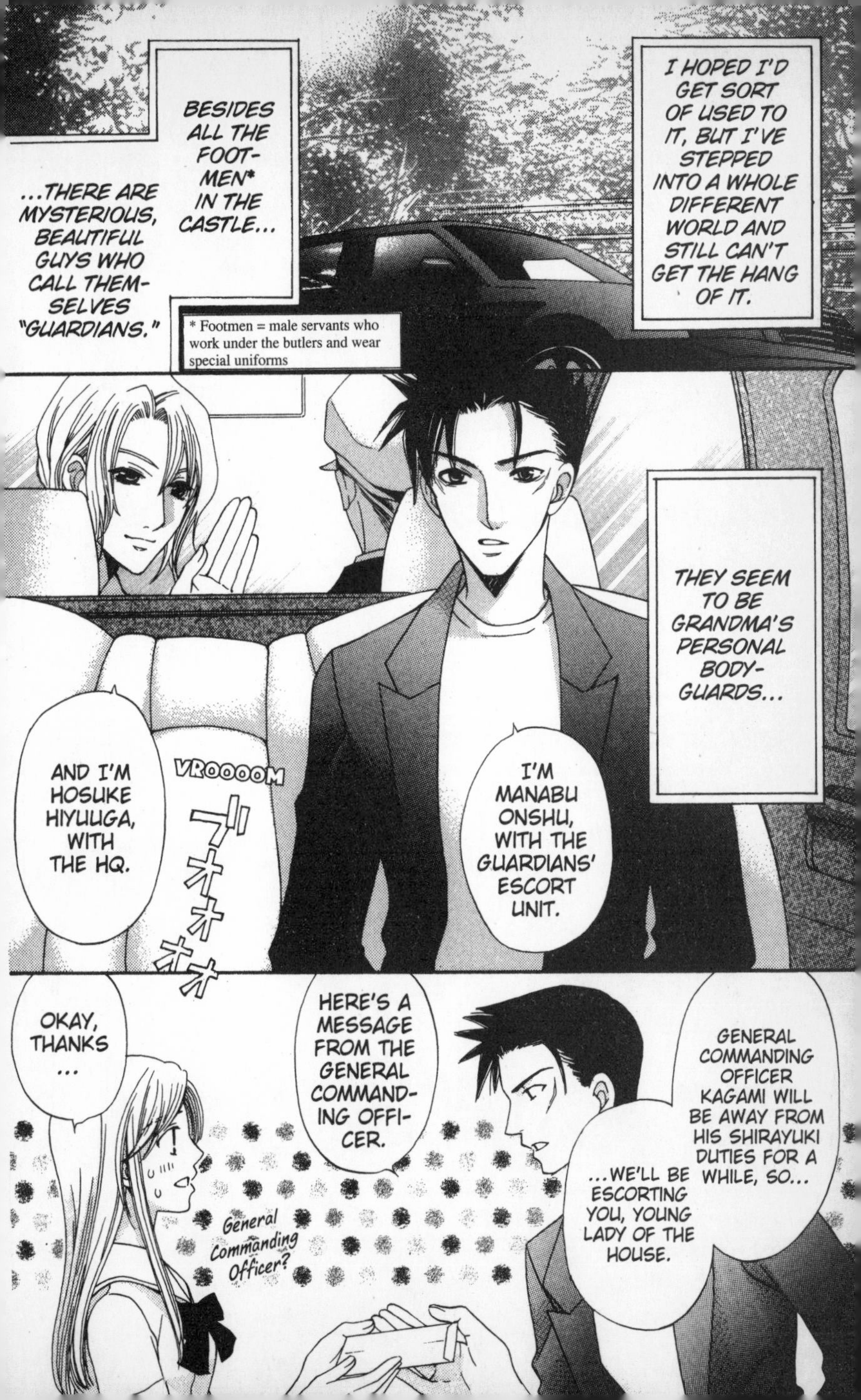
I HOPED I'D GET SORT OF USED TO IT, BUT I'VE STEPPED INTO A WHOLE DIFFERENT WORLD AND STILL CAN'T GET THE HANG OF IT.
BESIDES ALL THE FOOTMEN* IN THE CASTLE...
...THERE ARE MYSTERIOUS, BEAUTIFUL GUYS WHO CALL THEMSELVES "GUARDIANS."
THEY SEEM TO BE GRANDMA'S PERSONAL BODYGUARDS...
I'M MANABU ONSHU, WITH THE GUARDIANS' ESCORT UNIT.
VROOOOM
ブォオオオ
AND I'M HOSUKE HIYUUGA, WITH THE HQ.
GENERAL COMMANDING OFFICER KAGAMI WILL BE AWAY FROM HIS SHIRAYUKI DUTIES FOR A WHILE, SO...
...WE'LL BE ESCORTING YOU, YOUNG LADY OF THE HOUSE.
HERE'S A MESSAGE FROM THE GENERAL COMMANDING OFFICER.
OKAY, THANKS...
General Commanding Officer?

* Footmen = male servants who work under the butlers and wear special uniforms

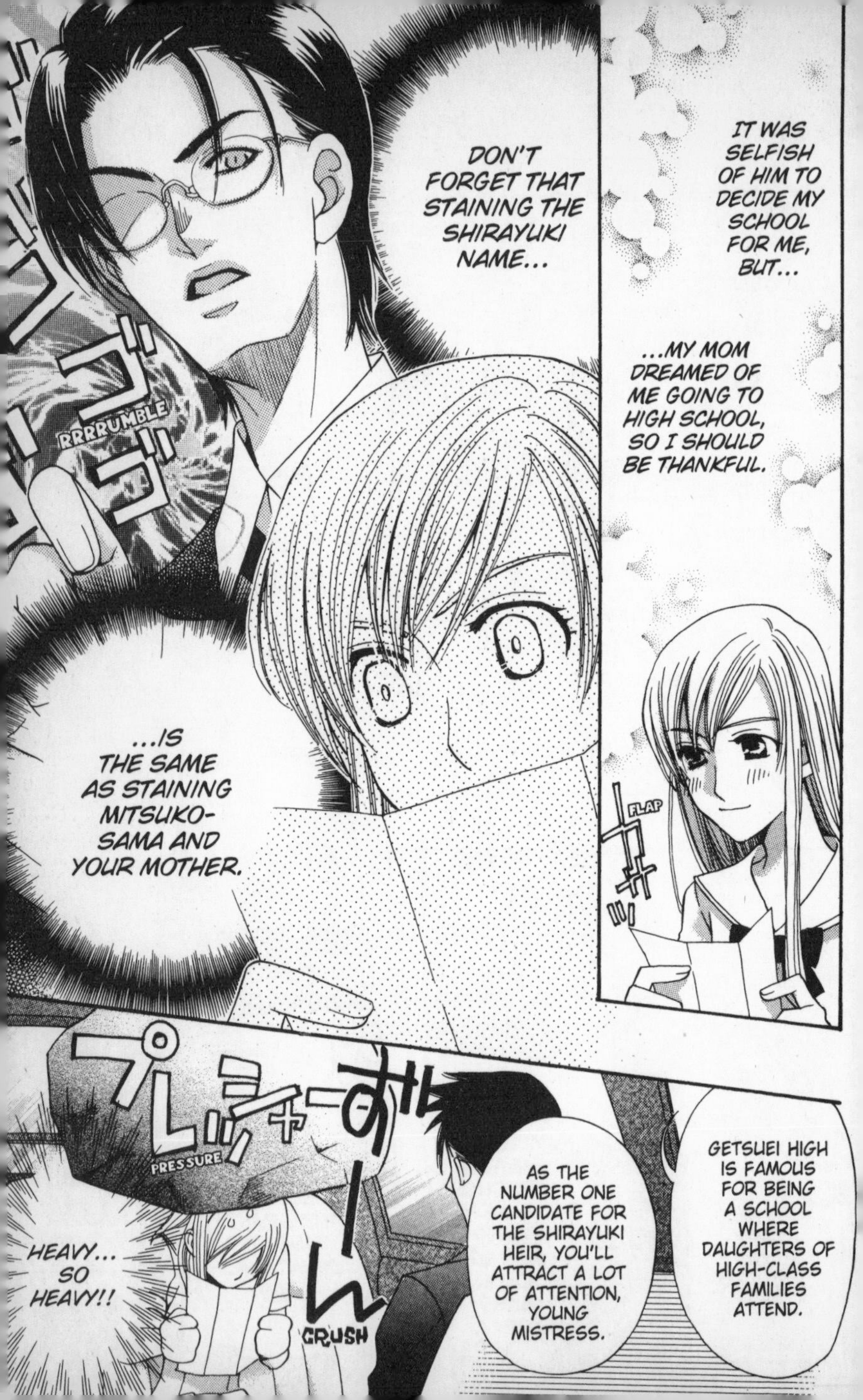
IT WAS SELFISH OF HIM TO DECIDE MY SCHOOL FOR ME, BUT...
...MY MOM DREAMED OF ME GOING TO HIGH SCHOOL, SO I SHOULD BE THANKFUL.
FLAP
DON'T FORGET THAT STAINING THE SHIRAYUKI NAME...
RRRRUMBLE
...IS THE SAME AS STAINING MITSUKO-SAMA AND YOUR MOTHER.
GETSUEI HIGH IS FAMOUS FOR BEING A SCHOOL WHERE DAUGHTERS OF HIGH-CLASS FAMILIES ATTEND.
AS THE NUMBER ONE CANDIDATE FOR THE SHIRAYUKI HEIR, YOU'LL ATTRACT A LOT OF ATTENTION, YOUNG MISTRESS.
PRESSURE
CRUSH
HEAVY... SO HEAVY!!

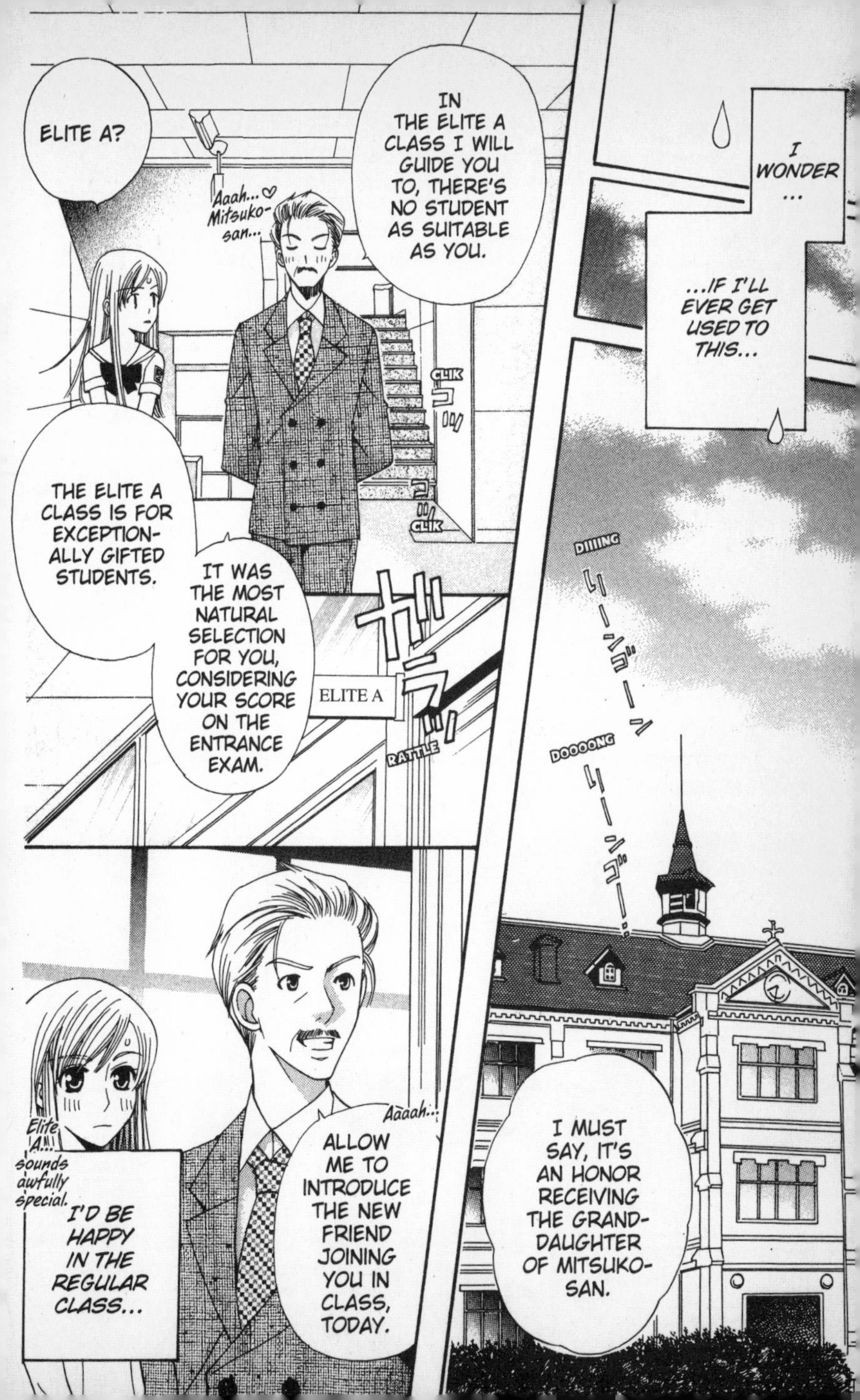
I WONDER ...
...IF I'LL EVER GET USED TO THIS...
DIIIING
DOOOONG
I MUST SAY, IT'S AN HONOR RECEIVING THE GRAND-DAUGHTER OF MITSUKO-SAN.
IN THE ELITE A CLASS I WILL GUIDE YOU TO, THERE'S NO STUDENT AS SUITABLE AS YOU.
Aaah...♡ Mitsuko-san...
ELITE A?
CLIK
CLIK
THE ELITE A CLASS IS FOR EXCEPTION-ALLY GIFTED STUDENTS.
IT WAS THE MOST NATURAL SELECTION FOR YOU, CONSIDERING YOUR SCORE ON THE ENTRANCE EXAM.
RATTLE
ELITE A
Aaaah...
ALLOW ME TO INTRODUCE THE NEW FRIEND JOINING YOU IN CLASS, TODAY.
Elite A... sounds awfully special.
I'D BE HAPPY IN THE REGULAR CLASS...

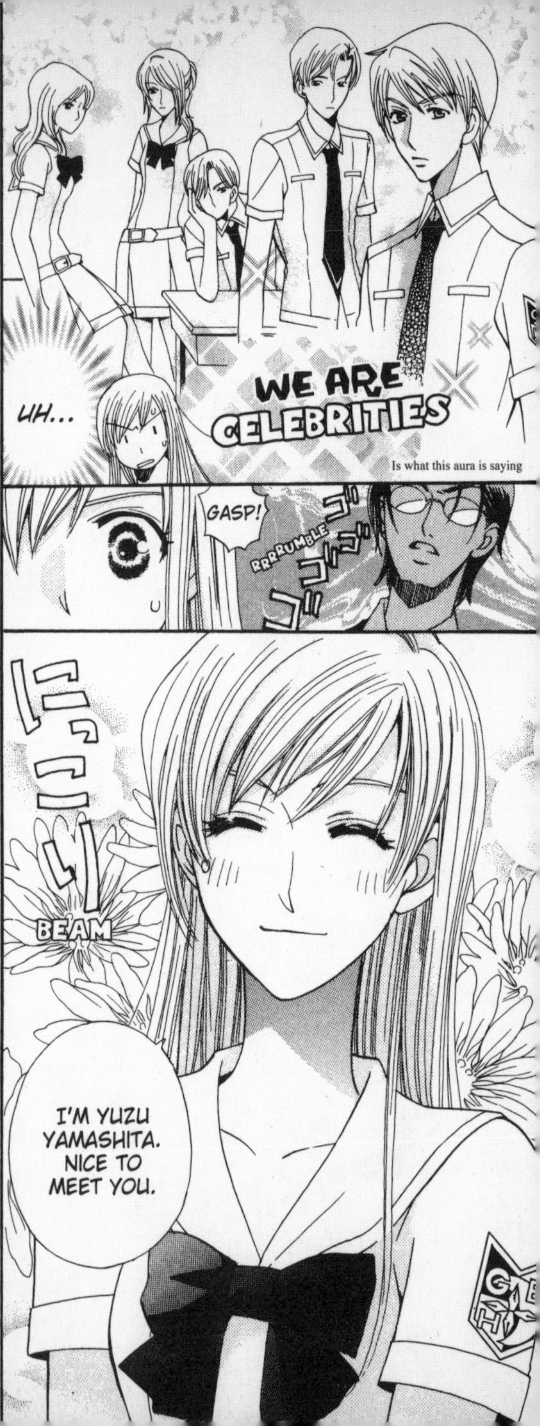
WE ARE CELEBRITIES
Is what this aura is saying
UH...
RRRRUMBLE
GASP!
BEAM
I'M YUZU YAMASHITA. NICE TO MEET YOU.

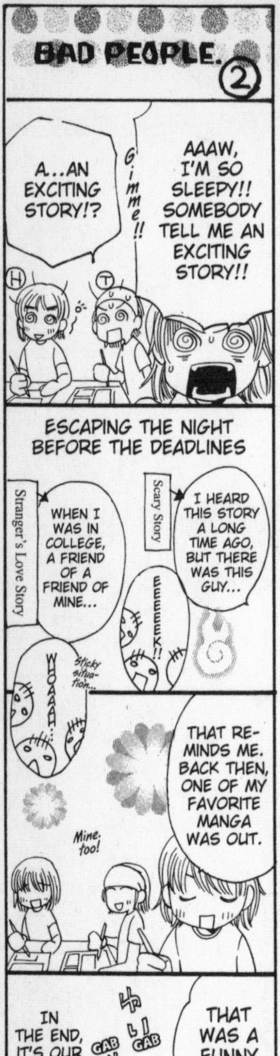
BAD PEOPLE. 2
AAAW, I'M SO SLEEPY!! SOMEBODY TELL ME AN EXCITING STORY!!
Gimme!!
A...AN EXCITING STORY!?
H
T
ESCAPING THE NIGHT BEFORE THE DEADLINES
Scary Story
I HEARD THIS STORY A LONG TIME AGO, BUT THERE WAS THIS GUY...
Stranger's Love Story
WHEN I WAS IN COLLEGE, A FRIEND OF A FRIEND OF MINE...
EEEEEK!!
Sticky situation...
WHOAAAH...
THAT RE-MINDS ME. BACK THEN, ONE OF MY FAVORITE MANGA WAS OUT.
Mine. too!
THAT WAS A FUNNY ONE, WASN'T IT?
I LOVED THAT CERTAIN CHARACTER!
GAB GAB GAB GAB GAB
IN THE END, IT'S OUR OTAKU STORIES THAT ARE THE MOST EXCITING ...
AT LEAST WE'RE NOT TIRED, ANYMORE.

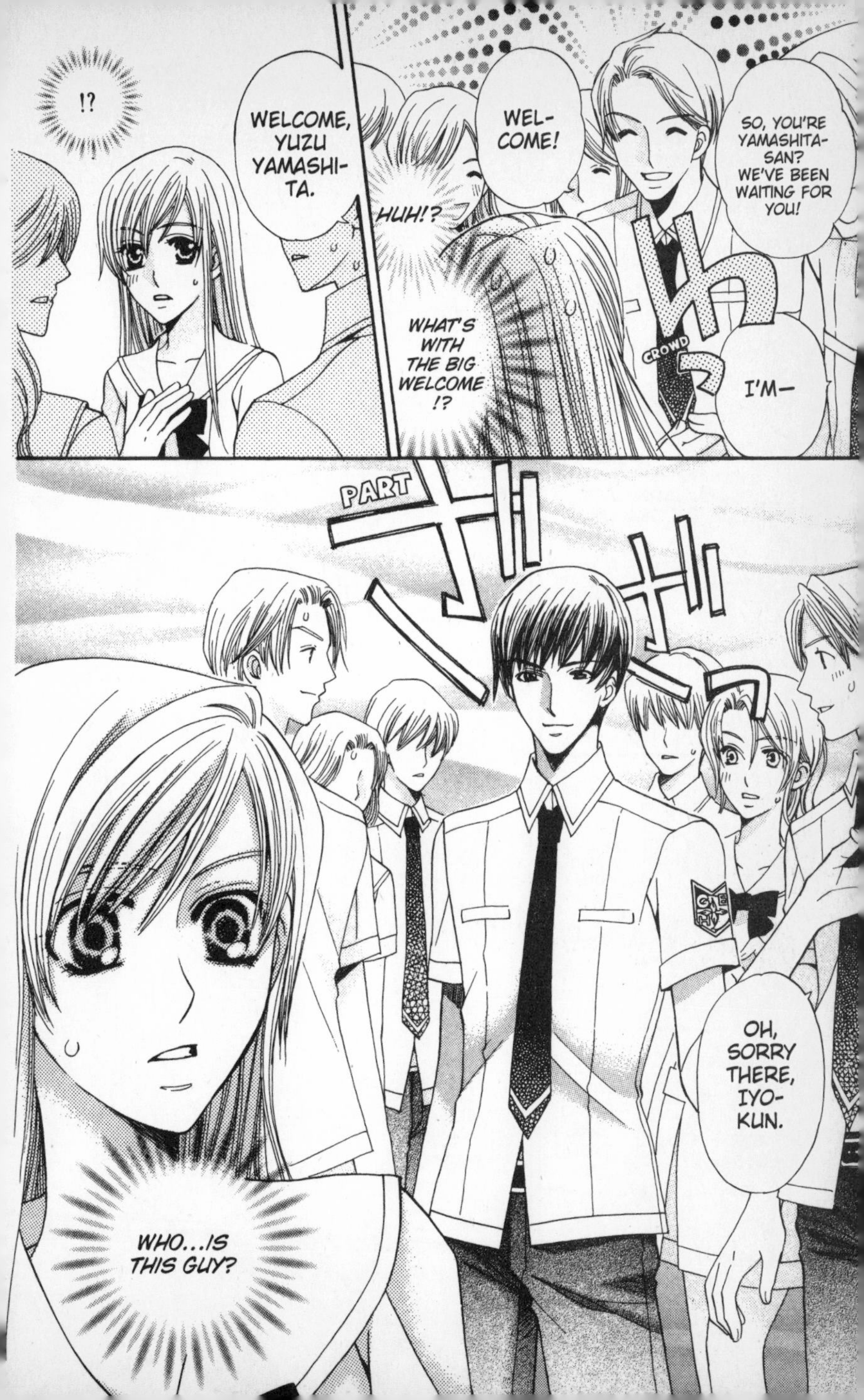
SO, YOU'RE YAMASHITA-SAN? WE'VE BEEN WAITING FOR YOU!
WEL-COME!
HUH!?
CROWD
I'M—
WHAT'S WITH THE BIG WELCOME !?
WELCOME, YUZU YAMASHITA.
!?
PART
OH, SORRY THERE, IYO-KUN.
WHO...IS THIS GUY?

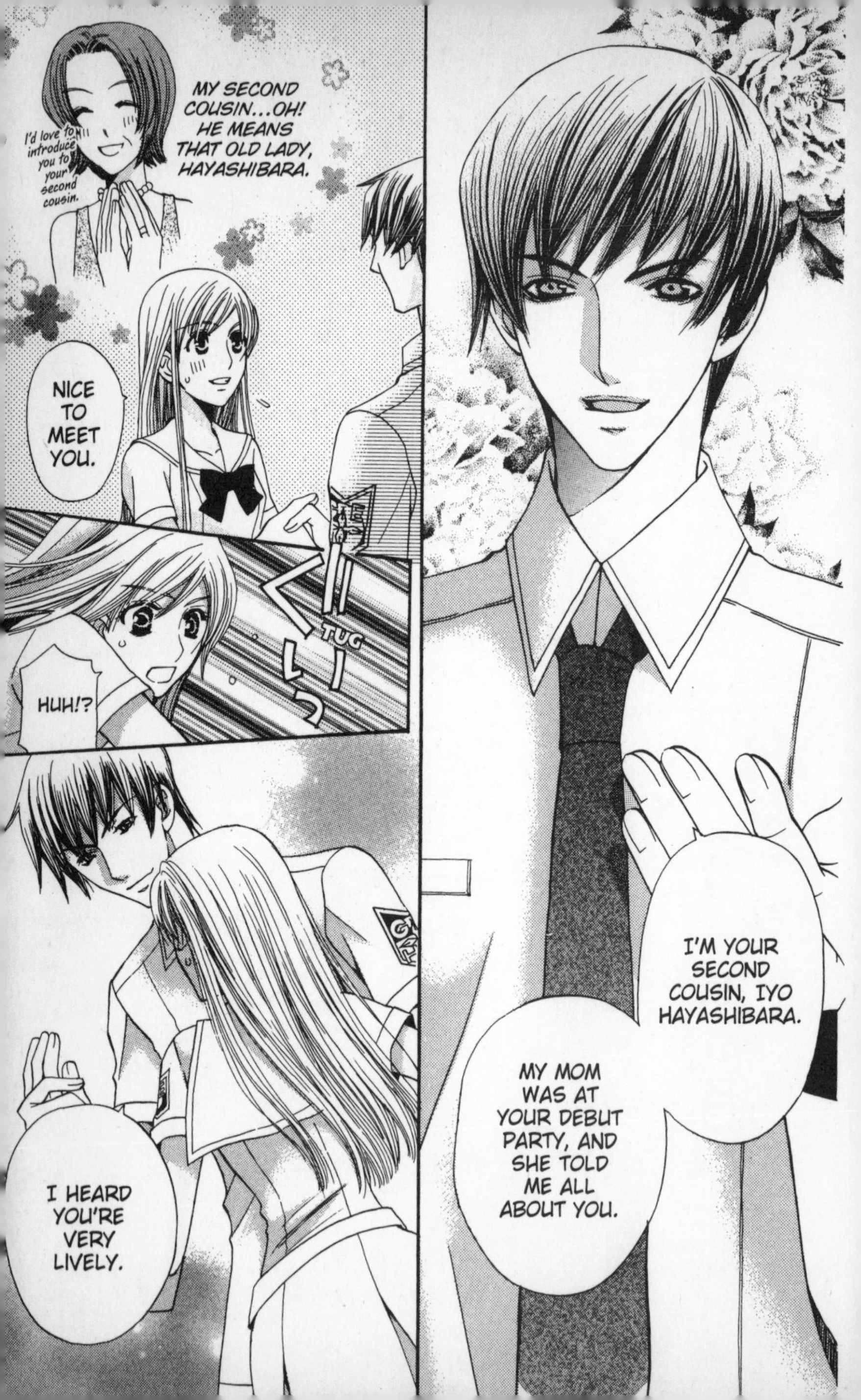
I'M YOUR SECOND COUSIN, IYO HAYASHIBARA.
MY MOM WAS AT YOUR DEBUT PARTY, AND SHE TOLD ME ALL ABOUT YOU.
MY SECOND COUSIN...OH! HE MEANS THAT OLD LADY, HAYASHIBARA.
I'd love to introduce you to your second cousin.
NICE TO MEET YOU.
TUG
HUH!?
I HEARD YOU'RE VERY LIVELY.

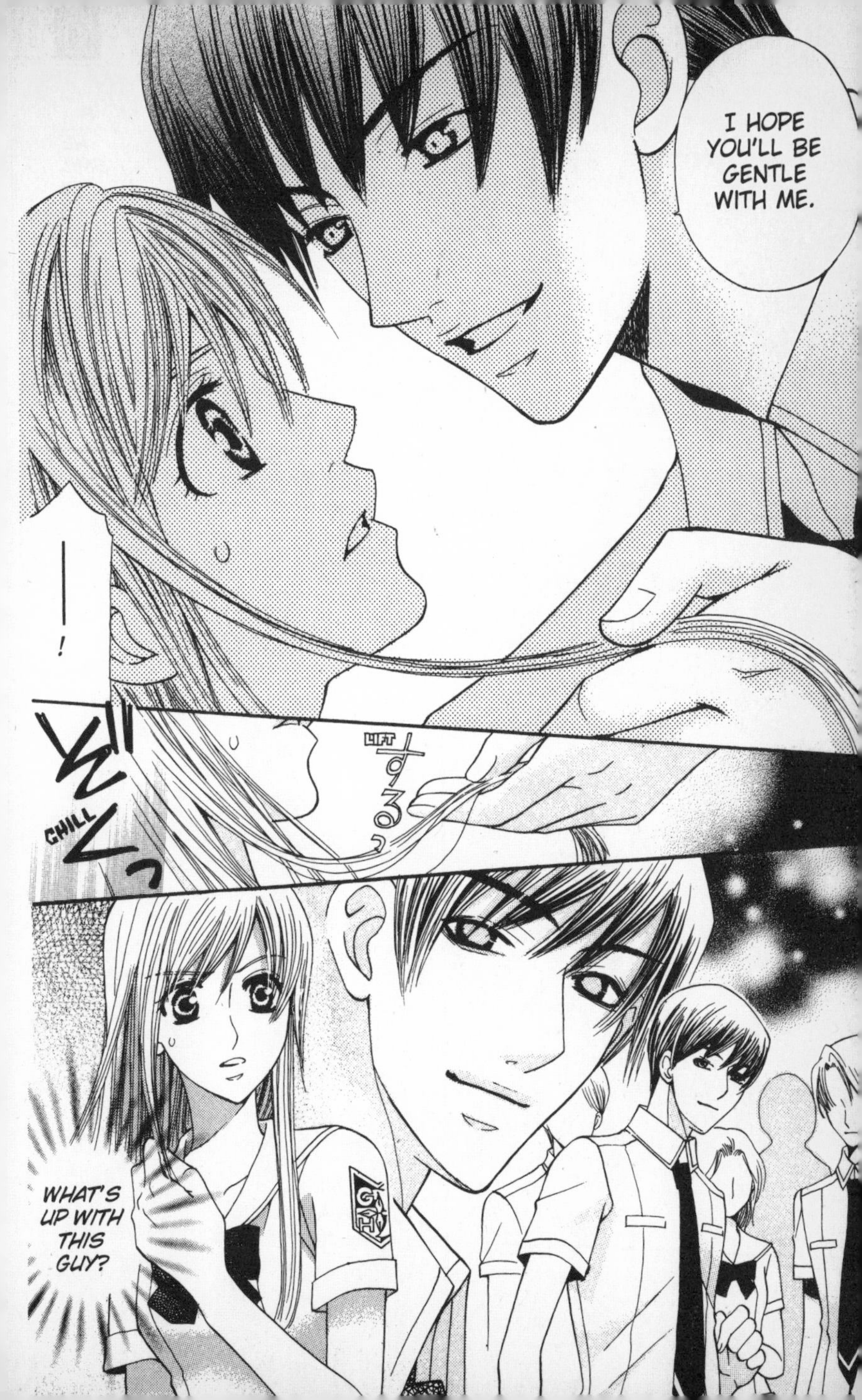
I HOPE YOU'LL BE GENTLE WITH ME.
——!
LIFT
するっ
CHILL
ぞくっ
WHAT'S UP WITH THIS GUY?

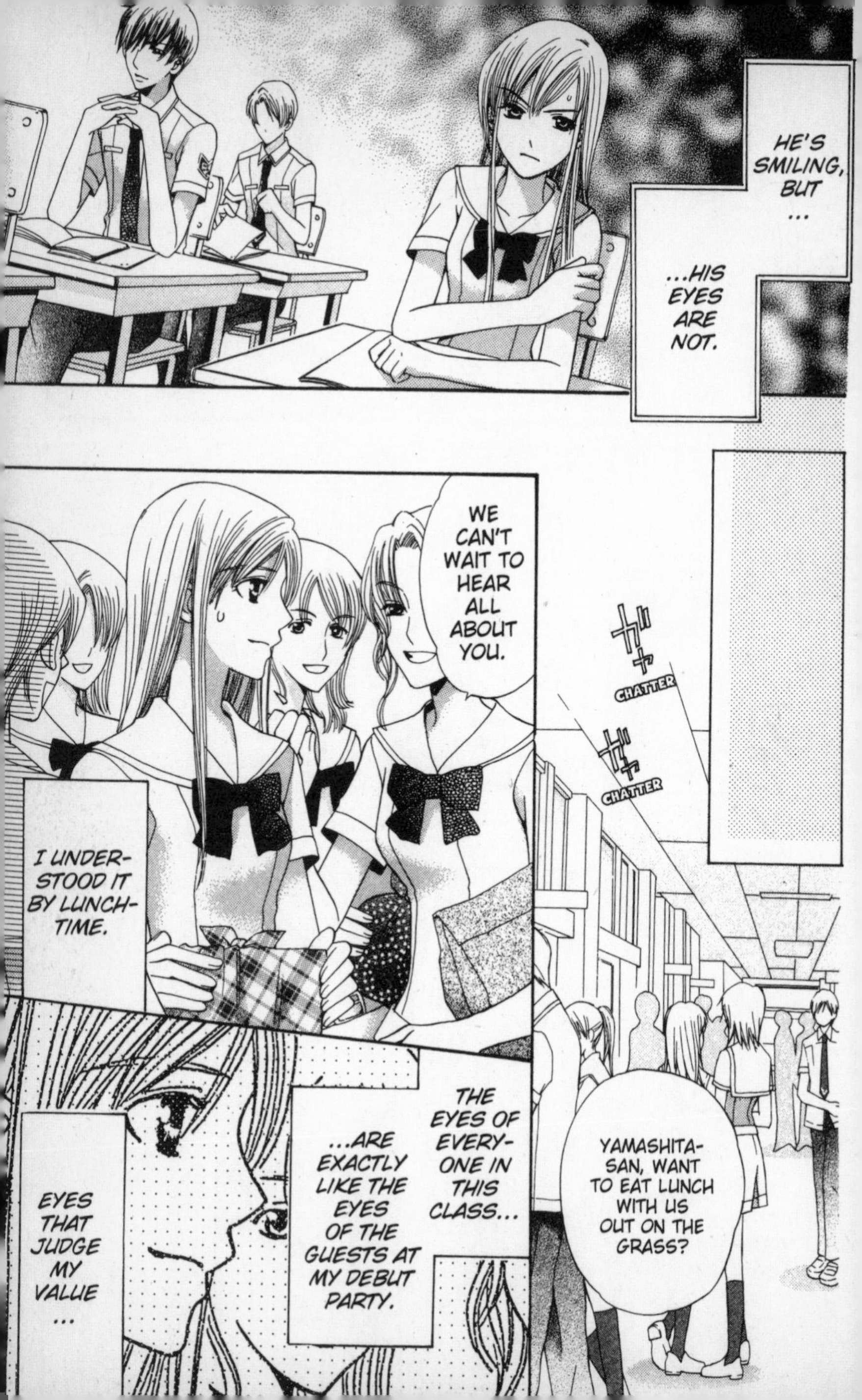

HE'S SMILING, BUT ...
...HIS EYES ARE NOT.
CHATTER
CHATTER
YAMASHITA-SAN, WANT TO EAT LUNCH WITH US OUT ON THE GRASS?
WE CAN'T WAIT TO HEAR ALL ABOUT YOU.
I UNDERSTOOD IT BY LUNCHTIME.
THE EYES OF EVERYONE IN THIS CLASS...
...ARE EXACTLY LIKE THE EYES OF THE GUESTS AT MY DEBUT PARTY.
EYES THAT JUDGE MY VALUE ...

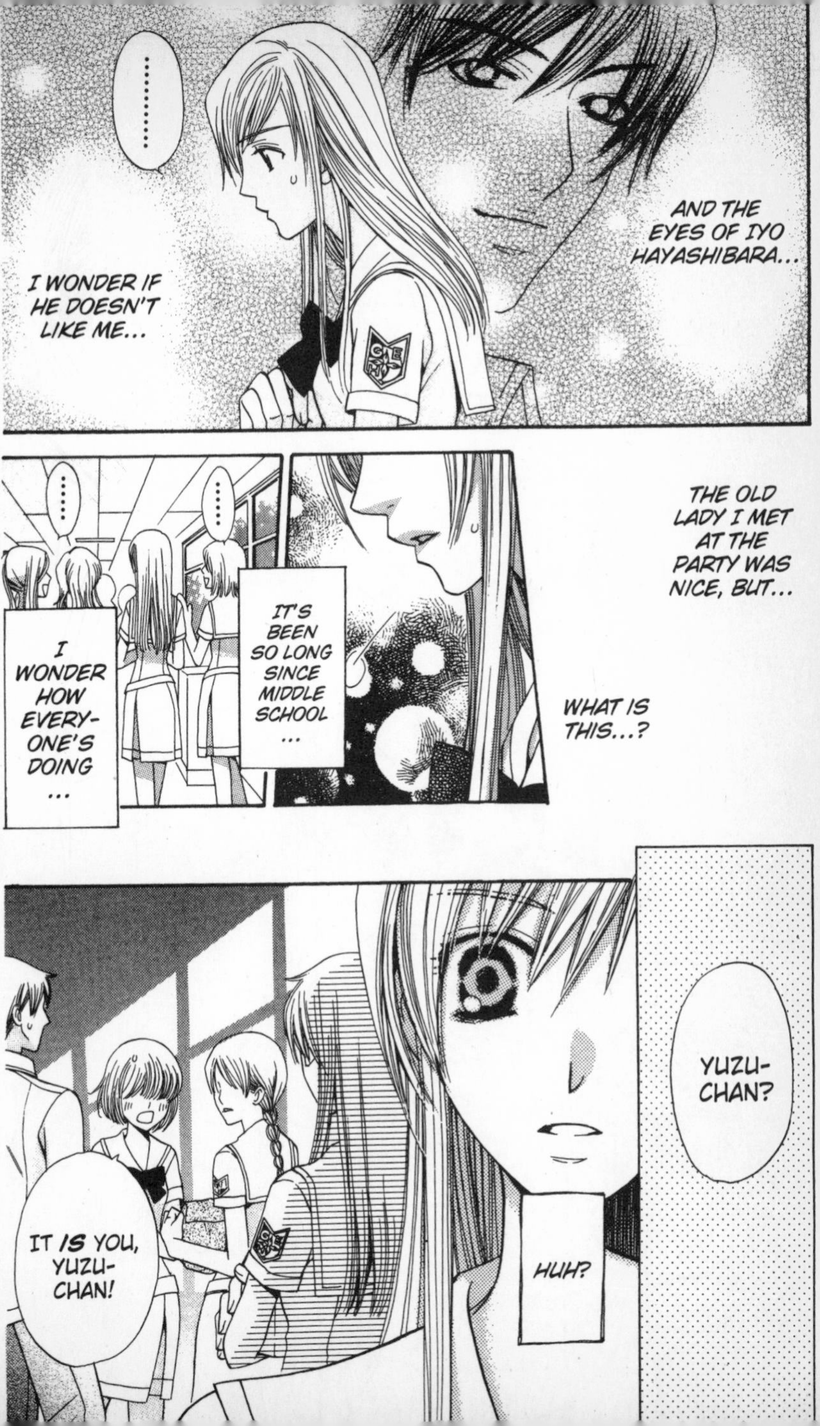
AND THE EYES OF IYO HAYASHIBARA...
......
I WONDER IF HE DOESN'T LIKE ME...
THE OLD LADY I MET AT THE PARTY WAS NICE, BUT...
WHAT IS THIS...?
IT'S BEEN SO LONG SINCE MIDDLE SCHOOL...
......
......
I WONDER HOW EVERY-ONE'S DOING...
YUZU-CHAN?
HUH?
IT *IS* YOU, YUZU-CHAN!

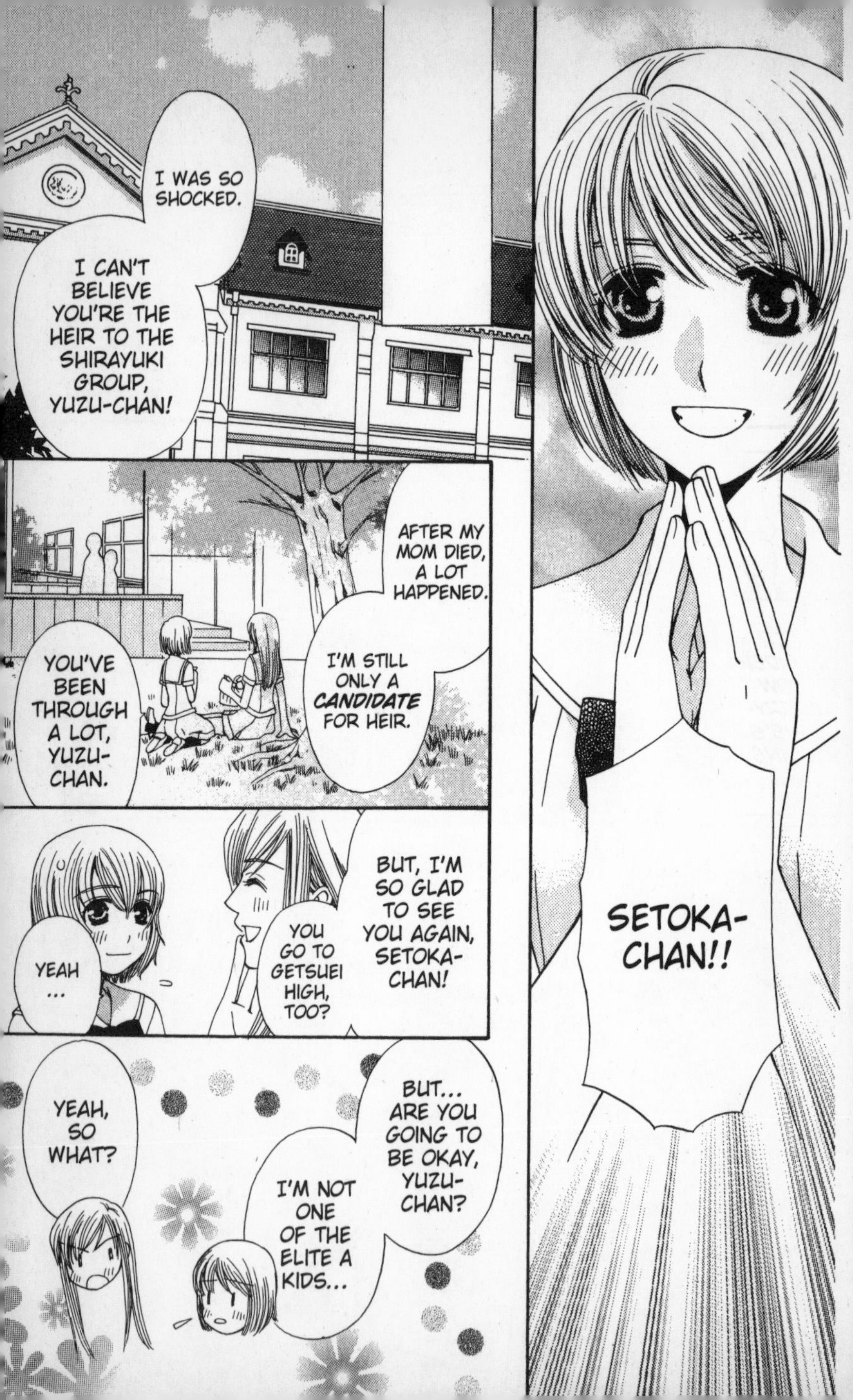
SETOKA-CHAN!!
I WAS SO SHOCKED.
I CAN'T BELIEVE YOU'RE THE HEIR TO THE SHIRAYUKI GROUP, YUZU-CHAN!
AFTER MY MOM DIED, A LOT HAPPENED.
I'M STILL ONLY A *CANDIDATE* FOR HEIR.
YOU'VE BEEN THROUGH A LOT, YUZU-CHAN.
BUT, I'M SO GLAD TO SEE YOU AGAIN, SETOKA-CHAN!
YOU GO TO GETSUEI HIGH, TOO?
YEAH...
BUT... ARE YOU GOING TO BE OKAY, YUZU-CHAN?
I'M NOT ONE OF THE ELITE A KIDS...
YEAH, SO WHAT?

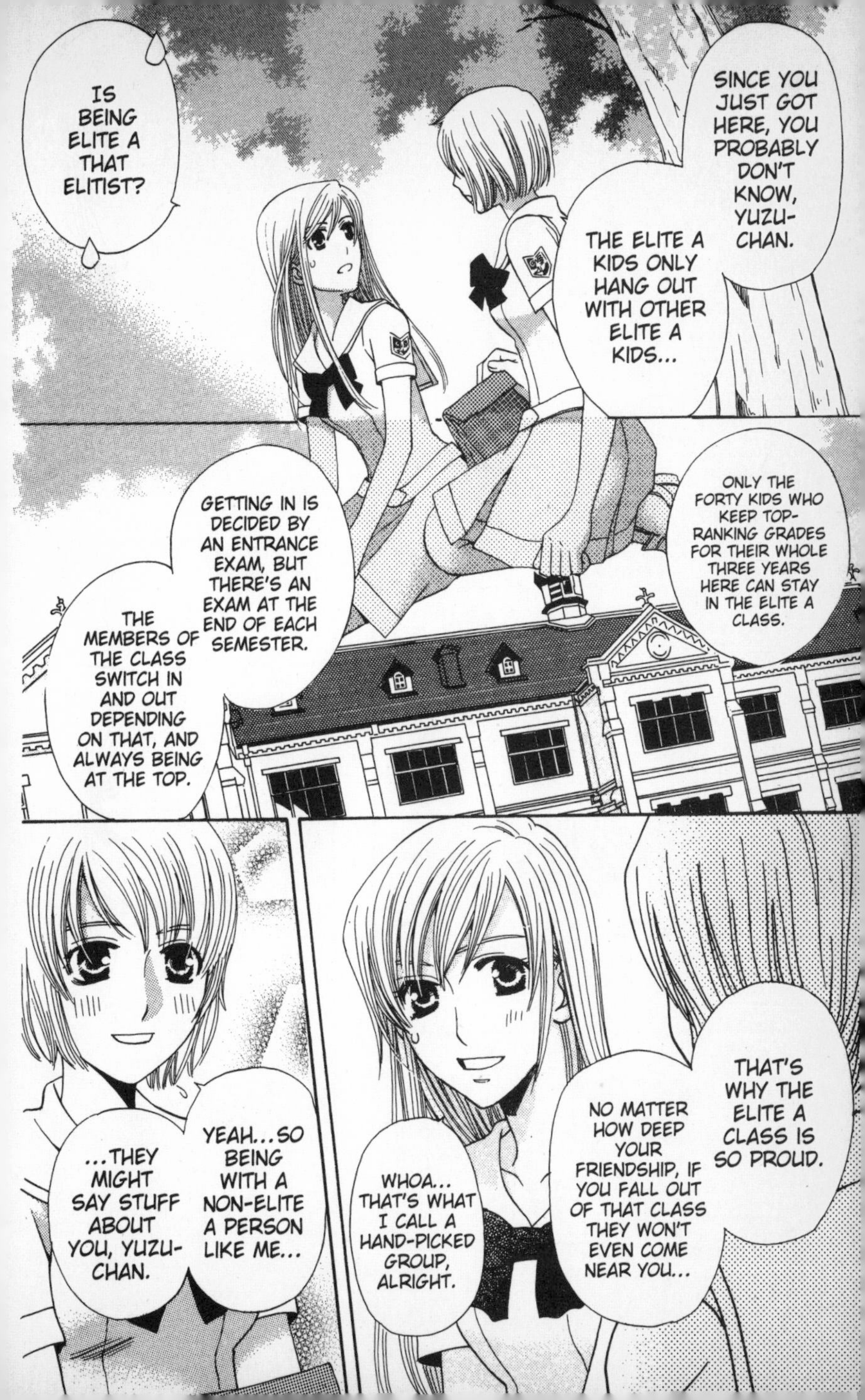
SINCE YOU JUST GOT HERE, YOU PROBABLY DON'T KNOW, YUZU-CHAN.
THE ELITE A KIDS ONLY HANG OUT WITH OTHER ELITE A KIDS...
IS BEING ELITE A THAT ELITIST?
ONLY THE FORTY KIDS WHO KEEP TOP-RANKING GRADES FOR THEIR WHOLE THREE YEARS HERE CAN STAY IN THE ELITE A CLASS.
GETTING IN IS DECIDED BY AN ENTRANCE EXAM, BUT THERE'S AN EXAM AT THE END OF EACH SEMESTER.
THE MEMBERS OF THE CLASS SWITCH IN AND OUT DEPENDING ON THAT, AND ALWAYS BEING AT THE TOP.
THAT'S WHY THE ELITE A CLASS IS SO PROUD.
NO MATTER HOW DEEP YOUR FRIENDSHIP, IF YOU FALL OUT OF THAT CLASS THEY WON'T EVEN COME NEAR YOU...
WHOA... THAT'S WHAT I CALL A HAND-PICKED GROUP, ALRIGHT.
YEAH...SO BEING WITH A NON-ELITE A PERSON LIKE ME...
...THEY MIGHT SAY STUFF ABOUT YOU, YUZU-CHAN.

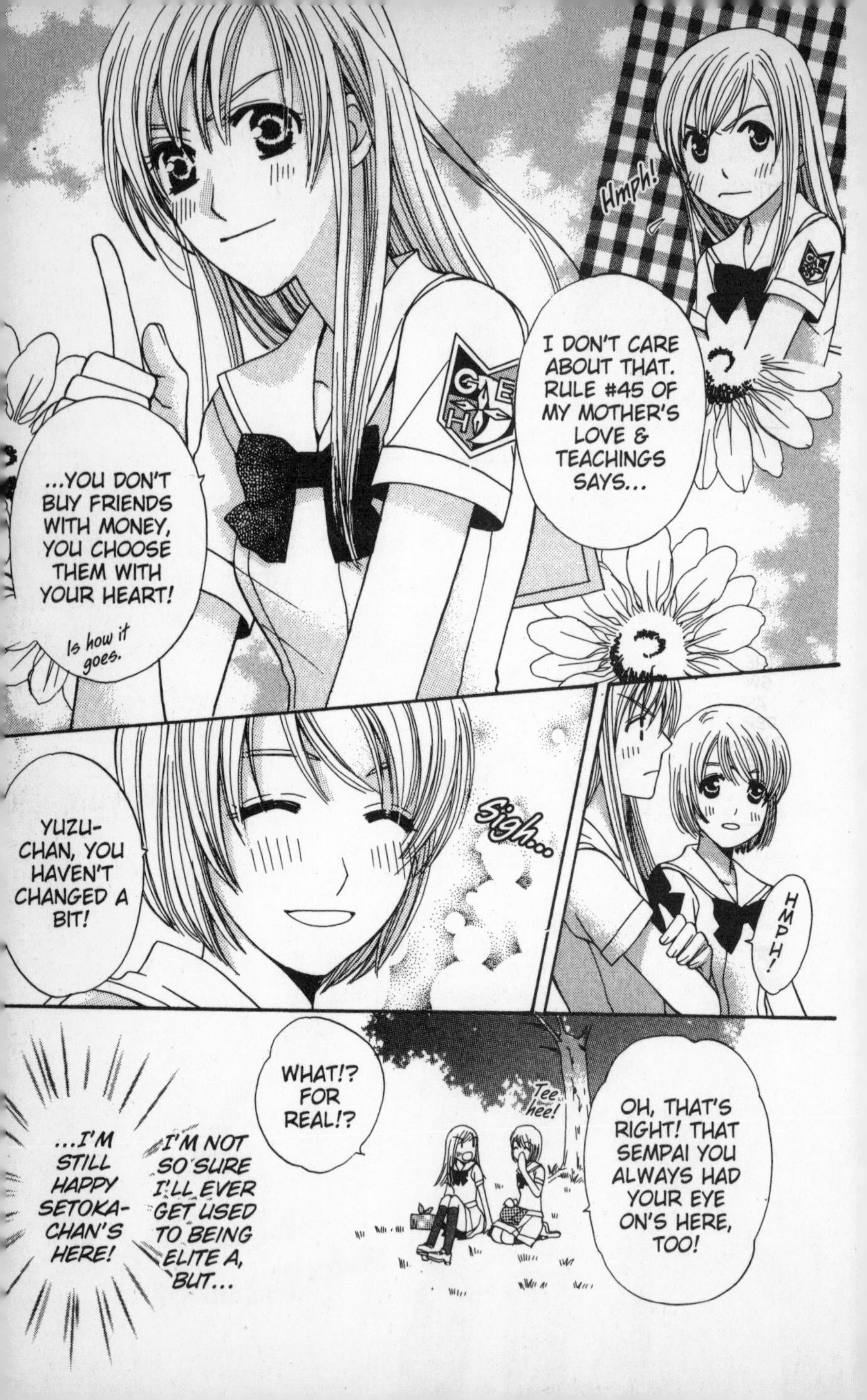
Hmph!
I DON'T CARE ABOUT THAT. RULE #45 OF MY MOTHER'S LOVE & TEACHINGS SAYS...
...YOU DON'T BUY FRIENDS WITH MONEY, YOU CHOOSE THEM WITH YOUR HEART!
Is how it goes.
HMPH!
Sigh...
YUZU-CHAN, YOU HAVEN'T CHANGED A BIT!
OH, THAT'S RIGHT! THAT SEMPAI YOU ALWAYS HAD YOUR EYE ON'S HERE, TOO!
Tee hee!
WHAT!? FOR REAL!?
I'M NOT SO SURE I'LL EVER GET USED TO BEING ELITE A, BUT...
...I'M STILL HAPPY SETOKA-CHAN'S HERE!

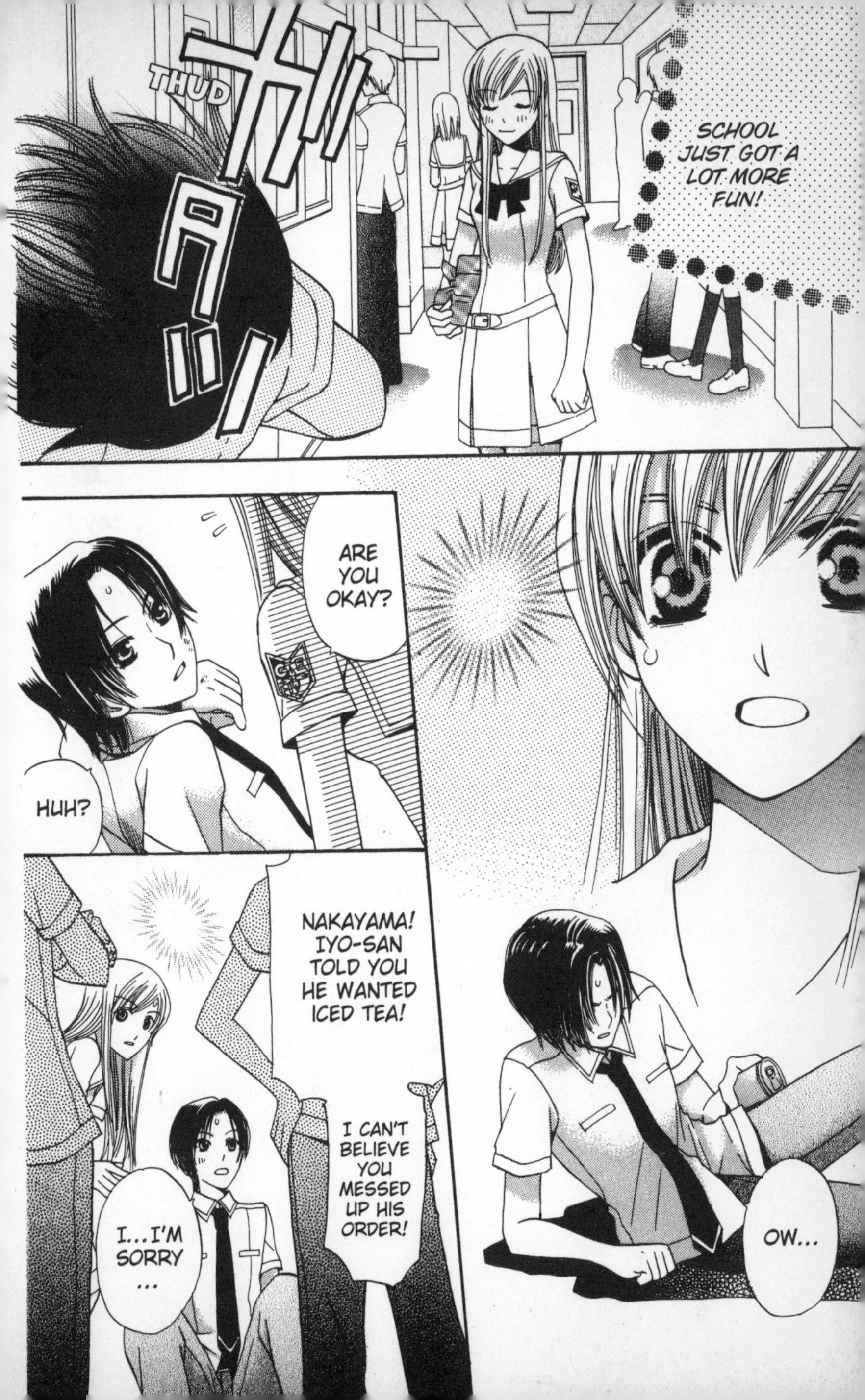
SCHOOL JUST GOT A LOT MORE FUN!
THUD
ARE YOU OKAY?
HUH?
OW...
NAKAYAMA! IYO-SAN TOLD YOU HE WANTED ICED TEA!
I CAN'T BELIEVE YOU MESSED UP HIS ORDER!
I...I'M SORRY ...

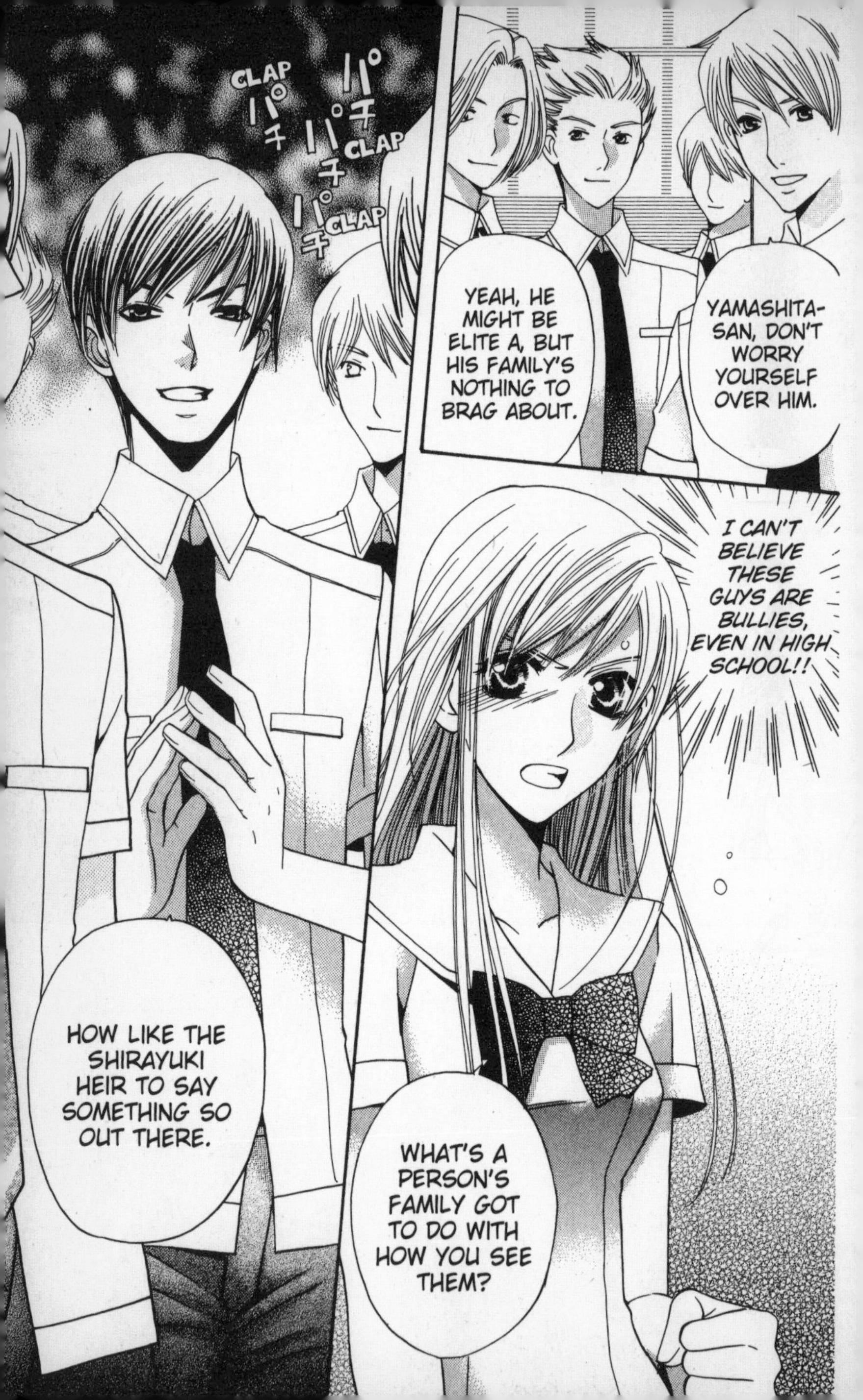
YAMASHITA-SAN, DON'T WORRY YOURSELF OVER HIM.
YEAH, HE MIGHT BE ELITE A, BUT HIS FAMILY'S NOTHING TO BRAG ABOUT.
I CAN'T BELIEVE THESE GUYS ARE BULLIES, EVEN IN HIGH SCHOOL!!
WHAT'S A PERSON'S FAMILY GOT TO DO WITH HOW YOU SEE THEM?
パチ CLAP
パチ CLAP
パチ CLAP
パチ
HOW LIKE THE SHIRAYUKI HEIR TO SAY SOMETHING SO OUT THERE.

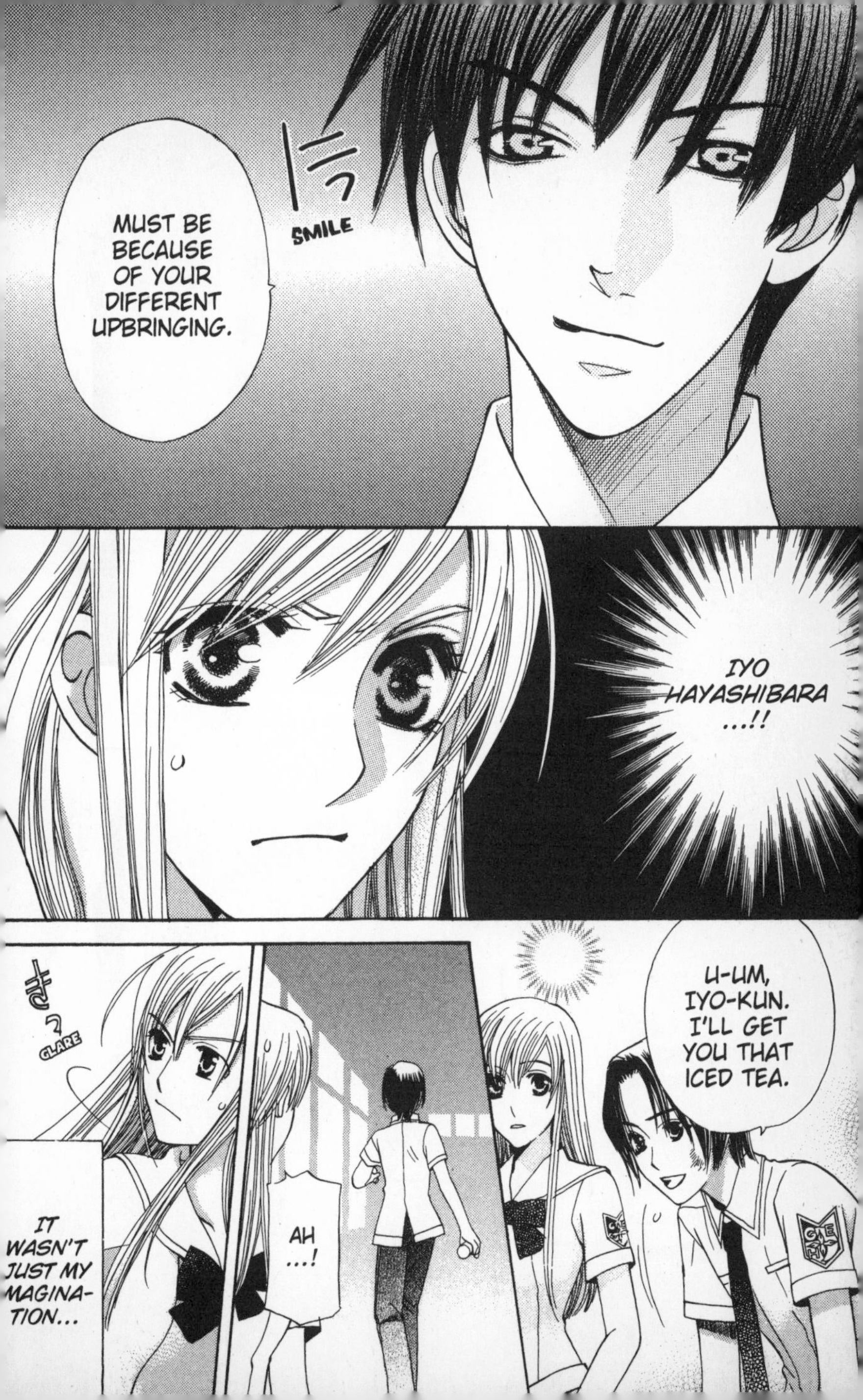
SMILE
MUST BE BECAUSE OF YOUR DIFFERENT UPBRINGING.
IYO HAYASHIBARA ...!!
U-UM, IYO-KUN. I'LL GET YOU THAT ICED TEA.
AH ...!
GLARE
IT WASN'T JUST MY MAGINA- TION...

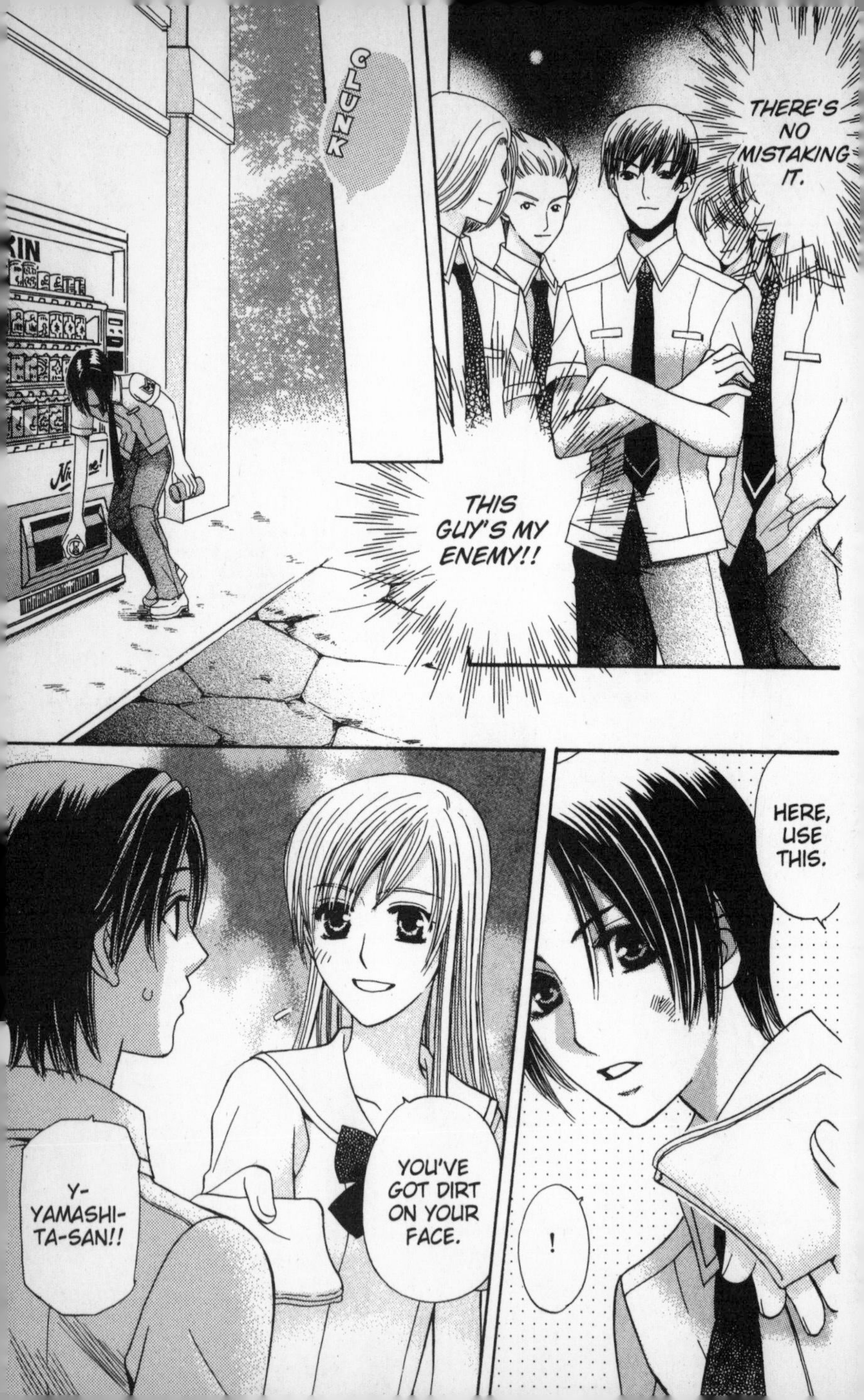
THERE'S NO MISTAKING IT.
THIS GUY'S MY ENEMY!!
CLUNK
HERE, USE THIS.
!
YOU'VE GOT DIRT ON YOUR FACE.
Y-YAMASHITA-SAN!!

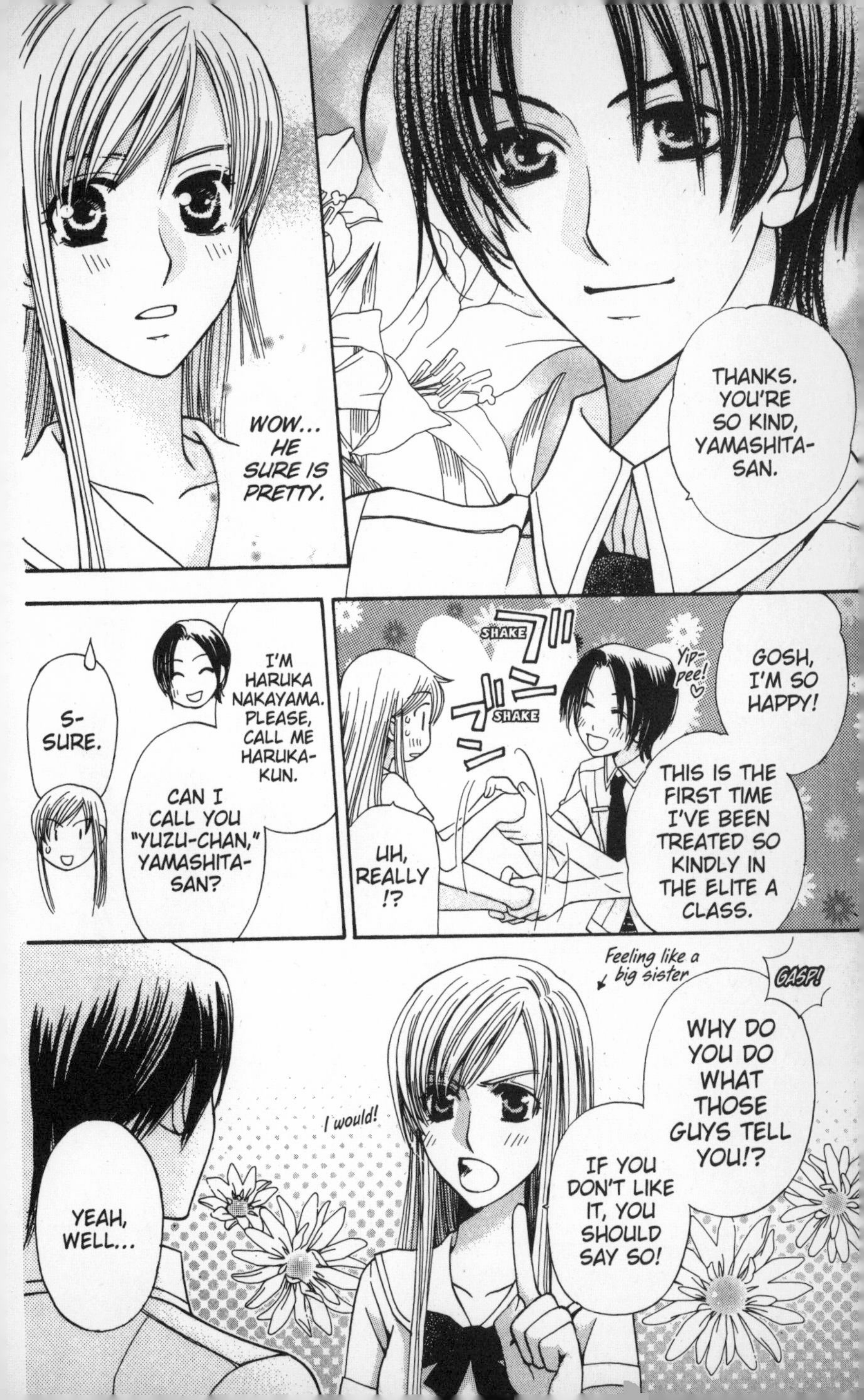

THANKS. YOU'RE SO KIND, YAMASHITA-SAN.
WOW... HE SURE IS PRETTY.
GOSH, I'M SO HAPPY!
Yip-pee!
SHAKE
SHAKE
THIS IS THE FIRST TIME I'VE BEEN TREATED SO KINDLY IN THE ELITE A CLASS.
UH, REALLY!?
I'M HARUKA NAKAYAMA. PLEASE, CALL ME HARUKA-KUN.
CAN I CALL YOU "YUZU-CHAN," YAMASHITA-SAN?
S-SURE.
Feeling like a big sister
GASP!
WHY DO YOU DO WHAT THOSE GUYS TELL YOU!?
IF YOU DON'T LIKE IT, YOU SHOULD SAY SO!
I would!
YEAH, WELL...

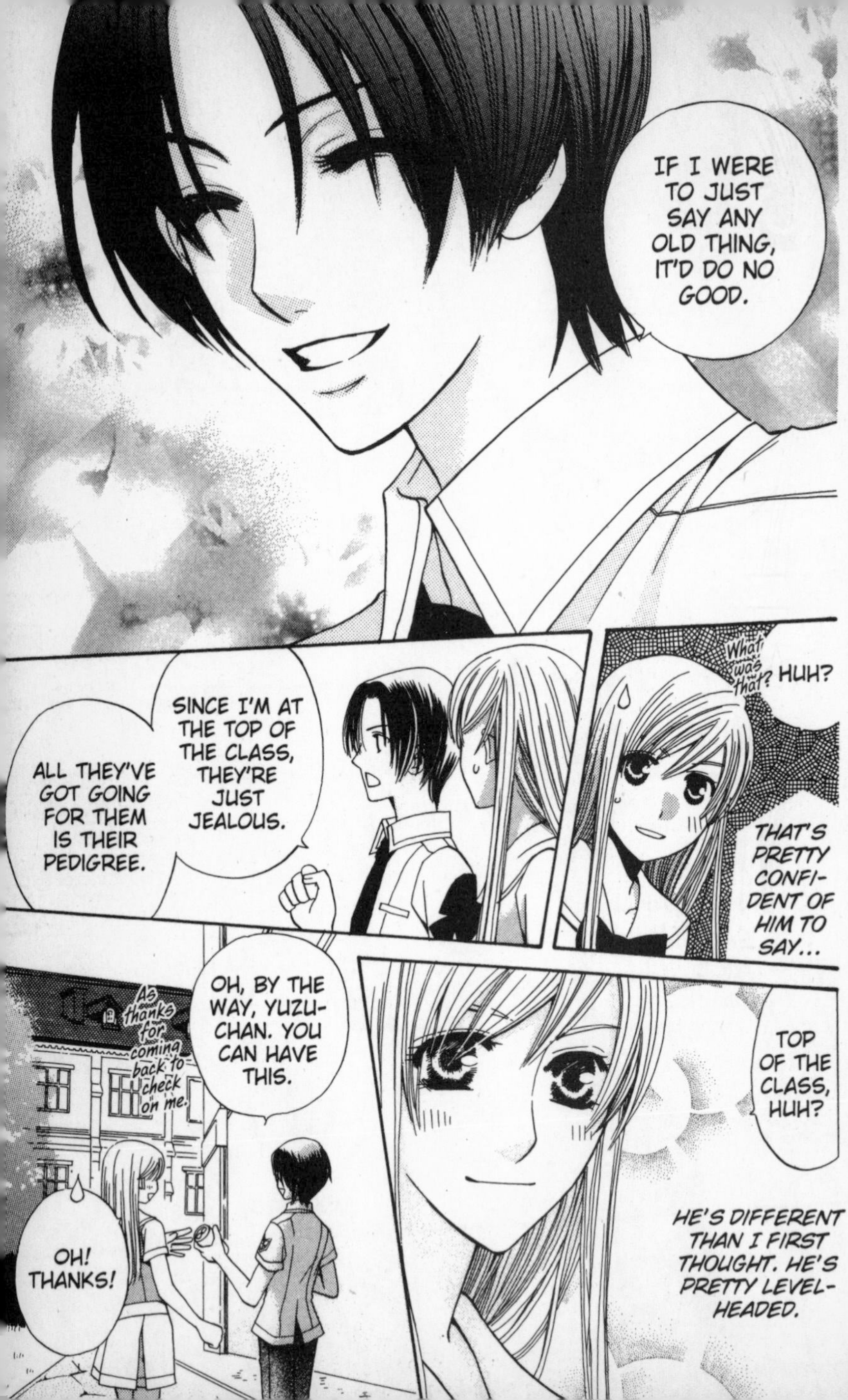
IF I WERE TO JUST SAY ANY OLD THING, IT'D DO NO GOOD.
What was that?
HUH?
THAT'S PRETTY CONFIDENT OF HIM TO SAY...
SINCE I'M AT THE TOP OF THE CLASS, THEY'RE JUST JEALOUS.
ALL THEY'VE GOT GOING FOR THEM IS THEIR PEDIGREE.
TOP OF THE CLASS, HUH?
HE'S DIFFERENT THAN I FIRST THOUGHT. HE'S PRETTY LEVEL-HEADED.
OH, BY THE WAY, YUZU-CHAN. YOU CAN HAVE THIS.
As thanks for coming back to check on me.
OH! THANKS!

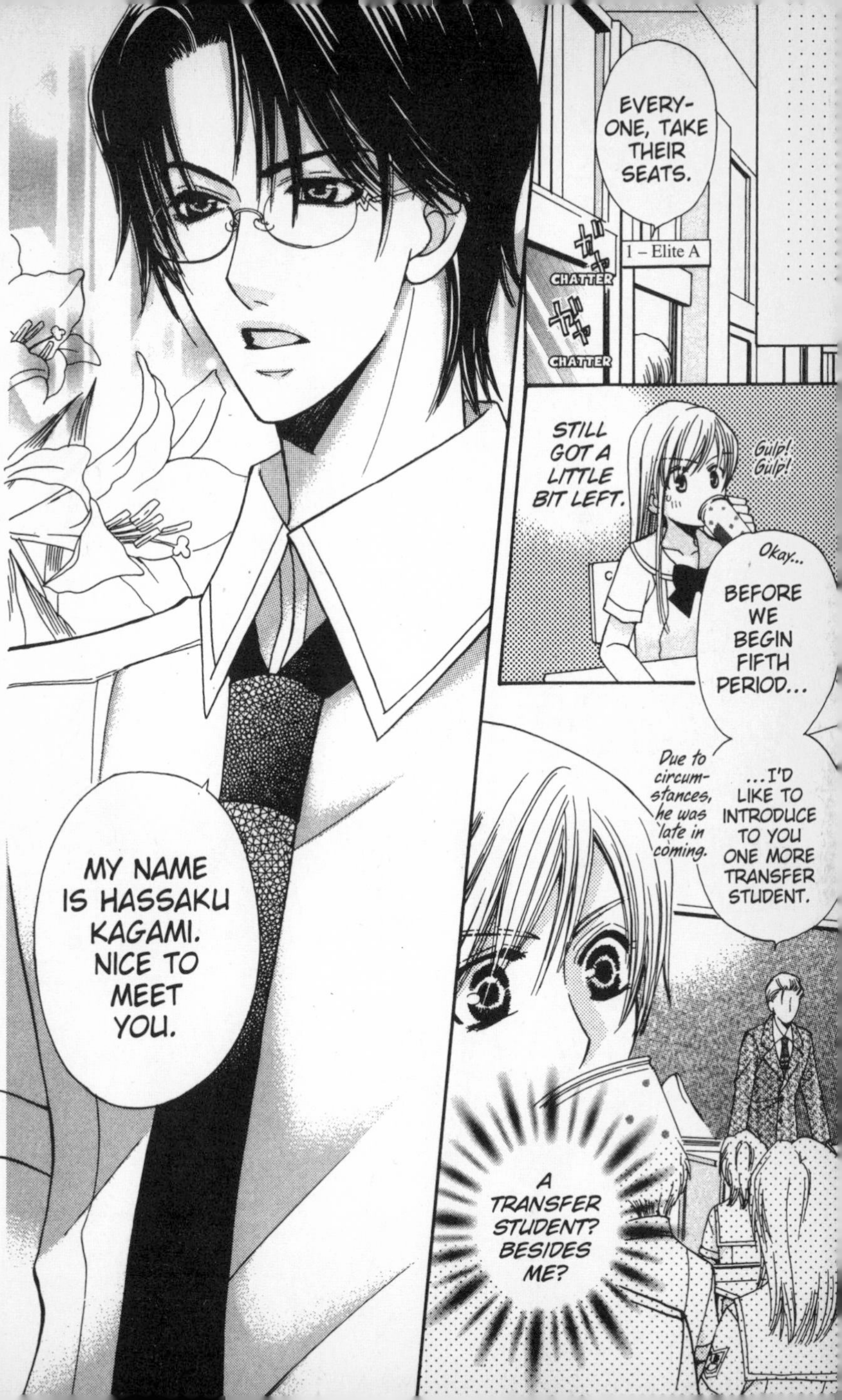
EVERY-ONE, TAKE THEIR SEATS.
1 – Elite A
CHATTER
CHATTER
Gulp! Gulp!
STILL GOT A LITTLE BIT LEFT.
Okay...
BEFORE WE BEGIN FIFTH PERIOD...
...I'D LIKE TO INTRODUCE TO YOU ONE MORE TRANSFER STUDENT.
Due to circumstances, he was late in coming.
A TRANSFER STUDENT? BESIDES ME?
MY NAME IS HASSAKU KAGAMI. NICE TO MEET YOU.

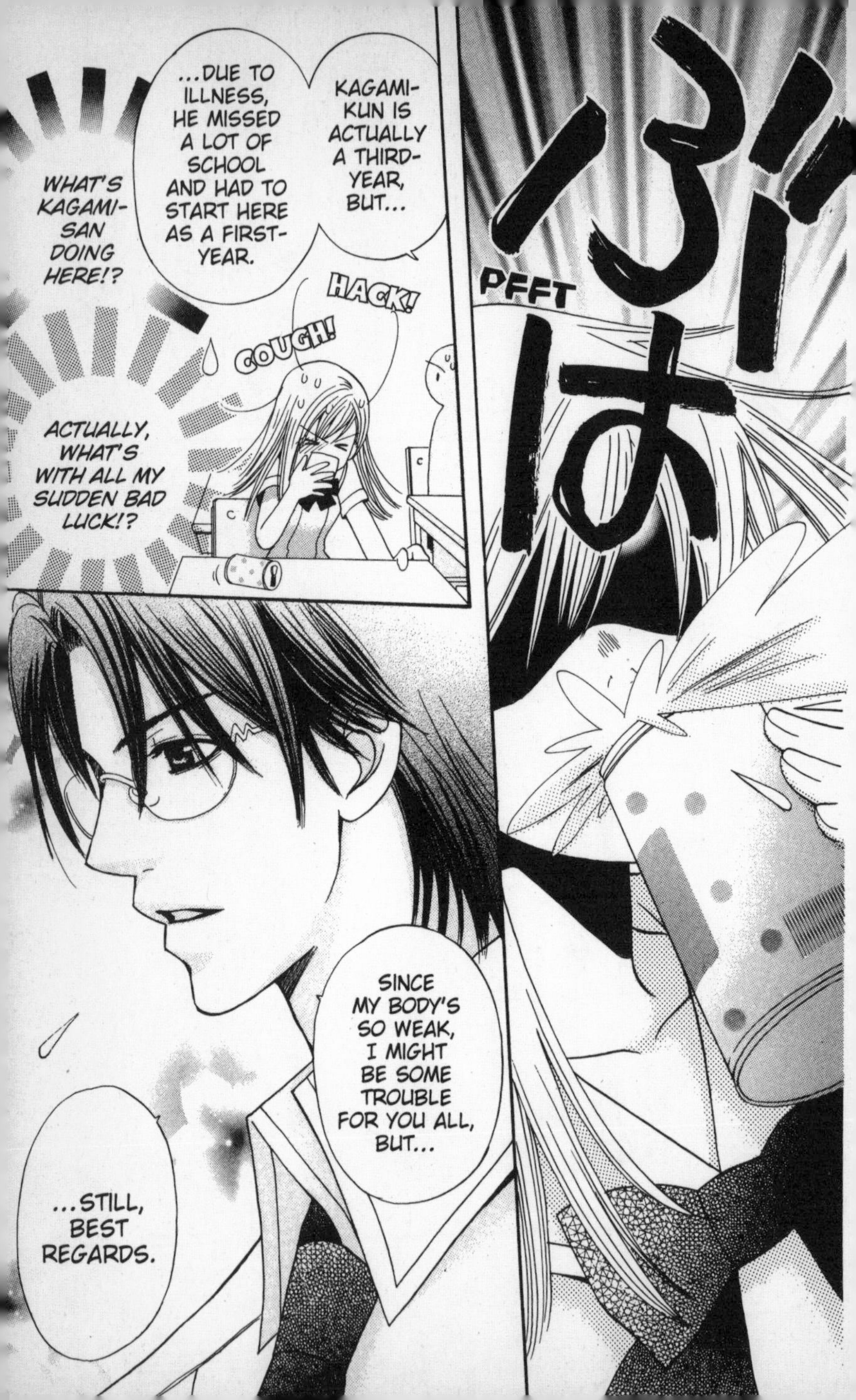
PFFT
KAGAMI-KUN IS ACTUALLY A THIRD-YEAR, BUT...
...DUE TO ILLNESS, HE MISSED A LOT OF SCHOOL AND HAD TO START HERE AS A FIRST-YEAR.
WHAT'S KAGAMI-SAN DOING HERE!?
HACK!
COUGH!
ACTUALLY, WHAT'S WITH ALL MY SUDDEN BAD LUCK!?
SINCE MY BODY'S SO WEAK, I MIGHT BE SOME TROUBLE FOR YOU ALL, BUT...
...STILL, BEST REGARDS.

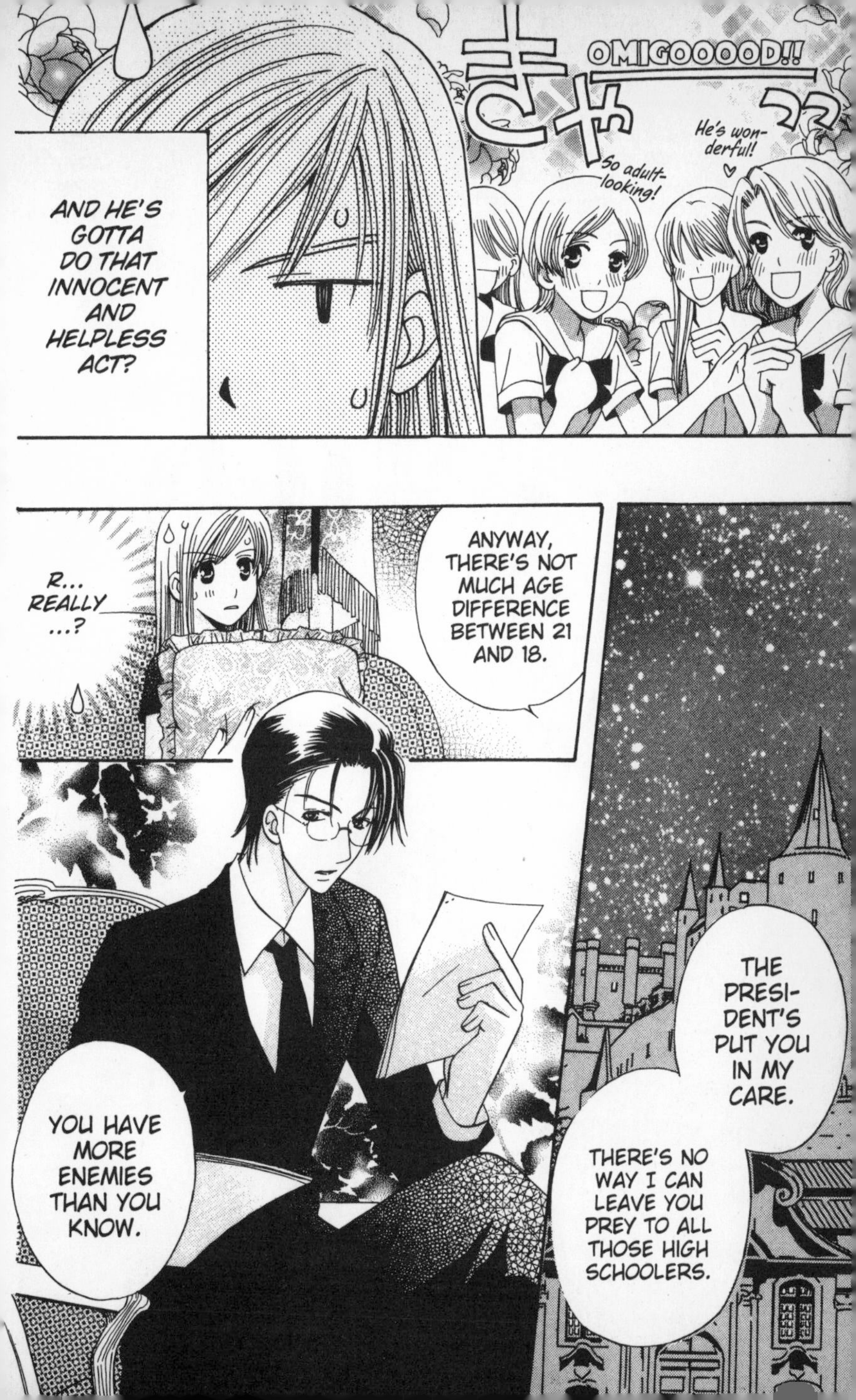
OMIGOOOOD!!
He's wonderful!
So adult-looking!
AND HE'S GOTTA DO THAT INNOCENT AND HELPLESS ACT?
THE PRESIDENT'S PUT YOU IN MY CARE.
THERE'S NO WAY I CAN LEAVE YOU PREY TO ALL THOSE HIGH SCHOOLERS.
ANYWAY, THERE'S NOT MUCH AGE DIFFERENCE BETWEEN 21 AND 18.
R... REALLY...?
YOU HAVE MORE ENEMIES THAN YOU KNOW.

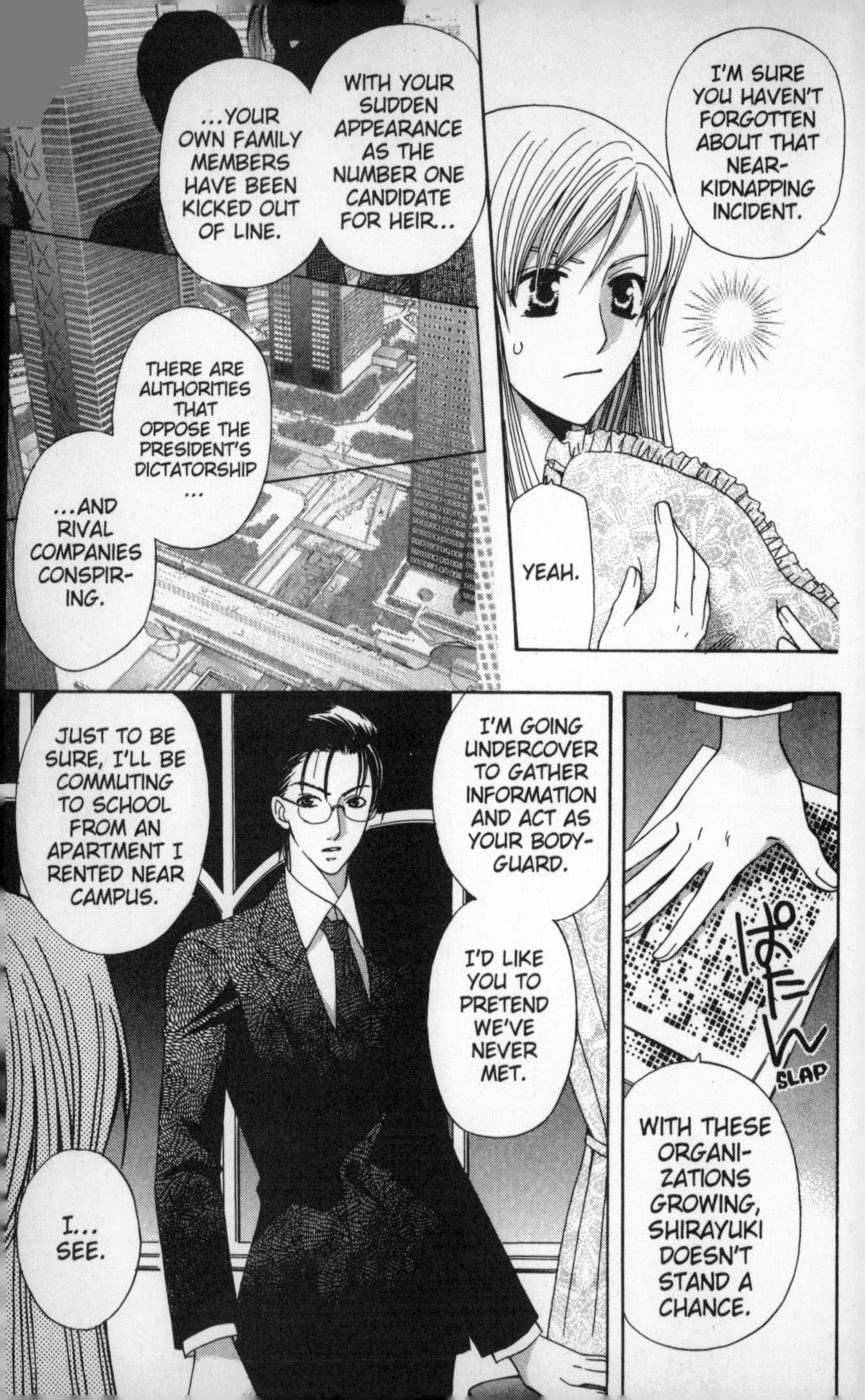
I'M SURE YOU HAVEN'T FORGOTTEN ABOUT THAT NEAR-KIDNAPPING INCIDENT.
YEAH.
WITH YOUR SUDDEN APPEARANCE AS THE NUMBER ONE CANDIDATE FOR HEIR...
...YOUR OWN FAMILY MEMBERS HAVE BEEN KICKED OUT OF LINE.
THERE ARE AUTHORITIES THAT OPPOSE THE PRESIDENT'S DICTATORSHIP...
...AND RIVAL COMPANIES CONSPIRING.
ぱたん
SLAP
WITH THESE ORGANIZATIONS GROWING, SHIRAYUKI DOESN'T STAND A CHANCE.
I'M GOING UNDERCOVER TO GATHER INFORMATION AND ACT AS YOUR BODYGUARD.
I'D LIKE YOU TO PRETEND WE'VE NEVER MET.
JUST TO BE SURE, I'LL BE COMMUTING TO SCHOOL FROM AN APARTMENT I RENTED NEAR CAMPUS.
I... SEE.

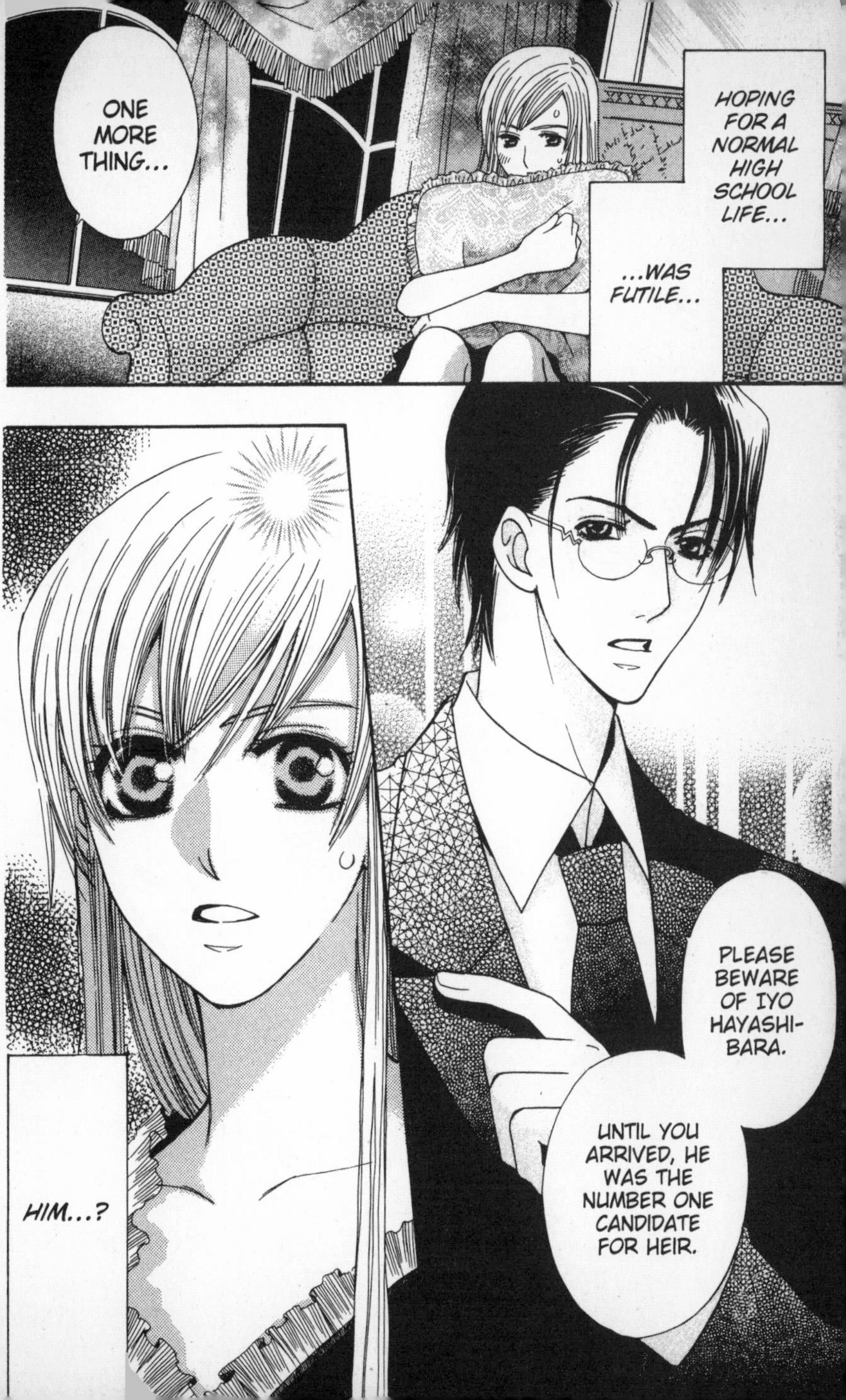
HOPING FOR A NORMAL HIGH SCHOOL LIFE...
...WAS FUTILE...
ONE MORE THING...
PLEASE BEWARE OF IYO HAYASHI-BARA.
UNTIL YOU ARRIVED, HE WAS THE NUMBER ONE CANDIDATE FOR HEIR.
HIM...?

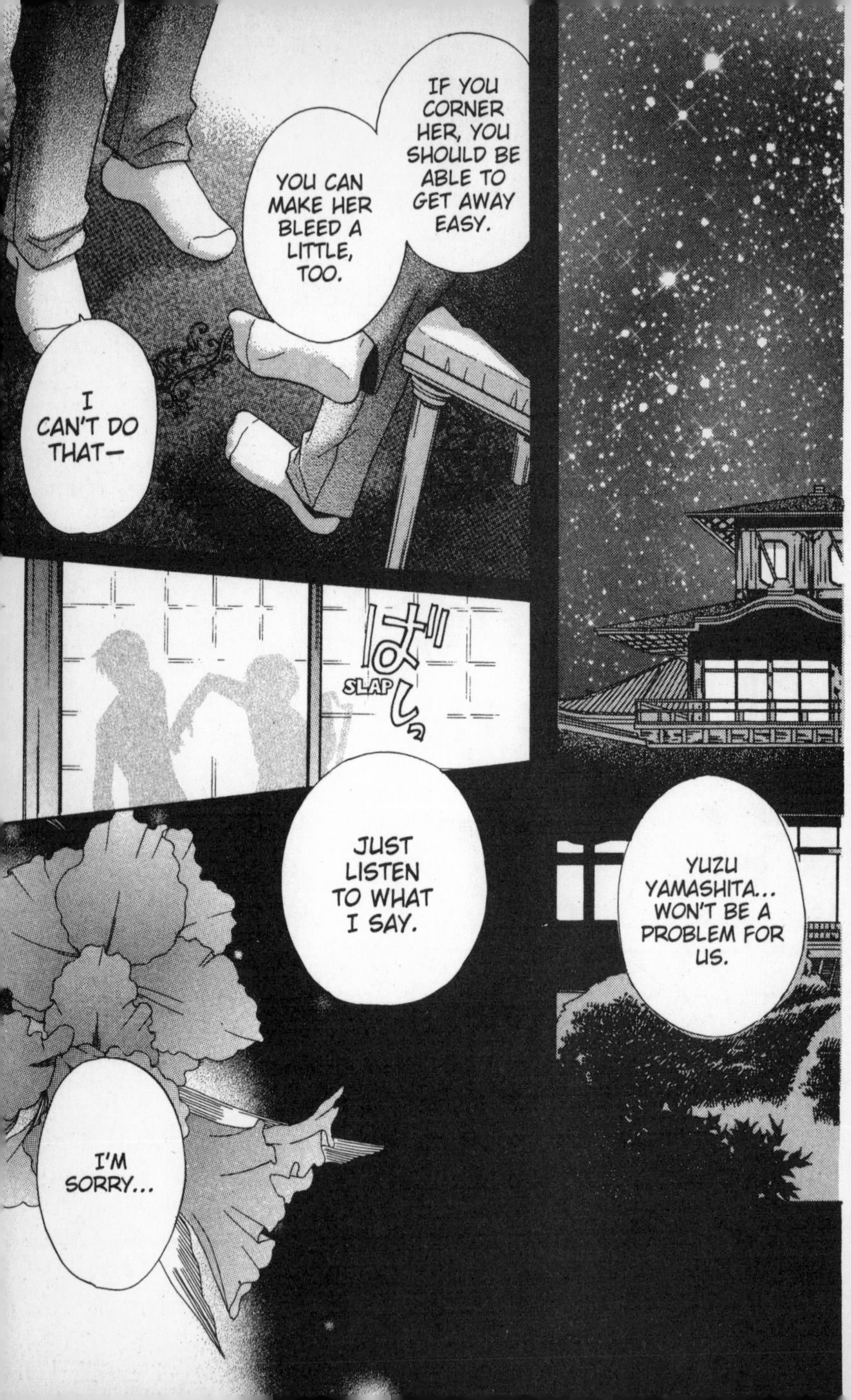
YUZU YAMASHITA... WON'T BE A PROBLEM FOR US.
IF YOU CORNER HER, YOU SHOULD BE ABLE TO GET AWAY EASY.
YOU CAN MAKE HER BLEED A LITTLE, TOO.
I CAN'T DO THAT—
ばしっ
SLAP
JUST LISTEN TO WHAT I SAY.
I'M SORRY...

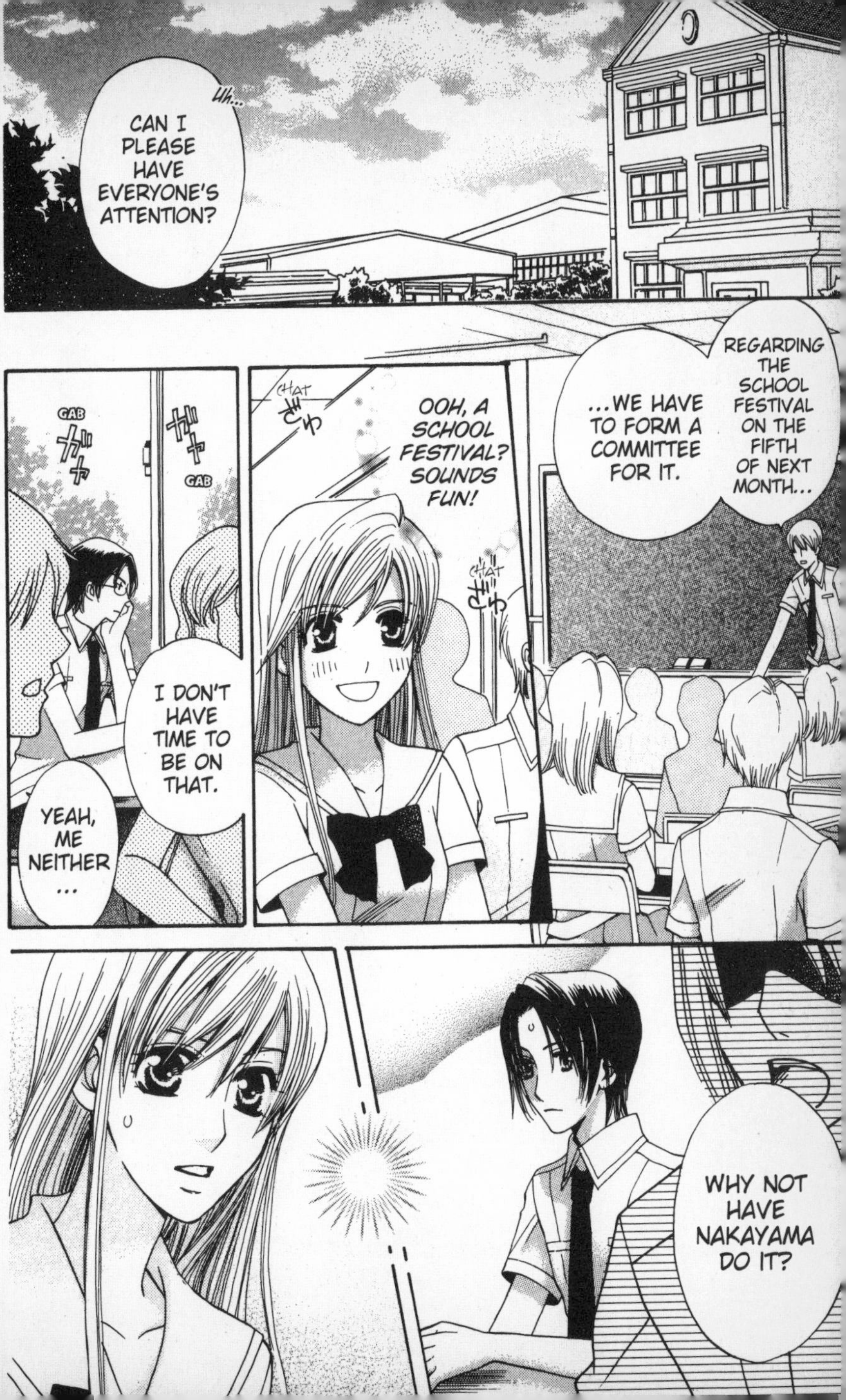
Uh...
CAN I PLEASE HAVE EVERYONE'S ATTENTION?
REGARDING THE SCHOOL FESTIVAL ON THE FIFTH OF NEXT MONTH...
...WE HAVE TO FORM A COMMITTEE FOR IT.
CHAT
ざわ
OOH, A SCHOOL FESTIVAL? SOUNDS FUN!
CHAT
ざわ
GAB
ガヤ
GAB
ガヤ
I DON'T HAVE TIME TO BE ON THAT.
YEAH, ME NEITHER...
WHY NOT HAVE NAKAYAMA DO IT?

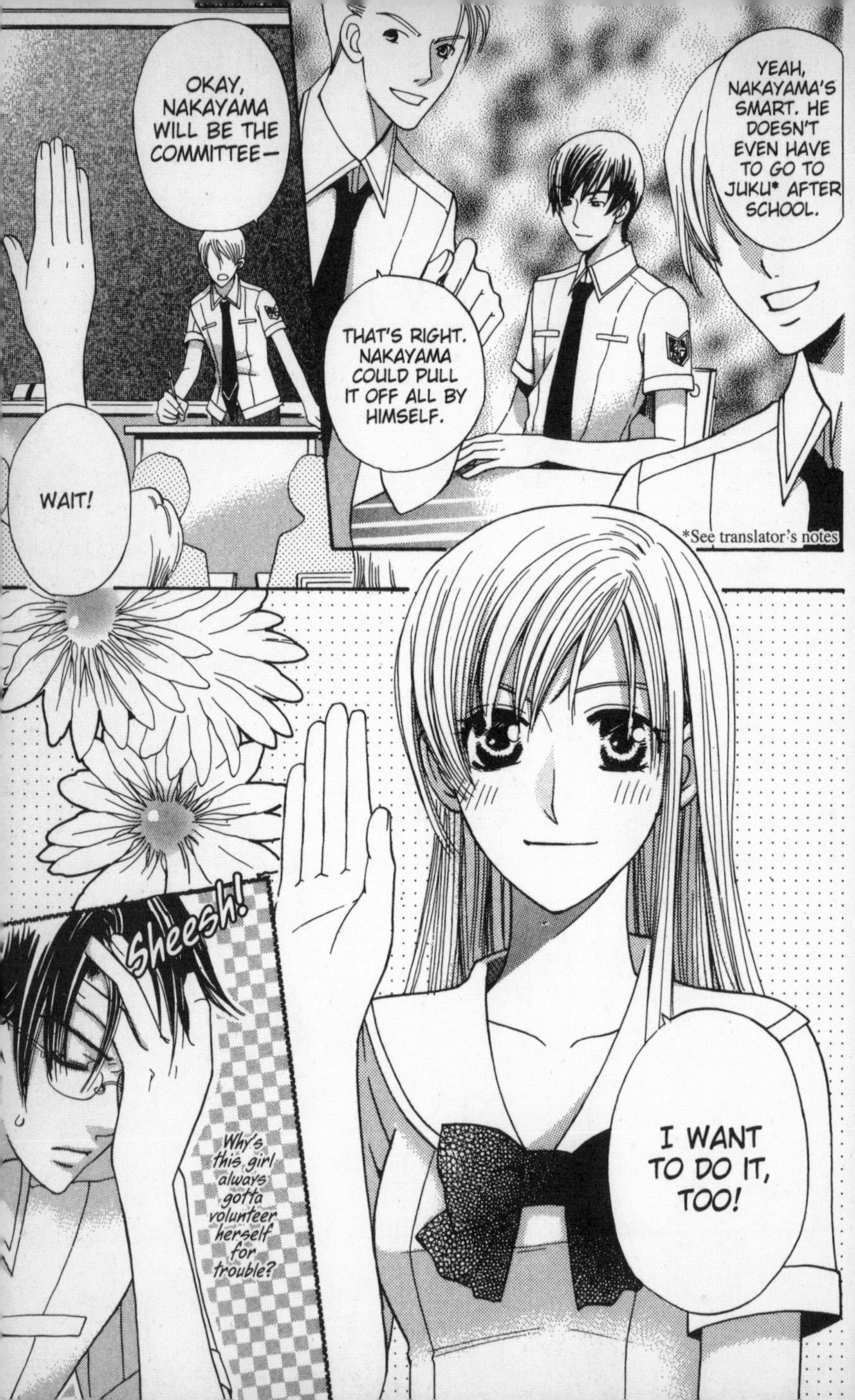
YEAH, NAKAYAMA'S SMART. HE DOESN'T EVEN HAVE TO GO TO JUKU* AFTER SCHOOL.
THAT'S RIGHT. NAKAYAMA COULD PULL IT OFF ALL BY HIMSELF.
*See translator's notes
OKAY, NAKAYAMA WILL BE THE COMMITTEE—
WAIT!
I WANT TO DO IT, TOO!
Sheesh!
Why's this girl always gotta volunteer herself for trouble?

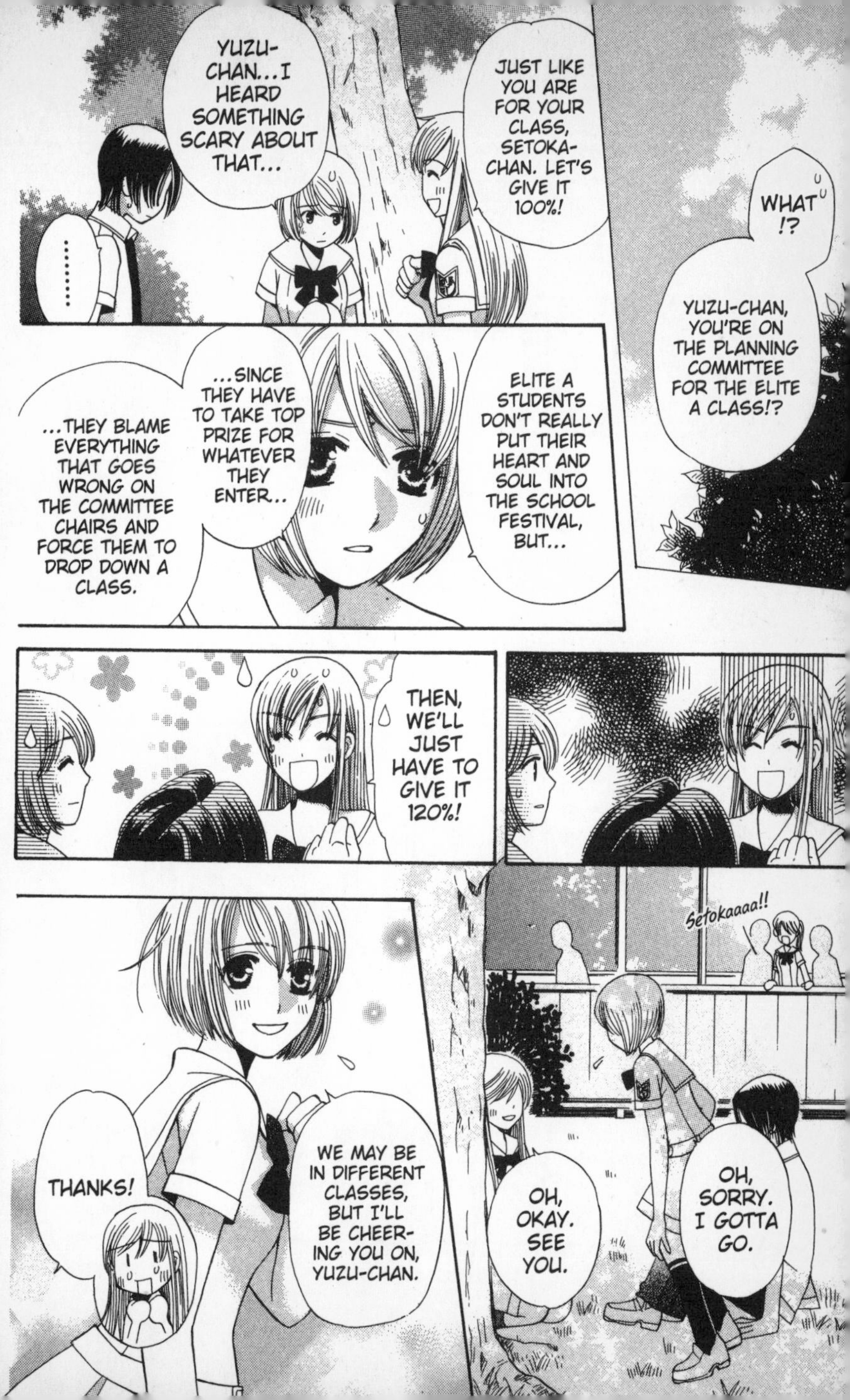
WHAT!?
YUZU-CHAN, YOU'RE ON THE PLANNING COMMITTEE FOR THE ELITE A CLASS!?
JUST LIKE YOU ARE FOR YOUR CLASS, SETOKA-CHAN. LET'S GIVE IT 100%!
YUZU-CHAN...I HEARD SOMETHING SCARY ABOUT THAT...
....
ELITE A STUDENTS DON'T REALLY PUT THEIR HEART AND SOUL INTO THE SCHOOL FESTIVAL, BUT...
...SINCE THEY HAVE TO TAKE TOP PRIZE FOR WHATEVER THEY ENTER...
...THEY BLAME EVERYTHING THAT GOES WRONG ON THE COMMITTEE CHAIRS AND FORCE THEM TO DROP DOWN A CLASS.
THEN, WE'LL JUST HAVE TO GIVE IT 120%!
Setokaaaa!!
OH, SORRY. I GOTTA GO.
OH, OKAY. SEE YOU.
WE MAY BE IN DIFFERENT CLASSES, BUT I'LL BE CHEERING YOU ON, YUZU-CHAN.
THANKS!

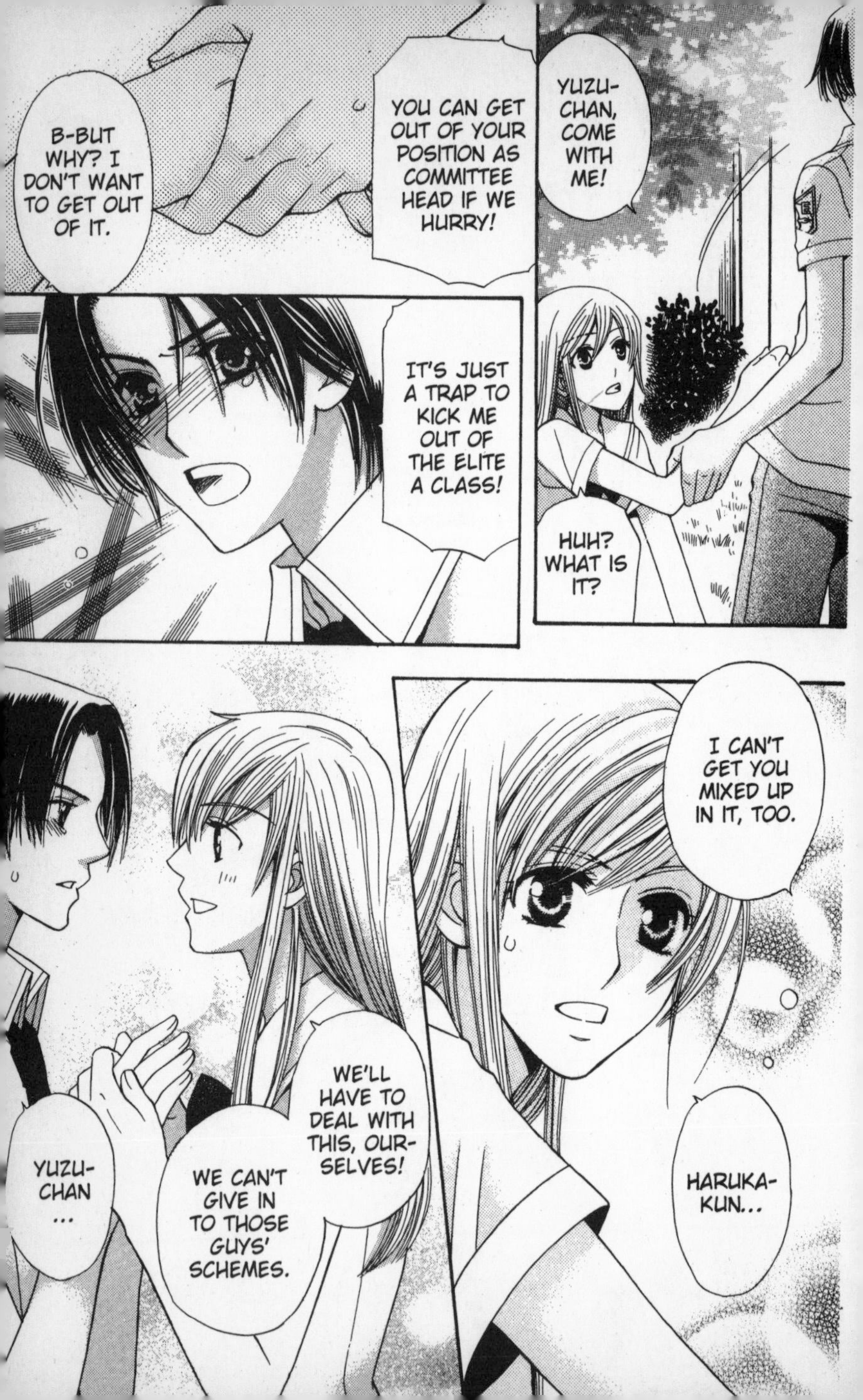
YUZU-CHAN, COME WITH ME!
HUH? WHAT IS IT?
YOU CAN GET OUT OF YOUR POSITION AS COMMITTEE HEAD IF WE HURRY!
B-BUT WHY? I DON'T WANT TO GET OUT OF IT.
IT'S JUST A TRAP TO KICK ME OUT OF THE ELITE A CLASS!
I CAN'T GET YOU MIXED UP IN IT, TOO.
HARUKA-KUN...
WE'LL HAVE TO DEAL WITH THIS, OUR-SELVES!
WE CAN'T GIVE IN TO THOSE GUYS' SCHEMES.
YUZU-CHAN
...

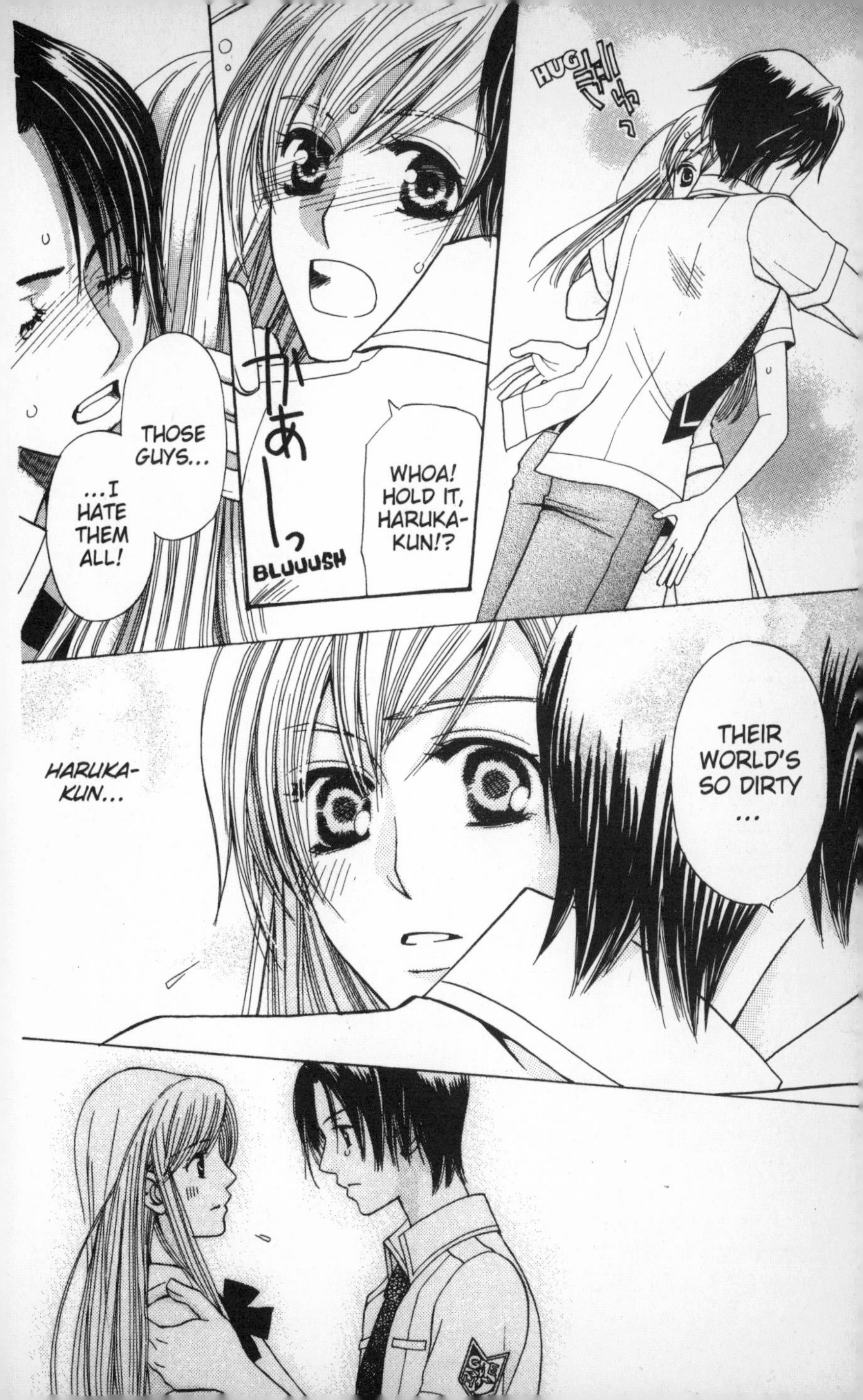

HUG
WHOA! HOLD IT, HARUKA-KUN!?
かぁーっ
BLUUUSH
THOSE GUYS...
...I HATE THEM ALL!
THEIR WORLD'S SO DIRTY ...
HARUKA-KUN...

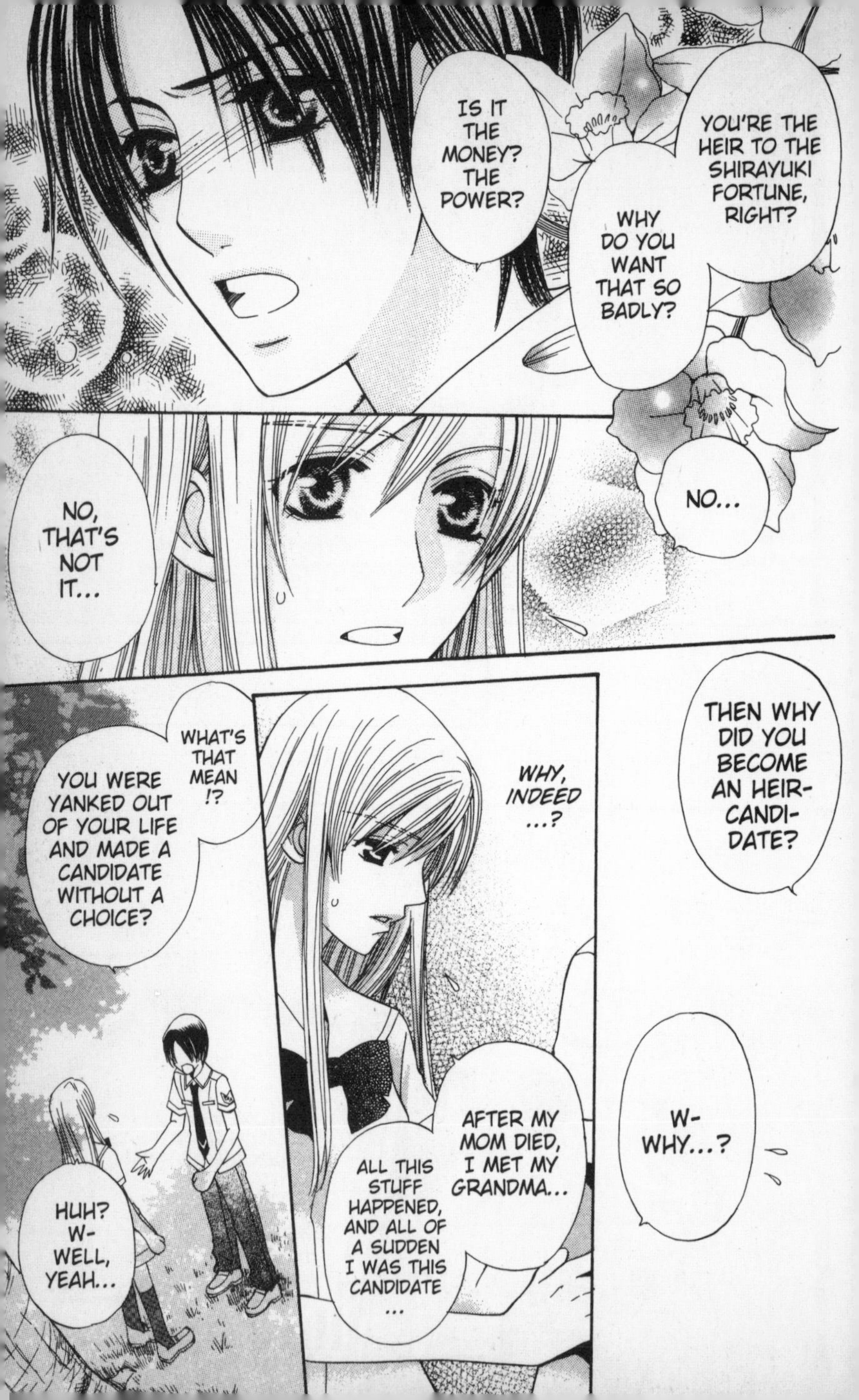
YOU'RE THE HEIR TO THE SHIRAYUKI FORTUNE, RIGHT?
WHY DO YOU WANT THAT SO BADLY?
IS IT THE MONEY? THE POWER?
NO...
NO, THAT'S NOT IT...
THEN WHY DID YOU BECOME AN HEIR-CANDIDATE?
W-WHY...?
WHY, INDEED ...?
AFTER MY MOM DIED, I MET MY GRANDMA...
ALL THIS STUFF HAPPENED, AND ALL OF A SUDDEN I WAS THIS CANDIDATE ...
WHAT'S THAT MEAN !?
YOU WERE YANKED OUT OF YOUR LIFE AND MADE A CANDIDATE WITHOUT A CHOICE?
HUH? W-WELL, YEAH...

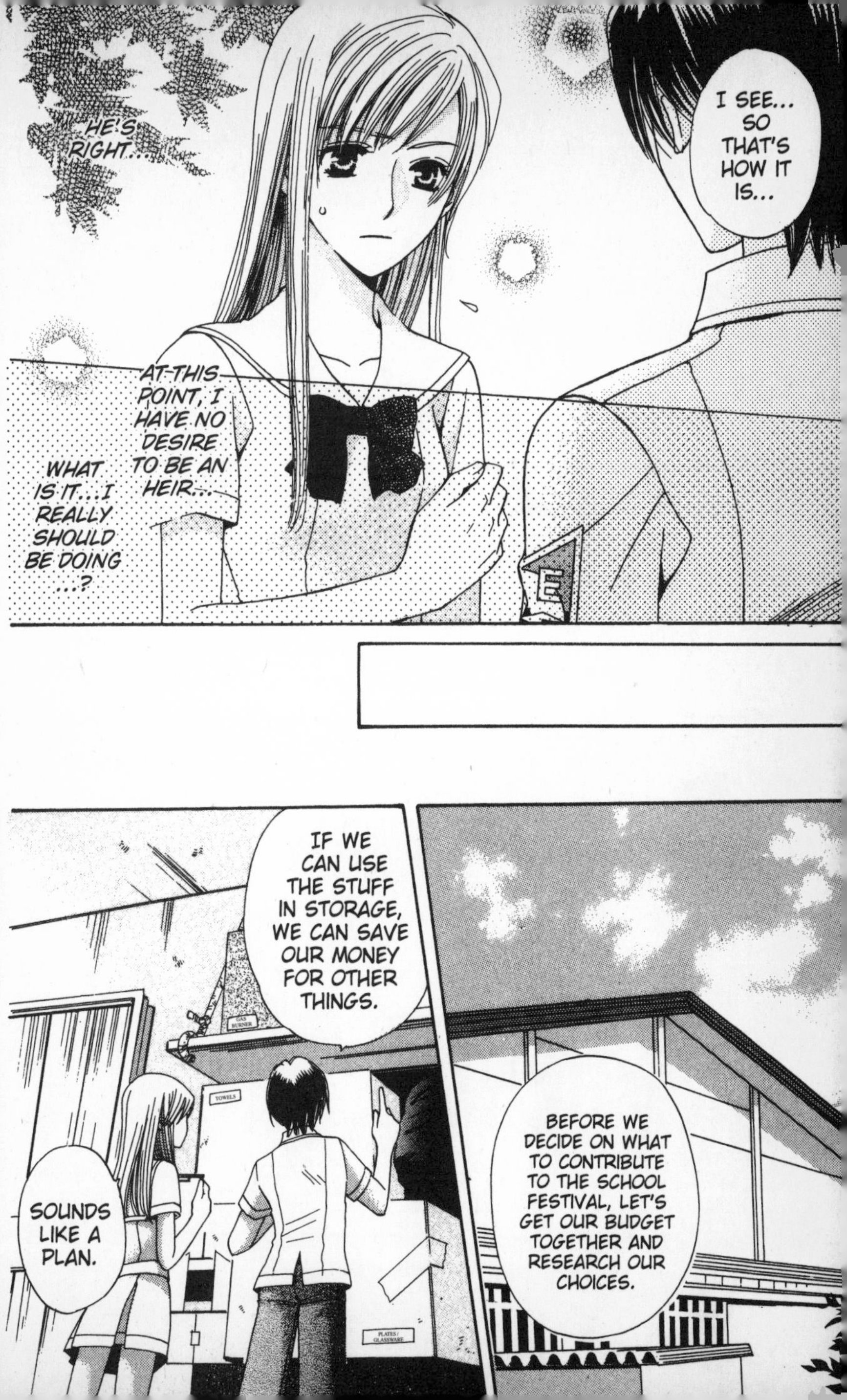
I SEE... SO THAT'S HOW IT IS...
HE'S RIGHT...
AT THIS POINT, I HAVE NO DESIRE TO BE AN HEIR...
WHAT IS IT...I REALLY SHOULD BE DOING ...?
BEFORE WE DECIDE ON WHAT TO CONTRIBUTE TO THE SCHOOL FESTIVAL, LET'S GET OUR BUDGET TOGETHER AND RESEARCH OUR CHOICES.
IF WE CAN USE THE STUFF IN STORAGE, WE CAN SAVE OUR MONEY FOR OTHER THINGS.
GAS BURNER
TOWELS
PLATES / GLASSWARE
SOUNDS LIKE A PLAN.

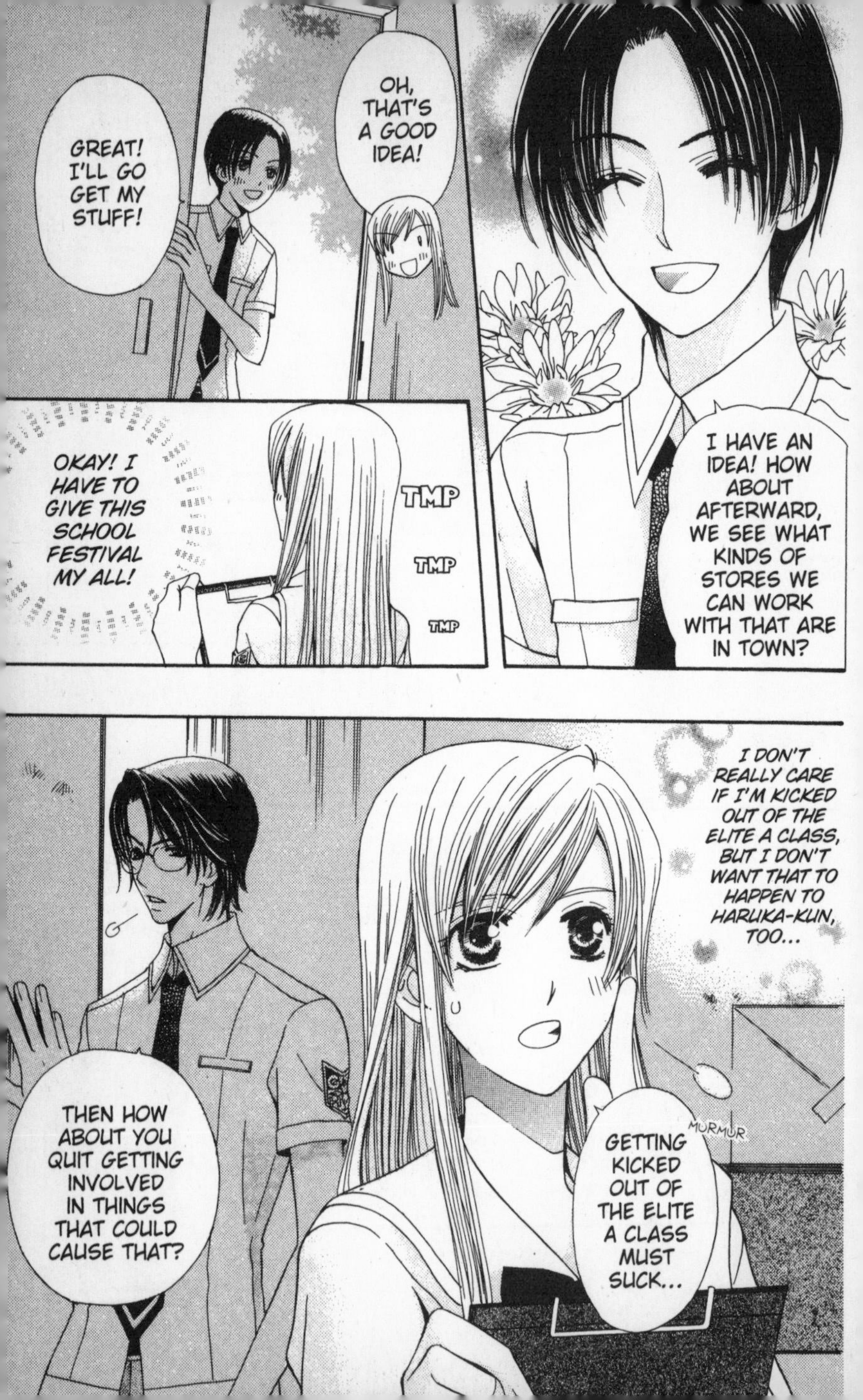
I HAVE AN IDEA! HOW ABOUT AFTERWARD, WE SEE WHAT KINDS OF STORES WE CAN WORK WITH THAT ARE IN TOWN?
OH, THAT'S A GOOD IDEA!
GREAT! I'LL GO GET MY STUFF!
TMP
TMP
TMP
OKAY! I HAVE TO GIVE THIS SCHOOL FESTIVAL MY ALL!
I DON'T REALLY CARE IF I'M KICKED OUT OF THE ELITE A CLASS, BUT I DON'T WANT THAT TO HAPPEN TO HARUKA-KUN, TOO...
MURMUR
GETTING KICKED OUT OF THE ELITE A CLASS MUST SUCK...
THEN HOW ABOUT YOU QUIT GETTING INVOLVED IN THINGS THAT COULD CAUSE THAT?

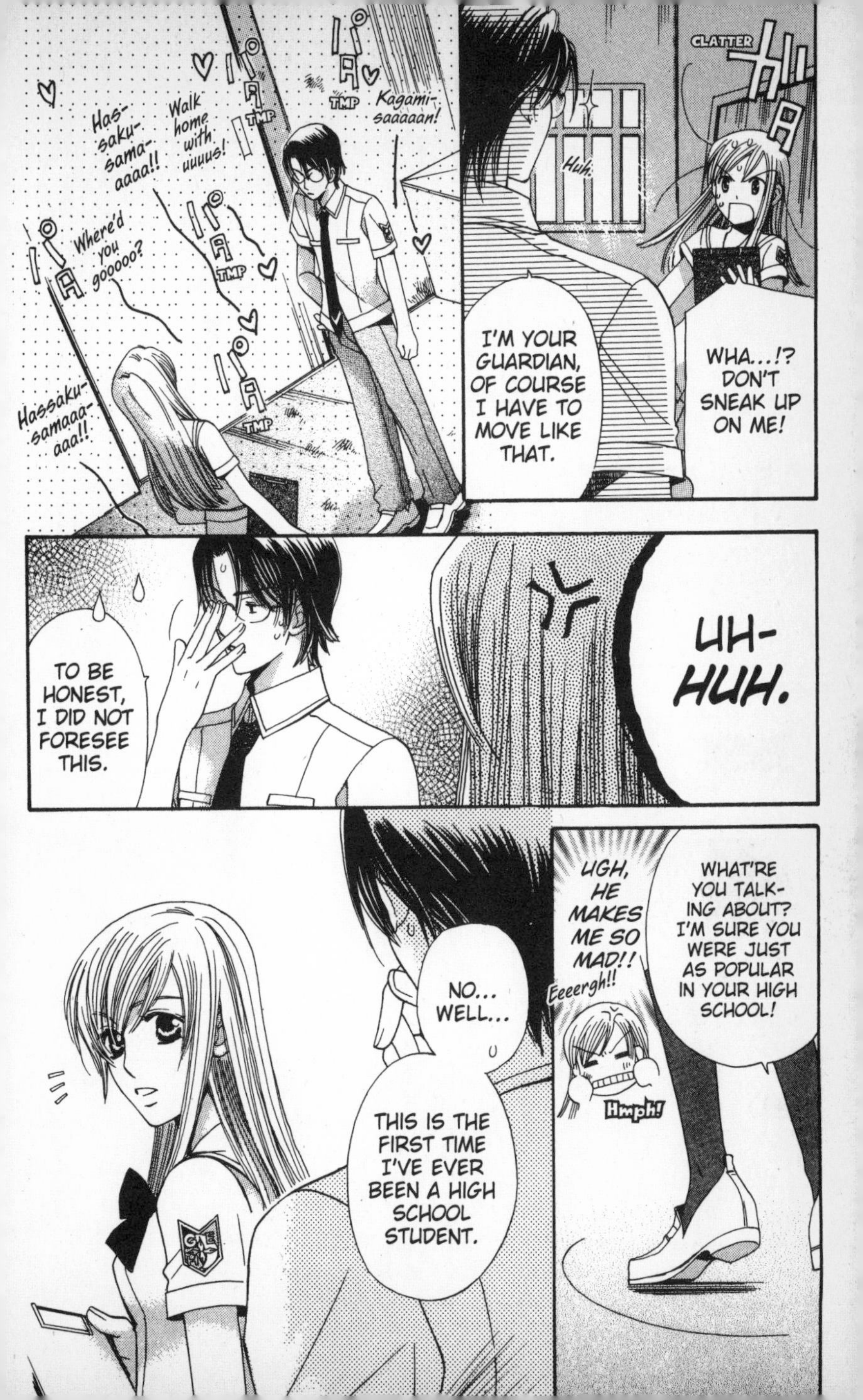
CLATTER
Huh.
WHA...!? DON'T SNEAK UP ON ME!
I'M YOUR GUARDIAN, OF COURSE I HAVE TO MOVE LIKE THAT.
Kagami-saaaaan!
TMP
Walk home with uuuuus!
Has-saku-sama-aaaa!!
TMP
Where'd you gooooo?
TMP
Hassaku-samaaaaaaa!!
TMP
UH-HUH.
TO BE HONEST, I DID NOT FORESEE THIS.
WHAT'RE YOU TALKING ABOUT? I'M SURE YOU WERE JUST AS POPULAR IN YOUR HIGH SCHOOL!
UGH, HE MAKES ME SO MAD!!
Eeeergh!!
Hmph!
NO... WELL...
THIS IS THE FIRST TIME I'VE EVER BEEN A HIGH SCHOOL STUDENT.

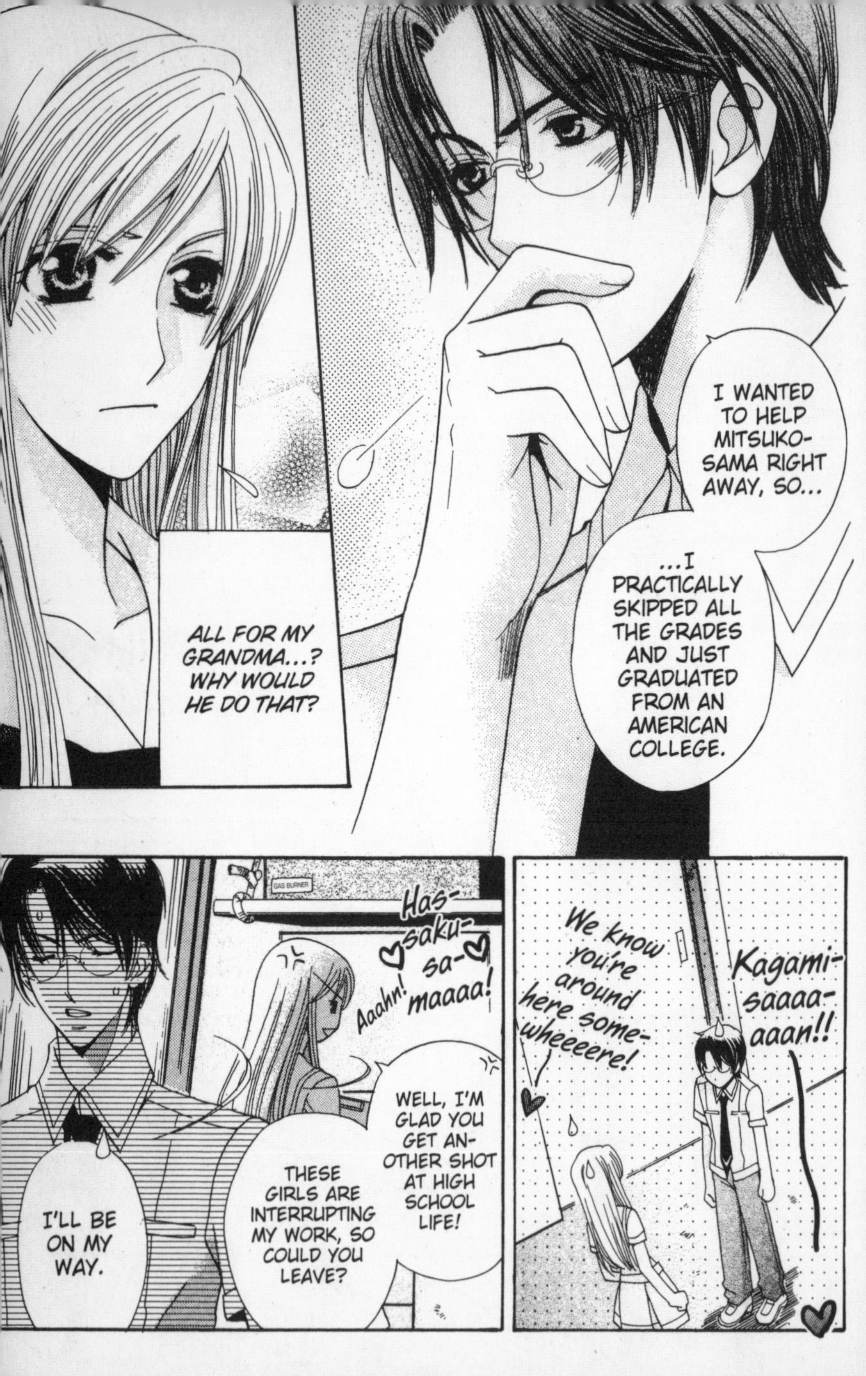
I WANTED TO HELP MITSUKO-SAMA RIGHT AWAY, SO...
...I PRACTICALLY SKIPPED ALL THE GRADES AND JUST GRADUATED FROM AN AMERICAN COLLEGE.
ALL FOR MY GRANDMA...? WHY WOULD HE DO THAT?
Kagami-saaaa-aaan!!
We know you're around here some-wheeeeere!
Has-saku-sa-maaaa!
Aaahn!
GAS BURNER
WELL, I'M GLAD YOU GET AN-OTHER SHOT AT HIGH SCHOOL LIFE!
THESE GIRLS ARE INTERRUPTING MY WORK, SO COULD YOU LEAVE?
I'LL BE ON MY WAY.

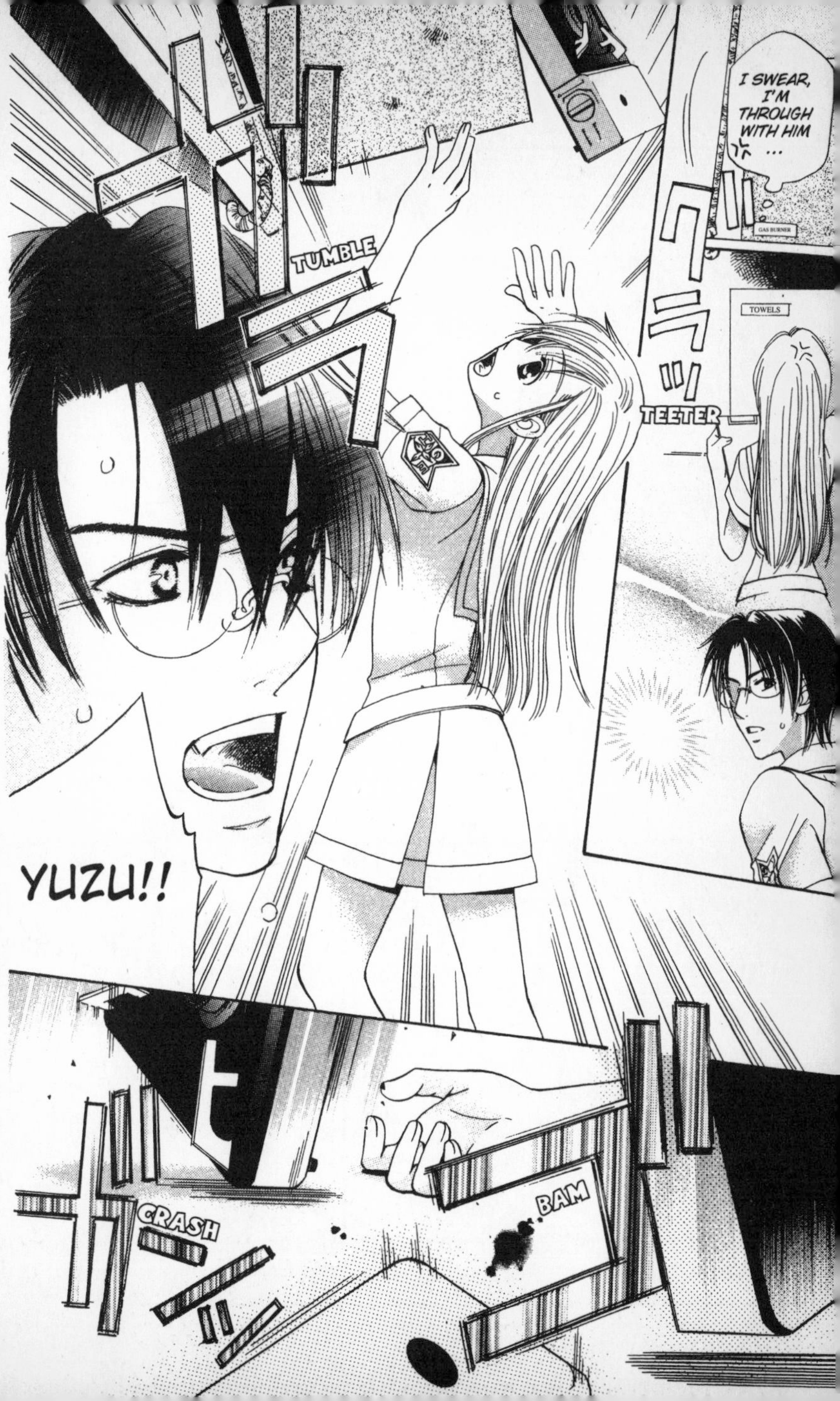
I SWEAR, I'M THROUGH WITH HIM ...
GAS BURNER
TOWELS
TEETER
TUMBLE
YUZU!!
BAM
CRASH

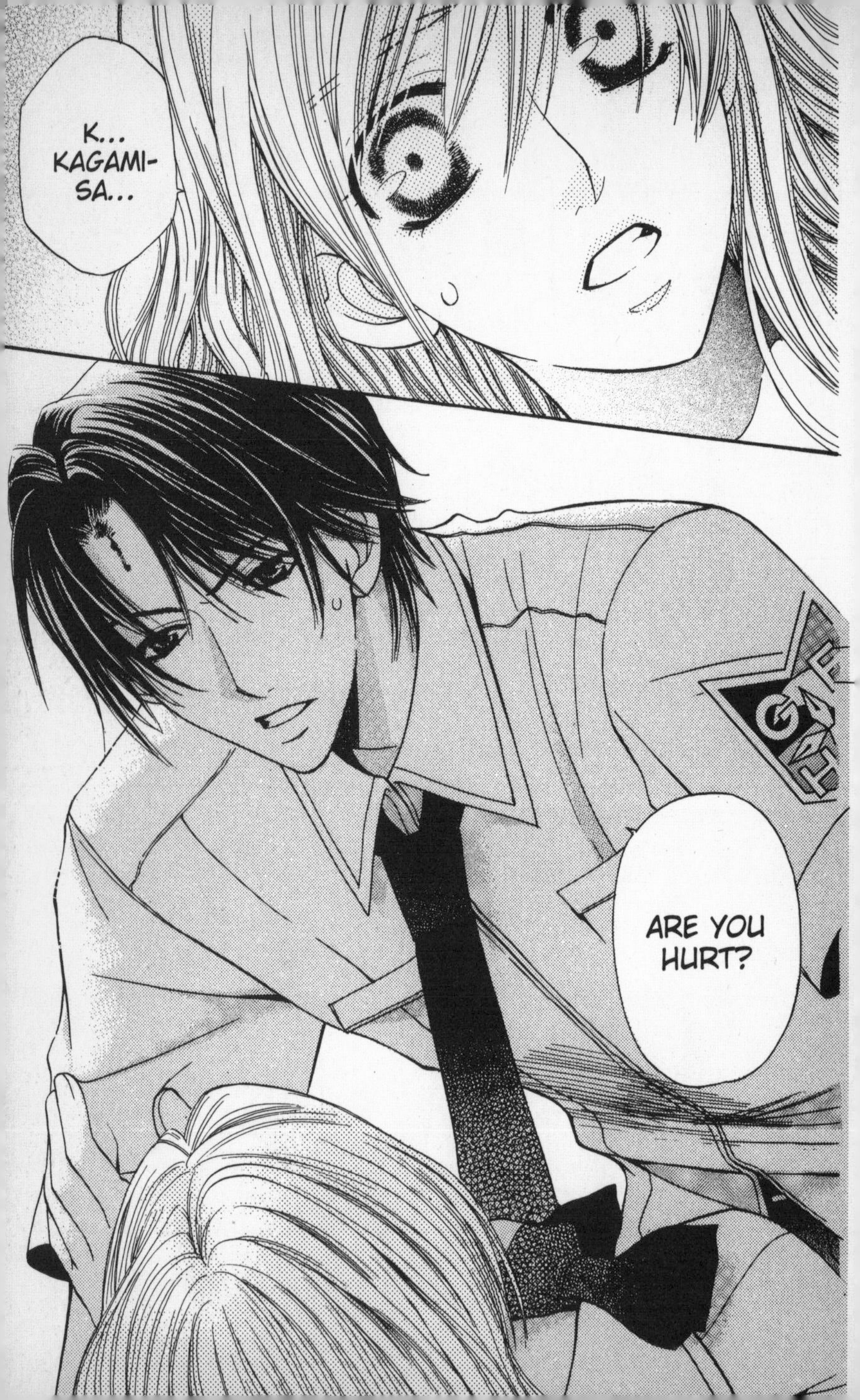
K... KAGAMI-SA...
ARE YOU HURT?

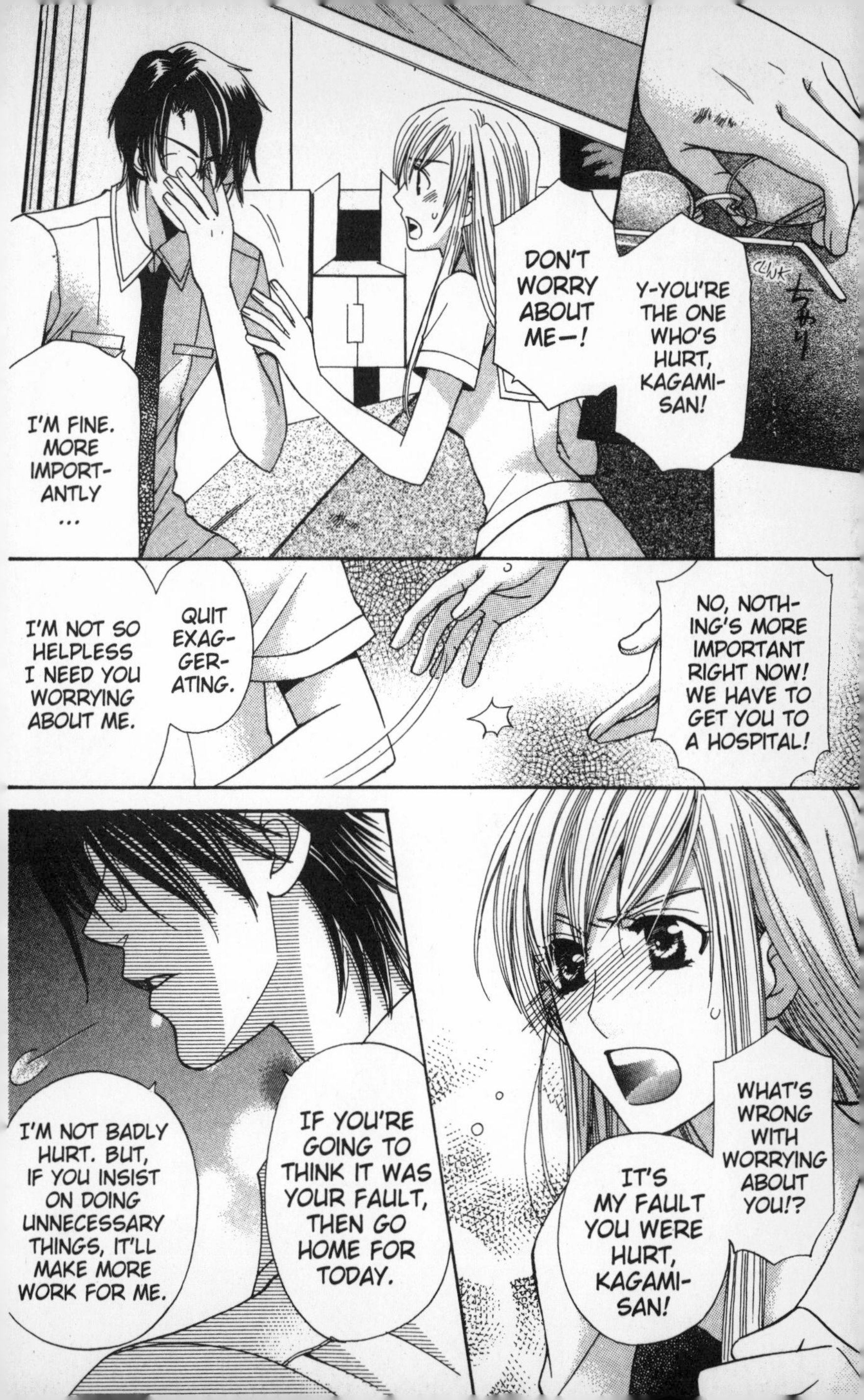
CLINK
ちゃり
Y-YOU'RE THE ONE WHO'S HURT, KAGAMI-SAN!
DON'T WORRY ABOUT ME—!
I'M FINE. MORE IMPORT-ANTLY ...
NO, NOTHING'S MORE IMPORTANT RIGHT NOW! WE HAVE TO GET YOU TO A HOSPITAL!
QUIT EXAG-GER-ATING.
I'M NOT SO HELPLESS I NEED YOU WORRYING ABOUT ME.
WHAT'S WRONG WITH WORRYING ABOUT YOU!?
IT'S MY FAULT YOU WERE HURT, KAGAMI-SAN!
IF YOU'RE GOING TO THINK IT WAS YOUR FAULT, THEN GO HOME FOR TODAY.
I'M NOT BADLY HURT. BUT, IF YOU INSIST ON DOING UNNECESSARY THINGS, IT'LL MAKE MORE WORK FOR ME.

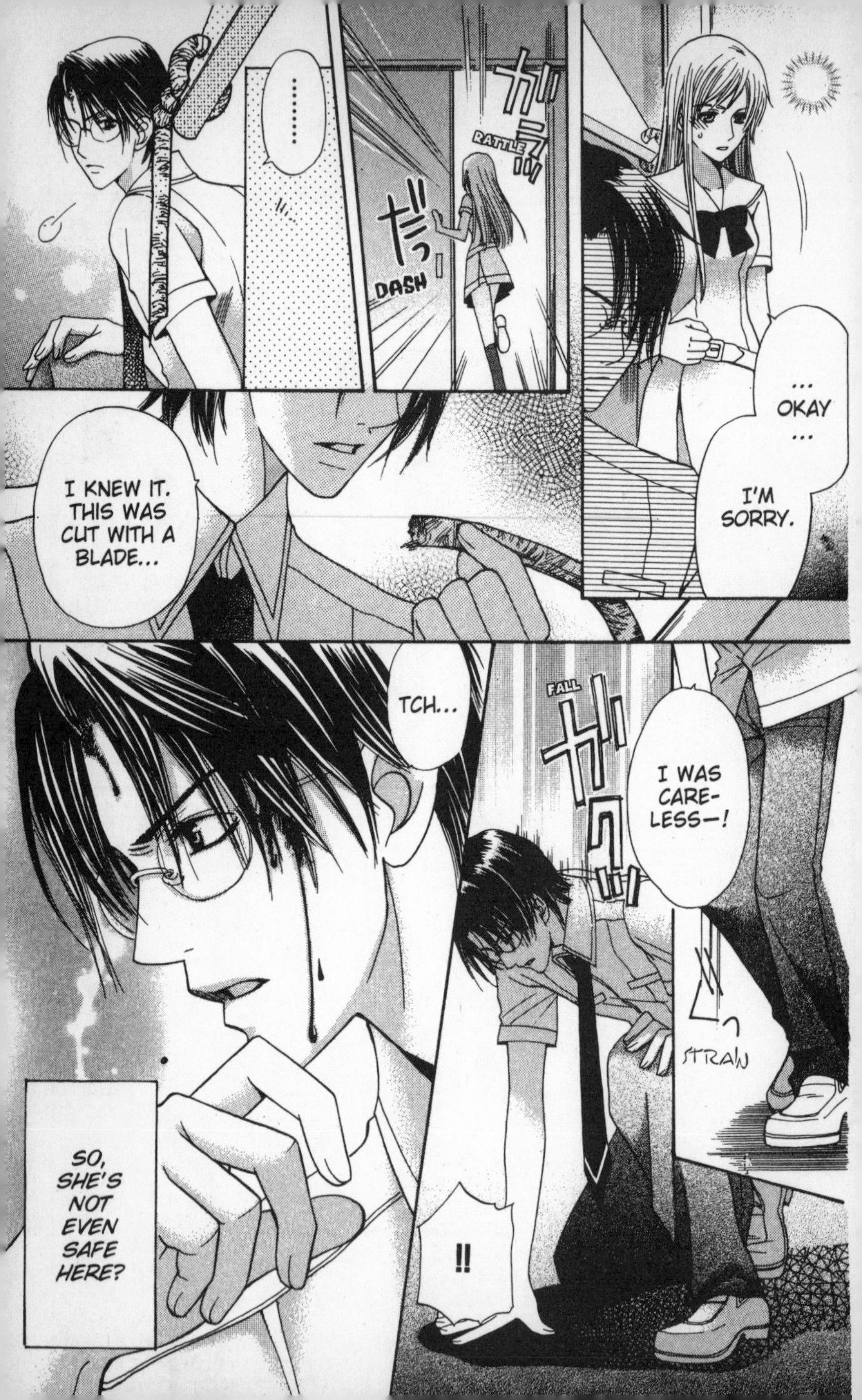
... OKAY ...
I'M SORRY.
ガラッ
RATTLE
だっ
DASH
......
I KNEW IT. THIS WAS CUT WITH A BLADE...
FALL
ガクッ
I WAS CARE-LESS—!
STRAIN
!!
TCH...
SO, SHE'S NOT EVEN SAFE HERE?

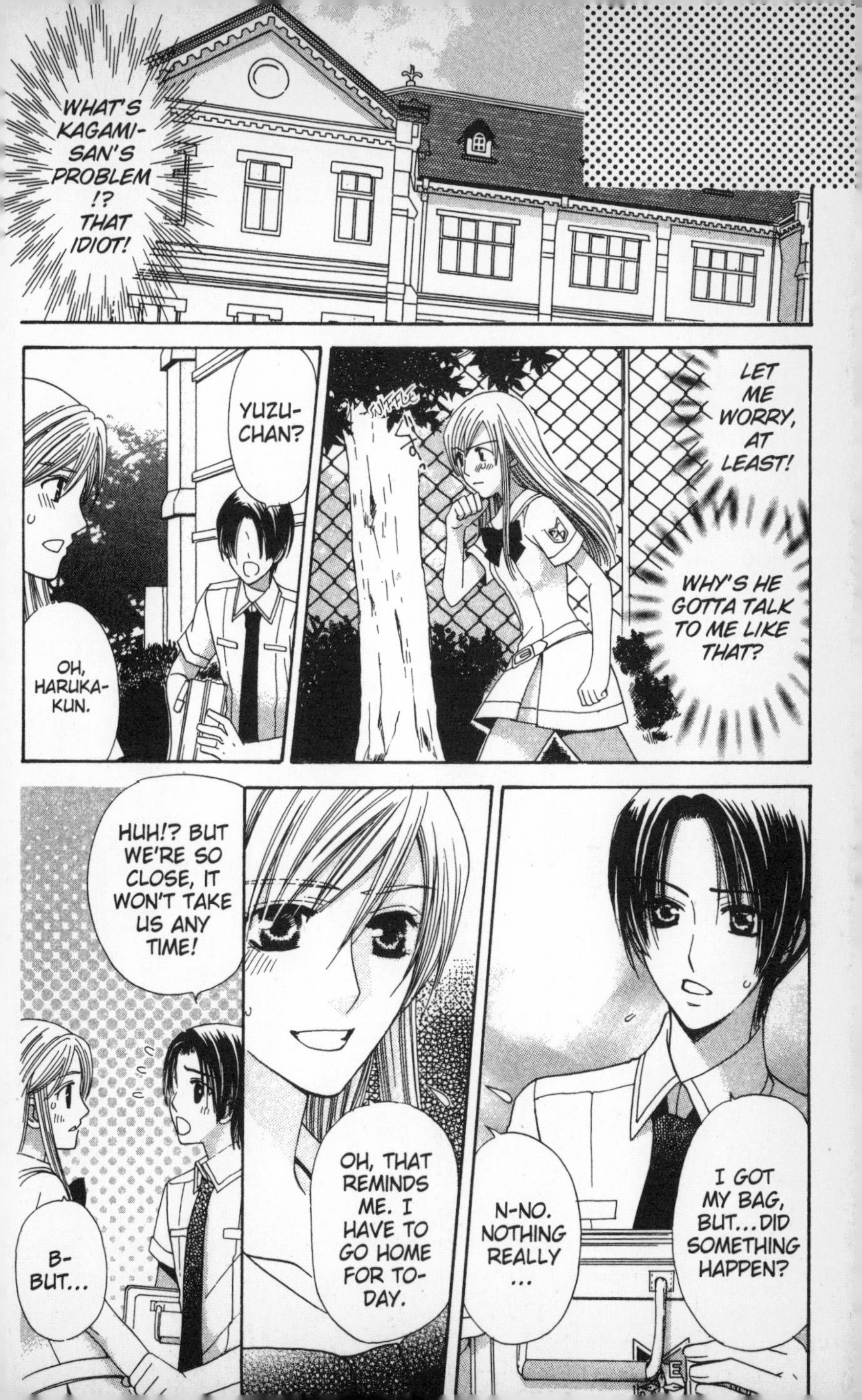
WHAT'S KAGAMI-SAN'S PROBLEM!? THAT IDIOT!
LET ME WORRY, AT LEAST!
WHY'S HE GOTTA TALK TO ME LIKE THAT?
YUZU-CHAN?
OH, HARUKA-KUN.
I GOT MY BAG, BUT...DID SOMETHING HAPPEN?
N-NO. NOTHING REALLY ...
OH, THAT REMINDS ME. I HAVE TO GO HOME FOR TO-DAY.
HUH!? BUT WE'RE SO CLOSE, IT WON'T TAKE US ANY TIME!
B-BUT...

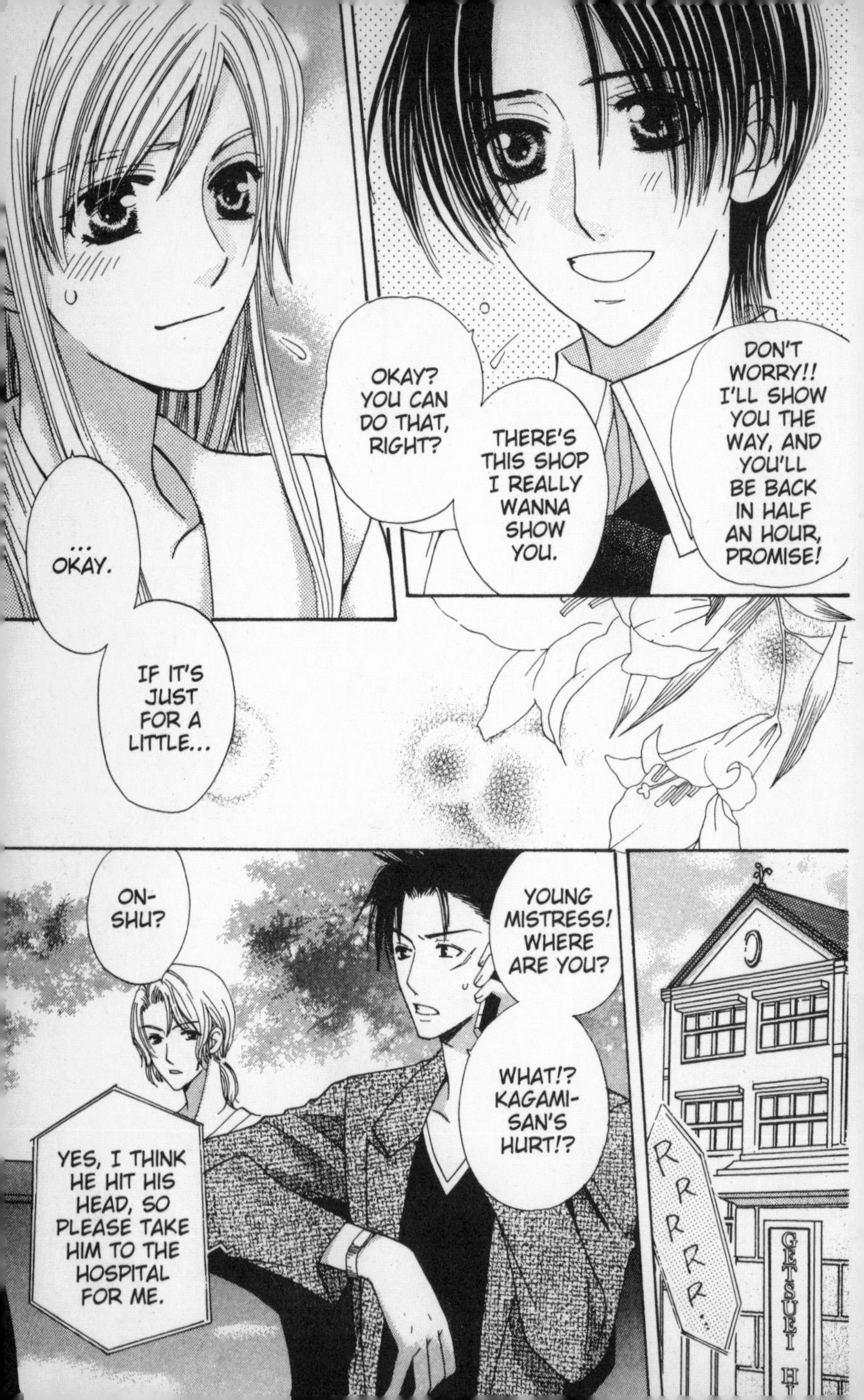
DON'T WORRY!! I'LL SHOW YOU THE WAY, AND YOU'LL BE BACK IN HALF AN HOUR, PROMISE!
THERE'S THIS SHOP I REALLY WANNA SHOW YOU.
OKAY? YOU CAN DO THAT, RIGHT?
... OKAY.
IF IT'S JUST FOR A LITTLE...
RRRR...
GETSUEI H
YOUNG MISTRESS! WHERE ARE YOU?
ON-SHU?
WHAT!? KAGAMI-SAN'S HURT!?
YES, I THINK HE HIT HIS HEAD, SO PLEASE TAKE HIM TO THE HOSPITAL FOR ME.

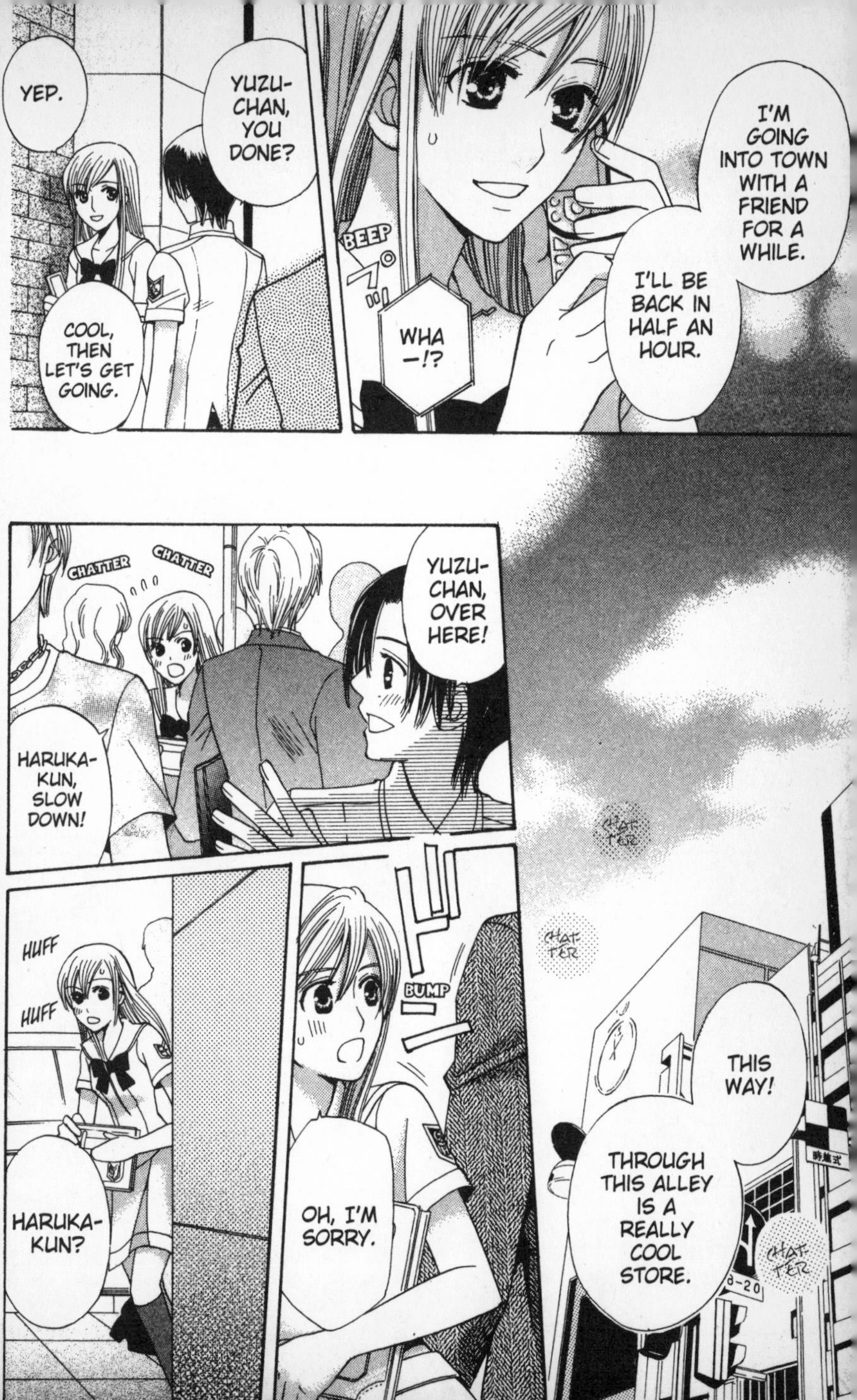
I'M GOING INTO TOWN WITH A FRIEND FOR A WHILE.
I'LL BE BACK IN HALF AN HOUR.
BEEP
WHA—!?
YUZU-CHAN, YOU DONE?
YEP.
COOL, THEN LET'S GET GOING.
CHAT-TER
CHAT-TER
THIS WAY!
THROUGH THIS ALLEY IS A REALLY COOL STORE.
CHAT-TER
YUZU-CHAN, OVER HERE!
CHATTER
CHATTER
HARUKA-KUN, SLOW DOWN!
BUMP
OH, I'M SORRY.
HUFF
HUFF
HARUKA-KUN?

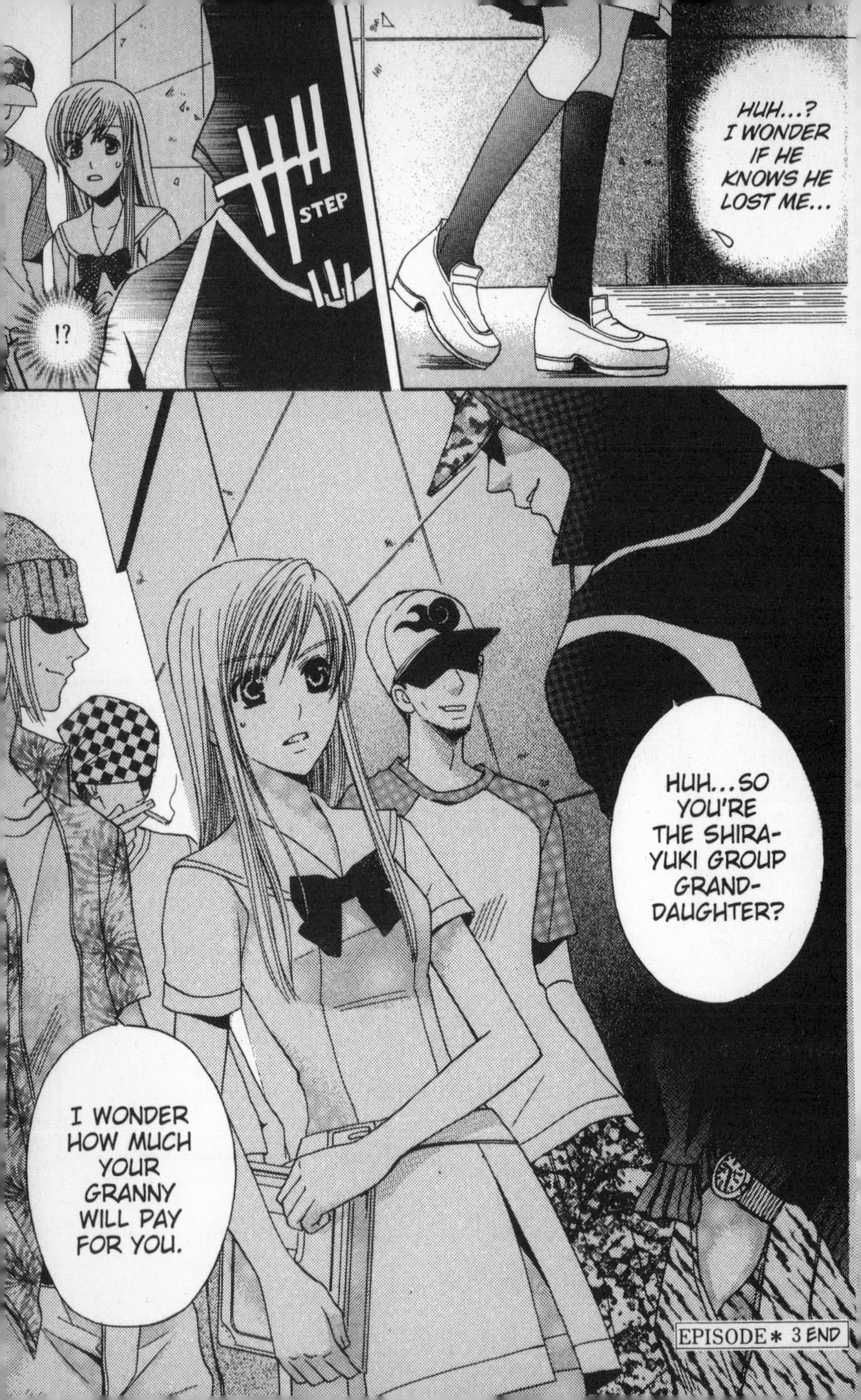
HUH...? I WONDER IF HE KNOWS HE LOST ME...
STEP
!?
HUH...SO YOU'RE THE SHIRA-YUKI GROUP GRAND-DAUGHTER?
I WONDER HOW MUCH YOUR GRANNY WILL PAY FOR YOU.
EPISODE * 3 END

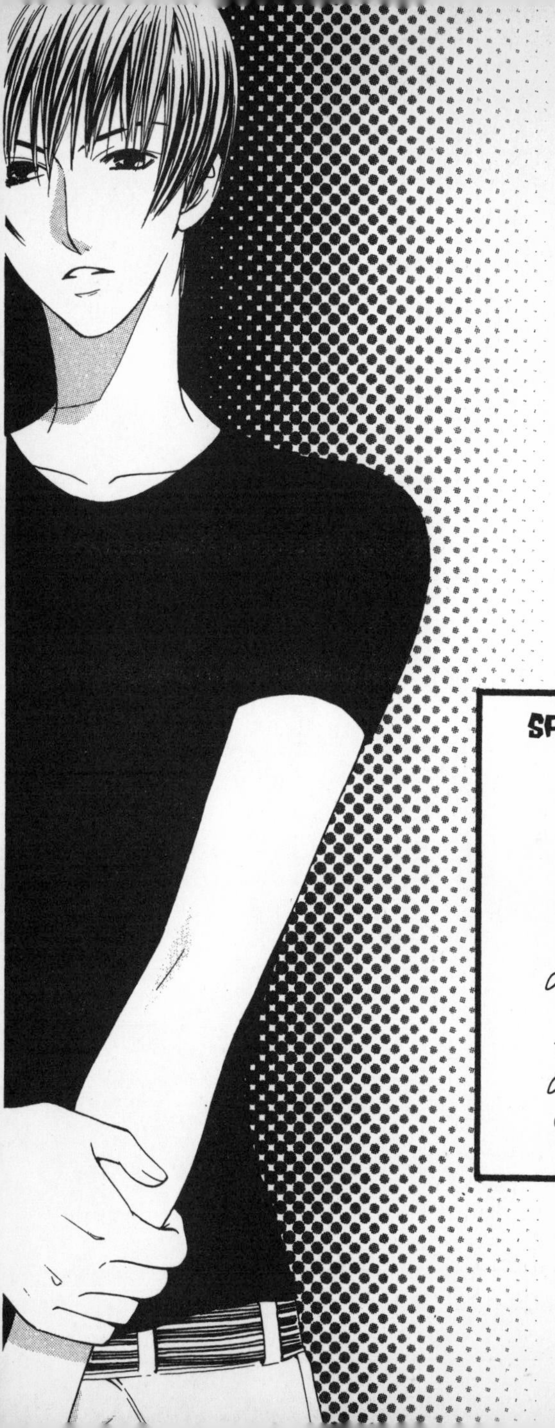

SPECIAL THANKS

Thanks for always saving my butt!

Hariguchi-san,
Fujiyama-san
My manager,
Kishima-san

And to everyone who read this book!
Thank you so much!
And best regards as you follow the story hereafter, too!

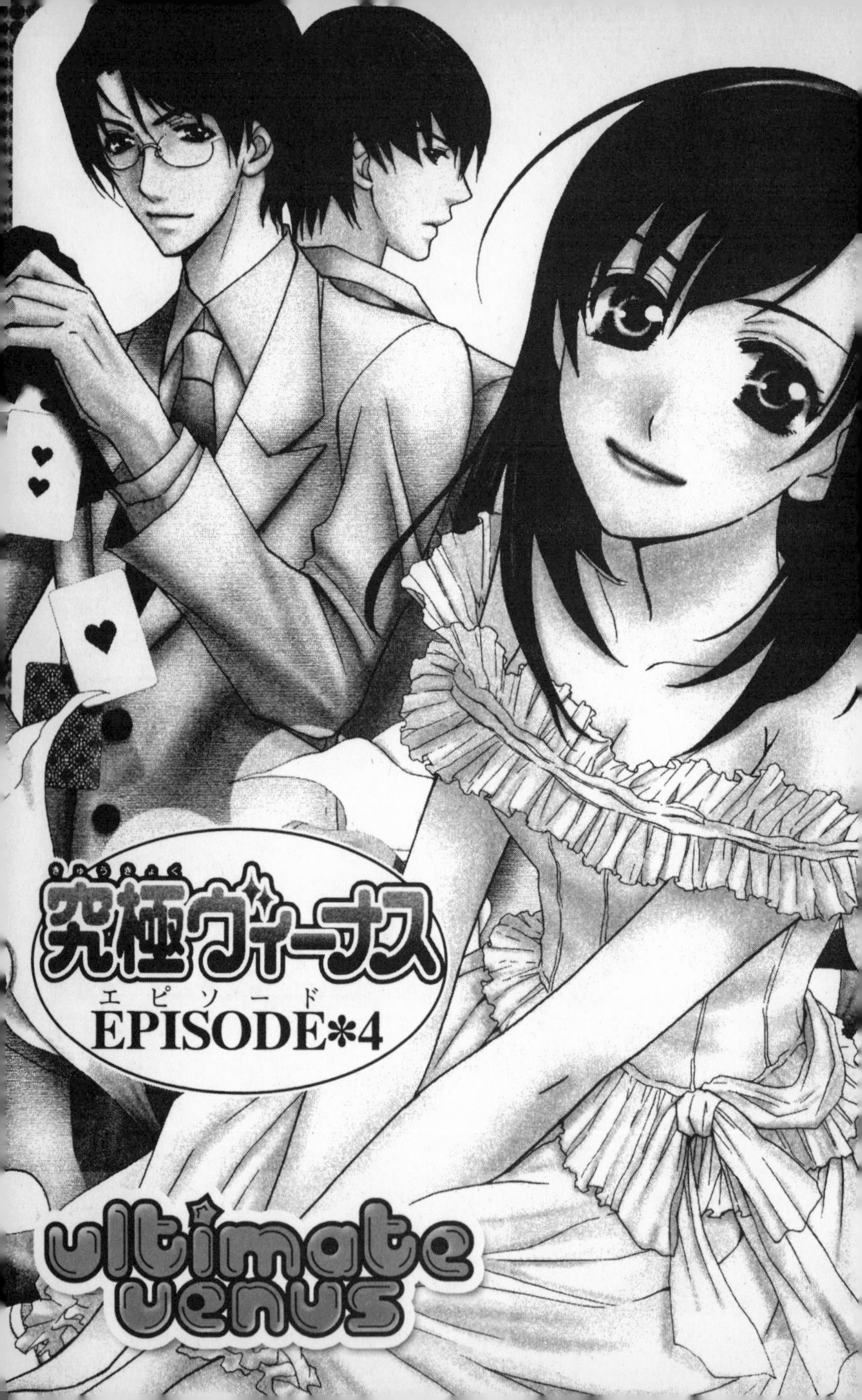
究極ヴィーナス
エピソード
EPISODE*4
ultimate venus

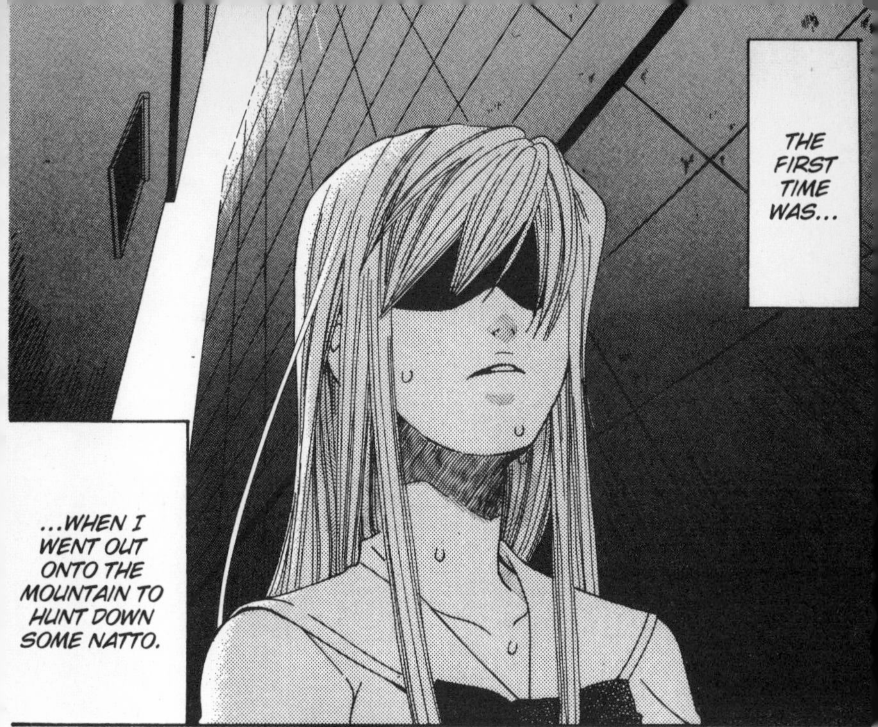
THE FIRST TIME WAS...
...WHEN I WENT OUT ONTO THE MOUNTAIN TO HUNT DOWN SOME NATTO.

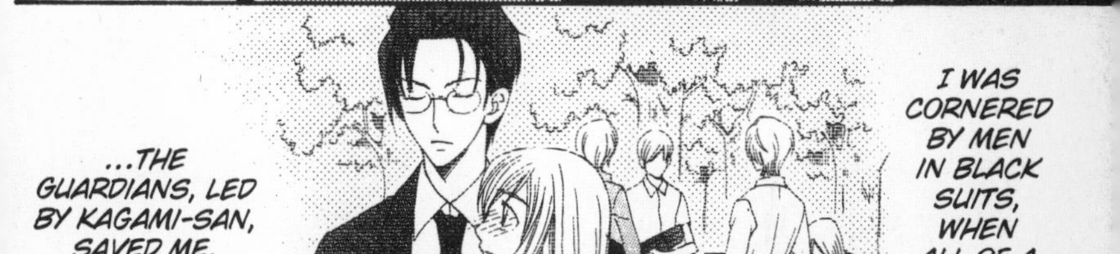
I WAS CORNERED BY MEN IN BLACK SUITS, WHEN ALL OF A SUDDEN...
...THE GUARDIANS, LED BY KAGAMI-SAN, SAVED ME.

Hassaku Kagami (age 21)

Birthday: June 17th

Blood Type: AB

Hobbies: Strategy, all martial arts

Has .8/.8 vision. At his job, since he's taken lightly for being so young, he wears glasses to seem older.

It's hard to write everything about his background...

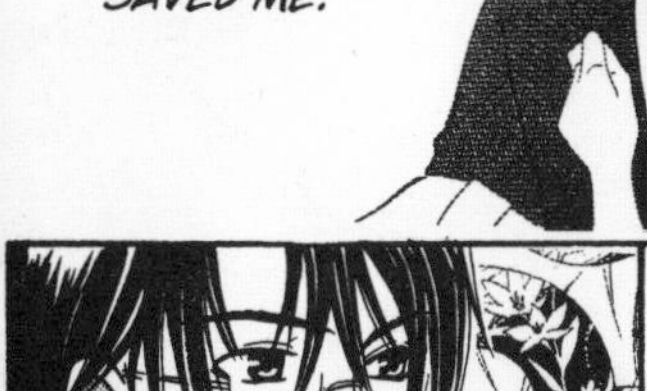

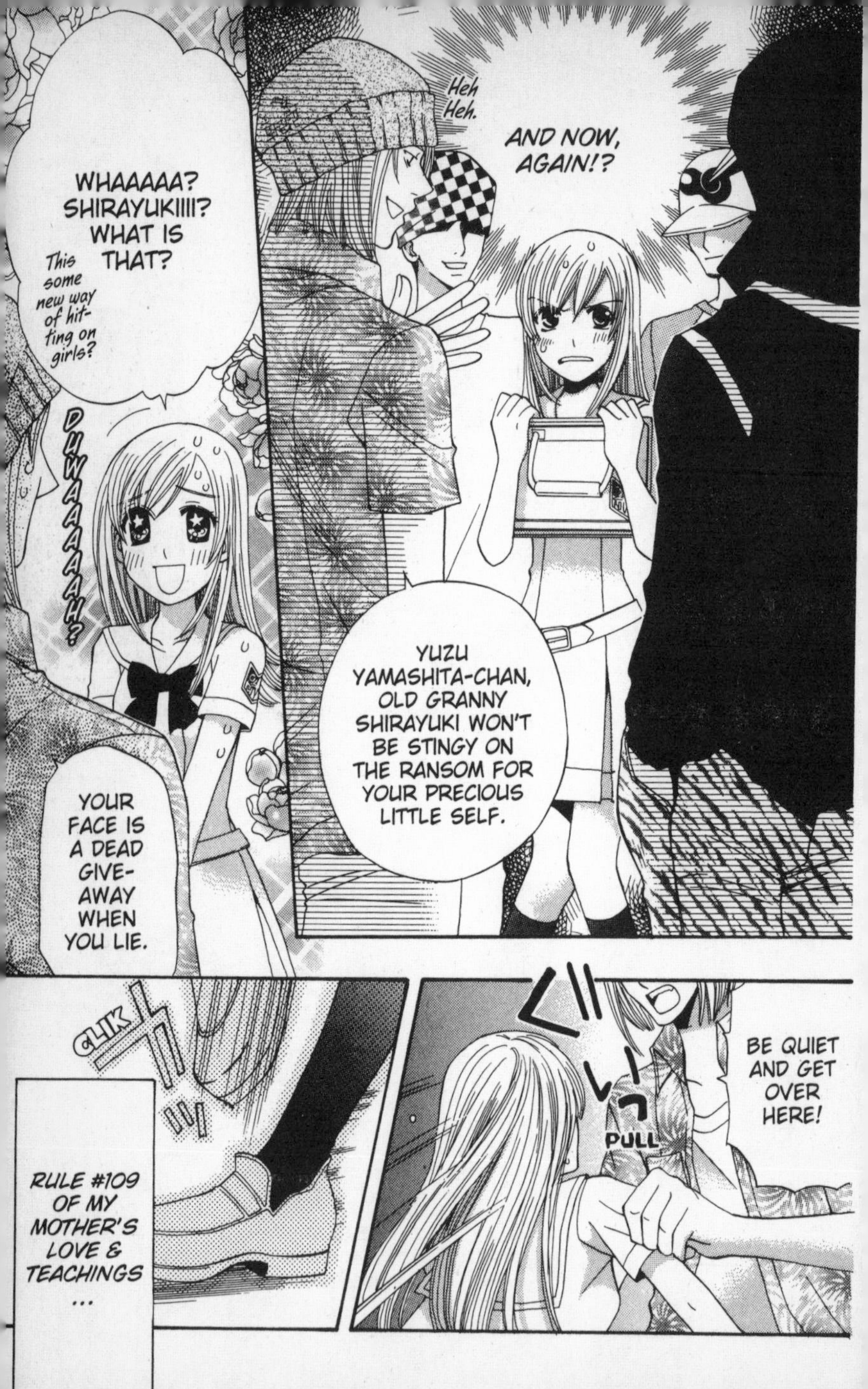
AND NOW, AGAIN!?
Heh Heh.
YUZU YAMASHITA-CHAN, OLD GRANNY SHIRAYUKI WON'T BE STINGY ON THE RANSOM FOR YOUR PRECIOUS LITTLE SELF.
WHAAAAA? SHIRAYUKIIII? WHAT IS THAT?
This some new way of hit-ting on girls?
DUWAAAAAAAH?
YOUR FACE IS A DEAD GIVE-AWAY WHEN YOU LIE.
BE QUIET AND GET OVER HERE!
PULL
CLIK
RULE #109 OF MY MOTHER'S LOVE & TEACHINGS ...

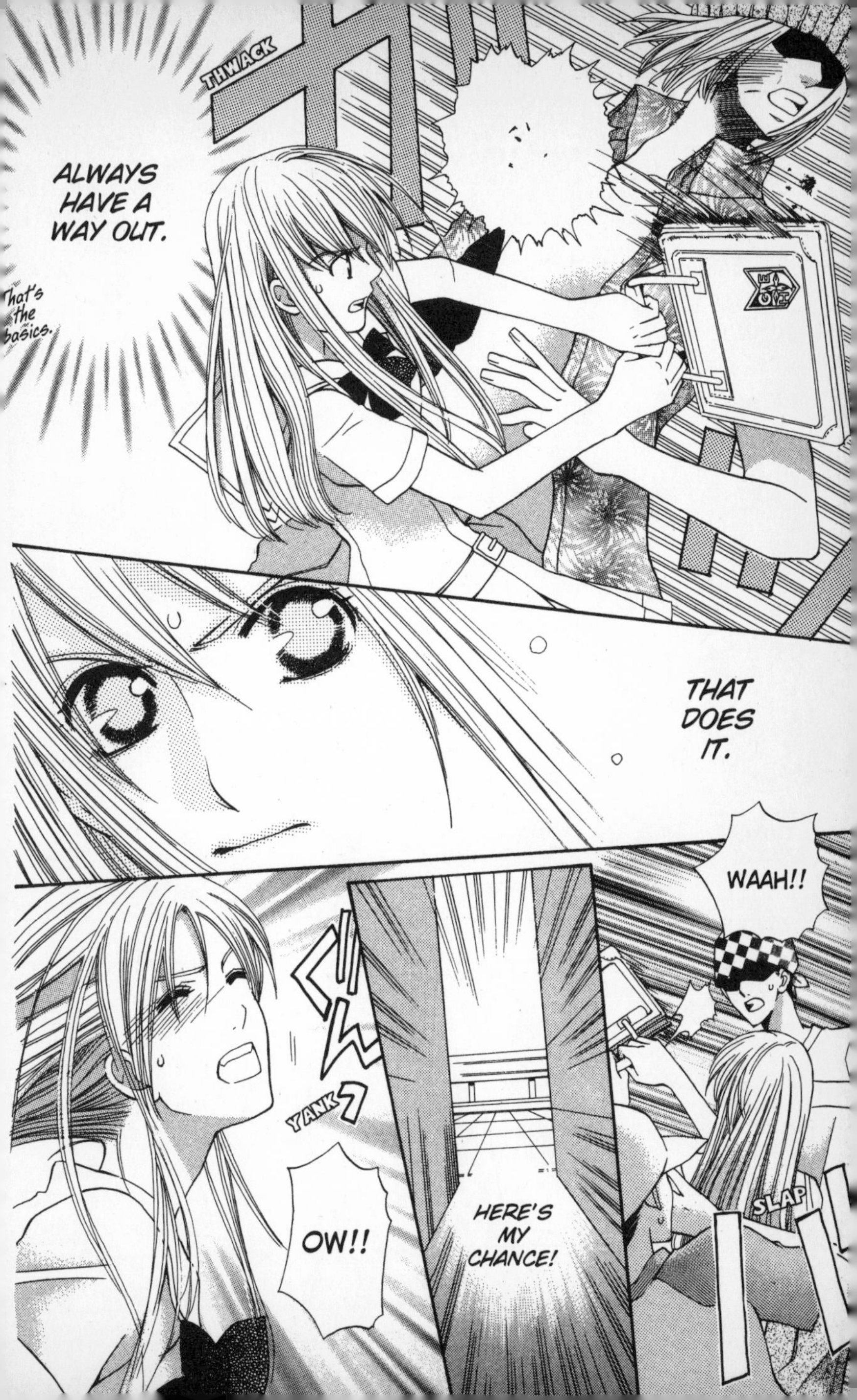
THWACK
ALWAYS HAVE A WAY OUT.
That's the basics.
THAT DOES IT.
WAAH!!
SLAP
HERE'S MY CHANCE!
YANK
OW!!

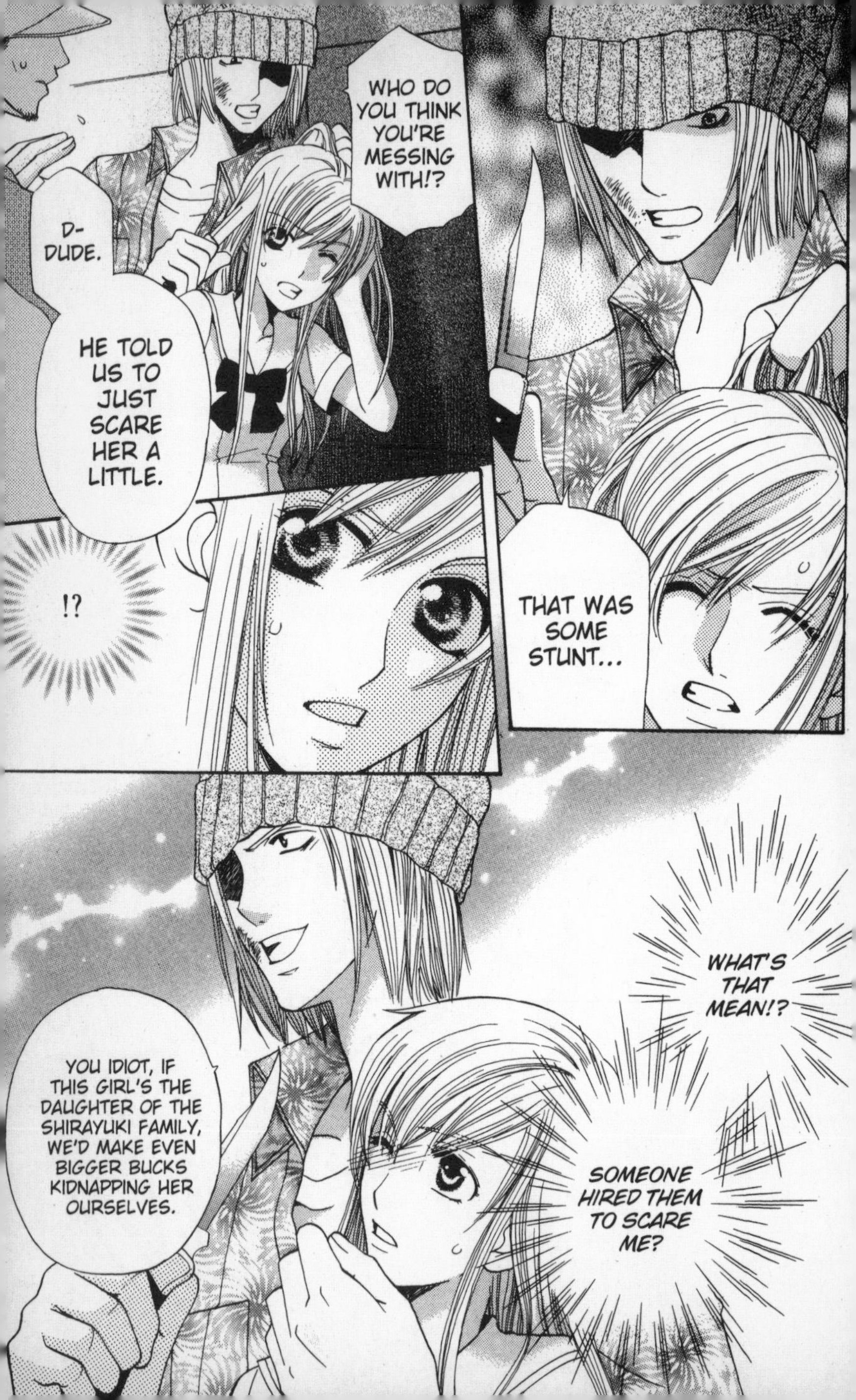
WHO DO YOU THINK YOU'RE MESSING WITH!?
D-DUDE.
HE TOLD US TO JUST SCARE HER A LITTLE.
THAT WAS SOME STUNT...
!?
WHAT'S THAT MEAN!?
YOU IDIOT, IF THIS GIRL'S THE DAUGHTER OF THE SHIRAYUKI FAMILY, WE'D MAKE EVEN BIGGER BUCKS KIDNAPPING HER OURSELVES.
SOMEONE HIRED THEM TO SCARE ME?

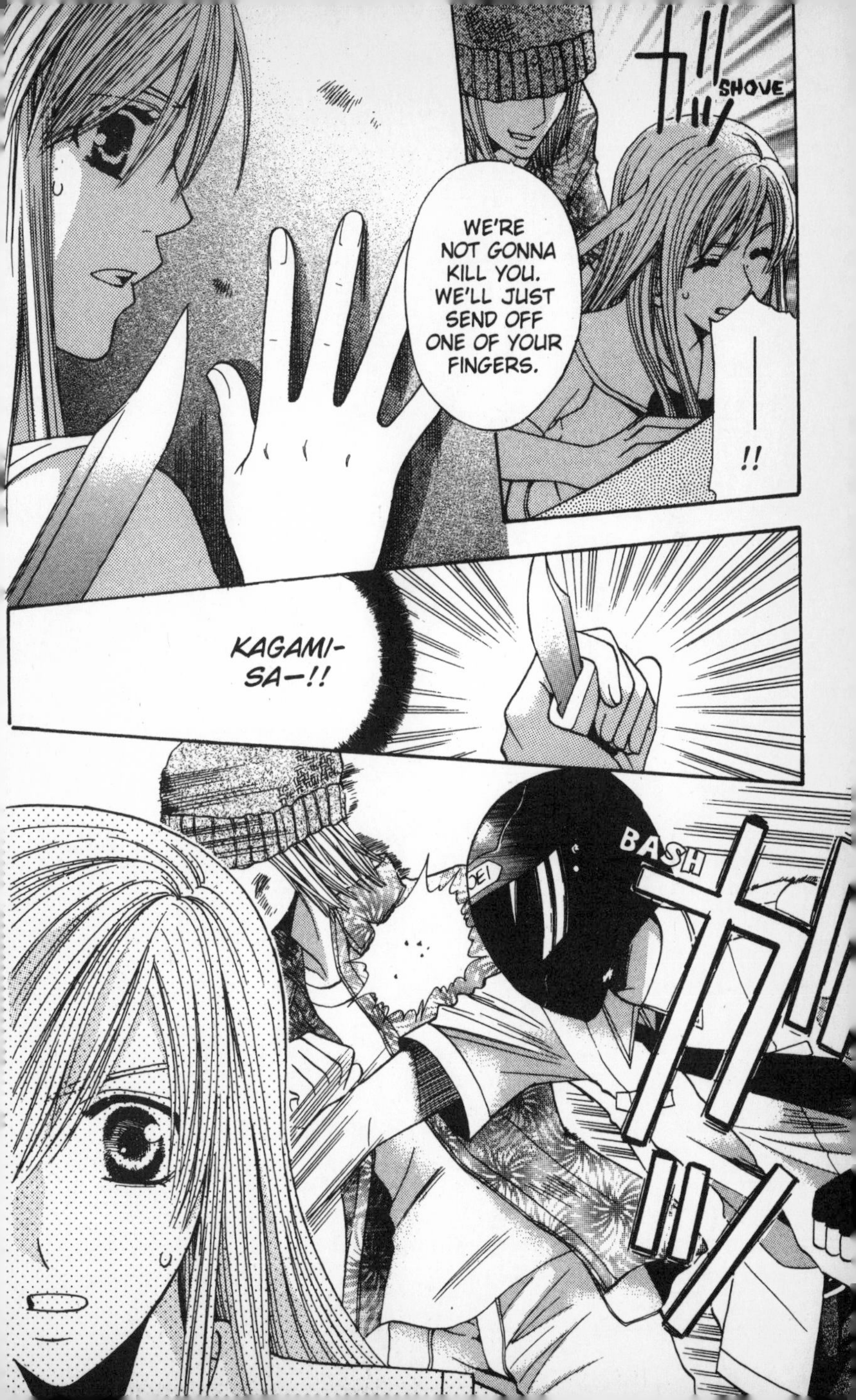

SHOVE
WE'RE NOT GONNA KILL YOU. WE'LL JUST SEND OFF ONE OF YOUR FINGERS.
!!
KAGAMI-SA-!!
BASH

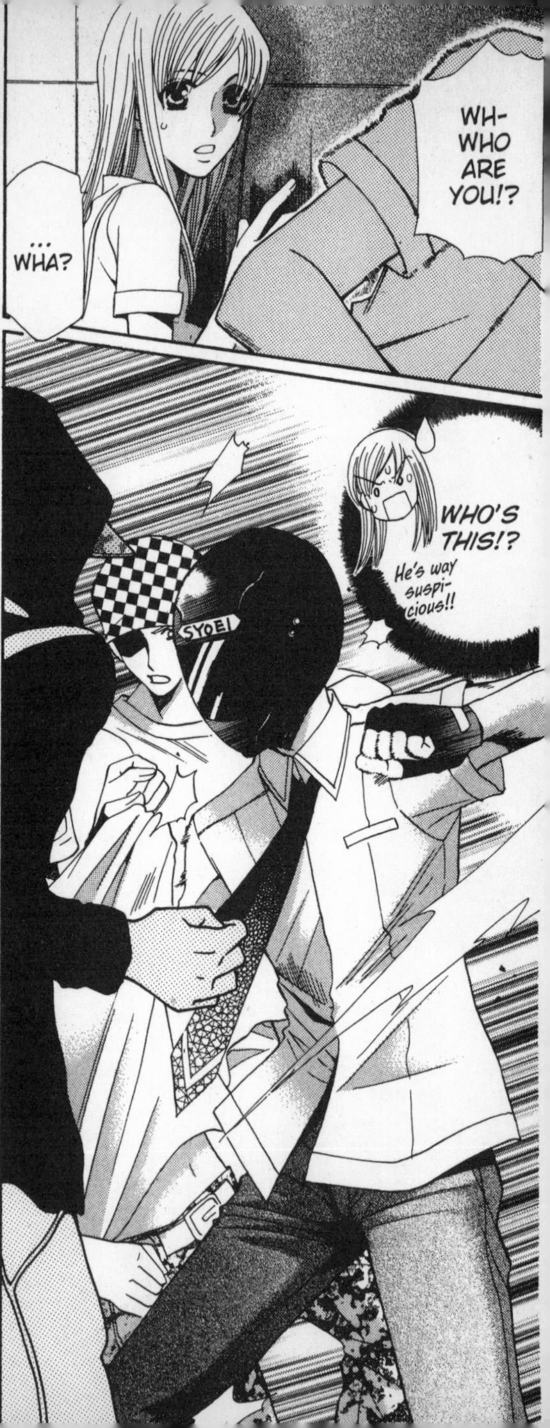
WH- WHO ARE YOU!?
... WHA?
WHO'S THIS!?
He's way suspicious!!
SYOEI

CURRENT OBSESSIONS

I just keep writing all over this manga, don't I? Currently, I'm challenging myself with reading a lot of Western books.

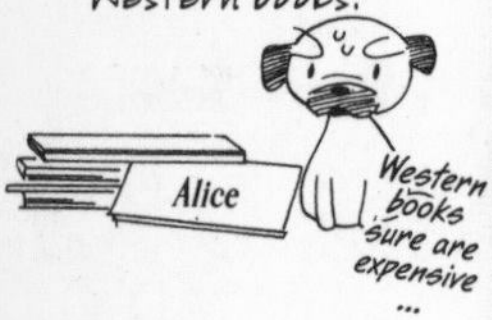
Alice
Western books sure are expensive ...

When I was a student, I was no good at English! I had very little confidence, so I read books at low-levels to improve, and eventually that lack of confidence went away. To be quite honest, I'm very happy with myself...
My dream is to one day read the sci-fi novel of a favorite author of mine who hasn't been translated yet...!!

Though it seems that'll take quite some time.

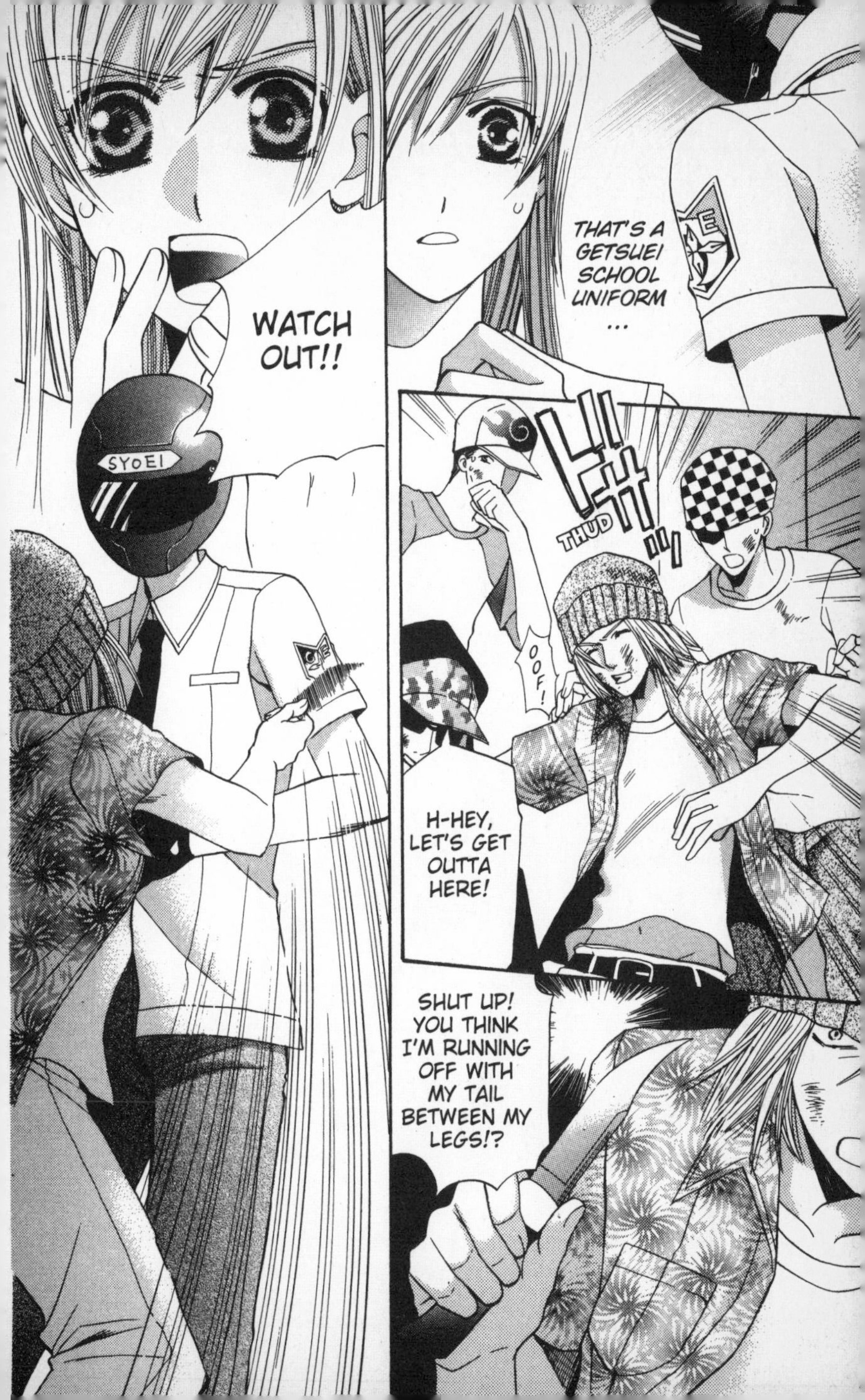
THAT'S A GETSUEI SCHOOL UNIFORM...
THUD
OOF!
H-HEY, LET'S GET OUTTA HERE!
SHUT UP! YOU THINK I'M RUNNING OFF WITH MY TAIL BETWEEN MY LEGS!?
WATCH OUT!!
SYOEI

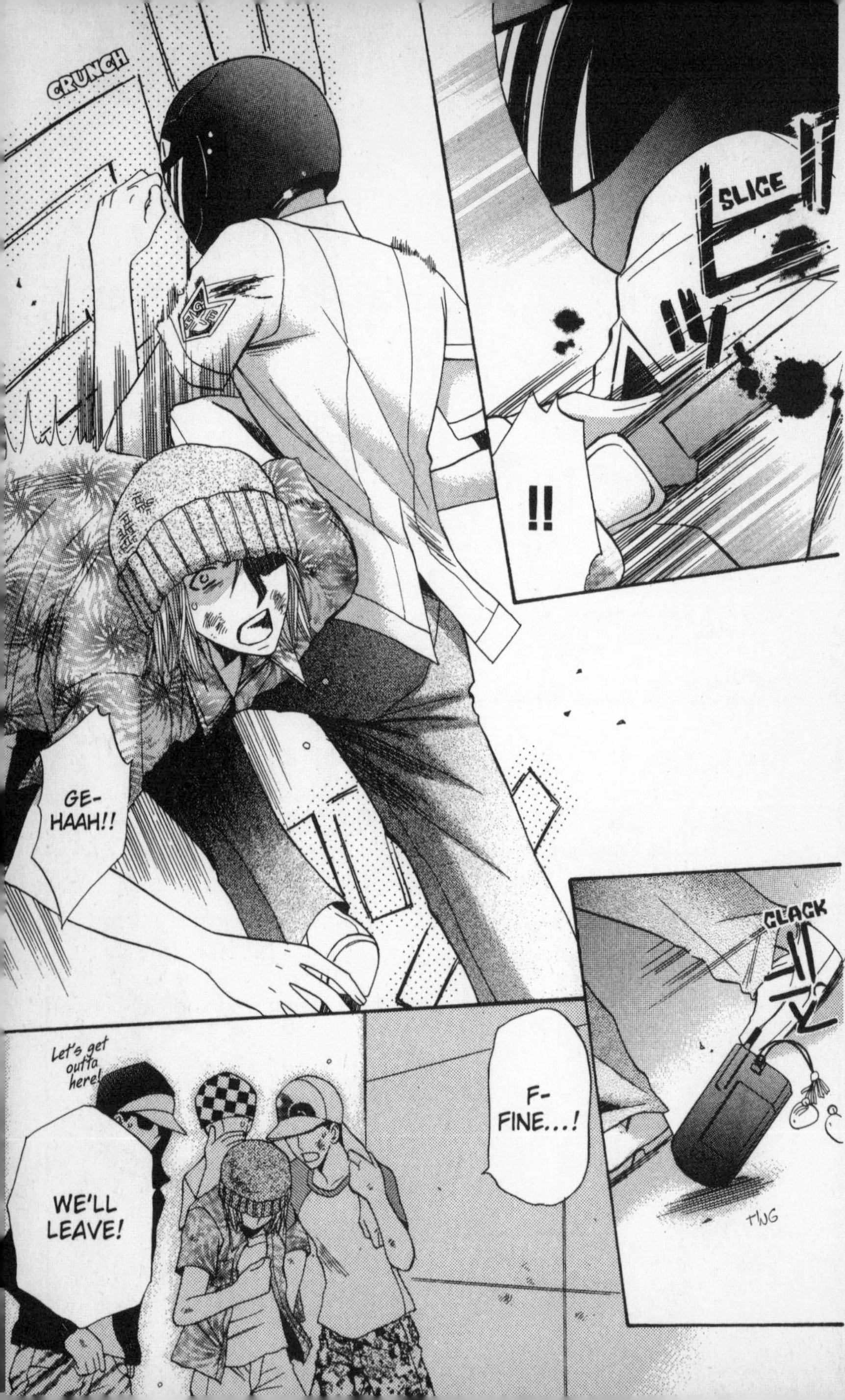
SLICE
!!
CRUNCH
GE-HAAH!!
CLACK
TING
F-FINE...!
Let's get outta here!
WE'LL LEAVE!

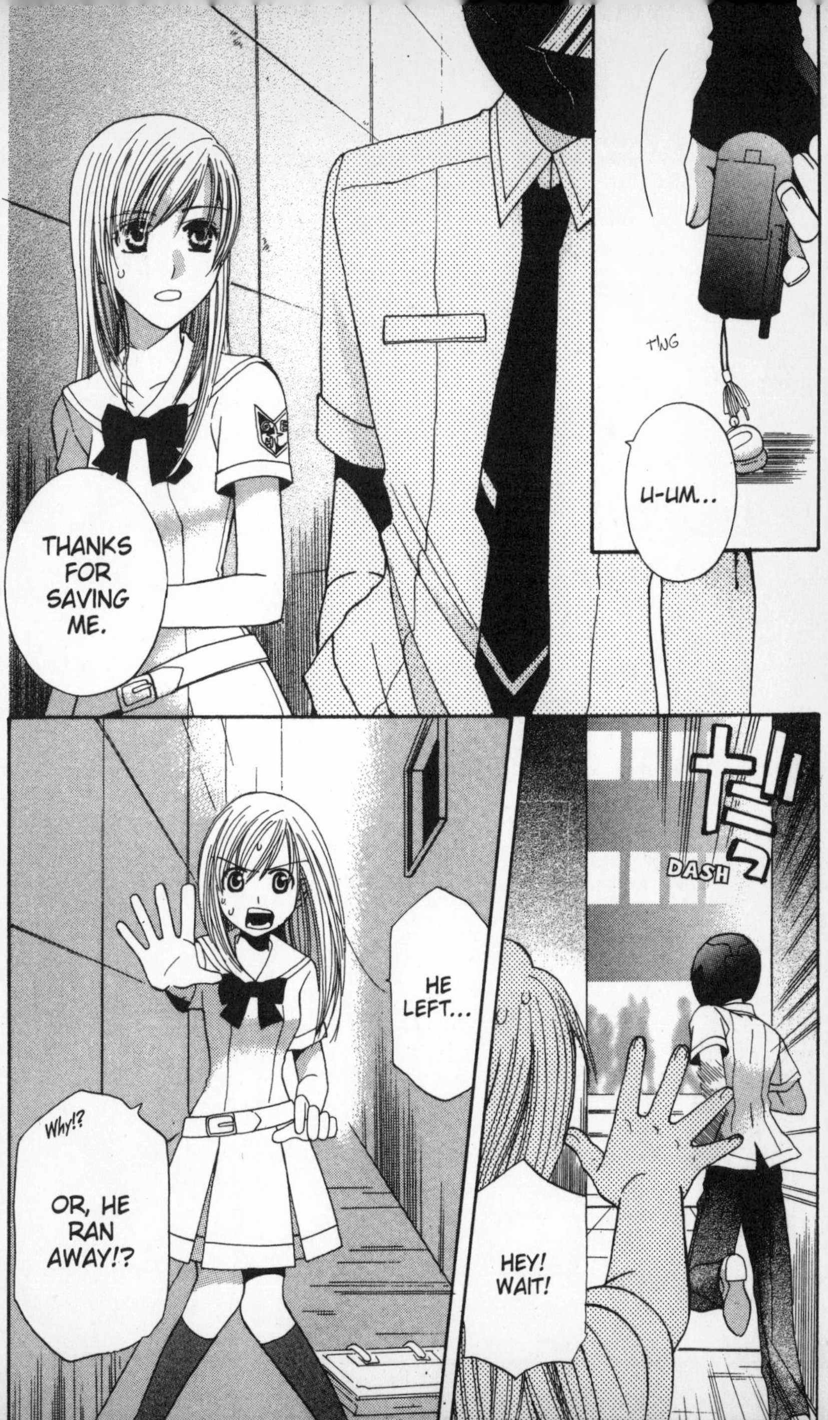

TWG
U-UM...
THANKS FOR SAVING ME.
DASH
HEY! WAIT!
HE LEFT...
Why!?
OR, HE RAN AWAY!?

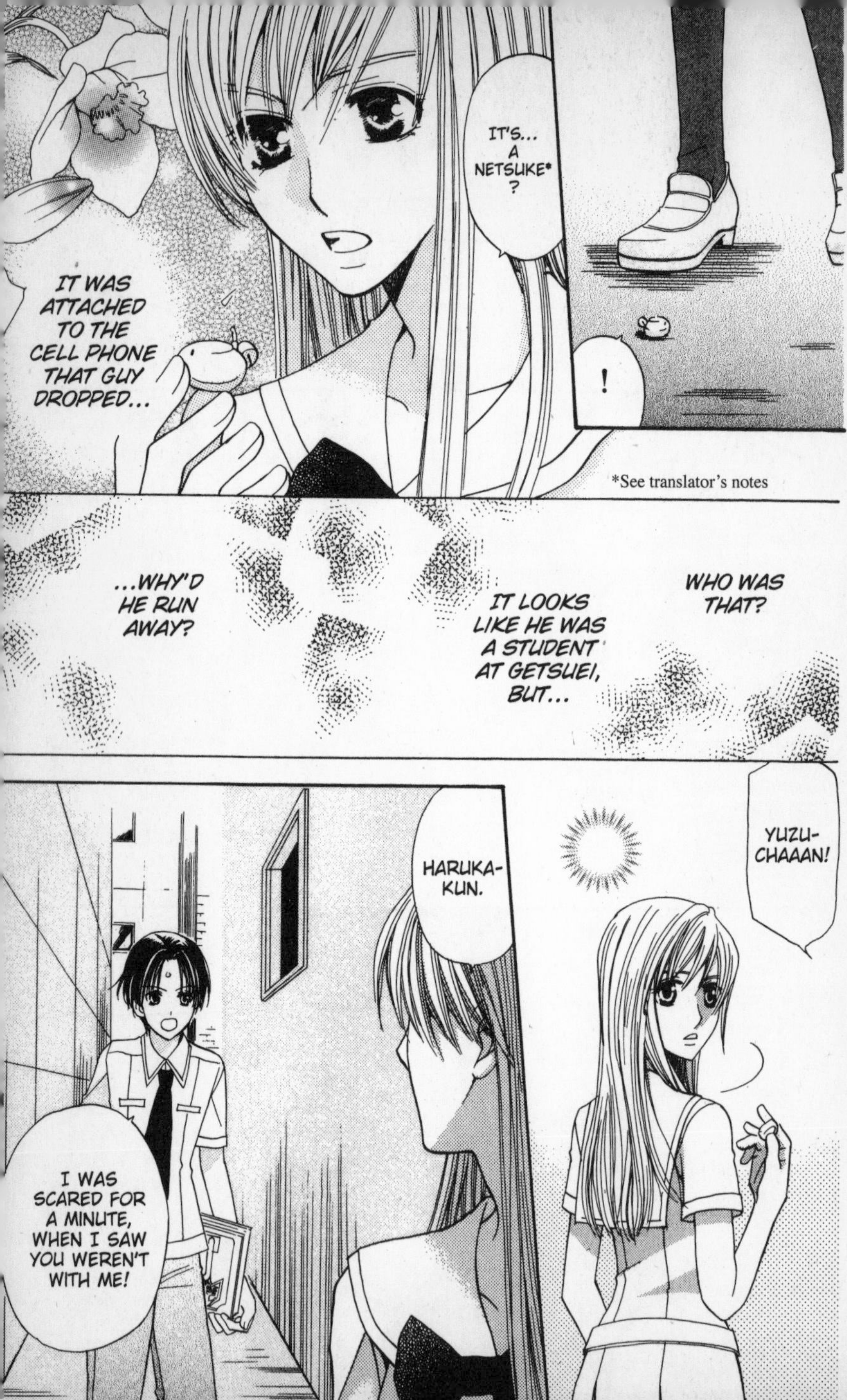
!
IT'S... A NETSUKE* ?
IT WAS ATTACHED TO THE CELL PHONE THAT GUY DROPPED...
WHO WAS THAT?
IT LOOKS LIKE HE WAS A STUDENT AT GETSUEI, BUT...
...WHY'D HE RUN AWAY?
YUZU-CHAAAN!
HARUKA-KUN.
I WAS SCARED FOR A MINUTE, WHEN I SAW YOU WEREN'T WITH ME!
*See translator's notes

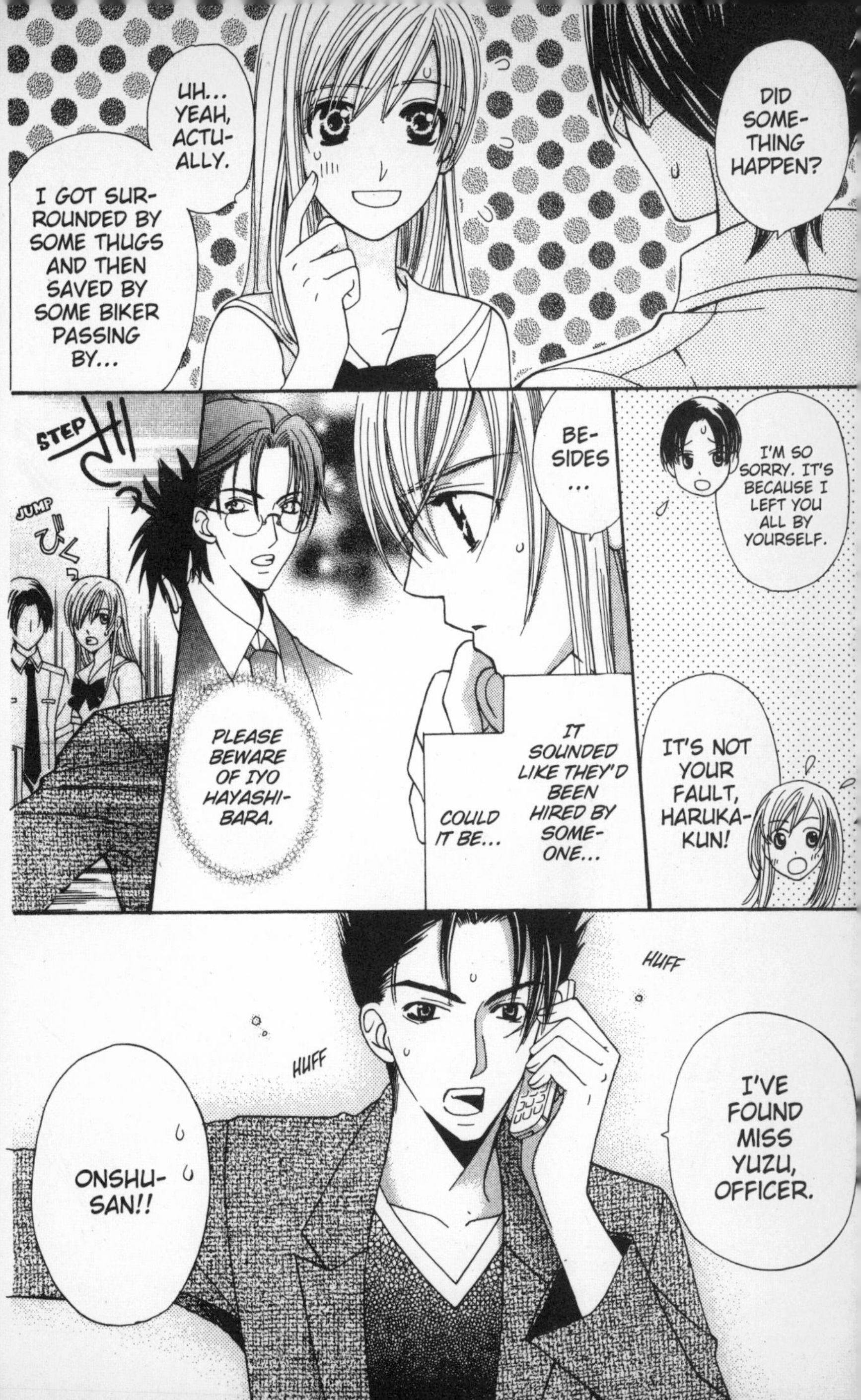
DID SOMETHING HAPPEN?
UH... YEAH, ACTUALLY.
I GOT SURROUNDED BY SOME THUGS AND THEN SAVED BY SOME BIKER PASSING BY...
I'M SO SORRY. IT'S BECAUSE I LEFT YOU ALL BY YOURSELF.
IT'S NOT YOUR FAULT, HARUKA-KUN!
BESIDES...
IT SOUNDED LIKE THEY'D BEEN HIRED BY SOMEONE...
COULD IT BE...
STEP
JUMP
PLEASE BEWARE OF IYO HAYASHIBARA.
HUFF
I'VE FOUND MISS YUZU, OFFICER.
HUFF
ONSHU-SAN!!

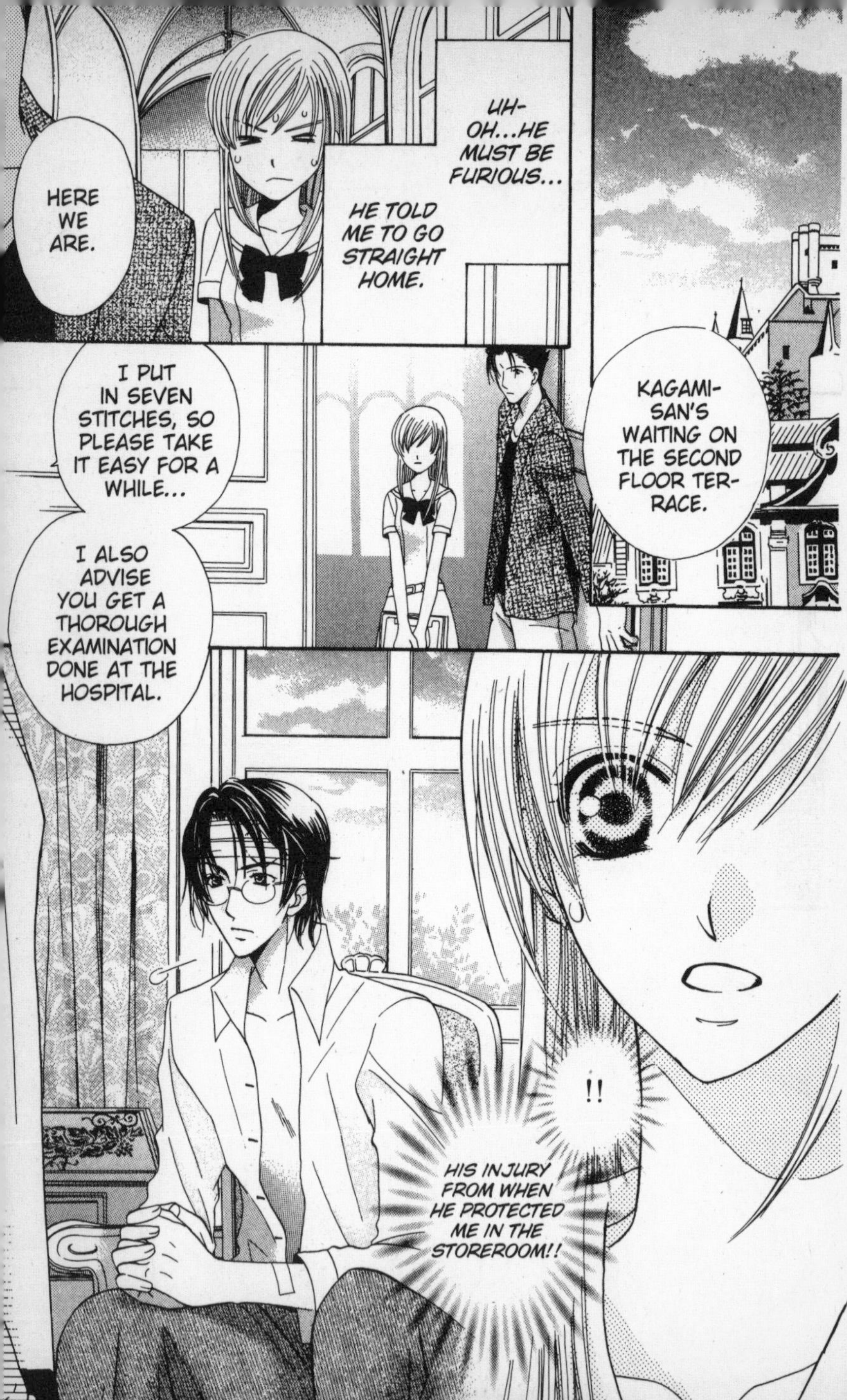
KAGAMI-SAN'S WAITING ON THE SECOND FLOOR TER-RACE.
UH-OH...HE MUST BE FURIOUS...
HE TOLD ME TO GO STRAIGHT HOME.
HERE WE ARE.
I PUT IN SEVEN STITCHES, SO PLEASE TAKE IT EASY FOR A WHILE...
I ALSO ADVISE YOU GET A THOROUGH EXAMINATION DONE AT THE HOSPITAL.
!!
HIS INJURY FROM WHEN HE PROTECTED ME IN THE STOREROOM!!

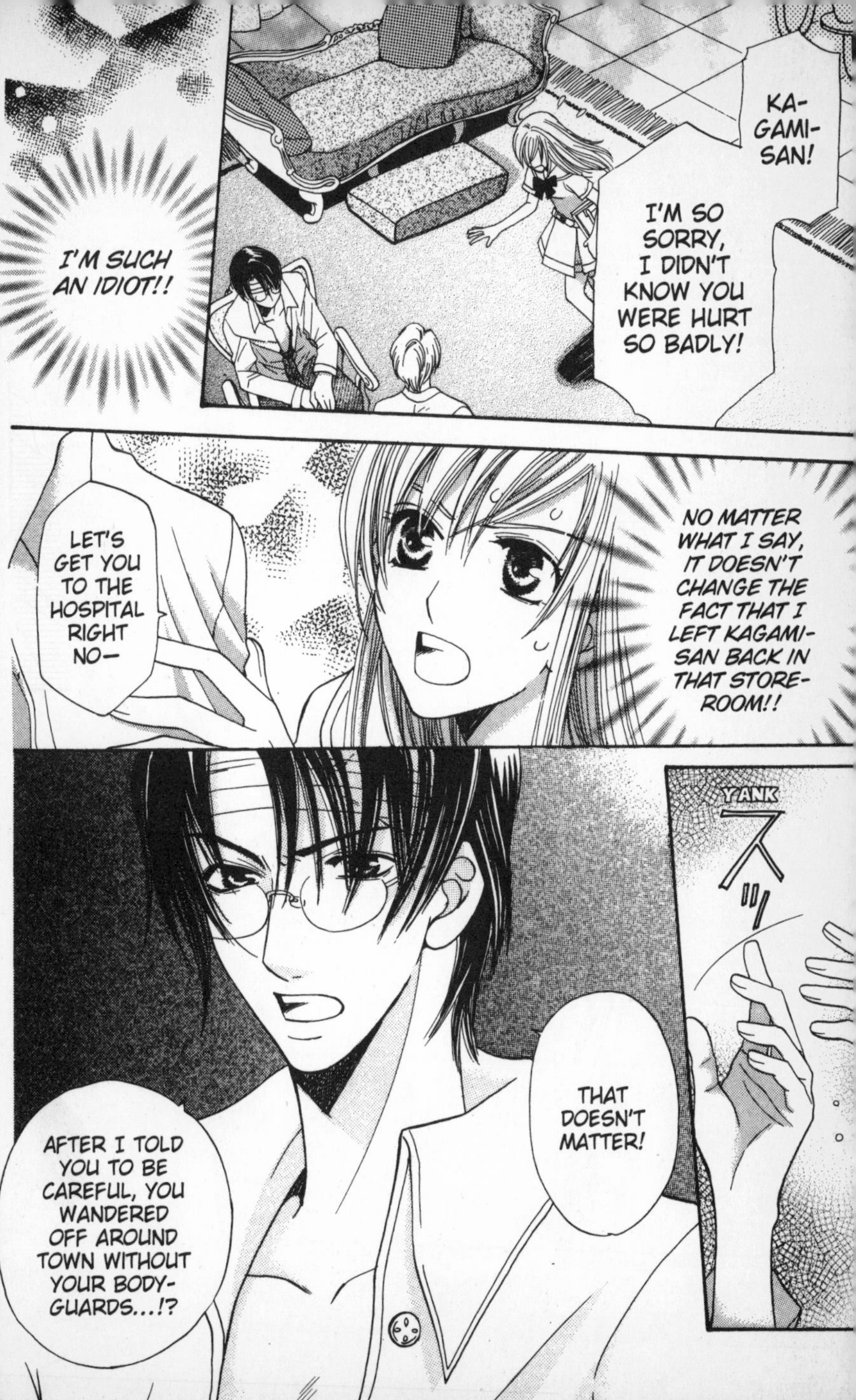
KA-GAMI-SAN!
I'M SO SORRY, I DIDN'T KNOW YOU WERE HURT SO BADLY!
I'M SUCH AN IDIOT!!
NO MATTER WHAT I SAY, IT DOESN'T CHANGE THE FACT THAT I LEFT KAGAMI-SAN BACK IN THAT STORE-ROOM!!
LET'S GET YOU TO THE HOSPITAL RIGHT NO—
YANK
THAT DOESN'T MATTER!
AFTER I TOLD YOU TO BE CAREFUL, YOU WANDERED OFF AROUND TOWN WITHOUT YOUR BODY-GUARDS...!?

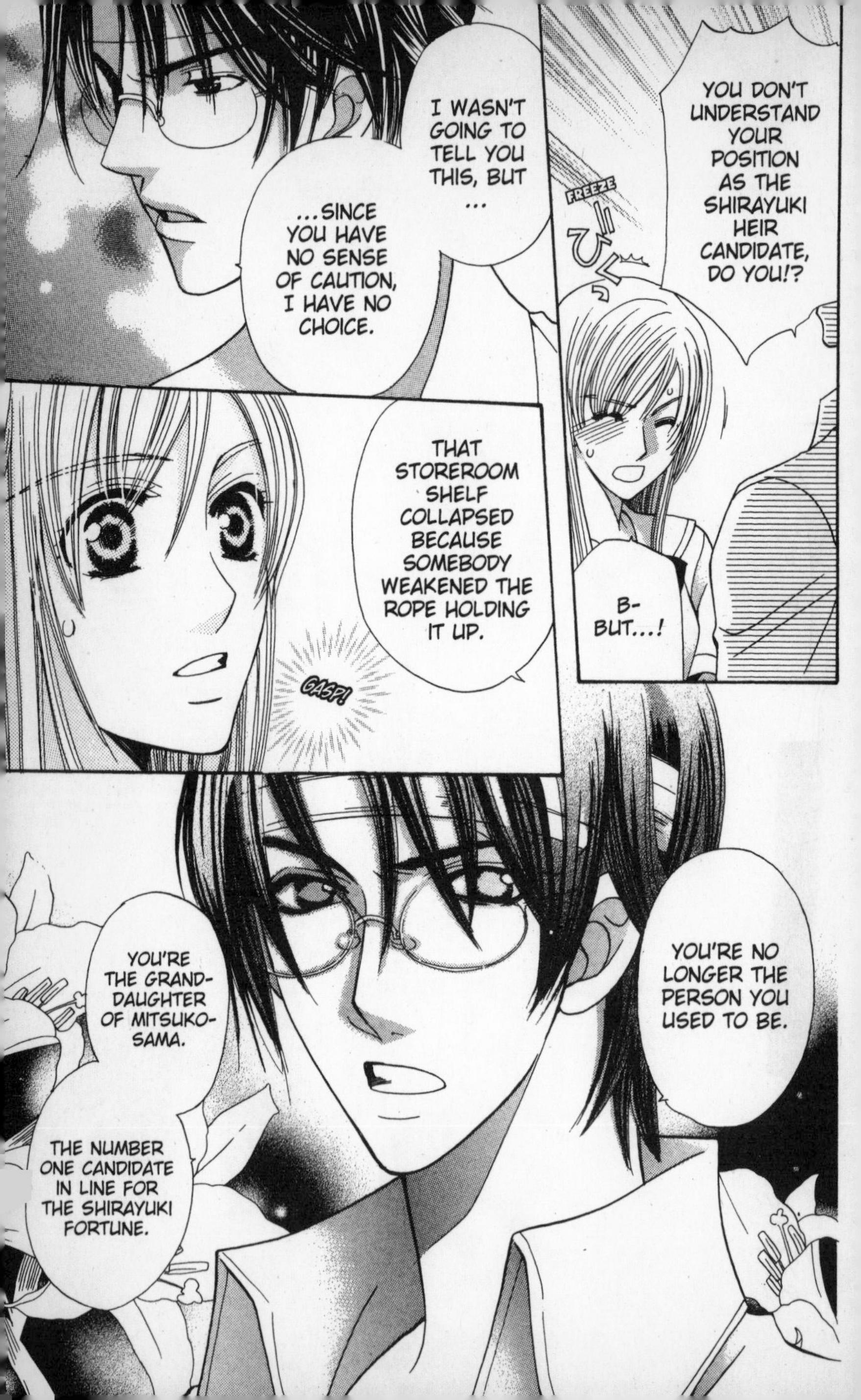
YOU DON'T UNDERSTAND YOUR POSITION AS THE SHIRAYUKI HEIR CANDIDATE, DO YOU!?
FREEZE
B-BUT...!
I WASN'T GOING TO TELL YOU THIS, BUT ...
...SINCE YOU HAVE NO SENSE OF CAUTION, I HAVE NO CHOICE.
THAT STOREROOM SHELF COLLAPSED BECAUSE SOMEBODY WEAKENED THE ROPE HOLDING IT UP.
GASP!
YOU'RE NO LONGER THE PERSON YOU USED TO BE.
YOU'RE THE GRAND-DAUGHTER OF MITSUKO-SAMA.
THE NUMBER ONE CANDIDATE IN LINE FOR THE SHIRAYUKI FORTUNE.

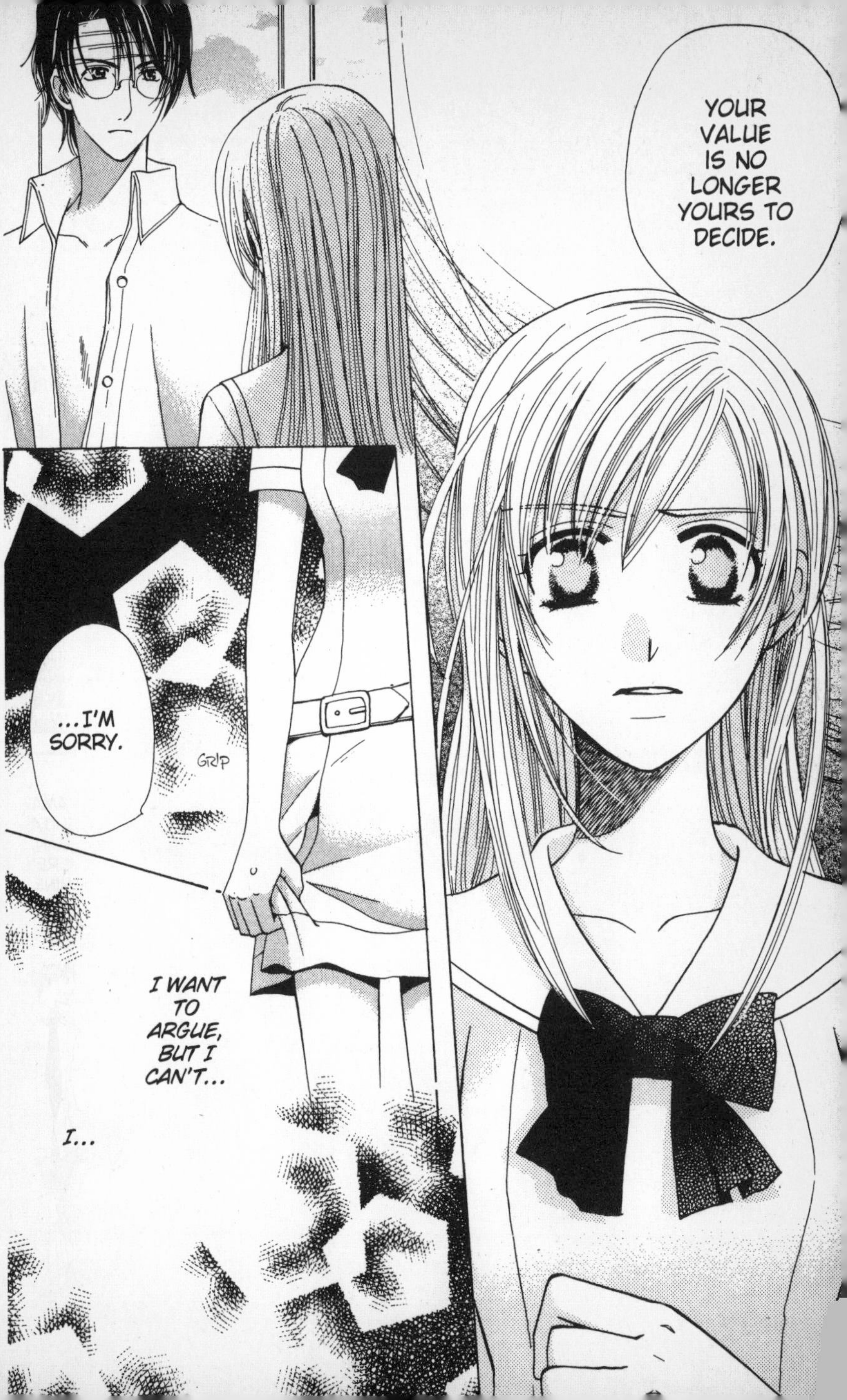
YOUR VALUE IS NO LONGER YOURS TO DECIDE.
...I'M SORRY.
GRIP
I WANT TO ARGUE, BUT I CAN'T...
I...

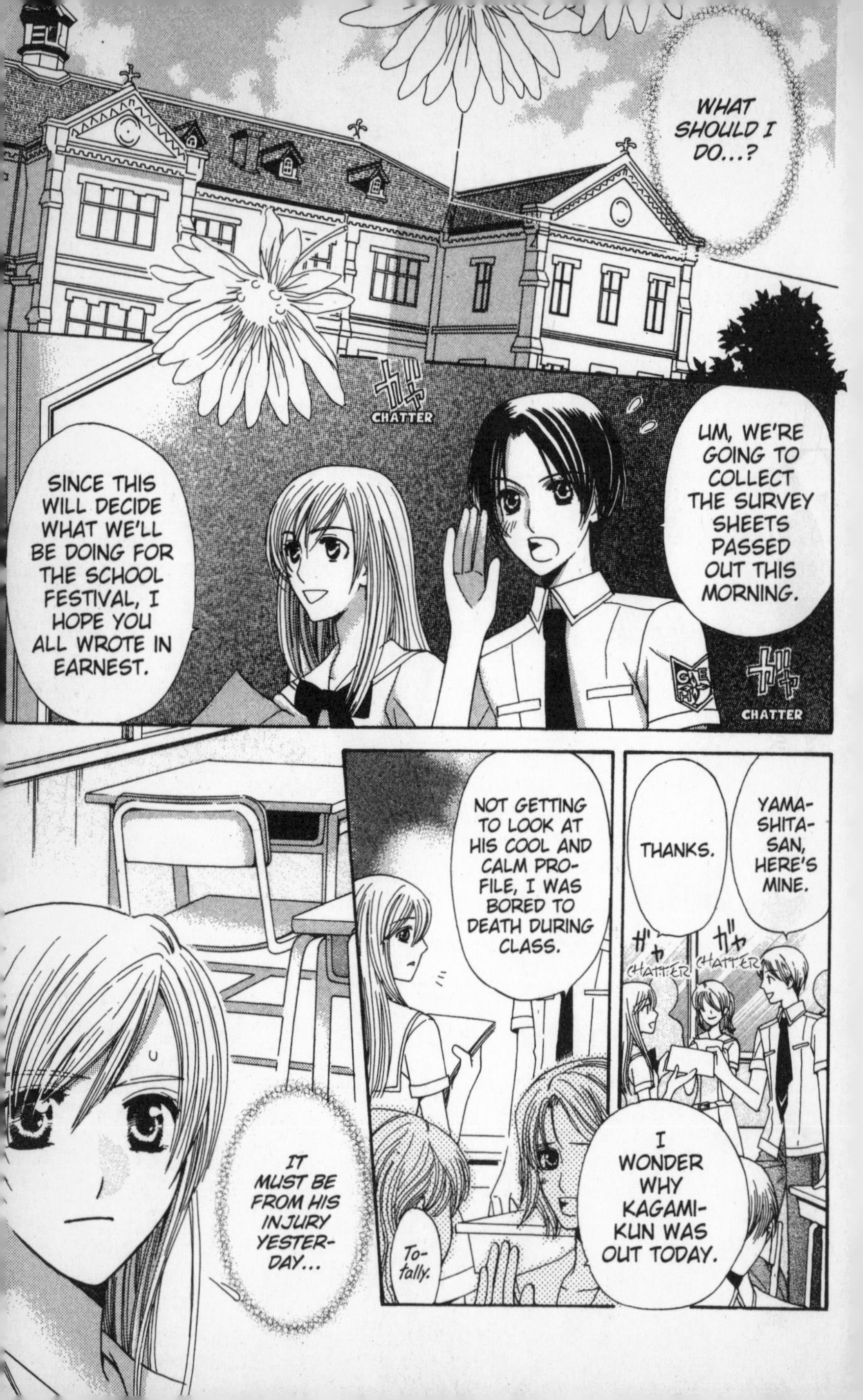
WHAT SHOULD I DO...?
CHATTER
UM, WE'RE GOING TO COLLECT THE SURVEY SHEETS PASSED OUT THIS MORNING.
CHATTER
SINCE THIS WILL DECIDE WHAT WE'LL BE DOING FOR THE SCHOOL FESTIVAL, I HOPE YOU ALL WROTE IN EARNEST.
YAMA-SHITA-SAN, HERE'S MINE.
THANKS.
CHATTER
CHATTER
I WONDER WHY KAGAMI-KUN WAS OUT TODAY.
NOT GETTING TO LOOK AT HIS COOL AND CALM PRO-FILE, I WAS BORED TO DEATH DURING CLASS.
To-tally.
IT MUST BE FROM HIS INJURY YESTER-DAY...

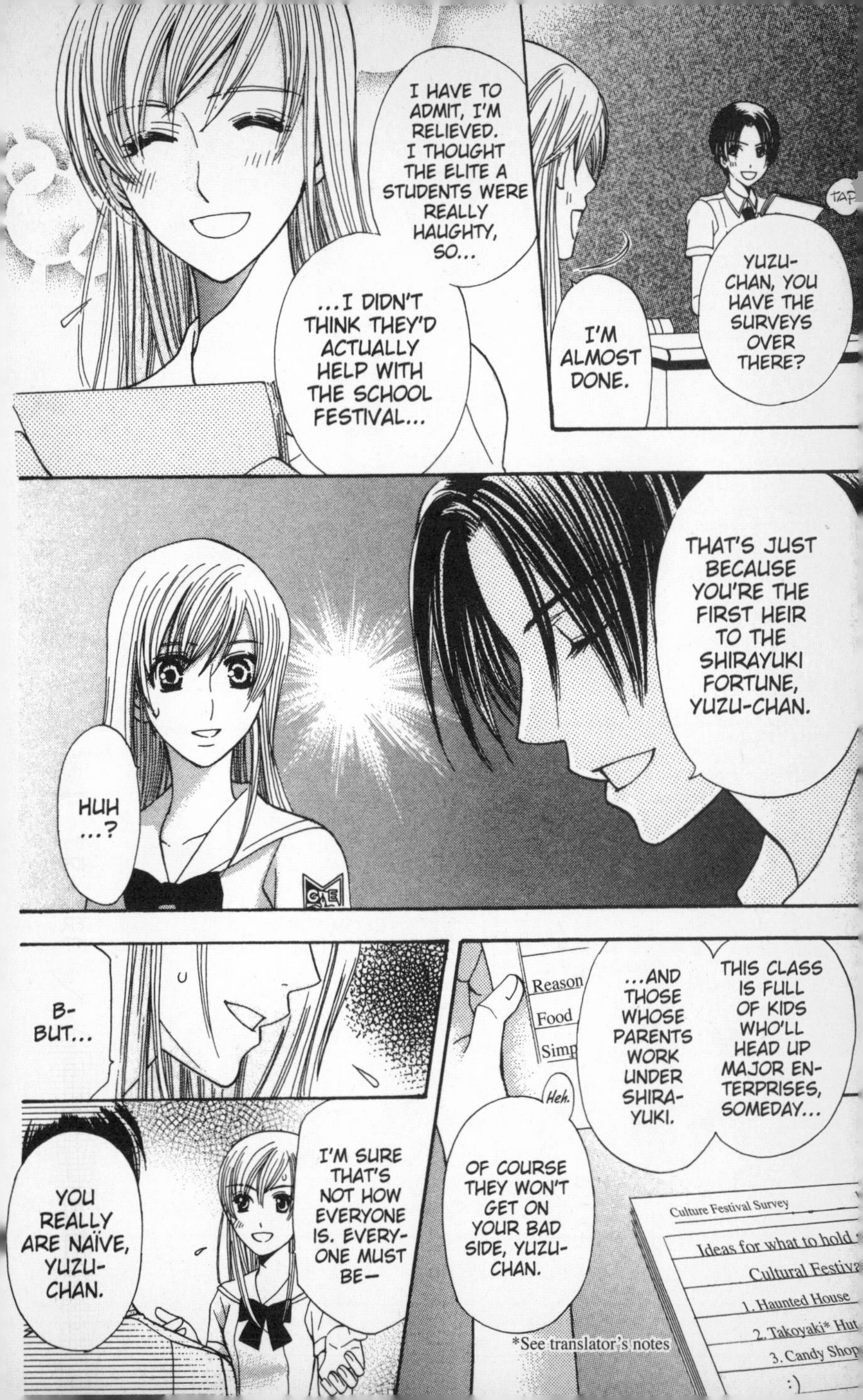
TAP
YUZU-CHAN, YOU HAVE THE SURVEYS OVER THERE?
I'M ALMOST DONE.
I HAVE TO ADMIT, I'M RELIEVED. I THOUGHT THE ELITE A STUDENTS WERE REALLY HAUGHTY, SO...
...I DIDN'T THINK THEY'D ACTUALLY HELP WITH THE SCHOOL FESTIVAL...
THAT'S JUST BECAUSE YOU'RE THE FIRST HEIR TO THE SHIRAYUKI FORTUNE, YUZU-CHAN.
HUH ...?
THIS CLASS IS FULL OF KIDS WHO'LL HEAD UP MAJOR EN-TERPRISES, SOMEDAY...
...AND THOSE WHOSE PARENTS WORK UNDER SHIRA-YUKI.
Reason
Food
Heh.
OF COURSE THEY WON'T GET ON YOUR BAD SIDE, YUZU-CHAN.
Culture Festival Survey
1. Haunted House
3. Candy Shop
B-BUT...
I'M SURE THAT'S NOT HOW EVERYONE IS. EVERY-ONE MUST BE—
YOU REALLY ARE NAÏVE, YUZU-CHAN.

*See translator's notes

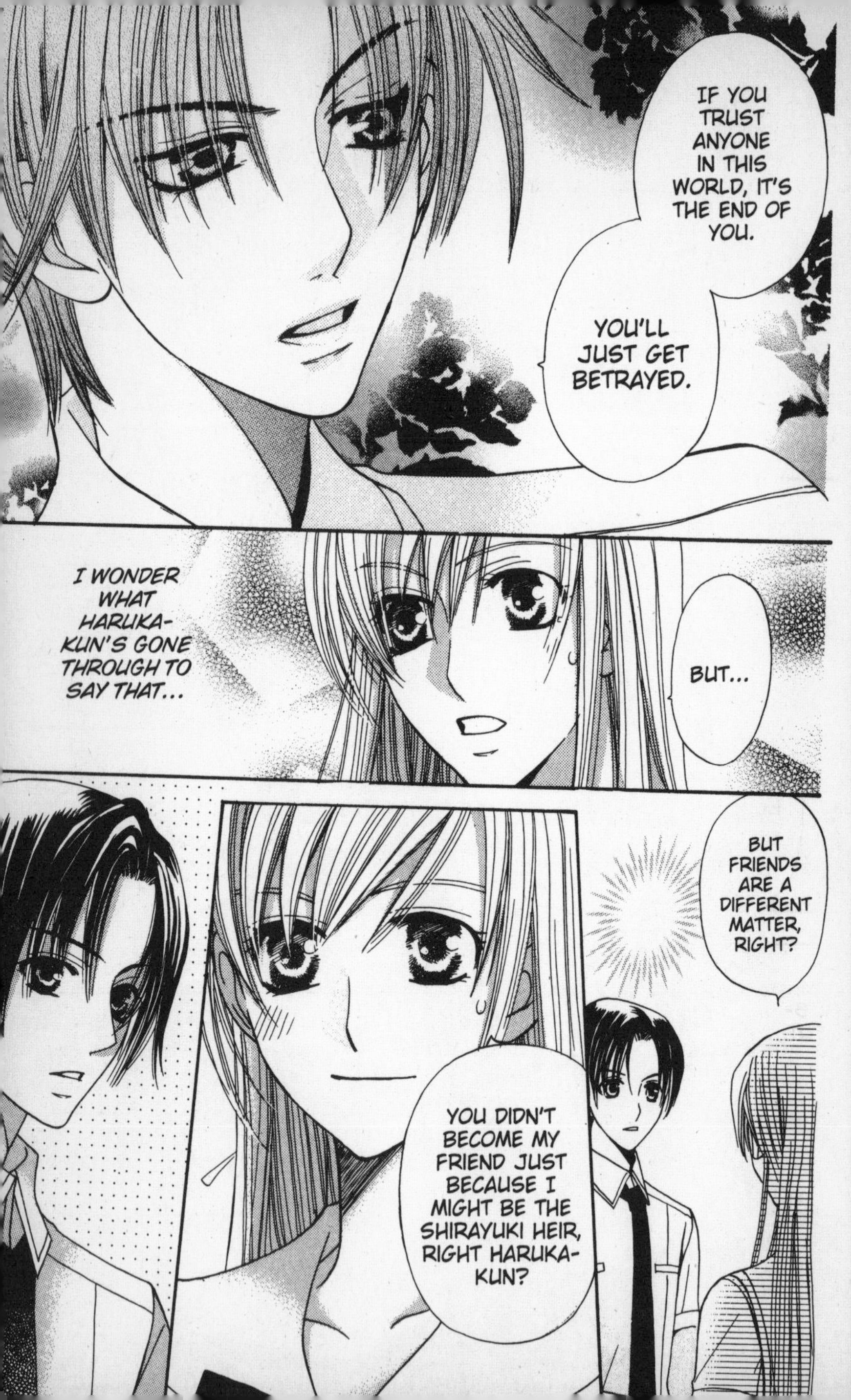
IF YOU TRUST ANYONE IN THIS WORLD, IT'S THE END OF YOU.
YOU'LL JUST GET BETRAYED.
BUT...
I WONDER WHAT HARUKA-KUN'S GONE THROUGH TO SAY THAT...
BUT FRIENDS ARE A DIFFERENT MATTER, RIGHT?
YOU DIDN'T BECOME MY FRIEND JUST BECAUSE I MIGHT BE THE SHIRAYUKI HEIR, RIGHT HARUKA-KUN?

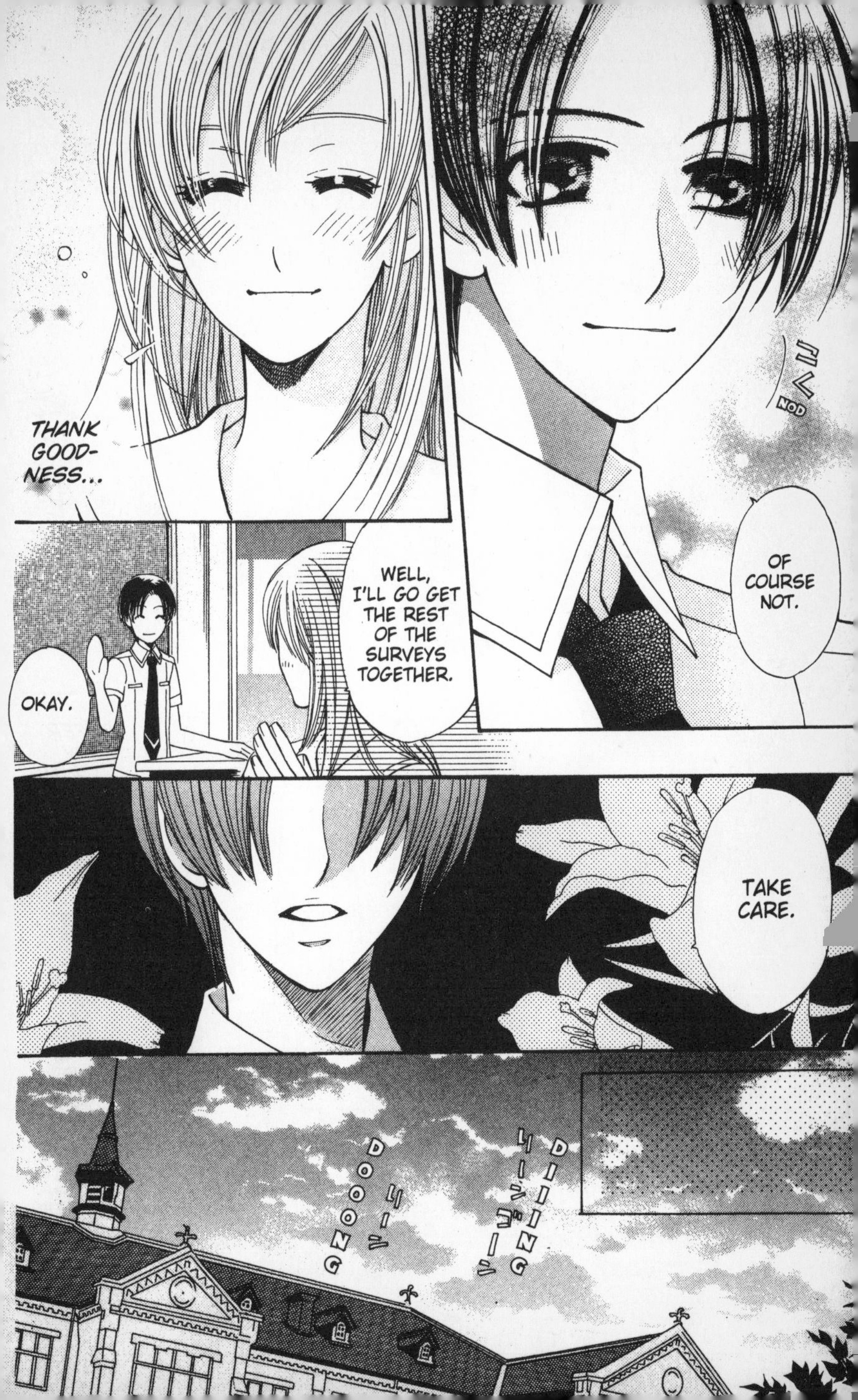
NOD
OF COURSE NOT.
THANK GOOD-NESS...
WELL, I'LL GO GET THE REST OF THE SURVEYS TOGETHER.
OKAY.
TAKE CARE.
DIIIING
DOOOONG

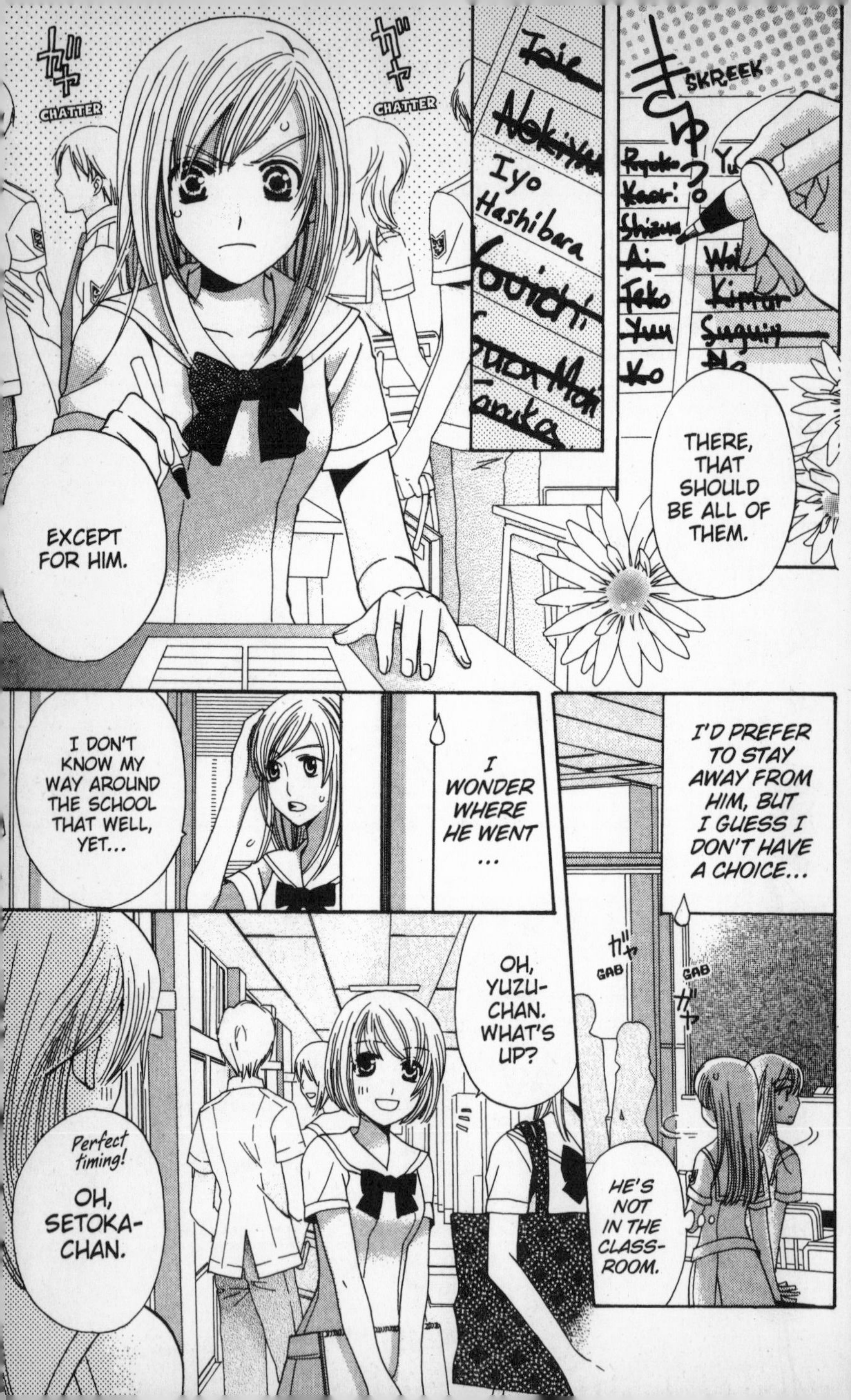
SKREEK
Iyo
Hashibara
THERE, THAT SHOULD BE ALL OF THEM.
CHATTER
CHATTER
EXCEPT FOR HIM.
I'D PREFER TO STAY AWAY FROM HIM, BUT I GUESS I DON'T HAVE A CHOICE...
I WONDER WHERE HE WENT...
I DON'T KNOW MY WAY AROUND THE SCHOOL THAT WELL, YET...
GAB
GAB
HE'S NOT IN THE CLASSROOM.
Perfect timing!
OH, SETOKA-CHAN.
OH, YUZU-CHAN. WHAT'S UP?

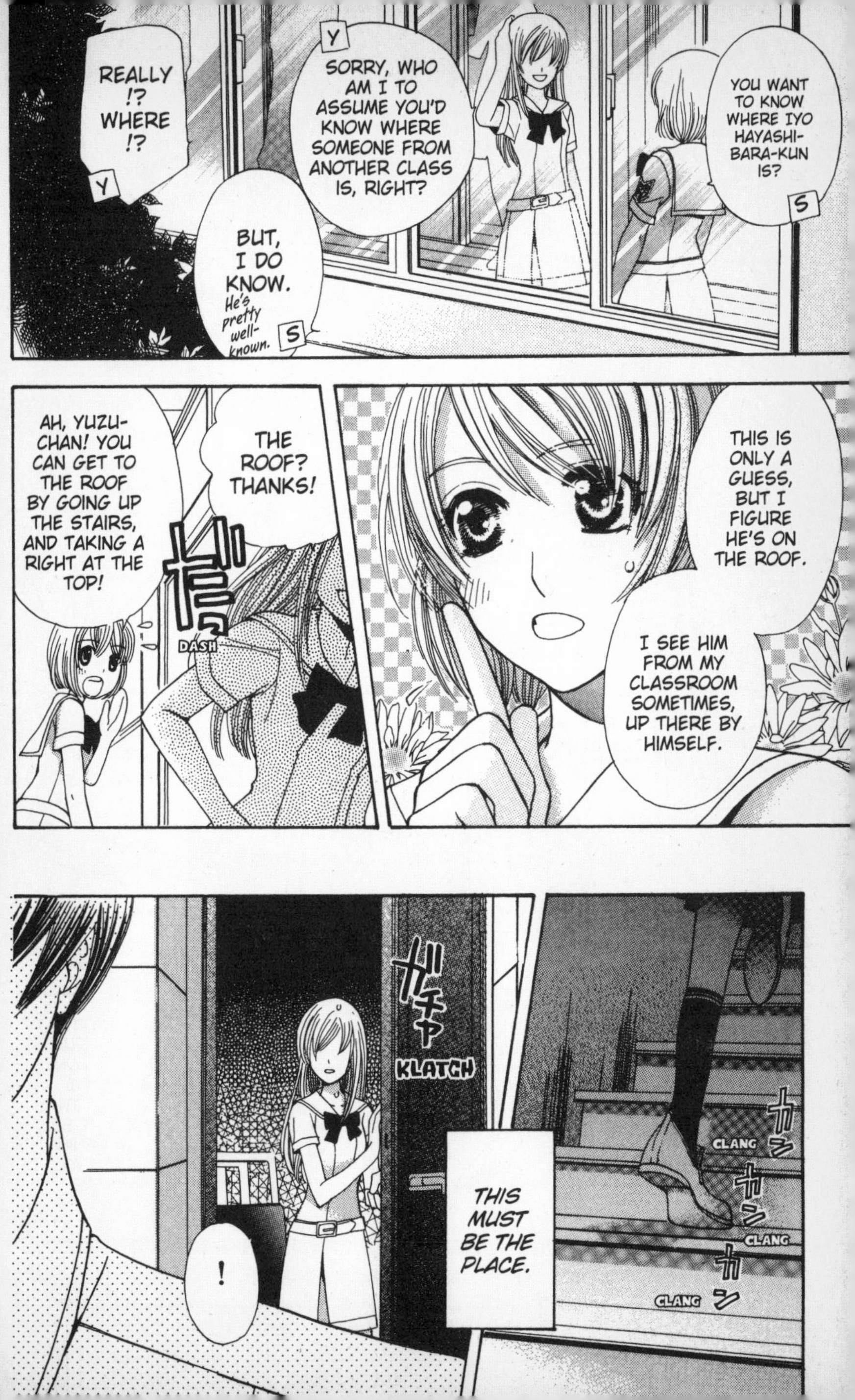
YOU WANT TO KNOW WHERE IYO HAYASHI-BARA-KUN IS?
SORRY, WHO AM I TO ASSUME YOU'D KNOW WHERE SOMEONE FROM ANOTHER CLASS IS, RIGHT?
BUT, I DO KNOW.
He's pretty well-known.
REALLY!? WHERE!?
THIS IS ONLY A GUESS, BUT I FIGURE HE'S ON THE ROOF.
I SEE HIM FROM MY CLASSROOM SOMETIMES, UP THERE BY HIMSELF.
THE ROOF? THANKS!
DASH
AH, YUZU-CHAN! YOU CAN GET TO THE ROOF BY GOING UP THE STAIRS, AND TAKING A RIGHT AT THE TOP!
CLANG
CLANG
CLANG
THIS MUST BE THE PLACE.
KLATCH
!

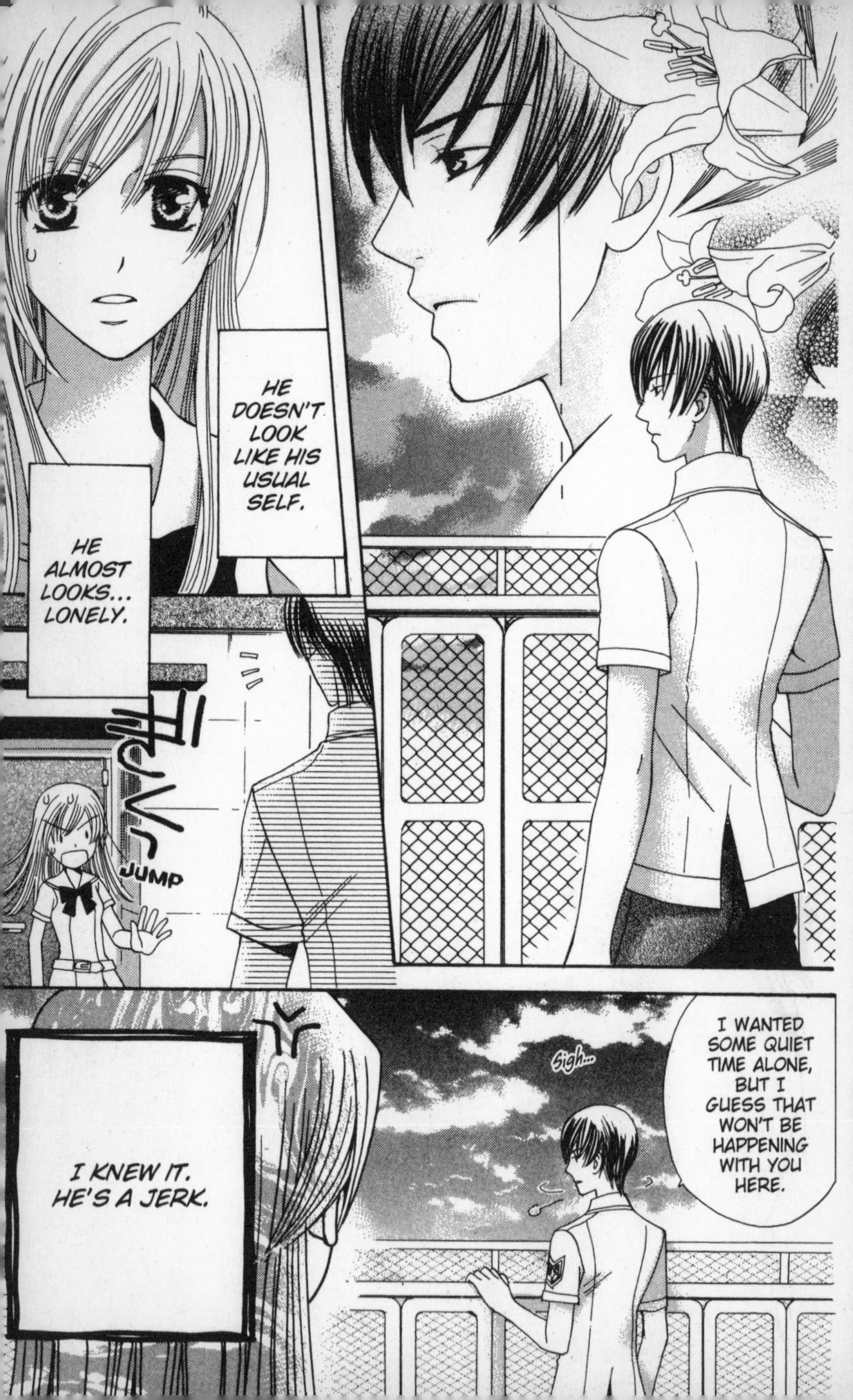
HE DOESN'T LOOK LIKE HIS USUAL SELF.
HE ALMOST LOOKS... LONELY.
JUMP
Sigh...
I WANTED SOME QUIET TIME ALONE, BUT I GUESS THAT WON'T BE HAPPENING WITH YOU HERE.
I KNEW IT. HE'S A JERK.

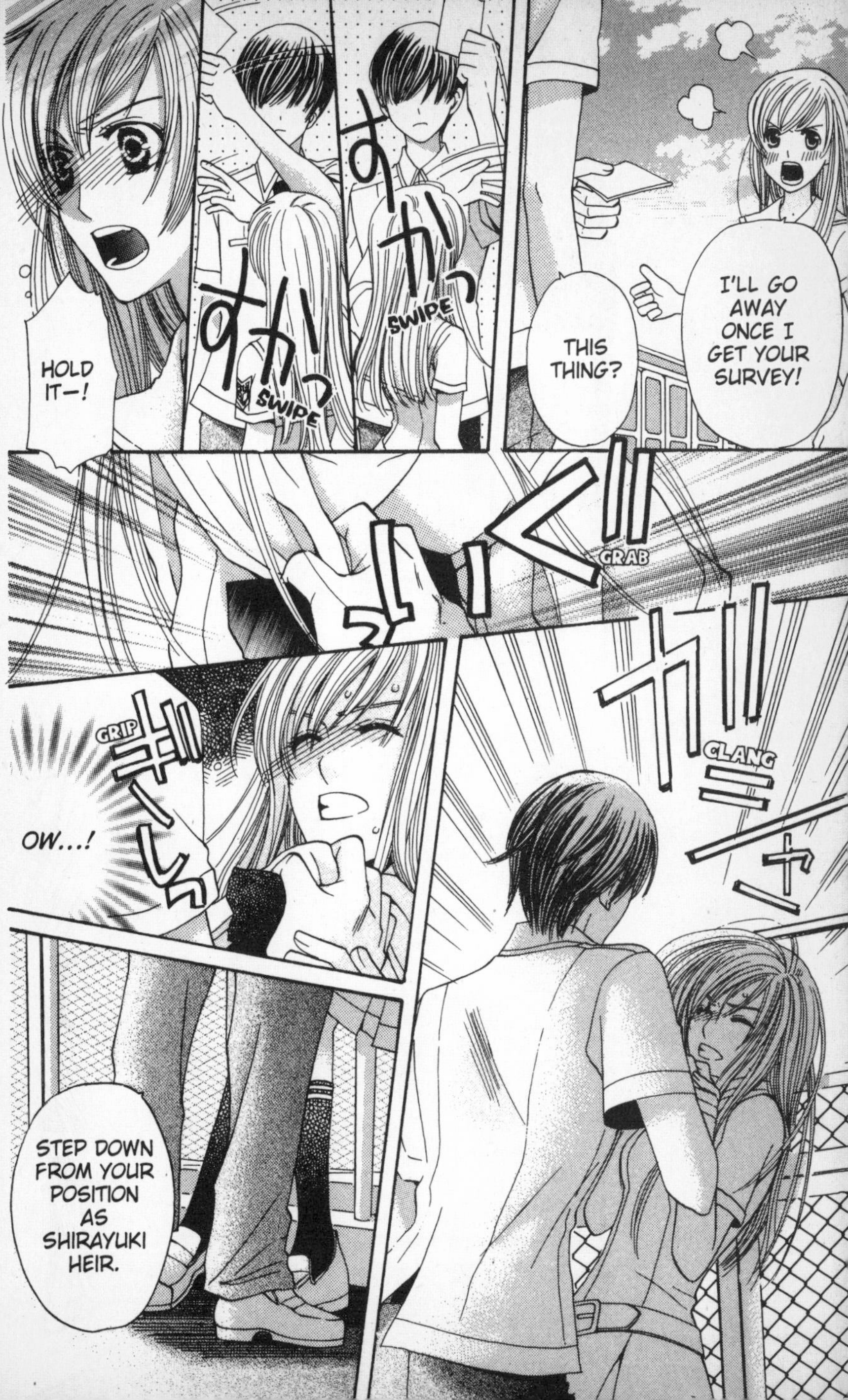
I'LL GO AWAY ONCE I GET YOUR SURVEY!
THIS THING?
SWIPE
SWIPE
HOLD IT—!
GRAB
CLANG
GRIP
OW...!
STEP DOWN FROM YOUR POSITION AS SHIRAYUKI HEIR.

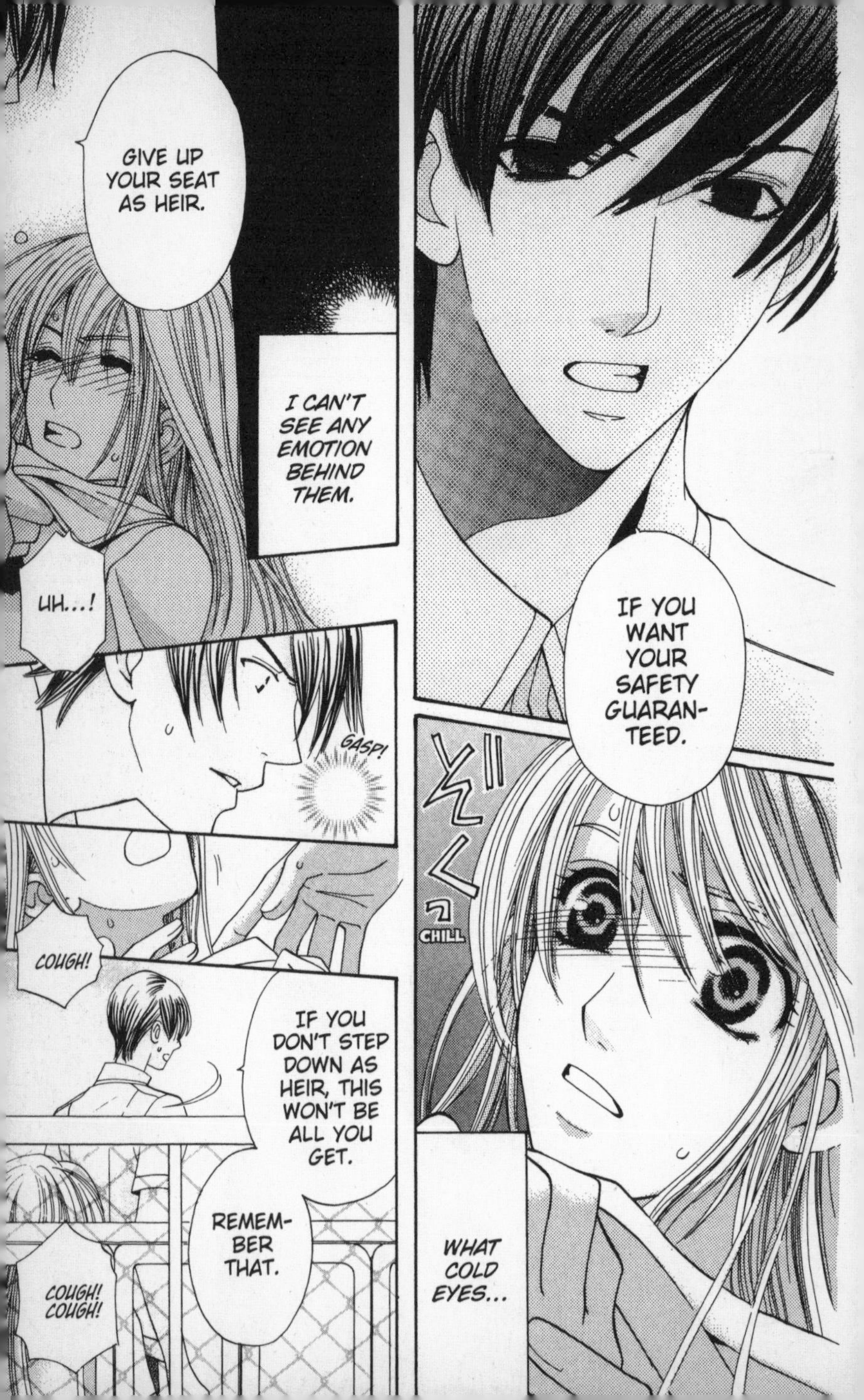
IF YOU WANT YOUR SAFETY GUARAN-TEED.
CHILL
WHAT COLD EYES...
GIVE UP YOUR SEAT AS HEIR.
I CAN'T SEE ANY EMOTION BEHIND THEM.
UH...!
GASP!
COUGH!
IF YOU DON'T STEP DOWN AS HEIR, THIS WON'T BE ALL YOU GET.
REMEM-BER THAT.
COUGH! COUGH!

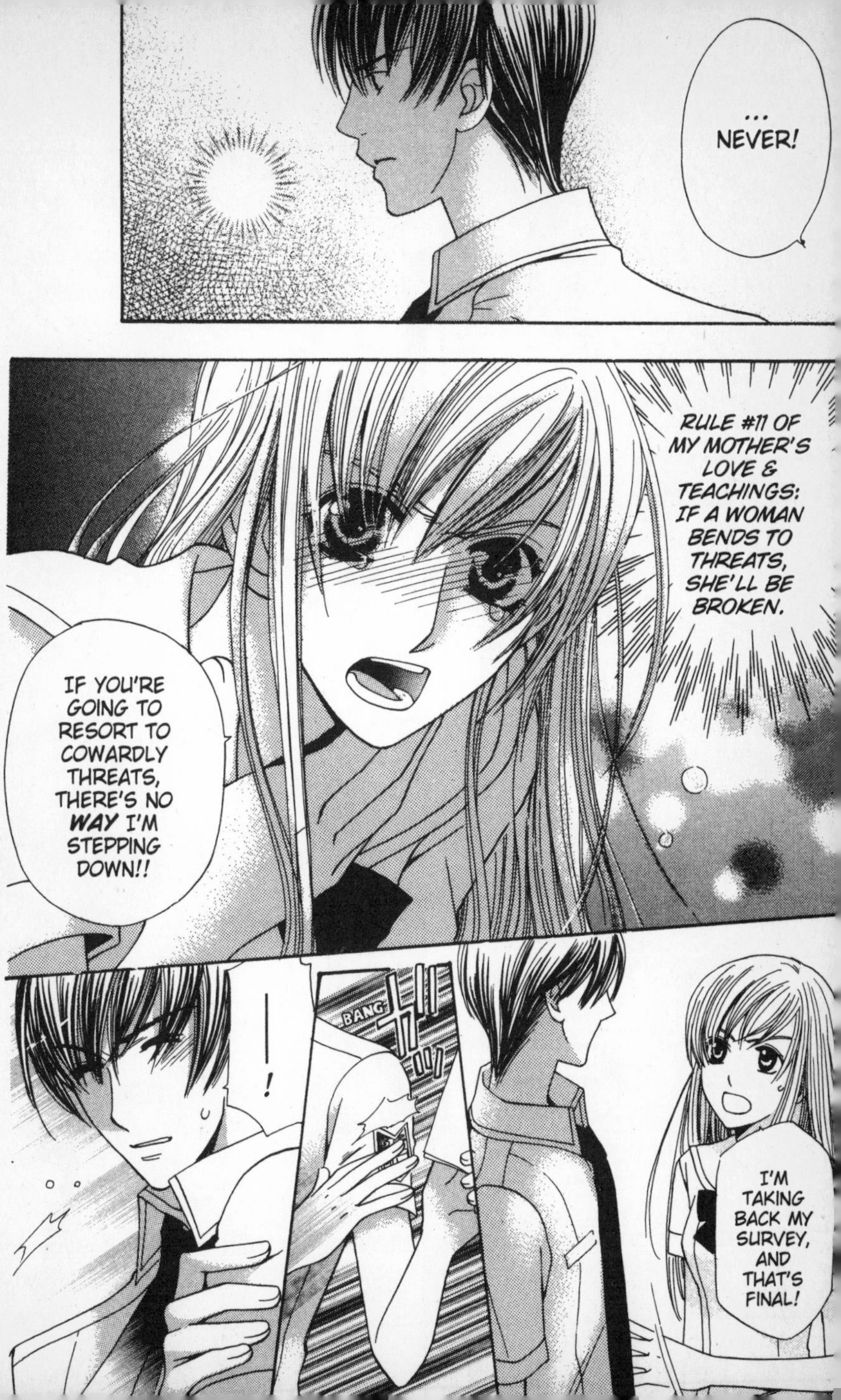
...NEVER!
RULE #11 OF MY MOTHER'S LOVE & TEACHINGS: IF A WOMAN BENDS TO THREATS, SHE'LL BE BROKEN.
IF YOU'RE GOING TO RESORT TO COWARDLY THREATS, THERE'S NO WAY I'M STEPPING DOWN!!
I'M TAKING BACK MY SURVEY, AND THAT'S FINAL!
BANG
—!

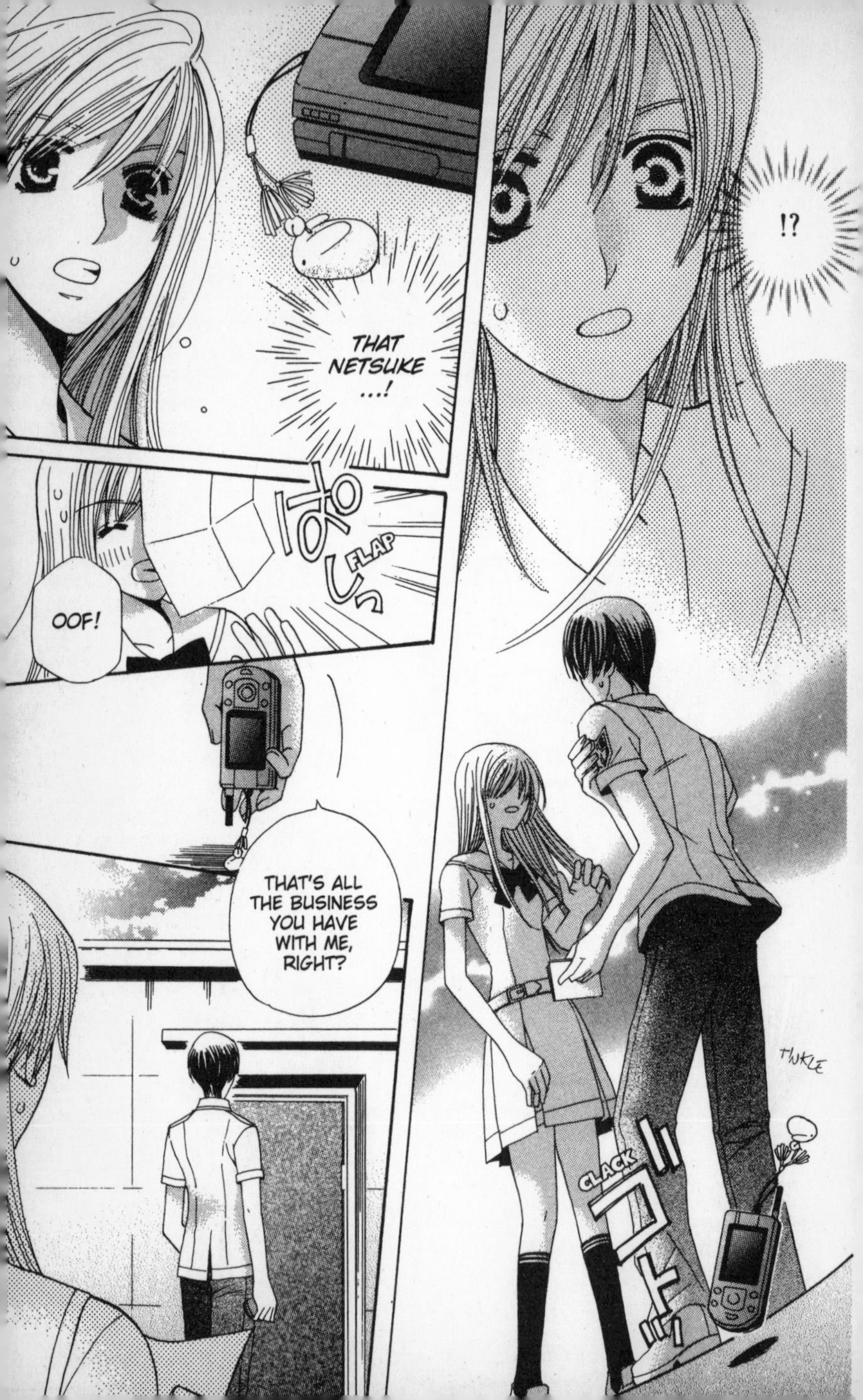
!?
TINKLE
CLACK
THAT NETSUKE ...!
FLAP
OOF!
THAT'S ALL THE BUSINESS YOU HAVE WITH ME, RIGHT?

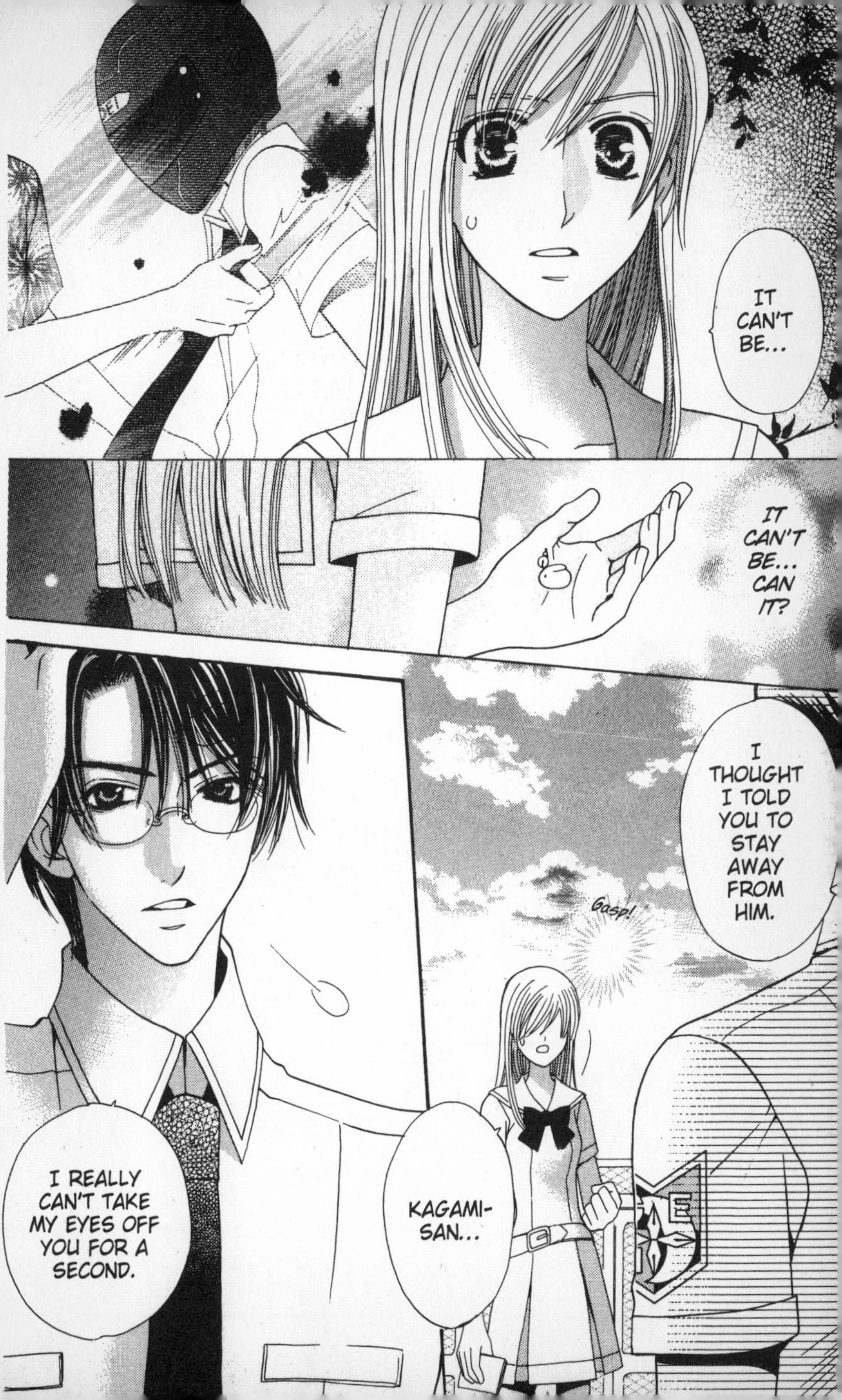
IT CAN'T BE...
IT CAN'T BE... CAN IT?
I THOUGHT I TOLD YOU TO STAY AWAY FROM HIM.
Gasp!
KAGAMI-SAN...
I REALLY CAN'T TAKE MY EYES OFF YOU FOR A SECOND.

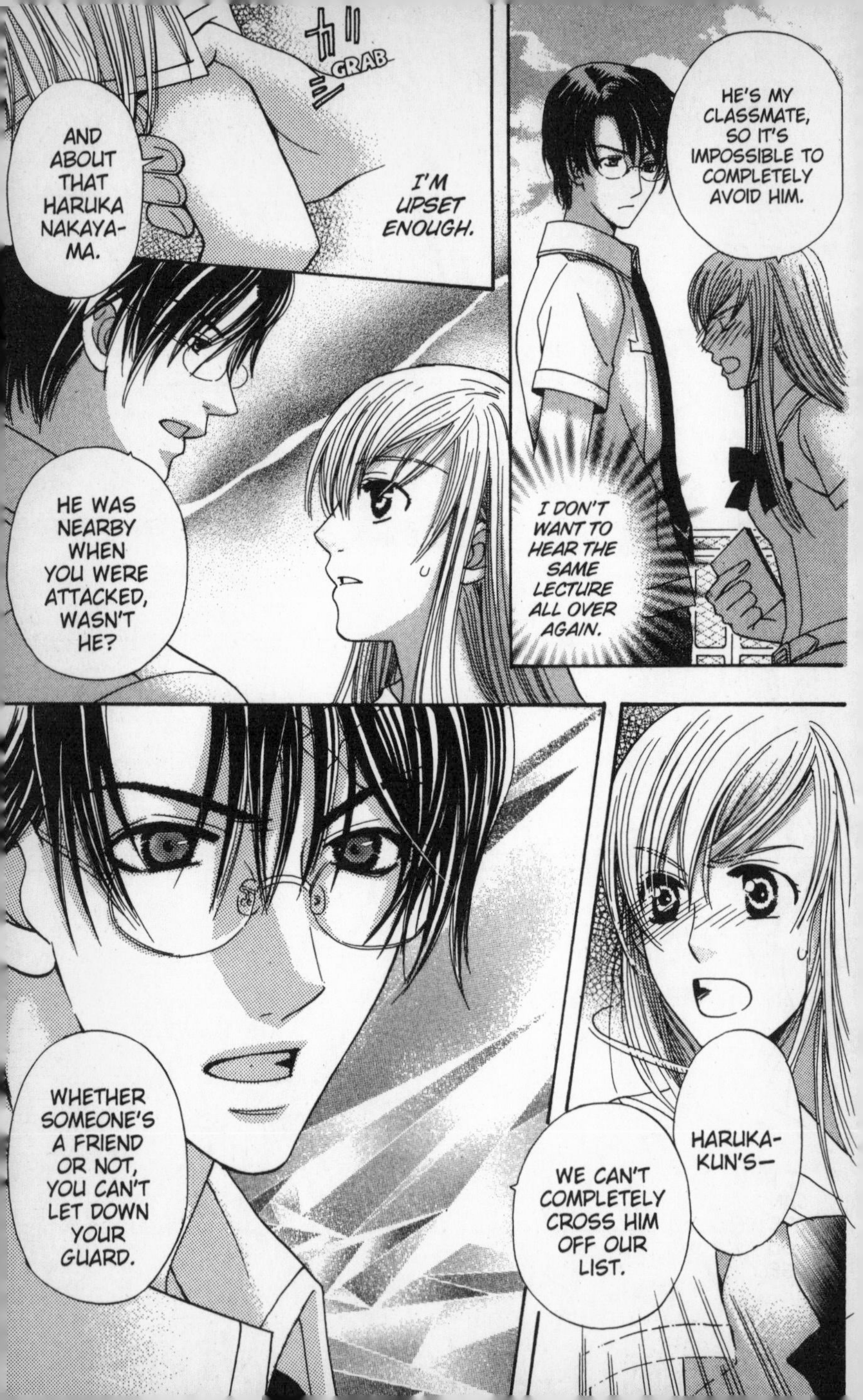
HE'S MY CLASSMATE, SO IT'S IMPOSSIBLE TO COMPLETELY AVOID HIM.
I DON'T WANT TO HEAR THE SAME LECTURE ALL OVER AGAIN.
カリ
GRAB
I'M UPSET ENOUGH.
AND ABOUT THAT HARUKA NAKAYA-MA.
HE WAS NEARBY WHEN YOU WERE ATTACKED, WASN'T HE?
HARUKA-KUN'S—
WE CAN'T COMPLETELY CROSS HIM OFF OUR LIST.
WHETHER SOMEONE'S A FRIEND OR NOT, YOU CAN'T LET DOWN YOUR GUARD.

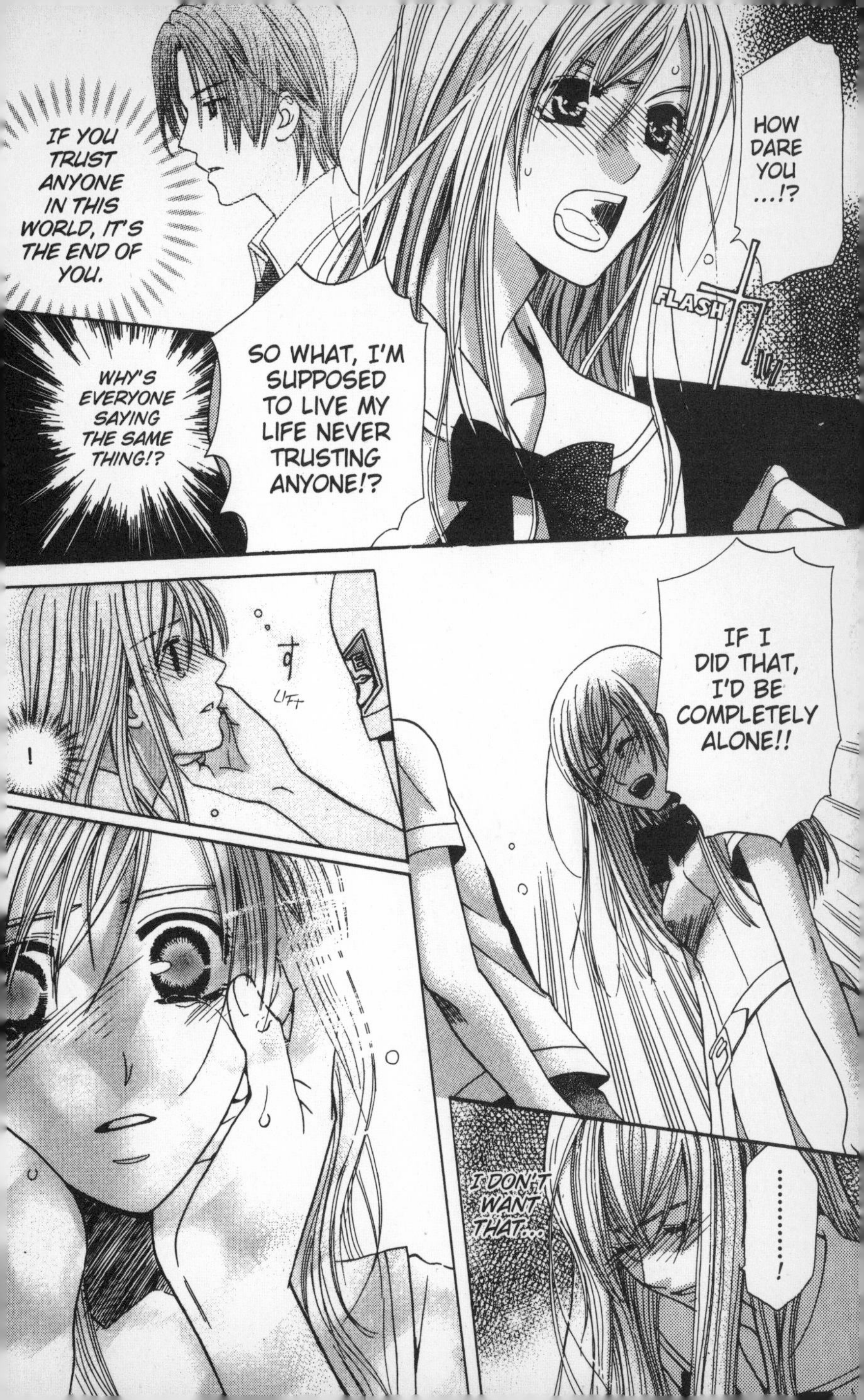
HOW DARE YOU ...!?
FLASH
IF YOU TRUST ANYONE IN THIS WORLD, IT'S THE END OF YOU.
SO WHAT, I'M SUPPOSED TO LIVE MY LIFE NEVER TRUSTING ANYONE!?
WHY'S EVERYONE SAYING THE SAME THING!?
IF I DID THAT, I'D BE COMPLETELY ALONE!!
!
す
LIFT
I DON'T WANT THAT...
......!

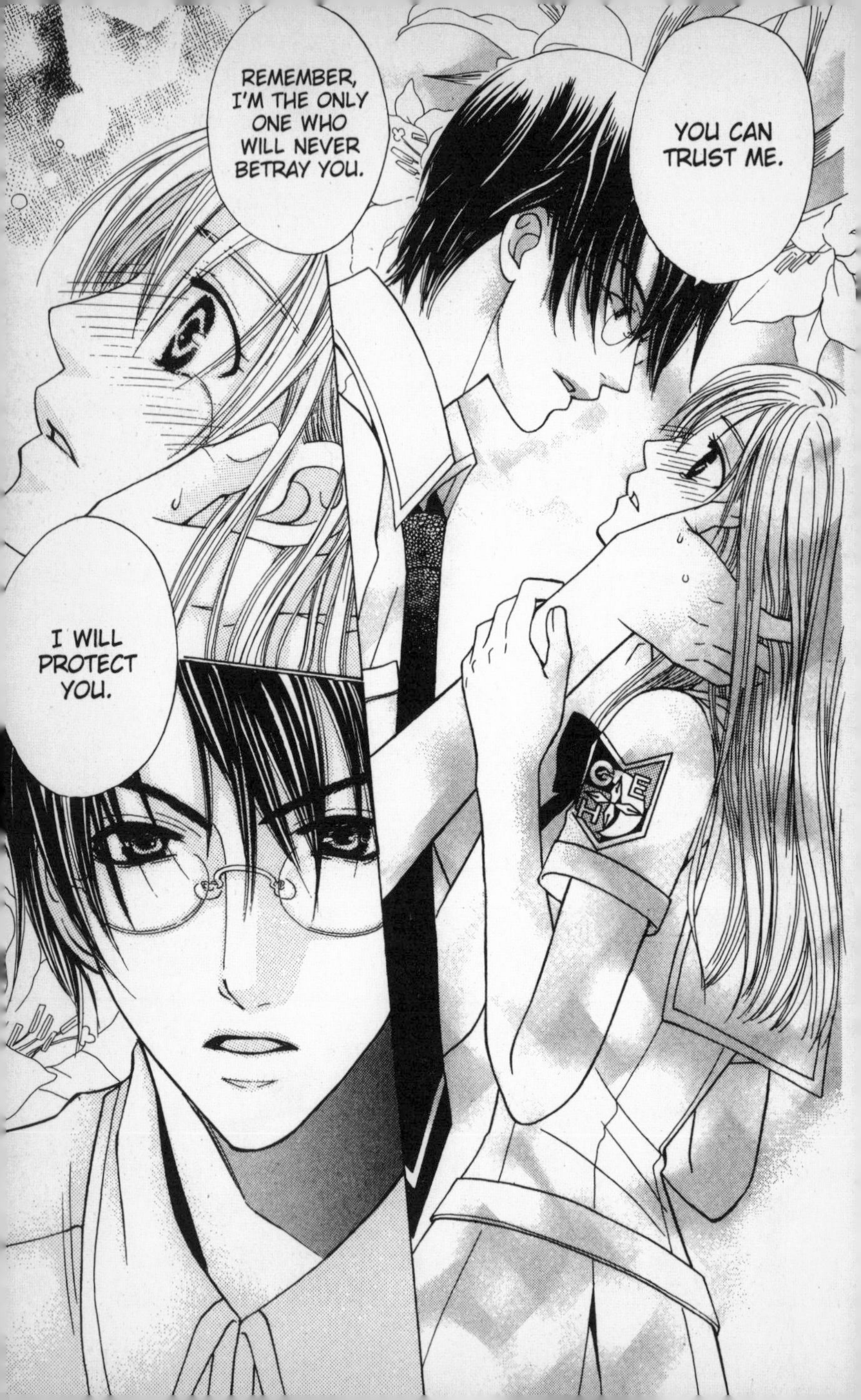
YOU CAN TRUST ME.
REMEMBER, I'M THE ONLY ONE WHO WILL NEVER BETRAY YOU.
I WILL PROTECT YOU.

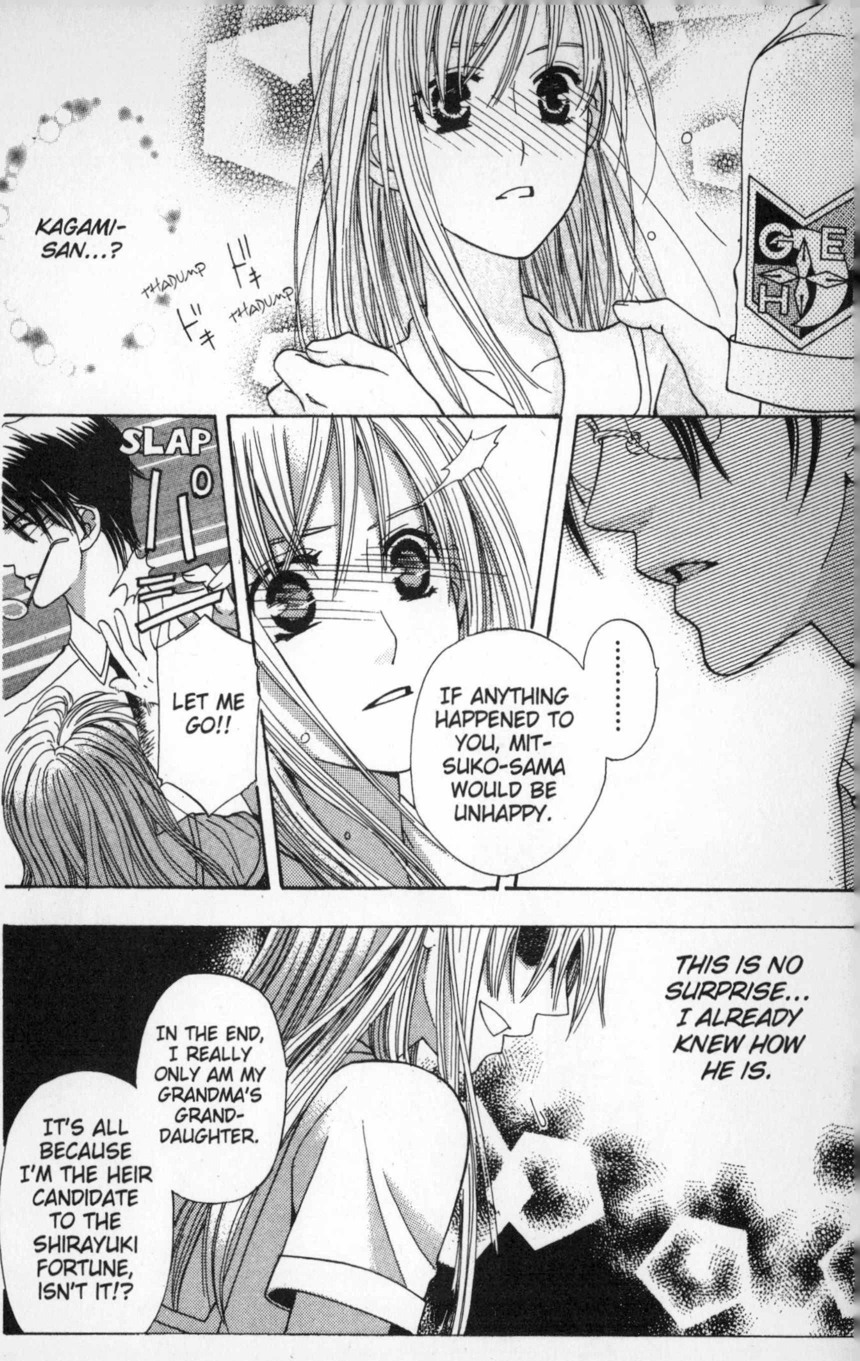
KAGAMI-SAN...?
THADUMP
THADUMP
SLAP
......
IF ANYTHING HAPPENED TO YOU, MIT-SUKO-SAMA WOULD BE UNHAPPY.
LET ME GO!!
THIS IS NO SURPRISE... I ALREADY KNEW HOW HE IS.
IN THE END, I REALLY ONLY AM MY GRANDMA'S GRAND-DAUGHTER.
IT'S ALL BECAUSE I'M THE HEIR CANDIDATE TO THE SHIRAYUKI FORTUNE, ISN'T IT!?

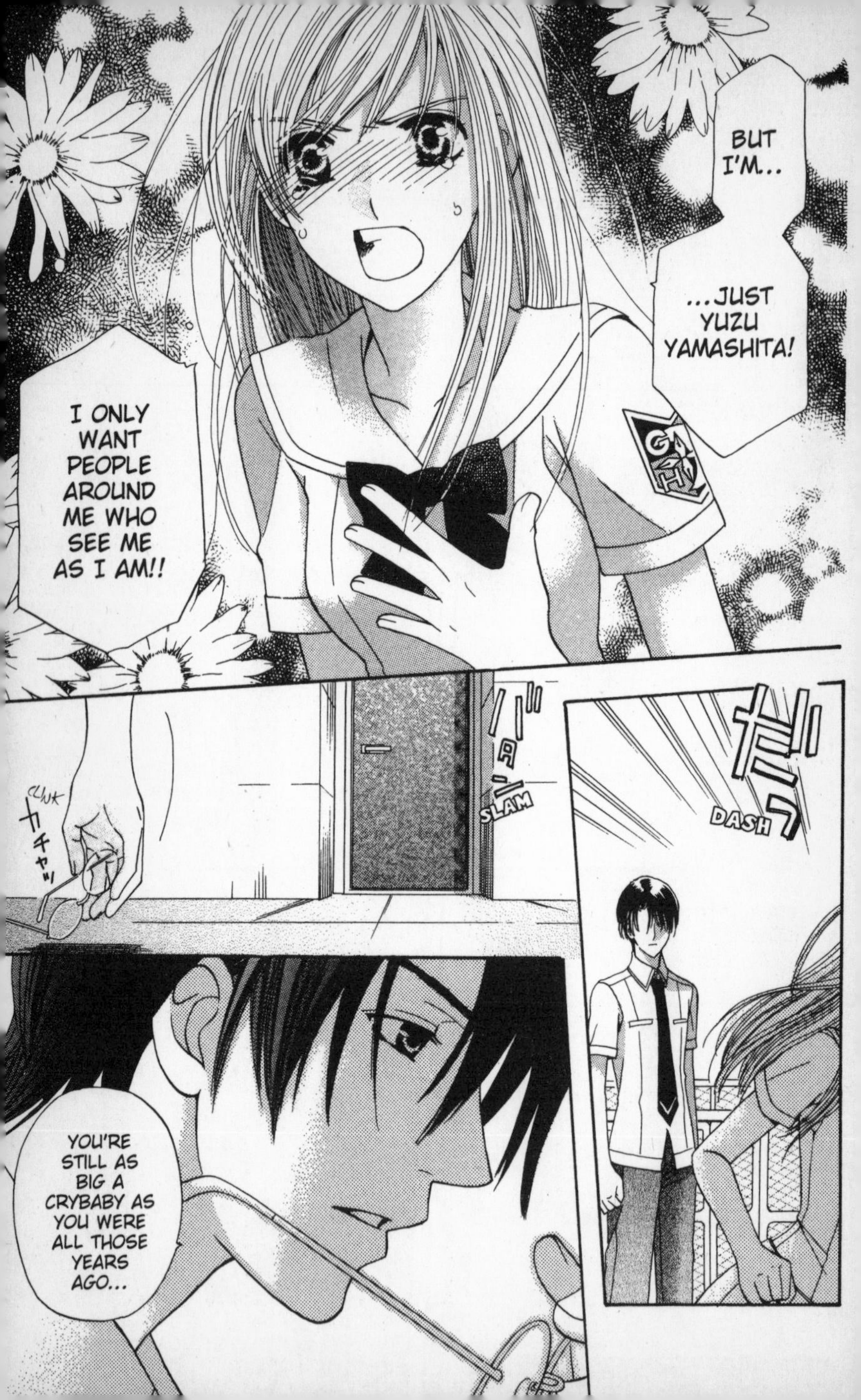
BUT I'M...
...JUST YUZU YAMASHITA!
I ONLY WANT PEOPLE AROUND ME WHO SEE ME AS I AM!!
DASH
SLAM
CLINK
YOU'RE STILL AS BIG A CRYBABY AS YOU WERE ALL THOSE YEARS AGO...

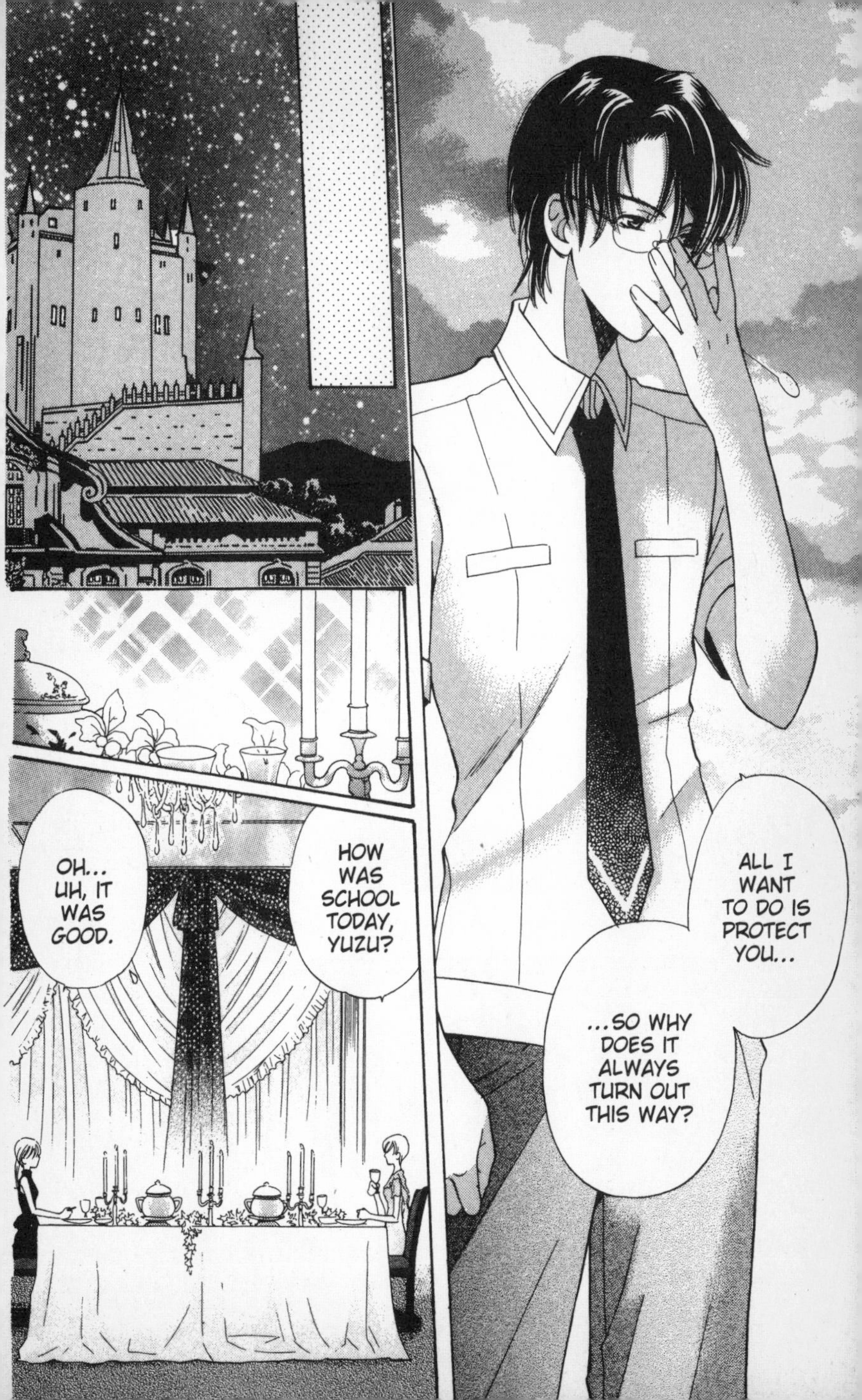
ALL I WANT TO DO IS PROTECT YOU...
...SO WHY DOES IT ALWAYS TURN OUT THIS WAY?
HOW WAS SCHOOL TODAY, YUZU?
OH... UH, IT WAS GOOD.

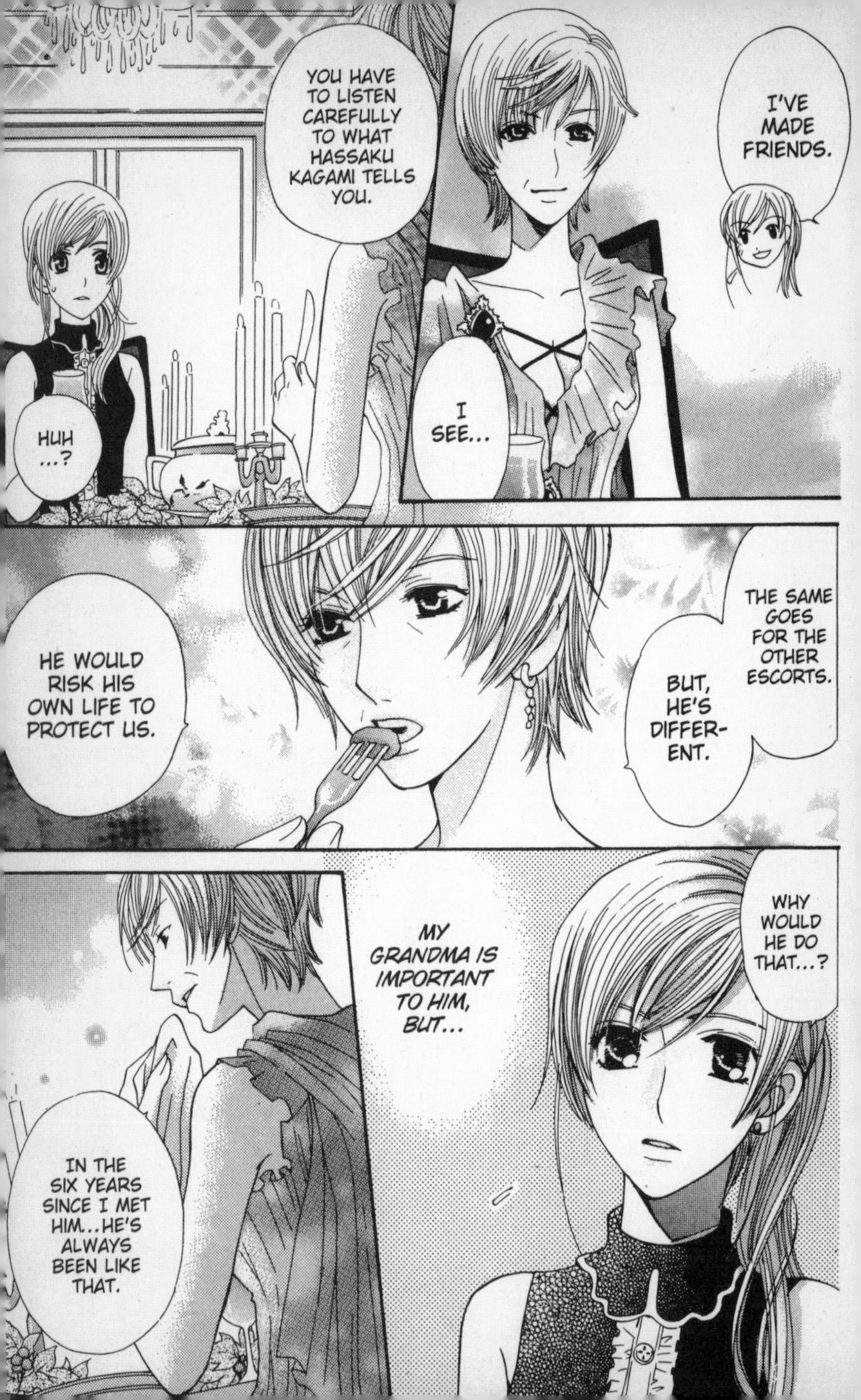
I'VE MADE FRIENDS.
I SEE...
YOU HAVE TO LISTEN CAREFULLY TO WHAT HASSAKU KAGAMI TELLS YOU.
HUH ...?
THE SAME GOES FOR THE OTHER ESCORTS.
BUT, HE'S DIFFER-ENT.
HE WOULD RISK HIS OWN LIFE TO PROTECT US.
WHY WOULD HE DO THAT...?
MY GRANDMA IS IMPORTANT TO HIM, BUT...
IN THE SIX YEARS SINCE I MET HIM...HE'S ALWAYS BEEN LIKE THAT.

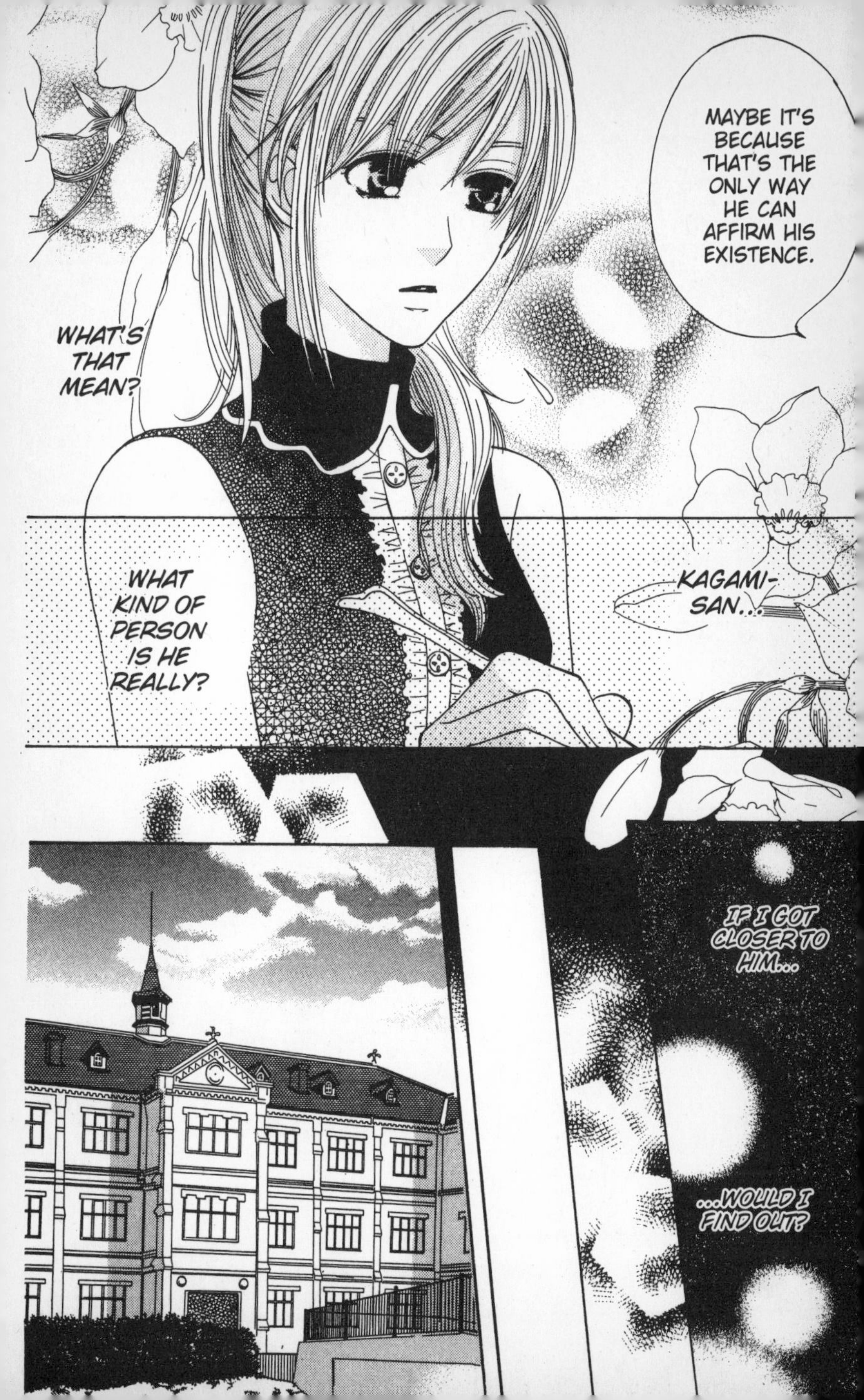
MAYBE IT'S BECAUSE THAT'S THE ONLY WAY HE CAN AFFIRM HIS EXISTENCE.
WHAT'S THAT MEAN?
KAGAMI-SAN...
WHAT KIND OF PERSON IS HE REALLY?
IF I GOT CLOSER TO HIM...
...WOULD I FIND OUT?

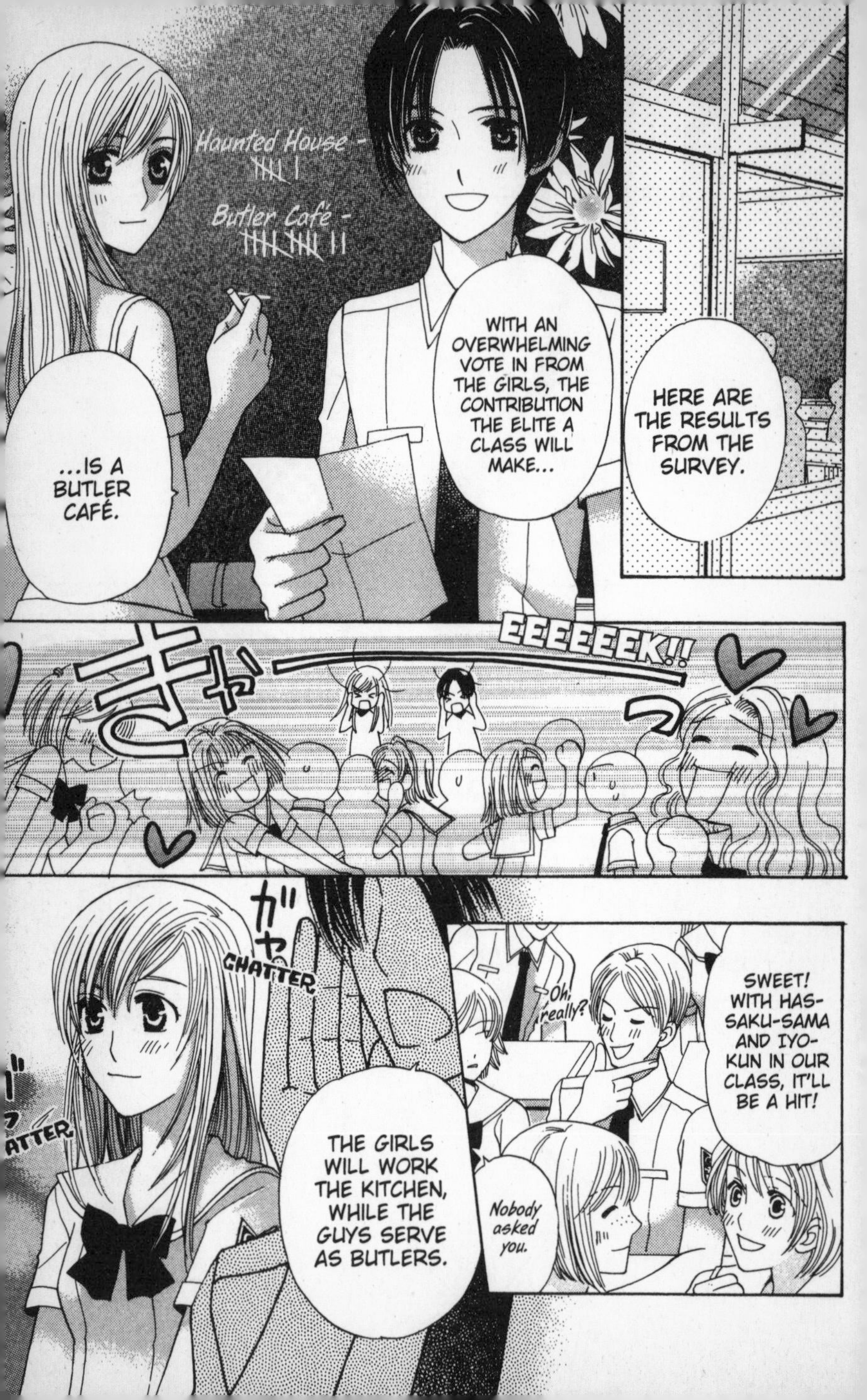
HERE ARE THE RESULTS FROM THE SURVEY.
Haunted House -
Butler Café -
WITH AN OVERWHELMING VOTE IN FROM THE GIRLS, THE CONTRIBUTION THE ELITE A CLASS WILL MAKE...
...IS A BUTLER CAFÉ.
EEEEEEK!!
きゃーっ
SWEET! WITH HAS-SAKU-SAMA AND IYO-KUN IN OUR CLASS, IT'LL BE A HIT!
Oh, really?
Nobody asked you.
ガヤ
CHATTER
ガヤ
CHATTER
THE GIRLS WILL WORK THE KITCHEN, WHILE THE GUYS SERVE AS BUTLERS.

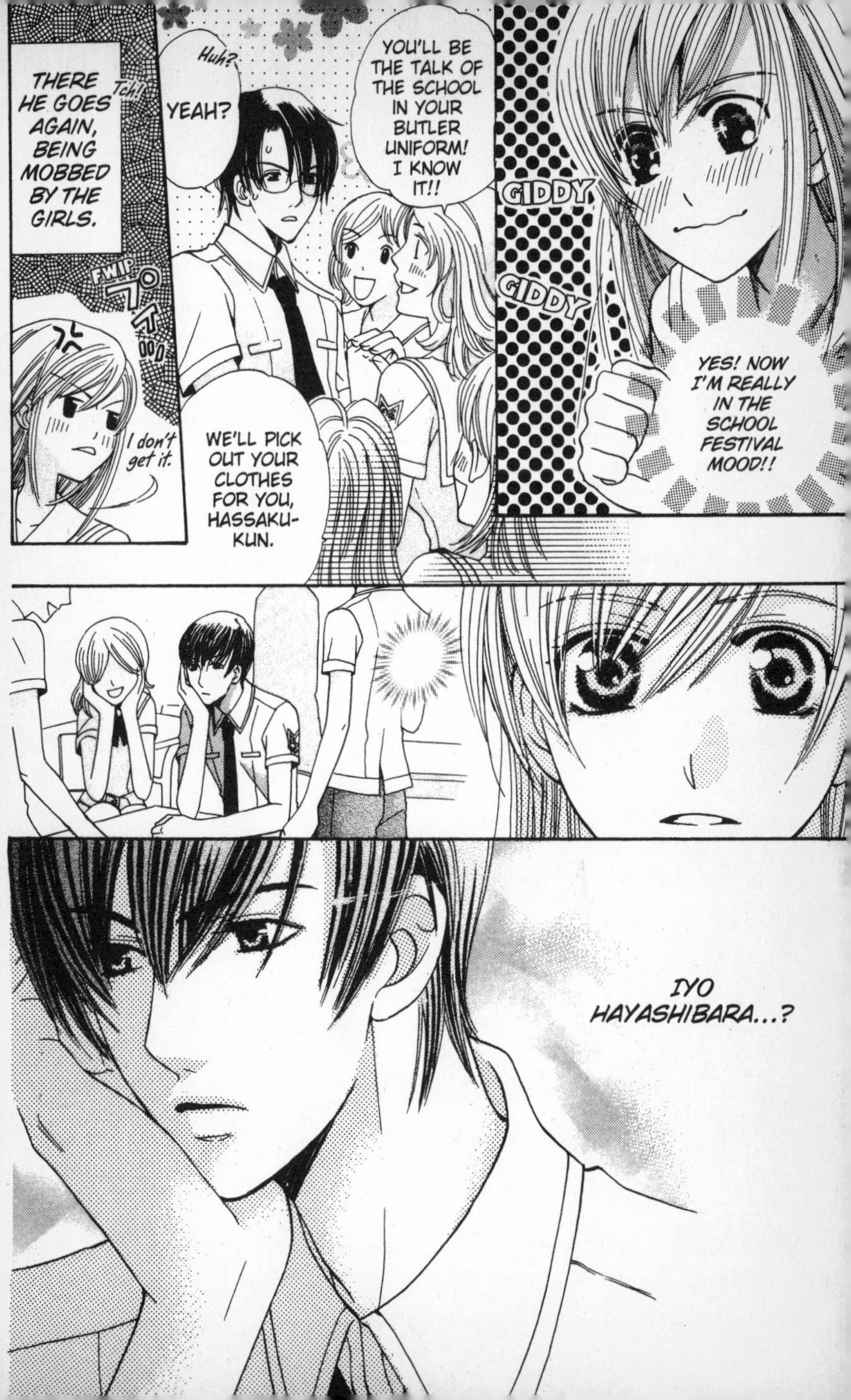
GIDDY
GIDDY
YES! NOW I'M REALLY IN THE SCHOOL FESTIVAL MOOD!!
YOU'LL BE THE TALK OF THE SCHOOL IN YOUR BUTLER UNIFORM! I KNOW IT!!
Huh?
YEAH?
Tch!
THERE HE GOES AGAIN, BEING MOBBED BY THE GIRLS.
WE'LL PICK OUT YOUR CLOTHES FOR YOU, HASSAKU-KUN.
FWIP
I don't get it.
IYO HAYASHIBARA...?

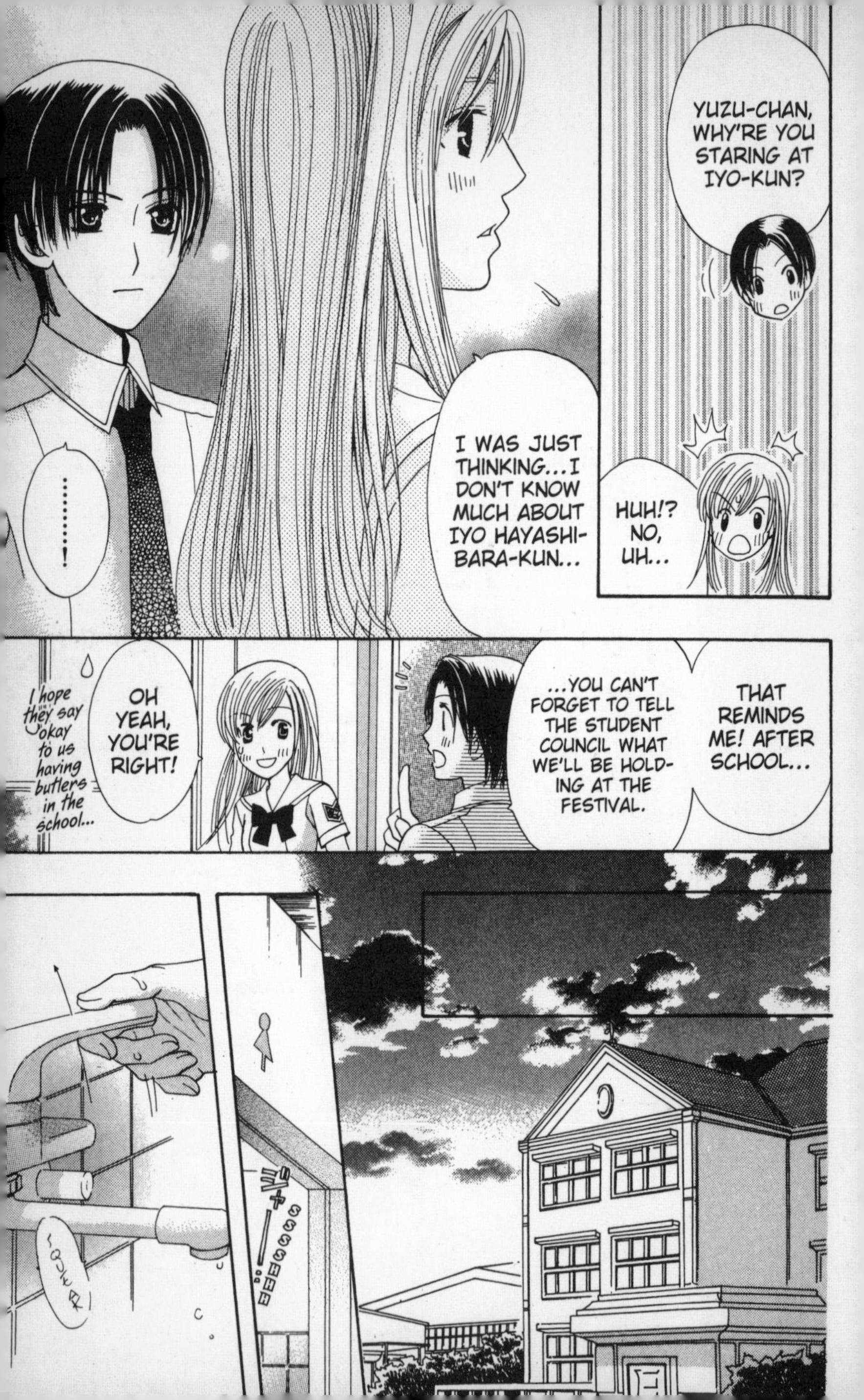

YUZU-CHAN, WHY'RE YOU STARING AT IYO-KUN?
HUH!? NO, UH...
I WAS JUST THINKING...I DON'T KNOW MUCH ABOUT IYO HAYASHI-BARA-KUN...
......!
THAT REMINDS ME! AFTER SCHOOL...
...YOU CAN'T FORGET TO TELL THE STUDENT COUNCIL WHAT WE'LL BE HOLD-ING AT THE FESTIVAL.
OH YEAH, YOU'RE RIGHT!
I hope they say okay to us having butlers in the school...
ジャー SSSSHHH!!

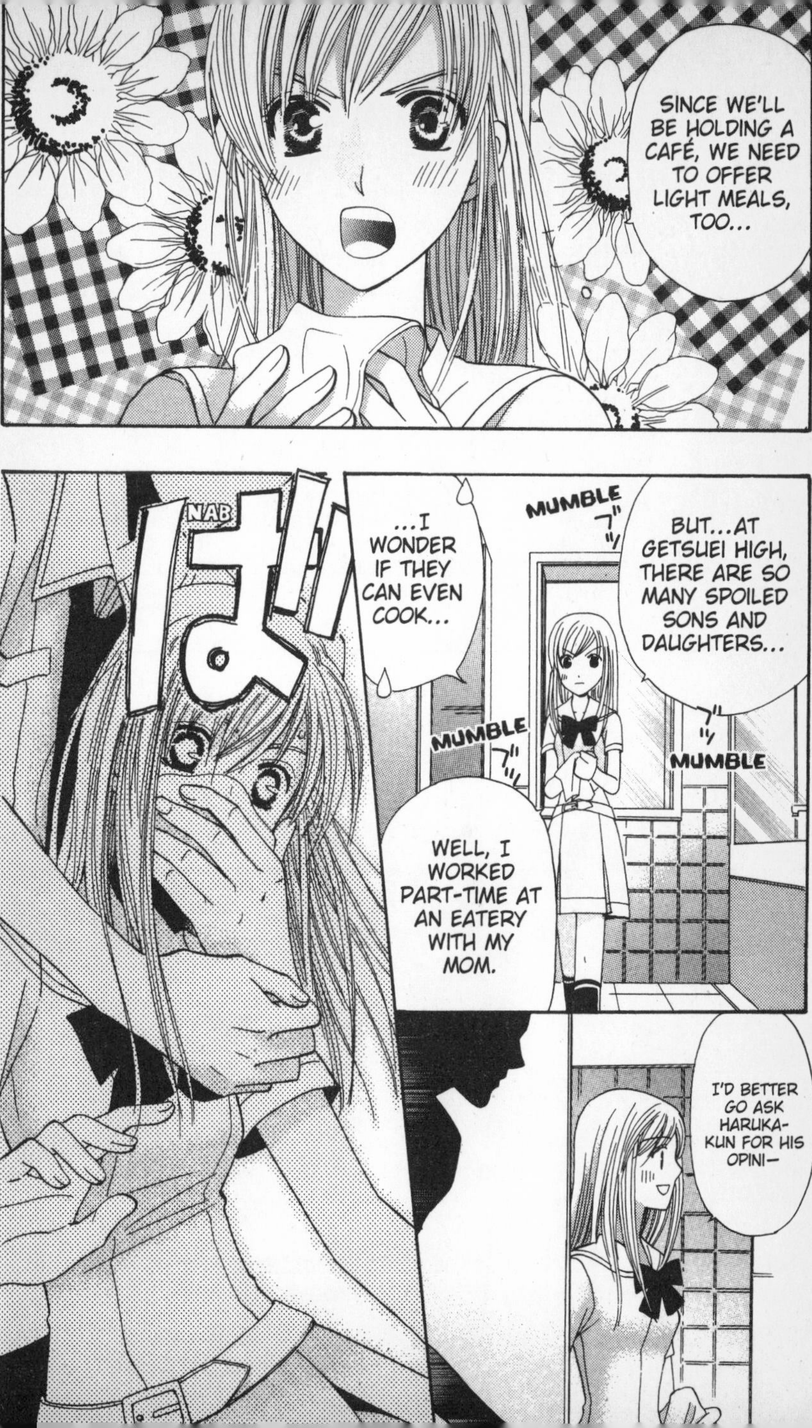
SINCE WE'LL BE HOLDING A CAFÉ, WE NEED TO OFFER LIGHT MEALS, TOO...
BUT...AT GETSUEI HIGH, THERE ARE SO MANY SPOILED SONS AND DAUGHTERS...
MUMBLE
MUMBLE
...I WONDER IF THEY CAN EVEN COOK...
MUMBLE
WELL, I WORKED PART-TIME AT AN EATERY WITH MY MOM.
I'D BETTER GO ASK HARUKA-KUN FOR HIS OPINI—
NAB

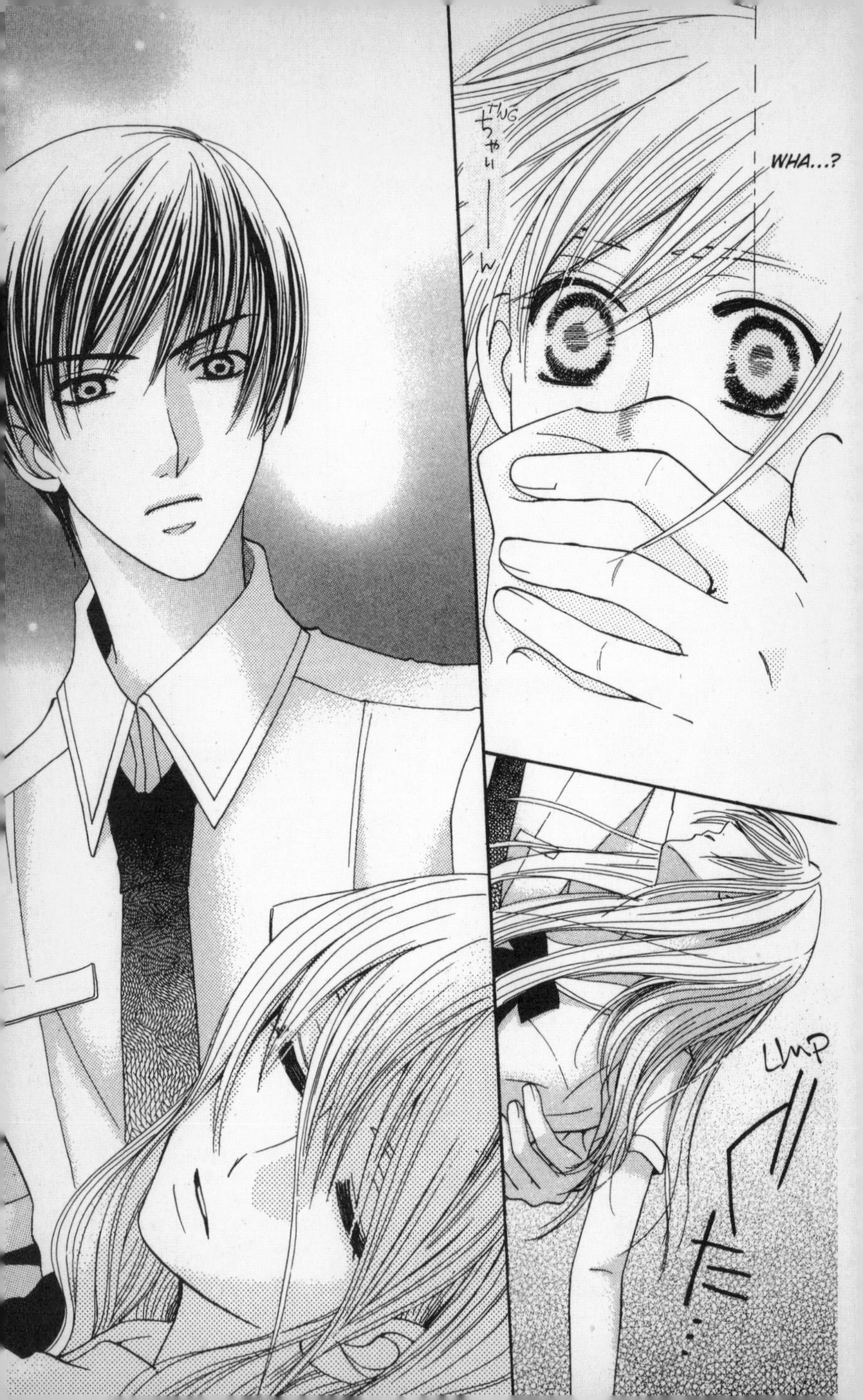

TING
ちゃりーん
WHA...?
LIMP
ぐた…

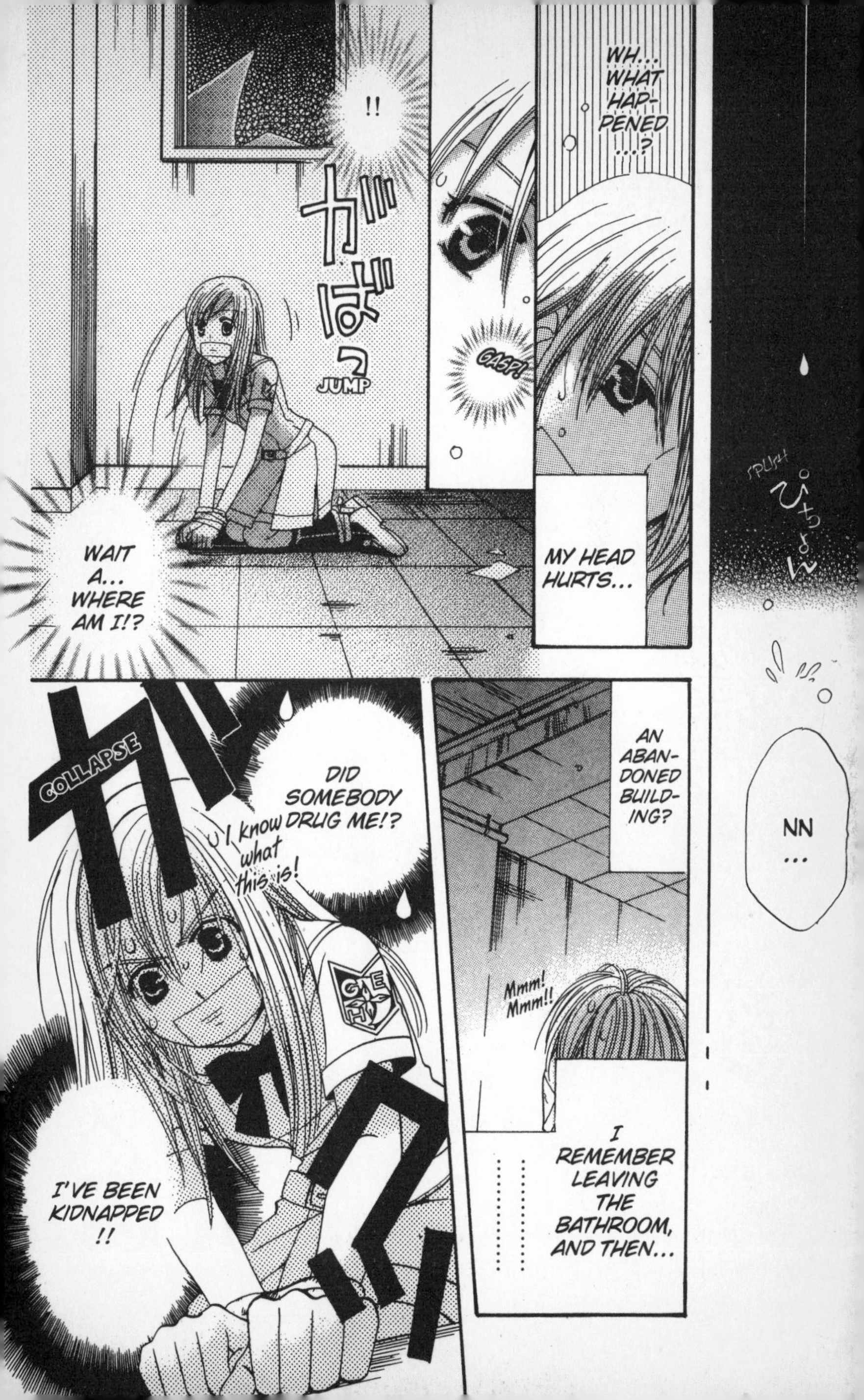
SPLISH
ぴちょん
NN...
WH... WHAT HAPPENED...?
GASP!
MY HEAD HURTS...
!!
がばっ
JUMP
WAIT A... WHERE AM I!?
AN ABANDONED BUILDING?
Mmm! Mmm!!
I REMEMBER LEAVING THE BATHROOM, AND THEN...
......
DID SOMEBODY DRUG ME!?
I know what this is!
COLLAPSE
I'VE BEEN KIDNAPPED!!

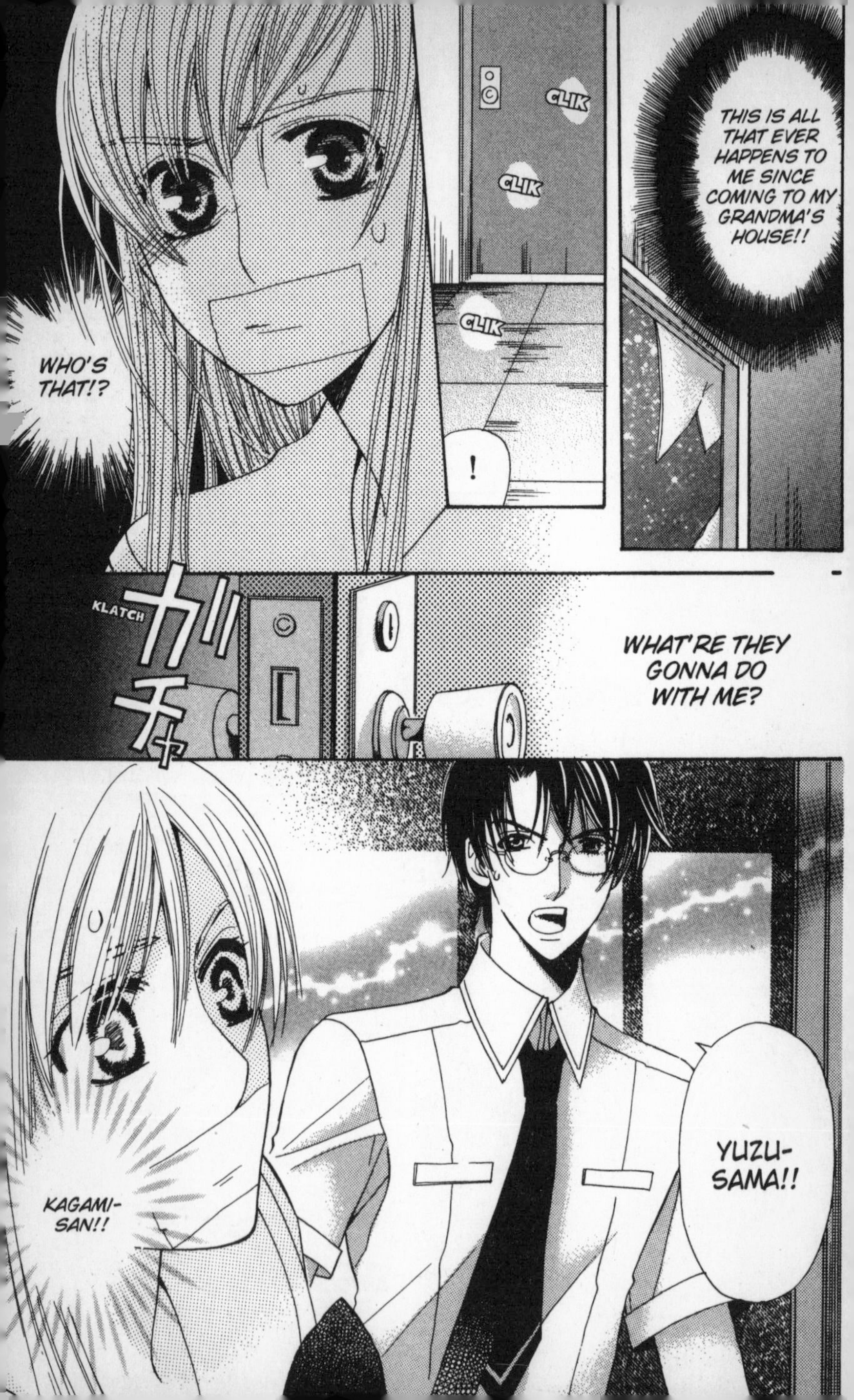

THIS IS ALL THAT EVER HAPPENS TO ME SINCE COMING TO MY GRANDMA'S HOUSE!!
CLIK
CLIK
CLIK
!
WHO'S THAT!?
WHAT'RE THEY GONNA DO WITH ME?
KLATCH
ガチャ
YUZU-SAMA!!
KAGAMI-SAN!!

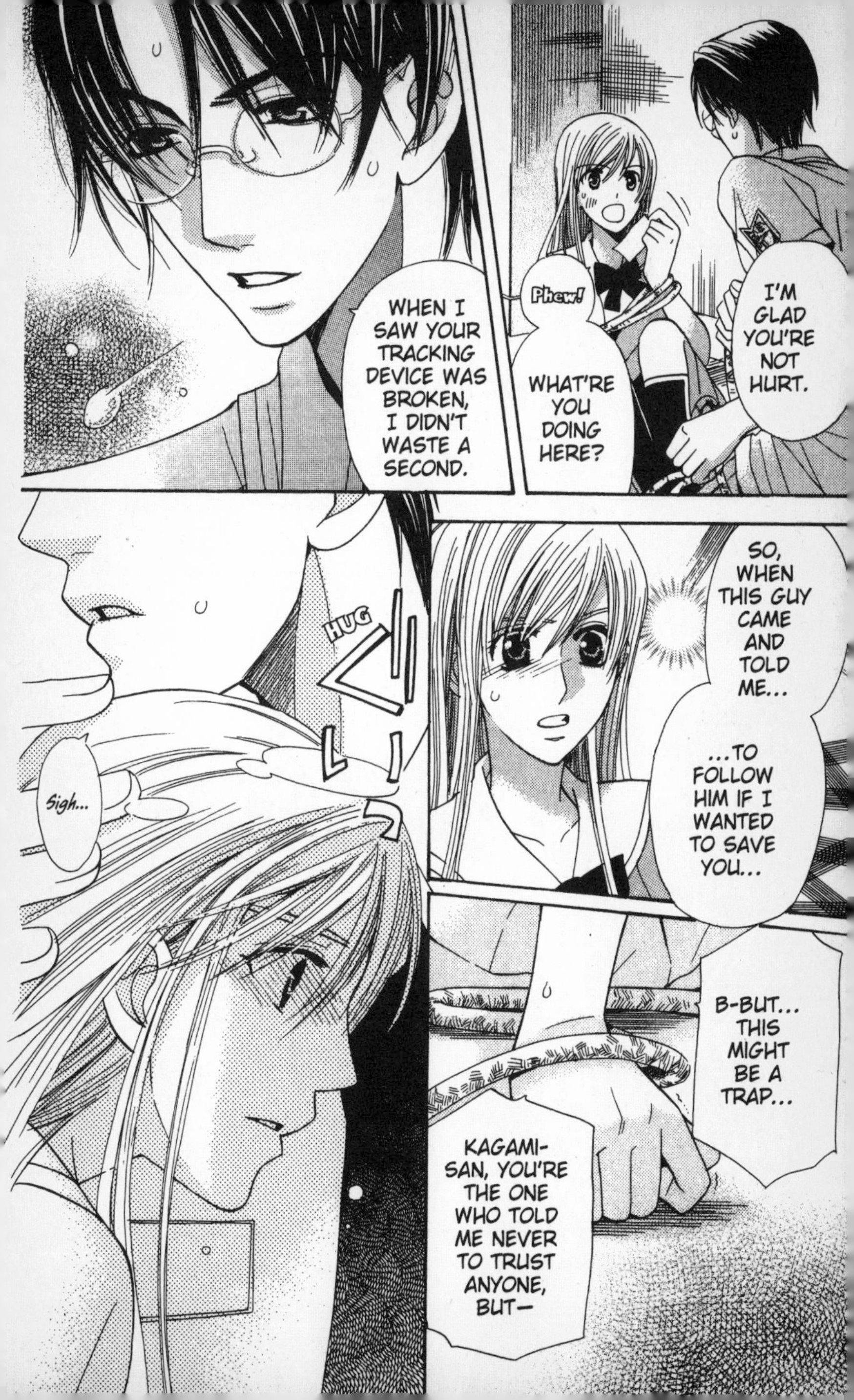
I'M GLAD YOU'RE NOT HURT.
Phew!
WHAT'RE YOU DOING HERE?
WHEN I SAW YOUR TRACKING DEVICE WAS BROKEN, I DIDN'T WASTE A SECOND.
SO, WHEN THIS GUY CAME AND TOLD ME...
...TO FOLLOW HIM IF I WANTED TO SAVE YOU...
B-BUT... THIS MIGHT BE A TRAP...
KAGAMI-SAN, YOU'RE THE ONE WHO TOLD ME NEVER TO TRUST ANYONE, BUT—
HUG
Sigh...

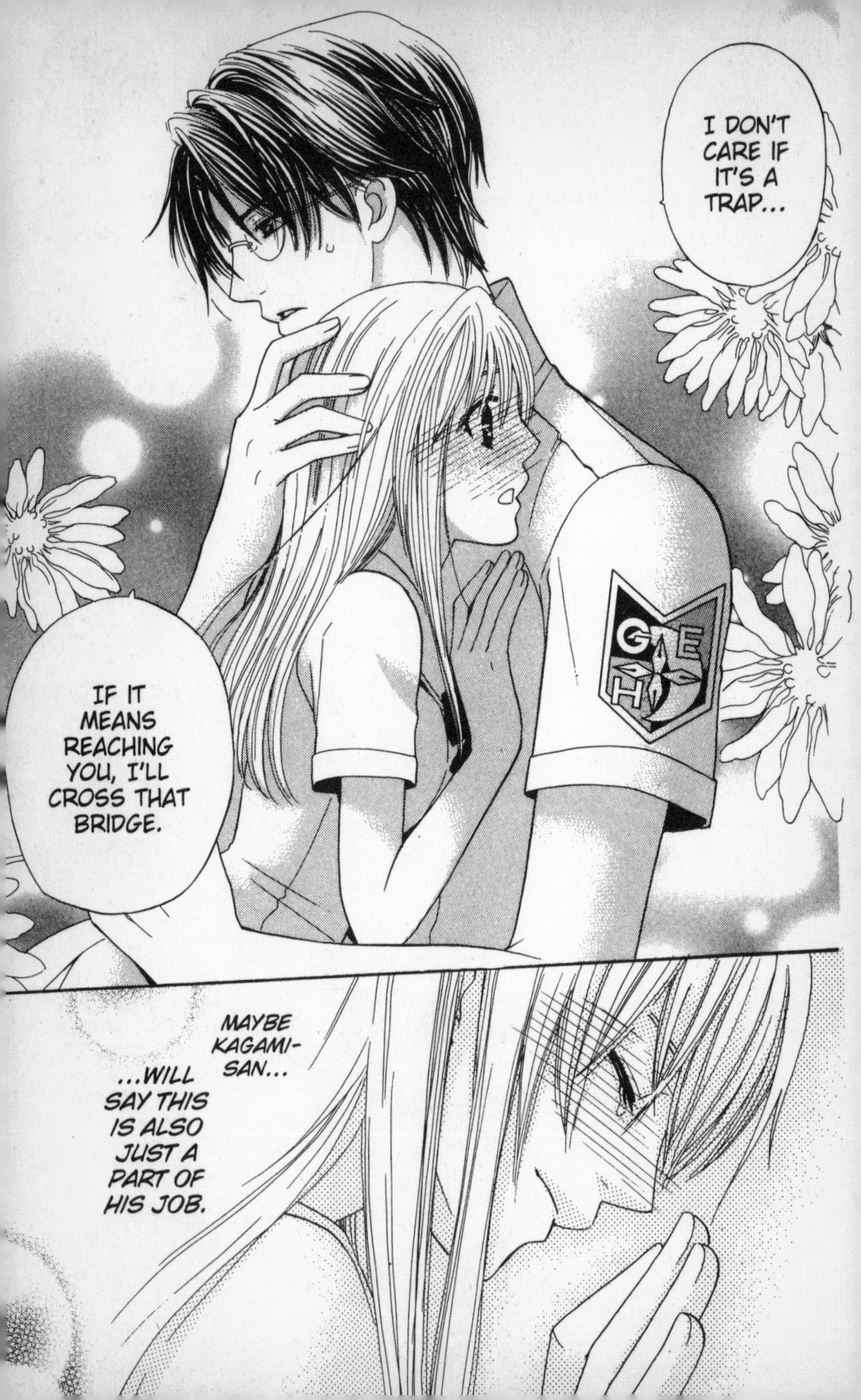
I DON'T CARE IF IT'S A TRAP...
IF IT MEANS REACHING YOU, I'LL CROSS THAT BRIDGE.
MAYBE KAGAMI-SAN...
...WILL SAY THIS IS ALSO JUST A PART OF HIS JOB.

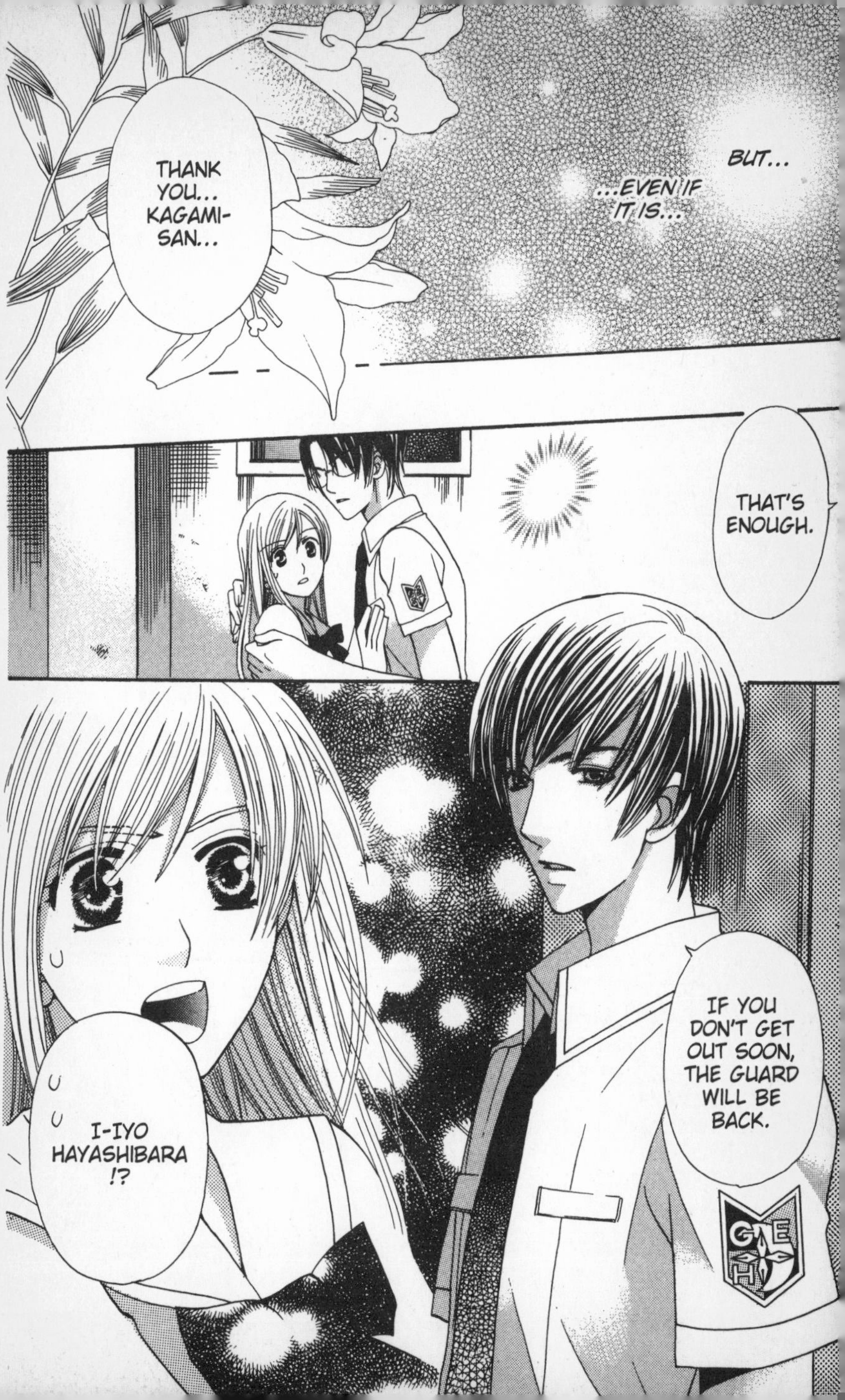

BUT...
...EVEN IF IT IS...
THANK YOU... KAGAMI-SAN...
THAT'S ENOUGH.
IF YOU DON'T GET OUT SOON, THE GUARD WILL BE BACK.
I-IYO HAYASHIBARA !?

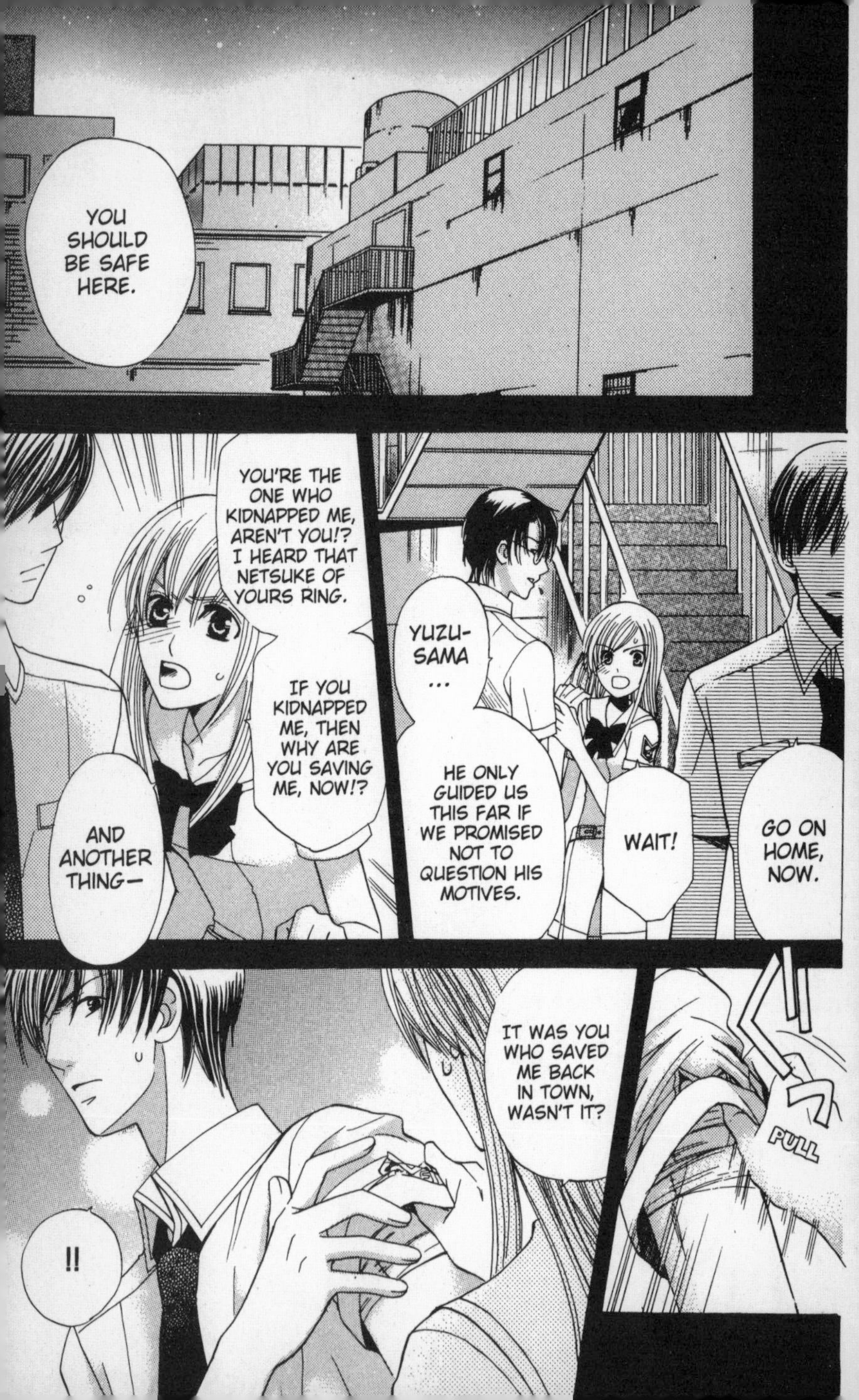
YOU SHOULD BE SAFE HERE.
GO ON HOME, NOW.
WAIT!
YUZU-SAMA ...
HE ONLY GUIDED US THIS FAR IF WE PROMISED NOT TO QUESTION HIS MOTIVES.
YOU'RE THE ONE WHO KIDNAPPED ME, AREN'T YOU!? I HEARD THAT NETSUKE OF YOURS RING.
IF YOU KIDNAPPED ME, THEN WHY ARE YOU SAVING ME, NOW!?
AND ANOTHER THING—
PULL
IT WAS YOU WHO SAVED ME BACK IN TOWN, WASN'T IT?
!!

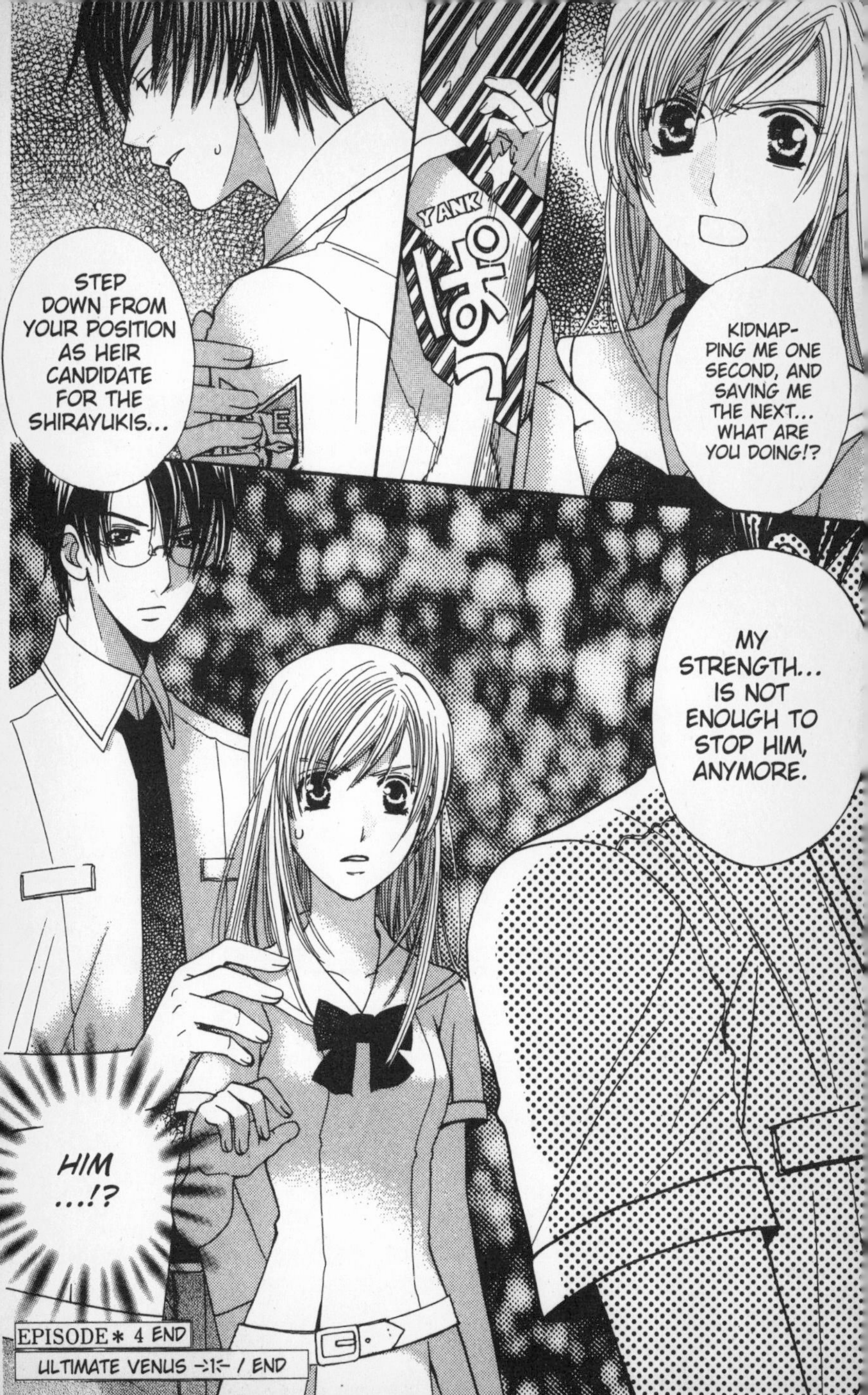
KIDNAP-PING ME ONE SECOND, AND SAVING ME THE NEXT... WHAT ARE YOU DOING!?
YANK
STEP DOWN FROM YOUR POSITION AS HEIR CANDIDATE FOR THE SHIRAYUKIS...
MY STRENGTH... IS NOT ENOUGH TO STOP HIM, ANYMORE.
HIM ...!?
EPISODE ✱ 4 END
ULTIMATE VENUS / END

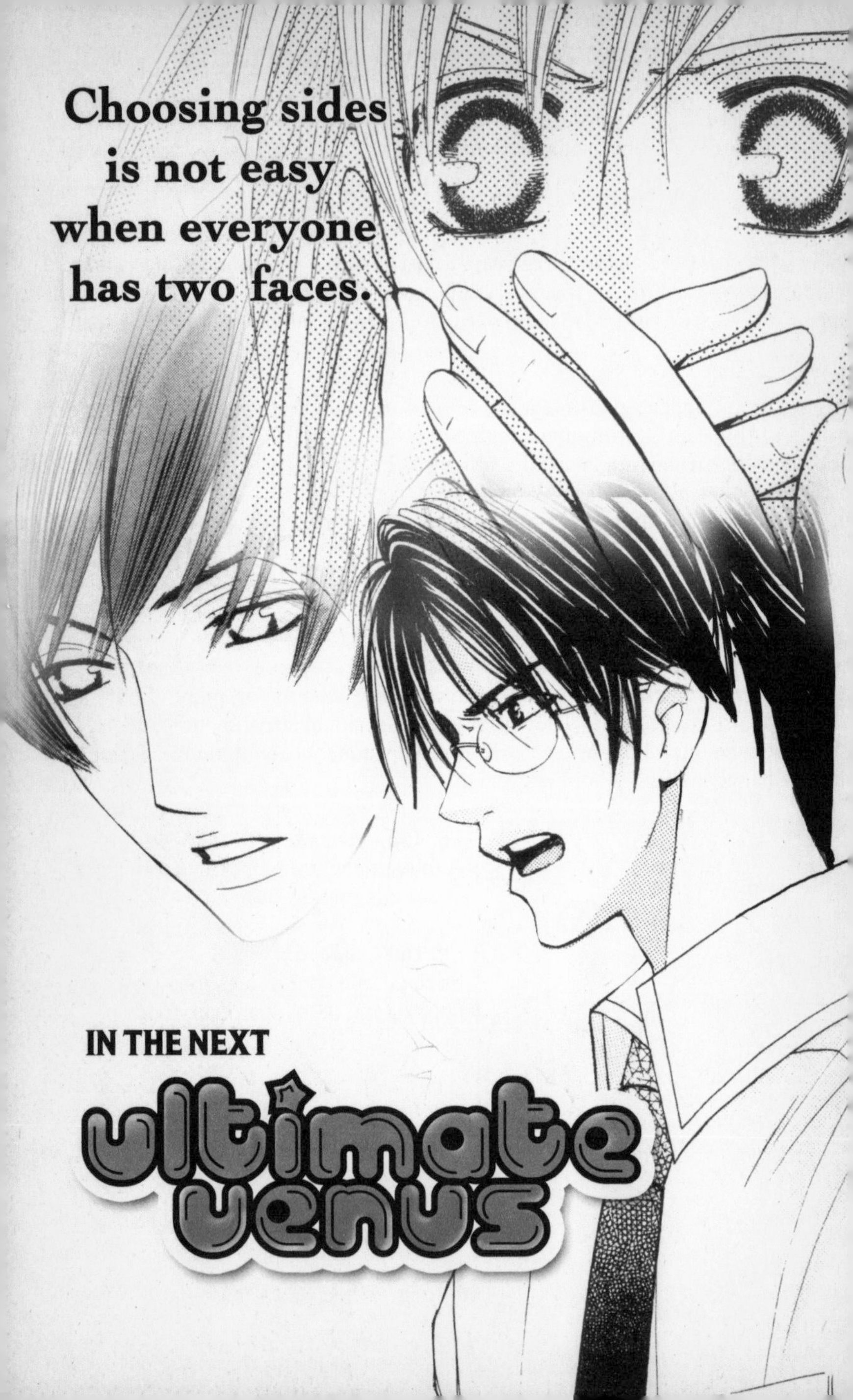
Choosing sides is not easy when everyone has two faces.
IN THE NEXT
ultimate venus

translator's notes:

'g. 32 – *hanko*
. *hanko* is a seal used by Japanese individuals and corporations to stamp a name ı ink onto a document. It is used as an equivalent to a signature or signing ne's initials.

g. 39 – "A peach tree takes three years to bear fruit, a persimmon takes eight."
'his Japanese idiom means that everything takes time. Yuzu's name also appens to mean a type of Japanese citrus fruit, fitting into the idiom quite well.

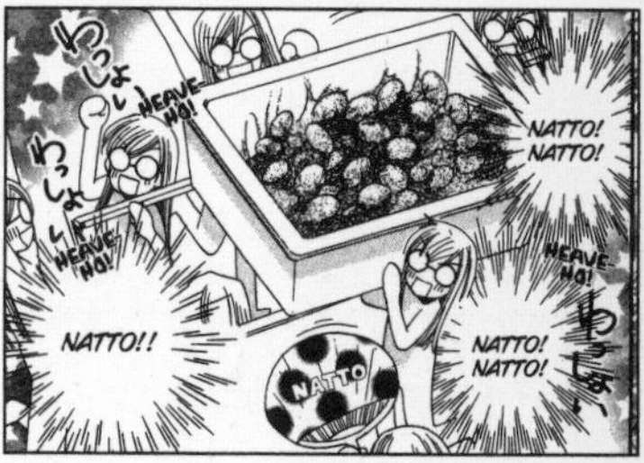
NATTO! NATTO!
HEAVE-HO!
NATTO! NATTO!
NATTO
NATTO!!
HEAVE-HO!
HEAVE-HO!

g. 72 – *natto*
his traditional Japanese dish is made of ermented soybeans. Its simultaneously icky and slippery nature, as well as potent nell, can be a real turn-off to many people, ut it's quite healthy and good for digestion. is also associated with a low-budget diet)r poor people.

g. 125 – *juku*
o get more organized teaching than what's offered at school, many Japanese udents take extra lessons after school in coaching schools (or, more often, cram schools") called *juku*. They offer more individual attention to students, elp those who are falling behind, and also prep students about to take difficult ıtrance exams to high school or college.

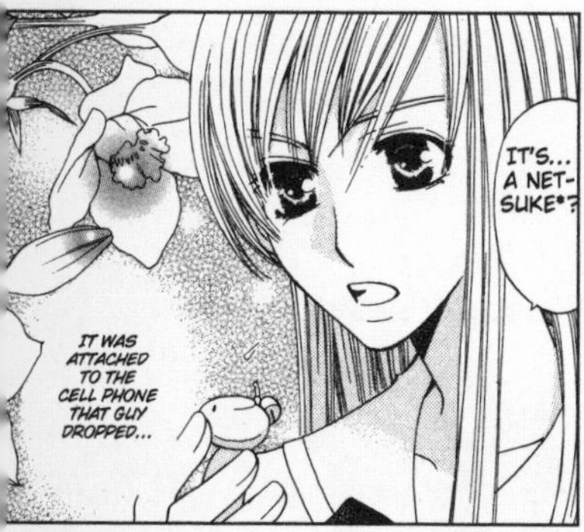
IT'S... A NET-SUKE*?
IT WAS ATTACHED TO THE CELL PHONE THAT GUY DROPPED...

Pg. 153 – *netsuke*
A miniature carving attached to the end of a cord hanging from a pouch.

Pg. 160 – *takoyaki*
Fried octopus dumplings that are a very popular and delicious snack food.